Praise for *THE PERFECTIONIST*

"Mr. Chelminski . . . knew Loiseau well. Better yet, he knows France well and the exalted role of fine dining in French culture. *The Perfectionist* tells, in rich detail, the story of Loiseau's rapid rise and desperate efforts to stay on top, but this cautionary tale is also a deeply informed guide to the last half century of French cuisine. . . ."

—William Grimes, *The New York Times*

"[Chelminski] has a moving story to tell, with universal implications: the downfall of the artist through perfectionism and paranoia."

—Adam Gopnik, *The New Yorker*

"*The Perfectionist* [delves] deep into the mad passion that seems to drive many master chefs. . . . Mouthwatering descriptions abound . . . the behind-the-scenes look at the kitchens of some of France's finest restaurants is fascinating . . . "

—*The Boston Globe*

" . . . illuminates the inner workings of French gastronomy . . . [and] the symbiotic relationship between restaurateur-chefs and food journalists."

—*San Francisco Chronicle*

"It's hard to imagine better ingredients for a riveting story. . . . *The Perfectionist* contains something to attract food fans, true-crime lovers, appreciators of rags-to-riches yarns, and collectors of the curious and disturbing."

—*New York Post*

"*The Perfectionist* effectively reveals the pressure-cooker atmosphere among a culinary elite dominated by intense rivalries, fickle reviewers, and hypercritical chefs for whom there is no such thing as second best."

—*Entertainment Weekly*

" . . . marvelously entertaining prose. . . . Even readers who don't know a thing about Loiseau or his famous restaurant . . . will get sucked into the chef's highs and lows . . . like a food-world *Behind the Music.* . . ."

—*Time Out New York*

Freelance writer and author **Rudolph Chelminski** has been living in Europe ever since the sixties, when he was sent to Paris as a writer for *LIFE* magazine. He has also written for *Smithsonian, Playboy, Reader's Digest, Wired, Atlantic Monthly, Town & Country, Fortune, Money, People, Time,* and many others.

The *Perfectionist*

LIFE AND DEATH IN HAUTE CUISINE

RUDOLPH CHELMINSKI

GOTHAM BOOKS

GOTHAM BOOKS
Published by Penguin Group (USA) Inc.
375 Hudson Street, New York, New York 10014, U.S.A.

Penguin Group (Canada), 90 Eglinton Avenue East, Suite 700, Toronto, Ontario, Canada M4P
2Y3 (a division of Pearson Penguin Canada Inc.); Penguin Books Ltd, 80 Strand, London
WC2R 0RL, England; Penguin Ireland, 25 St Stephen's Green, Dublin 2, Ireland (a division of
Penguin Books Ltd); Penguin Group (Australia), 250 Camberwell Road, Camberwell, Victoria
3124, Australia (a division of Pearson Australia Group Pty Ltd); Penguin Books India Pvt Ltd, 11
Community Centre, Panchsheel Park, New Delhi – 110 017, India; Penguin Group (NZ), cnr
Airborne and Rosedale Roads, Albany, Auckland 1310, New Zealand (a division of Pearson
New Zealand Ltd); Penguin Books (South Africa) (Pty) Ltd, 24 Sturdee Avenue, Rosebank,
Johannesburg 2196, South Africa

Penguin Books Ltd, Registered Offices: 80 Strand, London WC2R 0RL, England

Published by Gotham Books, a division of Penguin Group (USA) Inc.
Previously published as a Gotham Books hardcover edition.

First trade paperback printing, May 2006

1 3 5 7 9 10 8 6 4 2

Copyright © 2005 by Rudolph Chelminski
All rights reserved

Gotham Books and the skyscraper logo are trademarks of Penguin Group (USA) Inc.

The Library of Congress has cataloged the hardcover edition of this title as follows:
   Chelminski, Rudolph.
      The perfectionist: life and death in haute cuisine / by Rudolph Chelminski.
         p.   cm.
      ISBN 1-592-40107-4 (hardcover)   ISBN 1-592-40204-6 (paperback)
      1. Loiseau, Bernard, 1951–2003 2. Cooks—France—Biography. 3. Gastronomy.
   I. Title.
   TX649.L65C44 2005
   641.5'092—dc22   2004027853

Printed in the United States of America
Set in Electra with Trajan and Shelley Andante Script
Designed by Sabrina Bowers

This book is of course dedicated to the memory of Bernard Loiseau—a man who gave everything he had in pursuit of his dream, was often misunderstood for it, and in the end paid with his life for trying too hard to please too many people all the time. With all due modesty, I also offer his story as an expression of respect and admiration for the thousands of men and women whose talent, energy, and intelligence make France, today still, the world's epicenter of excellence in the restaurant business. From simplest *bistrot* to palace, they struggle daily with the same constraints, problems, and pressures that finally proved to be too much for their big, strong, but fragile *confrère*.

ACKNOWLEDGMENTS

$\mathscr{M}$y first and deepest thanks are owed to Dominique Loiseau, who accepted without reserve my project of a book showing her late husband as I had known him for more than thirty years, with his weaknesses and excesses as well as his incredible energy and the endless warmth of his simple humanity. Dominique spoke of herself, her husband, and their life together with unflinching sincerity. The staff of La Côte d'Or made me feel as if I were one of their own, speaking candidly of the boy-man who had been their boss, and to whom they continued to feel a fierce loyalty even after his death. Foremost among them was *premier maître d'hôtel* Hubert Couilloud, the rock on whom the entire service side of the house is built. His colleagues Eric Rousseau, Vincent Jousset, and Emmanuel Emonot offered equally precious insights, while Patrick Bertron in the kitchen found the time and patience to explain in minute detail the essence of *le style Loiseau*, as well as *le style Bertron*, which has now taken its place. Equally prodigal with help and articulate explanation was Dominique's assistant, Stéphanie Gaitey.

Bernard's parents, Pierre and Edith Loiseau, graciously received me twice at their home, and his brother Rémy and sister Catherine were equally forthcoming, as was Chantal, his first wife. Claude Verger, his surrogate father in the profession, and Bernard Fabre, his accountant, advisor, and friend, contributed precious character analysis and anecdotes that could not have come from any others associated with him.

Several gastronomic critics and editors of restaurant guides spoke with great eloquence and frankness about their own trade and the other one on which they sit as judges. Foremost were the last four editors of *Le Guide Michelin:* André Trichot, Bernard Naegellen, Derek Brown, and Jean-Luc Naret. René Gerbeau, an inspector in the sixties, gave me a fascinating account of life as a monk of gastronomy. Christian Millau, founder of the guide and magazine named after him and Henri Gault, spent an entire day spoon-feeding me a rich menu of his bottomless store of knowledge of food and wine, while Patrick Mayenobe, the latest boss of what remains of *GaultMillau,* gave a lively, detailed account of the operation today. François Simon of *Le Figaro* never shied from even the most challenging questions concerning his role in the tragedy, and was always helpful and gentlemanly when I came to him for further information. His predecessor on the paper's restaurant beat, Michel Piot, was avuncular, forthright, and knowledgeable. Philippe Couderc, the elegant, eloquent dean of restaurant critics, managed to squeeze an entire history semester (Gastronomy 101) into a single lunch. Thanks also to François Roboth, Gilles Pudlowski, and Albert Nahmias, all of whom gave of their time, opinions, and memories of Bernard.

In the miscellaneous category (i.e., not directly in the restaurant business themselves) I thank Alain Bories, Jean-Marc Catonné, Christophe Daguin, and Guillaume Potel of Architectes Associés. Thanks as well to Georges Duboeuf, Dr. Ladislas Kiss, Dr. Doron Zeeli, Avital Inbar, Bill Boyd, and Patrice Vappereau, mayor of Saulieu.

Unsurprisingly, Bernard's fellow restaurant professionals, especially the chefs, were a particularly rich vein of information. Foremost among them I must cite Pierre Troisgros, who along with his brother Jean took a rawboned teenager from the Auvergne and turned him into a cook. Pierre's marvelously keen memories and observations were bolstered by four men who shared apprenticeship with Bernard at Restaurant des Frères Troisgros: Bernard Chirent, Claude Perraudin, Jean Ramet, and Guy Savoy. Paul Bocuse, the idol that Bernard aspired to equal, was witty, intelligent, and perceptive, as usual, and Michel Guérard was a gold mine of historical and professional insights. So many others enlightened me that I would like to give them all three stars, but space here permits nothing more than an alphabetical listing of sincere thanks to: Jean Berteau, Georges Blanc, Michel Bras, Chantal Chagny, Suzanne Chapel, André Daguin, Alain Ducasse, Jean Ducloux, Henri Faugeron, Jean Fleury, Pierre Gagnaire, Guillaume Giblin, Jacques Guillo,

Philippe Jousse, Jean-Paul Lacombe, Jacques Lameloise, Claude Le Gall, Jean-Michel Lorain, Marc Meneau, Anne-Sophie Pic, Jean-Loup Prévost, Alain Senderens, Claude Terrail, Marc Veyrat, and Roger Vergé. *Un grand merci à tous et à toutes.*

From the point of view of my own profession, I am indebted to Bill Shinker of Gotham Books for having had faith in this book from the start, and to Lauren Marino and Hilary Terrell for unfailingly sticking with me to see it through to the end. And a final note of thanks to Matthew Guma of Inkwell Management, the guy who was behind this from the very first inkling of an idea. I wish all writers the good luck to have an agent like him.

CONTENTS

~

LUXE, CALME ET VOLUPTÉ

*O*n the Monday evening of February 24, 2003, a stupefying announcement broke into the 11 P.M. news bulletins throughout French radio and TV: Bernard Loiseau, chef and owner of the Côte d'Or restaurant in the Burgundy town of Saulieu, had been found dead in his home at age fifty-two, an apparent suicide. Tuesday morning, as more detail filtered out from police and gendarme reports, the earlier suicide speculation was confirmed: death by self-inflicted gunshot to the head. The arm was the victim's own shotgun—by cruel irony, a recent present from his wife.

France is a country where Latin hyperbole often colors judgments and pronouncements, but this time the population was truly shocked. More than a big story, this was an event of national and even international proportions. For several consecutive days Loiseau's death—no, not Loiseau's death, Loiseau's *suicide*, that was the part that was so staggering—continued to be the lead story in papers and prime-time TV shows from one end of the country to the other, shouldering aside George W. Bush, Saddam Hussein, and Donald Rumsfeld. For a nation that virtually defines itself by food, where restaurants are solemnly appraised, ranked, and debated the way football and soccer clubs are in less enlightened societies, where provincial chefs bathe in an esteem equal to that of the philosophers and essayists who strut and fret and solve the problems of the world in the Paris limelight, the news was inconceivable, a contradiction in terms.

This was not just some local notable, a mere politician, ecclesiastic, captain of industry, or other such inglorious *personage*. This was Bernard Loiseau the chef, arguably the most famous in France (and therefore the world), a man whose name-recognition score among the French general population—nine out of ten—was of presidential proportions. He was a cult figure of worldwide reputation, one of the gods of the trade, a man in the prime of life at the top of his profession, one of only twenty-five in the country then holding the coveted honor of a three-star rating in the *Guide Michelin*, the sole and true arbiter of the restaurant business. His hotel-restaurant complex at the gateway to the great Burgundy vineyards was more than luxurious. Simply put, it was perfection, or about as close to perfection as our poor human condition allows: thirty-two opulent suites of noble wood paneling, artisan tile, and polished marble, where authentic period furniture stood, cheek by jowl, with all the latest electronic gadgetry, Jacuzzis, and walk-in showers vast enough for a basketball team; a beautiful English garden custom-made for thinking green thoughts in a green shade while contemplating the swarm of infinitesimal bubbles aspiring heavenward in a *flûte* of champagne; a spa, workout room, and hammam; heated indoor and outdoor pools; an eighteenth-century billiards table; a library; a kiddies' playroom; one enormous fireplace in the bar-lounge and two smaller ones in intimate sitting rooms; and a monumental wooden staircase built by the *compagnons du devoir*, wrapped around a panoramic elevator. And, of course, there was the dining room—or, rather, three of them: two smaller ones for conferences and parties and the main one, a gorgeous hexagon overlooking the garden, where up to one hundred guests sat with a geometric latticework of wooden support beams above their heads and waxed stone *pavés* beneath their feet.

All of this was served by an ultramodern kitchen—a chef's glittering stainless steel dream equipped with every imaginable tool, machine, and instrument—and a twenty-five-strong cooking staff dedicated to turning out the signature *cuisine des essences* that had made the boss of the place a household name wherever in the world gourmets gathered to talk about great meals they had enjoyed or would be enjoying the day after tomorrow.

Bernard Loiseau had everything: a talent and drive that seemed inexhaustible; an eager young personnel that was entirely devoted to him and whose easygoing skill and aplomb was the envy of the trade; the (frequently jealous) recognition of his peers and the highest professional awards; the *légion d'honneur* personally pinned onto his lapel by the president of the republic in a gilt salon of the Élysée Palace in Paris; the respectful attention of journalists, universally intrigued by a personality so forceful and charismatic that he had achieved national stardom on radio and TV. The icing on the cake was his slim, attractive, and highly intelligent wife, Dominique, and the three bright, healthy young children she had given him. All this and he does away with himself! How could this happen? It was simply incomprehensible.

But of course there was more to it than the simple void of an enigma. Under the surface of Loiseau's brilliant success there lay a vast insecurity nervously cohabiting with a vast ambition. There was the ideal of a venerable tradition to be worthy of, or even surpass: the excellence in hospitality that over the years had made the French provinces synonymous with a warmth of welcome that put the snarling Parisians to shame and reconciled countless millions of visitors with the Gallic nation. There was a madly obsessive perfectionism in chasing that ideal. Obviously there was also human frailty. And there was the curse of Saulieu.

Perhaps the most disconcerting aspect of the tragedy, though, is this: Everything considered, it was not so surprising. Such a thing could have happened before, and it could happen again, because the world of *haute gastronomie française* in which Bernard Loiseau had been stewing for thirty-five years is a very particular, very peculiar kind of pressure cooker. To grasp a bit of the pleasures and satisfactions— but also the constraints, vexations, and pain—of that world, it is helpful to jump back in time. Half a century or so will do.

Là, tout n'est qu'ordre et beauté luxe, calme et volupté. It was with this bewitching phrase that a French writer, paraphrasing Baudelaire, had described another country inn 150 miles to the south of Saulieu in the mid-fifties. The place in question was the hotel-restaurant called La Pyramide, in the textile and leatherworking town of Vienne, lying on the banks of the Rhône south of Lyon. The owner and guiding genius of La Pyramide was a figure of near-legendary reputation, even in his lifetime: a huge, towering presence named Fernand Point. You can make a good case for saying that the story of Bernard Loiseau began there, because Fernand Point and La Pyramide remain, today still, the benchmarks against which French provincial inns, their proprietors, and the indefinable aura called style are inevitably measured. You cannot understand the saga of Bernard Loiseau—or, I daresay, the French themselves—without understanding something of Fernand Point, because, in this curious, toilsome line of business that they handle better than anyone else in the world, he incarnated the best qualities of a wonderfully talented, frequently endearing, but perpetually maddening people.

By today's standards, La Pyramide of Point's time probably would not be viewed as particularly plush. A three-story country manor faced with russet stucco and roofed with the rounded tiles characteristic of the southern half of France, its ground floor was almost entirely occupied by an airy, generously proportioned dining room, while outside, a wide terrace overlooked a sun-dappled garden interlaced with red clay pathways over which soared a magnificent stand of *platanes*, the plane trees that are to France what the great elms had been to America before the blight laid them low. It was in a corner of this garden that Point ritually began his day around 10 A.M., enveloped like a Christo wrapping in an immaculate white cloth as Monsieur Chazal, Vienne's number-one barber, proceeded with his matutinal shave. Close at hand, in one of the garden's several stone vases—this one left purposely free of flowers—a magnum of champagne exhaled its vapors over the shoal of cracked ice in which it bathed. In Point's hand was a Baccarat crystal *flûte* that ever and anon he raised to his lips.

"I enjoy a cup of champagne upon rising and a cup in the evening before turning in," Point used to say. "Nor do I fear to drink others between the two."

Point loved life, loved his trade and his restaurant, loved eating and drinking, and loved people—the perfect qualities to make an *aubergiste*. He instinctively understood that a great provincial restaurant was not a place for Parisian humbug and vanity but rather a refuge from the pressures and travails of workaday life, an island of tranquility where clients could snatch a few hours of civilized pleasure—precisely the *luxe, calme et volupté* that La Pyramide came to represent for two generations of French gourmets—at the cost of a few judiciously spent francs.

In 1933, when the Michelin guide first began ranking French restaurants in Paris and the provinces with its system of one, two, and three stars, La Pyramide fell quite naturally into the top three-star category. Point's cuisine was a personal, freewheeling derivation of the grand old Escoffier tradition, simplified and trimmed of the palatial ostentation common to big-city hotel restaurants where it held pride of place, and where he had learned the trade as apprentice, *commis*, and *sous-chef*. At the upper end, Point was perfectly capable of strutting his stuff with showpieces like *turbot à l'amiral*, which required two sauces, one based on white wine and the other on red, or the even more complex *filets de sole Brillat-Savarin*, a creamy lobster mousse jacketed in sliced truffles, surrounded by poached filets of sole on puff-pastry *croustades*, each filet topped with a lobster tail scallop and a ruinously thick slice of *T. melanosporum*, the black truffle that does for French cuisine what a Wonderbra does for an ambitious ingénue.

This was good, grand old nineteenth-century stuff, just right for eliciting an *oh, là là* chorus as the *maître d'hôtel* waltzed to the table with the platter, but it was relatively rare for Point. The dishes that are identified with his heritage today are the simple regional specialties that he brought to an apotheosis: *gratin* of crayfish tails, roast truffled chicken, foie gras encased in brioche. He did not fear to go simpler still, with various omelets, trout *au bleu* or just a hot Lyonnais sausage served with cubed potatoes. Whatever the dish, though, Point was intransigent when it came to total freshness; nothing was stocked, nothing prepared and left over from the day before. He insisted that his cooks begin each day with a naked kitchen and start all over again, and he took pleasure in patrolling the cooking premises, reaching high up on shelves and into cupboards to ensure that some wise guy hadn't squirreled away a work-saving container of *fond de volaille* or *glace de viande*. Point's stubbornness meant a lot of finicky handwork for the kitchen crew, but it guaranteed that only the freshest produce and top quality confections found their way onto his clients' plates.

Paul Bocuse, the ageless emperor of the French restaurant scene and Point's favorite apprentice, remembered the great man doing his daily marketing, selecting his fish, flesh, and fowl to be delivered to the cooks waiting in his kitchen while his wife, Mado, penned the day's menu in blue ink in her fine, strong script.

"It was *la cuisine du moment*," Bocuse explained. "In the big Paris restaurants where I worked afterward, the chef ordered provisions to fit the pre-established specialties already printed on the menu. Each morning the *maître d'hôtel* would come into the kitchen with a ritual question: 'What should we push today?' There was always food left over from the night before that they had to get rid of on a priority basis. Monsieur Point would have none of that. He made a fresh, clean start every morning."

Bocuse learned Point's lessons well and went on to apply them with tremendous success in his own restaurant in Collonges-au-Mont-d'Or on the banks of the Saône just north of Lyon. So well did Bocuse apply them, in fact, that he eventually surpassed his master in notoriety, and became the greatest international star of French cuisine of the postwar period—precisely the model that Bernard Loiseau chose to emulate a generation later. Bocuse's version of *la cuisine du moment* became a founding pillar of what was soon to be known as *la nouvelle cuisine française*. Much more than delicate little portions of pretty food on oversized plates, much more than sauces written in disappearing ink or the precious creations and daring (usually silly) combinations of ingredients by chefs who took themselves for *artistes*, the secret and soul of *nouvelle cuisine* lay in the simple act of following Point's insistence on cooking according to the day's market, cooking it at the last minute, individually for each client, and cooking it perfectly.

It was in Vienne under Point that Bocuse and a host of his brothers in arms learned the sophisticated simplicity that was to become the guiding principle of modern cooking. Point, a man who enjoyed maxims and aphorisms, never tired of telling his young pupils that it is the simplest dishes that are the hardest to master. To this end, he devised an infallible test for any passing professionals who entertained the idea of perhaps going to work for him: he asked them to fry an egg. Faced with the invariable failure, Point would cry "Stop, unhappy man—you are making a dog's bed of it!" And then he would proceed to demonstrate the one and only civilized manner of treating an egg:

Place a lump of fresh butter in a pan or egg dish and let it melt—that is, just enough for it to spread, and never, of course, to crackle or spit; open a very fresh egg onto a small plate or saucer and slide it carefully into the pan; cook it on heat so low that the white barely turns creamy, and the yolk becomes hot but remains liquid; in a separate saucepan, melt another lump of fresh butter; remove the egg onto a lightly heated serving plate; salt it and pepper it, then very gently pour this fresh, warm butter over it.*

"Du beurre! Donnez-moi du beurre! Toujours du beurre!" Point insisted: "Butter! Give me butter! Always butter!" As nutritionally incorrect as the battle cry may ring today in our cholesterol-obsessed times, he was only underlining an essential truth of the trade: French cuisine lives and breathes butter. Much fine cooking can be done without butter, but not the great syllabus of the French classics. Even Loiseau, who would go on to create a mini-revolution by largely eschewing fats with his *cuisine des essences*, had no choice but to sneak the magic ingredient into many of his dishes, if only by a discreet back door. Butter is elegance, suavity, and depth of flavor, even if you refuse to pronounce the B-word in public.

An astonishing number of figures in the pantheon of modern French cuisine spent their formative cooking years under Point's influence. Louis Outhier in La Napoule, Alain Chapel in Mionnay, François Bise in Talloires, and Claude Peyrot in Paris all went on to hold three Michelin stars; Maurice Coscuella in Gascony and Pierre

---

*Point's fussiness and arch-purism in the treatment of the humble egg would seem to be without equal, but a later chef—none other than Bernard Loiseau in Saulieu—was to go even further in finicky perfectionism. Loiseau did not even allow the egg to touch anything as vulgar as the direct heat of a pan. He cooked his egg, ever so slowly and ever so gently, in a buttered saucer reposing atop a saucepan of boiling water. (In a later refinement, he advised separating the yolk and the white, cooking them separately and reuniting them only at the end of the operation.) Can anyone go further than that? *Mais, bien sûr.* The celebrated Mme. Saint-Ange, author of a monumental tome of a home cookbook, picks one further bit of refinement: you must salt only the white, not the yolk, lest it leave unsightly spots.

Gaertner in Alsace made it as high as two stars, and still others contented themselves with one. But the most important of Point's pupils were three of the brightest three-star names associated with the *nouvelle cuisine* phenomenon: Paul Bocuse and the Troisgros brothers, Jean and Pierre. All three were to have a direct, indelible impact on Bernard Loiseau.

Of the three, it was Bocuse who bonded most thoroughly with Point, who considered him a surrogate son. Point and Bocuse's father, Georges, had toiled together in the same kitchen brigade of the Royal Hotel in Evian on Lake Geneva, but it was more than professional coincidence that brought mentor close to pupil. Point and the young Bocuse were both geniuses of cooking, both gifted with a sunny, sybaritic optimism and the natural, easygoing charisma of the born leader—and both shared a fiendishly active sense of humor. When Point honored a guest by inviting him into his kitchen for a preprandial drink, he brought him to the *garde-manger*, jammed him against the table with his great tum, and engaged him in loud, friendly conversation. A henchman, more often than not Paul Bocuse, crouched under the table with pot and brush, and whitewashed the victim's heels for his return to the dining room. Whenever a guest asked Point to prepare one of his famously succulent picnic baskets for the road, the guest became a potential victim: Point made sure that among the hard-boiled eggs there was always one that had been left treacherously raw.

The man had not an ounce of malevolence in him, though, and the pranks he inspired or committed were pure reflections of his enjoyment of life.* Peering amiably down from his height of six feet four, he addressed his clients as *"mon petit"* or, if he happened to be facing a member of one of the royal families that habitually took nourishment in Vienne, *"mon petit prince."* Accepting a free drink from Point could

---

*Occasionally he could come close to the red line, though. Bocuse recalled Point offering certain of his victims—those of the more stuffy or pompous sort—a curaçao cocktail so potent that the victim called out for some water to dilute it. "Certainly," said Point, obligingly handing him one of the soda water siphons that were common in the days before Perrier and other such bottled fizzy waters had made their breakthrough. This siphon was filled, of course, not with water but with white martini, a strong vermouth. The victim tottered back to his table with rather less dignity than when he had left it.

be hazardous, as a number of postmen and delivery boys discovered when they tarried for ten or fifteen minutes under the great man's friendly and time-consuming conversation—just long enough for Bocuse, the Troisgros brothers, or for Coscuella to paint his bike bright pink. Point became so notorious around town for his pranks that one afternoon—by bad luck, April the first—the local firemen laughed and hung up when he called them to extinguish a blaze in an upstairs bedroom. By the time he was able to persuade them that it was for real, the room was destroyed. Hoist by his own petard, Point could only laugh at the joke.

Food, on the other hand, was not a matter of levity. A famous tale, now ennobled high among the legends of French gastronomy, has it that shortly after the war Point forcibly expelled from his restaurant a couple of luckless Americans who came up with the unfortunate idea of ordering Cokes with their lunch. There was none of the vile brew in his place, anyway, but a principle was a principle—he personally threw the Yanks out of the place. Many years later Mado Point, then a widow, told me the story wasn't true, but I still like to think of her denial as a bit of ex-post-facto diplomacy.

Far ahead of his time, Point was intractable about the incompatibility of smoking and eating. Living in an age when smoking was not just socially acceptable but actually viewed as a mark of distinction, he left standing orders with his staff to immediately deliver the bill and a cup of coffee to any client who lit up between courses. "Oh, we thought you had finished," he would explain innocently. During the war, his intransigence frequently landed him in trouble with the authorities. Most memorable was the time he was haled before a collaborationist kangaroo court for frequenting the black market to buy a bucket of the *crème fraîche* he needed for one of his most celebrated specialties.

"No one," he roared incontrovertibly in his defense, "has the right to betray a *gratin dauphinois!*"

Unlike his skinny, marathon-running, wheat germ-chomping successors of today, Point entirely looked the part of the great traditional chef. Big and fat and triple-chinned, he was an imposing, pachydermous figure who flowed around his restaurant with stately grace. "My weight is confidential," he used to say, "but if you wish to obtain my volume, you have only to multiply the surface of my base by my height and divide by three."

For all his fame and exposure to the press, though, there is only one image of Point that perfectly captures his presence—a marvelously clever photo taken of him one day in the fifties by Robert Doisneau, the chronicler par excellence of the artists and artisans of an old French way of life that has mostly disappeared today.

On assignment for some now-forgotten newspaper story, Doisneau arrived at La Pyramide at about eleven in the morning for his appointment with the great man. "Come in, young man, come in," said Point, and before Doisneau quite knew what was happening he had a glass of champagne in his hand. "You are here for the photo, is it not?"

He was—and it was love at first sight, because nothing delights a photographer more than the instant flash of recognition that tells him exactly how he should compose his picture. *Lemme see now . . . Point,* La Pyramide . . . *Of course—Point the pyramid!* Doisneau grabbed a wide-angle lens, got down on the ground, and shot upward, filling two thirds of the frame with the vast expanse of the regal tummy encased in a black suit and vest, sloping upward and back toward Point's eternal polka-dot *lavalière* necktie and, above that, to the august countenance of Monsieur Fernand himself, gazing downward at these baffling photographic shenanigans.

Thrilled, Doisneau knew he had a great picture, and he wanted to get it developed and printed before Point figured out how he had been used. But that was not reckoning with his subject's totalitarian ways.

"*On ne part pas de chez Point sans déjeuner*"—"No one leaves Point's place without eating lunch"—he decreed, so in the same morning Doisneau had the picture of his life and the lunch of his life, without laying out a *sou* for either. "I was afraid they would be mad at me when the picture came out," Doisneau told me many years later, "but they loved it. Madame Point asked me for a blowup and invited me back for another free meal."

Grace and generosity like that was typical of *la maison Point.* At any one time, it was said in those days, a third or even a half of the guests—and "guests" is exactly the right word—in his dining room would be eating for free, because above all things, Fernand Point enjoyed making people happy. His pupils, and then the pupils of his pupils, carried the master's style of warmth, largesse, and good humor right on into the twenty-first century, most notably through the example of Paul Bocuse and Jean and Pierre Troisgros—all the way through, in fact, to Bernard Loiseau, spiritual grandson of *le grand Fernand*.

Worn out by too much work, too much champagne, and too much good living, Point died in 1956, a mere fifty-six years old. So many eminent doctors and professors of medicine had lunched and supped for free at his table that he was attended at his deathbed by a veritable all-star team of French medicine.

"I have been so well cared for," he whispered with one terminal wisecrack, "that I am certain to die in perfect health."

By the time Point went to his reward, Paul Bocuse had returned to the family inn in Collonges-au-Mont-d'Or and Jean and Pierre Troisgros had heeded their father's call to give up the pleasures of Paris, where they had been rubbing shoulders with the gentry in places like Maxim's and the Hôtel Crillon, and come back to Roanne to run the kitchen of the Hôtel Moderne. It had all the looks of a professional demotion, because Roanne, a manufacturing city on the Loire northeast of Lyon, is an exquisitely undistinguished kind of place, but papa was a boss who brooked no refusal. Year by year, as the young chefs gained confidence and progressively imposed their personal touches on the cuisine they had learned from Point and the *brigades* where they had labored in Paris, they began catching the attention of the locals. The word passed to the gastronomic grapevine that some extraordinary things were happening, and almost immediately the alerts reached Paris—the grapevine works with lightning speed where food is concerned in France. Soon the Michelin inspectors were nosing around, and soon the stars began to fall: a first one for the Troisgros brothers in 1955 and then for Paul Bocuse in 1958, at a time when his guests were still eating with stainless-steel silverware, wiping their mouths with paper napkins, and walking out into the courtyard for the toilets. More stars and greater distinctions were on their way just over the horizon: Nothing could stop talents like Bocuse and the Troisgros boys.

Things were shaping up fast. As France headed into *les trente glorieuses*, the thirty glorious years of economic expansion from the sixties to the nineties, the concomitance of vastly increased spending power, and the advent of a Europe-wide automobile culture, opened the floodgates to a new age of gastronomic nomadism: Dawn was breaking for the country inn. Before the Second World War, the automobile had been the virtually exclusive privilege of the wealthy—the torpedoes, phaetons, and limousines that in the thirties crunched the gravel outside of Point's gateway belonged to princes, movie stars, industrialists, and other such monied swells. The forties brought war, death, and deprivation, while the mostly chaotic fifties saw the start of rebuilding the national order. By the sixties, though, France had set a determined course for the same socioeconomic development that in America had made the private car a truly popular item that rapidly changed from an affordable luxury to a mundane necessity. By the mid-sixties the entire country was madly, passionately, on the road; the government of Charles de Gaulle had launched a major construction program of autoroutes, the limited-access superhighways that today crisscross the country; and French drivers were already carving out the reputation that they still proudly uphold today as the worst menaces on the entire European highway system.

Ornery as they are, though, French drivers also have a pronounced tendency to get hungry, and if there is one thing that a Frenchman or Frenchwoman enjoys more than driving at breakneck speed, it is lunch at a snail's pace. Nor do they disdain dinner, if truth be told. As the *trente glorieuses* began, then, the flow of automobiles turned into a flood, and French ingenuity was inventing ever more creative ways of commemorating something or other to create the *ponts*—bridges—that turn ordinary weekends into minivacation getaways to the *résidences secondaires* that five out of six French people seem to possess.

The roads, the gas stations, and the autoroute toll stations were booming, though, and opportunity knocked loud and clear for the hotel and restaurant trade. Suddenly thousands of *automobilistes* began discovering the wonderful but obscure little mom and pop country inns located in out-of-the-way places that until then had been the quasi-confidential clubs of wealthy gourmets who toured for pleasure, salesmen who traveled for work, or the lucky local notables who took their succulent cuisine for granted—places like Darroze in Villeneuve de Marsan deep in the southwest, where commercial men on tight budgets might find themselves before unimaginably generous portions of foie gras or, if the season was right and the market not too dear, steam-ing plates of *ortolans**—bunting—the tiny birds that were reputed to be France's greatest single delicacy before they became protected and disappeared from menus; like La Mère Blanc in Vonnas, where Madame Blanc herself, aided by a couple of village grannies, served mountains of scarlet crayfish in a peppery *nage*—mouthwatering po-tato pancakes and sautéed chicken in a cream sauce so delicious as to suggest some arcane conspiracy theory; or, indeed, the Hôtel Moderne in Roanne, soon to be rebaptized in the name of its gastronomically sainted owners, where the Troisgros family was cooking chicken with vinegar and a profusion of garlic cloves, salmon with sorrel, and grind-ing up thousands of darling little thrushes into a pâté[†] that caused grown men to shed bitter tears for not having known the address earlier.

As the gastronomy of the road became a profitable way of life, the mom and pop bistros expanded and took on more personnel, and with the passing years, grew progressively more luxurious; a new generation of energetic young cooks spotted opportunity and set up their estab-lishments. Soon there was hardly a village in France without a restau-rant serving true French food—not always necessarily sublime, but

---

*The *ortolan* is one of the great mythic creatures of French country cuisine. Trapped in nets and fattened up for several months, then smothered to death in wine, cognac, or vinegar, they could be prepared in any number of ways, but con-noisseurs tended to prefer them wrapped in a grape leaf and quick-roasted in a hot oven. A whole ceremony attended their consumption, regarded as the absolute acme of *gourmandise*. As plates of the bite-sized delicacies were delivered, diners covered their heads with towels and leaned forward like supplicants to capture every last savory vapor rising upward, then seized each critter by the feet and chomped it whole in one mighty munch, spitting out the beak and delicately returning its tiny feet to the plate before moving on to the next. Former president François Mit-terrand, at death's door with cancer, is said to have ordered a plate of *ortolans* for his last supper. In one of the legal pirouettes that this country handles with such ease, it is now against the law to sell them in France—but not to eat them.

[†]By offering *pâté de grives* on their card, the Troisgros were flying deliberately in the face of a hoary old legend well known to everyone in France. On the (some-times legitimate) assumption that many of the less rectitudinous caterers and *char-cutiers* push thriftiness to extreme limits, the legend postulates a standard professional list of ingredients required for the *pâté*: one thrush, one horse; one thrush, one horse . . .

light years above the pizza and burger chains that are doing their best to blight the landscape today.

One of the first of this new breed of entrepreneurs of top-quality eating, and one of the smartest and most admirable, was Jean Ducloux, a tough, wisecracking, no-nonsense character from the little city of Tournus on the river Saône, approximately halfway between the vineyards of Burgundy and the golden hills of the Beaujolais. Ducloux, too, shared a chunk of history with Bernard Loiseau, even if he was old enough to have been his father, because his path had taken him to the very same kitchen in Saulieu where young Bernard was to make his professional life and where, after nearly three decades of flailing and fighting, he would choose to end it.

Along with Bocuse and the Troisgros brothers, Ducloux was the third leg of the trio of chefs whom Loiseau took as models and mentors. Amiably presiding over his Restaurant Greuze (two Michelin stars) well past his eightieth year before finally selling it and taking a well-earned retirement in 2003, he became something of a French icon, as indelibly identified with Tournus as the fortresslike St. Philibert church, a Romanesque masterpiece that is the city's architectural pride and joy. He was a man of the old school, this Ducloux, and he had learned the trade the old way, the hard way—what is known as *l'école des coups de pied au cul*—the school of kicks in the ass. Not lucky enough to have the professional benevolence of Fernard Point close at hand, he had been delivered, still in shorts and his voice not yet broken, by his mother to the doorstep of a celebrated restaurant in Dijon on the day he turned thirteen.

Few among us can set a precise date to the end of our childhood, but for little Jean Ducloux, it happened on the first of September 1933, when he began his apprenticeship under Monsieur Henri Racouchot, chef and owner of the Trois Faisans. The very next morning he was hauling fifty-pound blocks of ice two flights upstairs to the cold room, then doing the same for the garbage cans, up from the basement and out to the sidewalk: fifteen of them in all, weighing between seventy-five and eighty pounds apiece. It is always the latest apprentice who inherits the worst chores, and he holds on to them until the next kid comes along. Bernard Loiseau was to get a similar welcome to the real world some thirty-five years later.

Apprentices of Ducloux's time worked from eight in the morning until ten thirty at night, with half a day off every week—unless, of course, they were held in for some egregious professional misdemeanor such as speaking without permission. The boys were unpaid, of course, but a long-standing tradition allowed them to earn a few coins by loading tubs of disgusting old kitchen greases into the restaurant's handcart and lugging them to the local soap factory. The handcart was something of a sacred relic for the Trois Faisans' apprentices, as the central instrument in a famous bit of heroics that had occurred ten years before Ducloux's arrival on the scene. Two brothers, the Parizot boys, who had been apprenticed there together, were dispatched to deliver a catered meal to a private Dijon home, using the very same handcart. Bad luck: They tipped the cart over en route. Faced with the truly horrifying prospect of returning to the Trois Faisans and telling the chef the dreadful truth, they somehow managed to scrape the *quenelles de brochet*, the lobster, and the filet of beef off the sidewalk, artfully rearrange it all back in the original containers, and deliver it up to the client. No one was the wiser; the client paid and sent his compliments to Monsieur Racouchot.

Ducloux spent two years at the Trois Faisans learning the basics of the trade, graduating from gutting fish and plucking partridges, pheasants, and larks, to preparing the *fumets*, the classical fish stocks used for poaching various types of seafood, and clarifying the *fonds de cuisine*, rich broths of meat trimmings simmered with aromatic herbs—then, as now, the fundamental building blocks for the sauces that set French cuisine apart from all others. Although apprentices never actually cooked any dishes—that was reserved for the big guys, the chef, the *sous-chefs*, and the *commis*—little Jean could at least feel that his work had contributed to the specialties that gourmets in Dijon were devouring in those days: the classical, inimitable *tournedos Rossini*, a *nouveau riche* fantasy of food heaven, all beef and truffles and foie gras aswim in Madeira sauce; thick Châteaubriand steaks with unspeakably seductive béarnaise, as yellow and unctuous as the egg yolks and butter that had built its velvety consistency, speckled with green flecks of tarragon and underlaid with just enough of the sharp, acid bite of vinegar, shallots, and white wine to give it the character of the aristocrat of sauces; *quenelles de brochet*, the lovely, tumescent pike "omelets" traditionally served with a creamy, pinkish sauce of the reduced essences of crayfish; hot, meaty pâtés, drenched in sauces derived from the very same *fonds de veau* that Jean had been clarifying; *Homard Gaston Gérard*, a lobster first brushed with olive oil and seared in a hot oven for ten minutes, then flambéd with cognac in a vegetable *mirepoix* and cooked on the stove for ten minutes more in a bath of the most excellent Burgundy that a judge, doctor, or wine merchant could afford.

It was good, rich, rib-sticking stuff in the grand old tradition of the Troisième République, when appetites were appetites, bellies were ample, and no one had heard of cholesterol—the same kinds of dishes, no doubt, that Toulouse-Lautrec and his friends might have been consuming in the gaslit restaurants in the Paris of the Belle Époque thirty or forty years earlier.

On October 15, 1935, Monsieur Racouchot signed a document certifying that after two years of practice, Jean Ducloux had reached the stage of *ouvrier cuisinier*—qualified kitchen worker. You didn't rise to the giddy rank of chef or *sous-chef*—not even *commis* (assistant)—so easily in those days. You had to get some experience first, and you worked your way up. As fate had it, Ducloux's next stop along the road of experience was the restaurant La Côte d'Or in Saulieu.

He was fifteen when he got there, and proud to be considered worthy of working in an establishment that was already a landmark of French *haute gastronomie* under its famous chef, Alexandre Dumaine. The building Ducloux saw when he walked up the hill from the station was a long, rectangular, three-story structure with a high tiled roof pierced by four chimneys, a stucco façade interrupted by four spacious arcaded windows, and a wide, triple-doored entryway, also arcaded. All in all, it was a sturdy, reassuringly comfortable kind of place, of the sort that commonly fronted on the main highways throughout France. Like the even larger Hôtel de la Poste across the street, it dated back to the eighteenth century and had been originally built as a post house to accommodate the many horse-drawn coaches that used to follow the old Route Nationale 6 (R.N. 6) from Paris by stages down to the Mediterranean via Fontainebleau, Sens, Auxerre, and Avallon. Saulieu had been a *ville étape*, or staging city, from earliest history, and the R.N. 6 faithfully followed the trace of the Romans' Via Agrippa. At each stage, coachmen could rest, water, and stable their horses for the night, discharging their passengers to the potluck victuals and the straw mattresses of the town's several inns, before leaving again at the crack of dawn the next morning.

It was a long, slow slog down to Avignon, Marseille, and Toulon, but the better-quality post houses made the trip bearable. As it had been in the eighteenth century, it was a very definite advantage for Alexandre Dumaine's place to be located in Saulieu, because the R.N. 6 ran smack through the middle of town and, as the private car became more and more commonplace, the logic of the road dictated that Saulieu, at 250 kilometers from Paris, would be a natural stopover point—for lunch if the *voyageurs* quit the capital in the morning, or for dinner and the night if they took their departure in the afternoon. Dumaine knew what he was doing when he bought the commerce from a retiring fellow chef. For locating a hotel-restaurant, Saulieu was a nearly cast-iron guarantee of a steady flow of customers, unless it repelled them with food that was absolutely horrible.

It wasn't. In fact, it was very, very good. Dumaine had been around the gastronomic establishment for many years before finally settling in Saulieu—notably in the vacation spots of the French North African colonies and aboard the big, prestigious ocean liners that had already made him something of an international star. The man knew a thing or two about fine cuisine and didn't exactly discourage headline writers from referring to him as Alexander the Great. Within only a few years of arriving in this otherwise godforsaken little town of 3,000—in fact in 1935, the very year he hired young Jean Ducloux—Dumaine was visited with the trade's equivalent of a papal blessing: three Michelin stars. Thus anointed, he became an official member of the Holy Trinity of French provincial cuisine.

That little phrase wasn't a joke. Once again, it was the logic of the pre-autoroute roads, the distances between stopping points, and the presence of three great chefs that turned three otherwise unremarkable towns—Saulieu, Vienne, and Valence—into centers of pilgrimage for those of the ingestive inclination. If Saulieu was Dumaine and Vienne was Point, Valence, approximately midway between Lyon and Avignon, was André Pic, a pure Escoffier man (*ballottine* of stuffed pigeons and truffles, woodcock terrine, *poularde à l'ancienne*) who bore a remarkable resemblance to Oliver Hardy, and who had earned his third Michelin star one year ahead of Dumaine. Point, Pic, and

Dumaine were the three great heroes of drivers who frequented the north-south axis of gastroland.

By the thirties, of course, the internal combustion engine had replaced horsepower, but the role of the *aubergistes* on the Route Nationale 6 remained remarkably similar to the old days. Chefs along the route could not hope to make a decent living from local customers alone—especially in Saulieu, by far the smallest of the three cities—so they relied on attracting travelers. France being France, they could buy most of their ingredients from the farms, villages, and open-air markets in the immediate vicinity of their restaurants, and their short daily menus reflected what they found: *Cuisine du terroir*—regional cooking—was king in those days. It was usually uncomplicated stuff, but in the hands of the men of the Holy Trinity it could be dazzling.

From day to day, Dumaine could never know whether the flow of cars and buses would bring him ten customers or fifty, so he laid in just enough victuals for a basic tourist menu, reserving complex creations for much more expensive gourmet dinners or, if he intended to really flex his culinary muscles, for special meals on command. On his first workday in Saulieu, Jean Ducloux discovered the *autocariste* menus for clients arriving by bus from Paris. There were three of them, priced at 18, 20, and 30 francs, and at first sight they might have appeared almost laughable compared to the sophisticated big-city cooking he had known at Les Trois Faisans. At 18 francs, the bottom menu offered:

Mixed hors d'oeuvres

Butter

Peasant omelet

Baby peas à la française

Roast chicken

Green salad

Cheeses

Selection of desserts

Fruit basket

The big menu, the 30-franc treatment for the big appetites, added a trout *meunière* and a *feuilleté* of crayfish tails after the hors d'oeuvres, and a *pâté en croûte* after the roast chicken. It was unpretentious country fare, the ingredients were irreproachable, and they all came from Saulieu and its environs.* Reminiscing years later, Ducloux dispelled any doubts about the comparison with Les Trois Faisans: "These dishes were masterpieces."

You will never impress food snobs with green salad and roast chicken, though, and Dumaine, being much closer to Paris than Point or Pic, was more frequently called upon to custom-build special meals for the rich and famous,† the sorts of things that no mere *autocariste* would ever see for their 20 or 30 francs. Charlie Chaplin, for instance, was partial to a deluxe version of Dumaine's *pâté en croûte*, featuring woodcock, truffles, and foie gras, while Curnonsky, the food chronicler known as "the prince of gastronomes," ordered his own version of *pochouse*, an elaborate freshwater fish stew cooked with white wine, the sauce thickened not with flour but "mounted" at the last minute with fresh, sweet butter, garnished with poached eggs, and served with grilled croutons, *very lightly* garlicked, please. Edouard Herriot, mayor of Lyon and president of parliament, habitually took a special pâté of pike and crayfish, served with a reduction of a white wine *fumet*. The khedive of Egypt liked to set his royal choppers into a *ballottine d'agneau*, a stuffed and braised shoulder of lamb, much more proper for the Muslim that he was than the roast suckling pig stuffed with *boudin noir*—black blood sausages—and *boudin blanc*—white veal sausages—that two aristocratic ladies, Louise de Vilmorin and Countess Mapie de Toulouse-Lautrec, were not afraid to challenge with their noble appetites.

During the war, times were tough and victuals were scarce. La Côte d'Or vegetated, surviving as best it could. Toward the end, with the Allies advancing toward Saulieu from both the north and the south,

---

*Although I have my doubts about the freshness of those baby peas, because young Jean Ducloux arrived at the Côte d'Or in November. But in the mid-thirties canned baby peas were actually considered rather *chic*, like smoking.

†"Paris–Dumaine, 250 kilometers" was a popular slogan among wealthy gastronomads of that time.

the countryside was in a panic: There were no more markets and peasants were zipped up tight in their farms, waiting it out (forget meat). Hardly anything was available at all—and just then Dumaine unexpectedly inherited a guest of great mark: Marshall Henri M. Philippe Pétain himself, head of the collaborationist regime installed by the Germans after France's terrible defeat of 1939.

On August 20, 1944, Pétain arrived in a black limousine with a small presidential entourage, escorted by an SS detachment. The pathetic remains of the Vichy government were on their way to a brief exile in the castle of Sigmaringen, across the German border on the other side of the Black Forest. Meanwhile, Dumaine had to feed his imposed guest. Scrounging around, he came up with enough material to make a decent menu for *Monsieur le Président*'s last dinner in France:

Vegetable soup

Mushroom omelet

Potato croquettes

Peasant salad

Cheese

Fruits from the neighbor's orchard

Within a few years of the German surrender, France's lush, heaven-blessed countryside was yielding up its bounty once again, and Dumaine could return to the kind of cooking that had made his reputation, notably his famous *poularde à la vapeur*, a truffled Bresse chicken seasoned inside with salt, spices, and marsala—truffle slices under the skin, whole truffles all around it—steam-cooked on a tripod over a rich meat broth of beef, veal, chicken, and salt pork. But when he had the chance for a truly big blowout, he set himself and his assistants to work on an *oreiller de la belle Aurore*. It was quite an operation—just the thing to impress the Club des Cent.

Le Club des Cent is France's snobbiest and richest eating club, limited to one hundred members, as its name indicates. It was founded by journalists, but over the years, as the expenses of its outings grew ruinous, the journalists slunk away, making room for the clique of bankers, stockbrokers, and publishers that forms the club membership today—men who can afford to pay for the kind of treatment to which they are accustomed. Just such a treatment was the *oreiller de la belle Aurore* with which Dumaine titillated their fancies. Imagined by Jean Anthelme Brillat-Savarin (1755–1826), judge, politician, and writer, whose *Physiologie du Goût* is one of France's great humanist documents, the *oreiller* was a pâté that could be served either hot or cold,* but one of such fiendishly complex construction that it required two days of work for seasoned professionals to put together.

It is shaped like a pillow (*oreiller* means pillow); Brillat-Savarin's mother and sister were both named Aurore. So there you are. The following is a very abridged description of what Dumaine put into it.

Filets of hare, partridge, chicken, and duck; fresh ham, veal, and pork. All these meats to be cut into strips not more than 2 centimeters thick. Scallops of foie gras, truffles, and pistachios.

TWO MARINADES:

> *White:* for the chicken, veal, and ham, with chopped shallots, white wine, a tablespoon of anise, and a teaspoon of lemon syrup; olive oil. Marinate for 24 hours
>
> *Brown:* for the partridge, duck, and hare: cognac, Madeira, and olive oil. Marinate for 24 hours

THREE STUFFINGS:

> *White*, made of veal, chicken, and pork
>
> *Brown*, made of partridge, duck, hare, and pork
>
> *Gratin*, made of salt pork, chicken livers, and foie gras, *flambé* with cognac and flavored with Madeira
>
> The various ingredients were artfully layered in a mold, alter-

---

*The admirable Gérard Besson in Paris, one of the rare men brave enough to 1) put in all the work required for this *chef d'oeuvre* and 2) to go against the grain of fashion, offers Dumaine's recipe on his menu today (hunting season only). He serves it hot, with a champagne-based sauce.

nating meat, stuffing, and more truffles, then oven-cooked
in a *bain marie*, unmolded, and then encased in a *pâte
feuilletée*, cooked again to brown the pastry shell, then injected with a rich broth of forest game and left to cool.

When finally served and cut open by a suitably ceremonious
maître d'hôtel, Dumaine's entire dining room turned fragrant with the
intoxicating perfume of truffles and meat broth. "Close the windows!"
cried one anguished club member, alarmed at the prospect of losing
the least atom of goodness.

In today's cooking crowd, a dish like this is generally viewed as a
museum piece, a reminder of the grandiose traditions of pompous
nineteenth-century masters like Carême and Escoffier, whether or not
it is delicious—which it is, of course. Rare are those who dare venture
into that terrain in these rock 'n' roll days of postmodern experimentation and gimmick. Times change, and tastes change with them. Ironically enough, the same Alexandre Dumaine who was viewed with
almost reverential awe just a couple of generations ago would doubtless catch hell from both sides of the critical divide today. His set-piece
creations like the *oreiller* would be hooted as wildly complicated and
pretentious, while his simpler menus would be dismissed as primitive.
Jean Ducloux remembered another lunch that the master put together
for the Club des Cent:

Consommé diablotins

Filets de truite florentine

Coq au Chambertin

Timbale de morilles châtelaine

Mousses d'écrevisses au Cliquot

Fromages

Coupe glacée aux fraises

Corbeille de fruits

If this was cutting-edge stuff in the early fifties, today it would certainly earn condescending smiles. A consommé with croutons? You can get that in Tashkent and Toledo. While it is hard to go wrong with a profligate heap of morel mushrooms or a well-handled and well-garnished mousse of crayfish tails, the idea of trout filets *florentine*—on a bed of buttered spinach and covered with a *sauce mornay*—would immediately set the eyes rolling. (A *mornay* contains flour, and if that was not shocking enough, the preparation would have been sprinkled with grated cheese and browned under a salamander grill.) And as for Dumaine's *coq au chambertin*, well! That was merely a high-class *coq au vin*, wasn't it? Any restaurateur of quality daring to serve a *coq au vin* today—or a *boeuf bourguignon*, or a *sole normande*—would deserve a medal for heroism. Dumaine's cheeses would probably pass muster, but the idea of just strawberries and ice cream for dessert would be something akin to culinary outrage. You have to try harder today. People expect more, and better (whatever the current definition for that happens to be).

And there's the rub: Fashions change, and nothing goes out of fashion as fast as fashion. Dumaine retired in 1964 and sold La Côte d'Or in a full blaze of glory, before he suffered the ignominy of going out of date. Bernard Loiseau, cooking in the very same kitchen forty years later, was destined to ride an exhilarating wind of triumph when it was his turn to be perfectly in tune with the latest avatars of taste and fashion, doing his part to change them and even, for a few giddy years, seeming to dictate them. But, slowly and imperceptibly at first, then accelerating and suddenly running out of control, out there beyond his ken, they twisted away from him and changed once again. And poor Bernard fell off the top of the world.

II

CLERMONT-FERRAND

*T*he year 1950 was not a good time for optimism. Trouble was everywhere. With the Iron Curtain clanged firmly shut and the Cold War at its frigid debut, the last illusions about anything resembling democracy for the U.S.S.R.'s Eastern European satellite states had dissipated. Mao's ragtag People's Army had already pushed the Nationalists into the sea and settled their domination over mainland China. The French were hopelessly bogged down in a neocolonialist struggle in Vietnam (which they were pleased to pass on to America a decade or so later), the Algerian war was brewing, and *le Parti Communiste Français* was seething with defiant confidence. Nerves were frayed on the other side of the Atlantic, too: NATO had been formed, President Truman had given the go-ahead for the development of the hydrogen bomb, and Senator Joseph McCarthy was braying to anyone who would listen that the U.S. State Department was a viper's nest of Reds. In June a surprise attack from Pyongyang set off the Korean War. Everything considered, it didn't seem much like a world worth bringing kids into, but life went on, as it always does. That same June, in Clermont-Ferrand, a twenty-seven-year-old shopkeeper named Edith Loiseau received the strongest possible reminder of life's forces: She discovered that she was pregnant with her first child.

Clermont-Ferrand is an odd kind of place, quite different from what most people would recognize as typically French. Capital city of the former countship of Auvergne, it sits smack in the middle of

France, ringed on three sides by the soft domes of ancient, long-extinct volcanoes that impart a kind of austere majesty to the area. Many of its churches, public buildings, and older houses are built of the gloomy black lava that once so liberally flowed throughout the region. It is a workaday, rather boring kind of place without much beauty or spark, and it certainly does not ring with the *joie de vivre* that characterizes so many other French cities. Neat enough, but just a little shabby and tattered at the edges. The soil of the surrounding countryside is generally poor, fit for little more than grazing cattle, and the *auvergnats* themselves have always been viewed in France as singular exceptions to the national Latin stereotype: dour, thrifty, industrious, and reserved as clams. Withal, the city is prosperous, thanks to its single employer, around whose factories and administration everything else revolves: the Michelin tire company, employer of 15,000-plus *clermontois*. Clermont-Ferrand is Michelin City.

Although she had always enjoyed a natter and a laugh—Edith Loiseau, *née* Rullière, was as thrifty and industrious as the best of the Clermont natives around her, even if she was not a true *auvergnate*. "I'm an *ardéchoise!*" she heavily insists whenever the question of her origin arises in conversation. The Ardèche, another of the ancient provinces that history subsumed into greater France, is an equally poor region of volcanic hills, valleys, and swift torrents, abutting the Auvergne to the southeast. Today still, the French remain extremely touchy and punctilious about their regional origins and talents, the character traits—and, of course, the styles of cuisine—that these geographic provenances are assumed to impart. Edith was and is no exception.

Her father was an outsider, an *ardéchois* butcher who migrated to Clermont and went on to own the biggest and (according to her, at any rate) best *charcuterie** in town, on the rue du Gras near the cathedral. Edith remembers her father as excessive, energetic, and hyperactive,

---

Charcuterie literally means a shop of cooked meat (*chair* = meat, *cuire* = to cook), and the basic element of a *charcuterie* has traditionally been pork—sausages, pâtés, terrines, and the like. In modern times they branched out to all kinds of cooked dishes and ready-to-eat meals, beautifully displayed in their show windows—a minor art form by themselves. The *charcuterie* might be termed a princely delicatessen.

most of the time charging around as if he meant to take over Clermont's entire *charcuterie* trade, but occasionally and inexplicably falling into black funks that left him listless and frail. Many years later, in view of the rise and fall of the grandson whom he never lived long enough to know, the suspicion of some kind of genetic behavioral link between the two was bound to arise.

He died when Edith was only sixteen. As the family's eldest child, it was her duty to drop everything and run the shop until her little brother grew old enough to assume the traditional male role of *chef de famille* and take command of the business. She was still proprietor pro tem when she met and married Pierre Loiseau, and so devoted to work that her first child was almost born on the floor of the *charcuterie*—there were always customers to be served, and she pushed her calculations a bit too close to the limit. On January 13, 1951, Pierre got her, just in time for birth, to the Clinique Sainte-Madeleine in Chamalières, the Clermont suburb where they owned an apartment. They named their baby boy Bernard. As soon as she was strong enough, Edith went back to work in the *charcuterie*.

The little four-room apartment of the Loiseau family on the avenue Franklin Roosevelt was typical of the urban dwellings of the French *petite bourgeoisie* of that era: neither shower nor bath, and communal toilets out in the hallway. Wash basins and the all-important *bidets* in the bedrooms and a trip to the public baths once a week for a good cleanup. The kitchen was the all-purpose room for cooking, washing, and family gatherings. The surroundings in which the baby grew to boyhood reflected neither poverty nor wealth but the normal middle-of-the-road comfort of the Clermont-Ferrand commercial class in the fifties.

Little Bernard spent his infancy practically under Edith's skirts in the *charcuterie*—either there or across the street, where a nice lady who owned a shoe store consented to watch the boy when Edith was too busy slicing ham and dishing out *champignons à la greque*. There was a Catholic day-care center in another part of town, but it was more convenient to have the child nearby. That was fine with Bernard, who much preferred being with Mama than with some social functionary. "I grew up between *terrines*, sausages and calves' heads," he remembered years later. "I watched how they made *andouilles* [tripe sausages] and pâtés. I liked to hide in the show window. It was fun and it smelled good."

The baby grew into a cheerful, gregarious, and indefatigably active boy, both outgoing and enthusiastic. He was so much a part of daily life among the *commerçants* of the old town section that he was regarded as something of a neighborhood mascot—*"l'enfant chéri du quartier,"* as Edith put it. Two years after his birth a second son, Rémy, was born, and he proved to be as calm, reserved, and introverted as Bernard was explosive. Where Bernard led, Rémy followed—he and their other friends, too. Bernard had the natural stuff of a leader. When, in 1962, Edith gave birth to Catherine, her only daughter, she finally quit the *charcuterie*, handed the keys to her brother, and moved back to Chamalières for good.

She was often alone in the apartment with her brood, because her husband was a traveling salesman, a "VRP"—*voyageur représentant placier*. He might have gone into the butchery business himself, because his family, too, was of the trade; his father owned a small *abattoir* in the village of Messeix in the hilly countryside west of Clermont. But Pierre preferred the open road to the knife and the blood of the slaughter, and he was happy to leave the *abattoir* to a younger brother. The life of a traveling man seemed more appealing and prestigious, and at any rate it was certainly much cleaner. The road was not as glamorous as all that, though. As a provincial VRP (also known, somewhat disparagingly, as *commis voyageur*), earnestly peddling ladies' hats and stockings, Pierre resembled nothing so much as a Gallic model of Arthur Miller's Willy Loman.

He began his professional life in 1947, in the *bonneterie* line: ladies' hats and hosiery. Hats were all the rage in the thirties and forties, and after the deprivations of the war, the fashion exploded again in the fifties— no self-respecting Frenchwoman of any *coquetterie* at all would venture into the street without some stylish *chapeau* perched on her head. Several hat factories and ateliers thrived in Clermont, and Pierre would load boxes upon boxes of samples into his little Peugeot, turn the crank to fire it up, and go puttering off north to visit *modiste* shops in the sector where he enjoyed exclusive sales rights. It was a big territory, taking him away from Clermont for two and three weeks at a time as he roamed as far as Lille, Tourcoing, and Valenciennes, way up by the Belgian border.

It was an unpredictable, chancy kind of business, because his entire income derived from commissions: If Pierre sold nothing he earned nothing. Very rapidly he learned the pasted-on smile and the commercial small talk required of anyone who hoped to make any progress against the eternal *moue* of dubiety of the ladies—it was always ladies—who ran the millinery shops. But Pierre was a believer—he had actually begun studies for the priesthood in his younger years—and one way or another, things always worked out. Until the sixties, that is: calamity arrived for the *bonneterie* trade when hats abruptly went out of fashion. The factories and ateliers closed down. Pierre had to find something else, fast. He bought a client list from a retiring colleague in the *layette* business: baby clothes.

This time, things weren't quite so risky. Whatever happened, there would always be babies, he reasoned, and they would always have to be clothed. Pierre signed up with a manufacturer named Ribambel, located in Roanne, 130 kilometers to the northeast over on the other side of the Black Woods and the Monts de la Madeleine. Pierre already knew the city well. Much smaller than Clermont, it was a center of light manufacturing, textiles, foundries, and notably, a national arsenal and factory where tanks and armored vehicles were built for the army. But much more important than all that, it had the Hôtel Moderne.

All the gentlemen of the road knew about the place, property of the Troisgros family. In the fifties and sixties it was probably the best *table d'hôte* in France. The saga had begun in the early thirties in Chalon-sur-Saône, a sleepy town between Tournus and the southern edge of the Burgundy vineyards, where Jean-Baptiste and Marie Troisgros ran the little Café des Négociants. With two infant boys taking up more and more room, Jean-Baptiste wanted something bigger and better, so he began looking around. Although it took him away from the wine fields that he dearly loved, he finally settled on the little four-story Hôtel des Platanes in Roanne. It had a very interesting location directly across from the railway station, and its plumbing was up-to-date. This was a man who knew a thing or two about marketing long before the word even existed. He changed the name of the place to Hôtel Moderne and appended a bit of alluring information to the sign by the front door: "Hot water on every floor. Renowned cuisine."

Very quickly it was appreciated, too, especially by the commercial gentlemen who soon adopted it as one of their preferred stopping points. Pierre Loiseau always looked forward to taking his seat at the Hôtel Moderne's big, convivial *table d'hôte*—sometimes as many as twenty or thirty of his colleagues would be there with him—because he knew that whatever was posted on the day's fixed menu, it was going to be first-rate eats. By the time he arrived on the scene Marie had left the kitchen, her place taken at the big coal-fired stove—*"le piano,"* as they call it in the trade—by a journeyman chef whom Jean-Baptiste hired in her stead. But the food remained of the same style, the bourgeois classics that countless generations revered and knew by heart: *soupe à l'oignon, blanquette de veau, fromage de tête*, calves' feet in *sauce gribiche*, roast beef with ratatouille, *gratin dauphinois, coq au vin*, and the like.

To wet his customers' whistles, Jean-Baptiste ordered barrels of Burgundy and Beaujolais, rolled them across from the station and down into his cellar, where he put them up in bottles himself—a chore he passed on to his sons as soon as they were old enough to handle the equipment properly. (In return, he gave them movie tickets.) Jean-Baptiste served his wines cool, at the temperature of the *cave*, rather than bothering to *chambrer* them up to room temperature. In itself this was already a departure from the standard practice of the day, but Jean-Baptiste had his way of doing things. In time, he would be viewed as something very much like a revolutionary.

"He had had no formal training in either cooking or wine," said Christian Millau, founder of the *Guide GaultMillau*, the bible of *nouvelle cuisine* in the seventies and eighties, "but he had the same kind of instinctive feel for cuisine that François Villon did for poetry. He was an extraordinary man. Couldn't cook a thing himself, but he was a genius of taste. I admired him greatly."

Sharp-tongued, peremptory of judgment, Jean-Baptiste proved to be as influential as Fernand Point and the prestigious Paris chefs under whom his sons had worked in developing the signature Troisgros cuisine—the "new" cuisine that would soon be setting gourmets atwitch from Paris to New York to Tokyo and points beyond. He was a tough, authoritarian little rooster of a man. He always knew exactly what he wanted, and he brooked no sass. When he sent his boys away to La Pyramide and thence to the big *brigades* in Paris to finish their training, he had already decided that they would return to Roanne and the Hô-tel Moderne—whether or not they had other plans. Like Jean Ducloux he was a man of the old school, and no one said no to Jean-Baptiste.

"He was the boss," Pierre Troisgros told me with a rueful laugh. "*Le Patron.* Our mother and father, we addressed them as '*patron*' and '*patronne*,' not Papa and Maman. I would never have been able to even say the word 'papa.' It was impossible. I would have been dishonored. It would have been the end of the world. You would have had to torture me to get the word 'papa' out of my mouth. *C'était le patron*, and that was that."

This commanding, demanding demeanor was not mere frivolity or some kind of ego trip on Jean-Baptiste's part, though. He earned it by the work he put in. The restaurant trade is a thing for perfectionists in the first place, and the Troisgros boys knew only too well from their ex-periences in Vienne and Paris to put in all the effort and attention to detail required to make faultless meals and please the customers twice a day. *Twice a day*—that's the nub, that's the thing restaurant profes-sionals always come back to when they talk about the trade. Do it right, get a little rest, then come back and do it all over again at night. No breaks, no taking the day off if you don't feel like it, no calling in sick unless you are comatose—and the Troisgros place was open seven days a week.

"They didn't have any time for a family life," Pierre says today. "My parents just crossed paths in the stairway, one coming up when the other was going down."

Jean-Baptiste brought his kids back home because he sensed exactly what he could do with them. "*Ils ont du talent, ces deux petits cons*," he grudgingly admitted to Millau one evening in the seventies—these two little jerks have got talent. All they needed was some guidance.

Jean-Baptiste guided effortlessly—first his wife, then the hired la-bor he brought in to fill the gap while Jean and Pierre were away at fin-ishing school rattling pots and pans, and then finally the kids themselves. In 1954 Pierre returned from Lucas-Carton and, six months later, Jean from the Crillon. Jean-Baptiste honored the return of the prodigals by renaming the establishment Les Frères Troisgros. It was a nice pat on the back, but that didn't mean that everything was shaped up and finished. Not yet. The stage was set for a confrontation.

"We thought we were the world champions," Pierre recalled. "There wasn't anyone who could teach us a thing. But when we started making the big classical dishes we had learned in the *brigades*—*selle de veau Orloff*, that kind of thing—he brought us right up short. *'C'est de la merde, ça,'* he said. *'C'est zéro.'* I was so mad and hurt that I spent a month without speaking to him—we literally communicated by notes back and forth, but it turned out that he was right."

Pierre's month-long pout turned out to be a learning experience. He watched his father circulating from table to table, chatting up the clients, grilling them about their preferences, then darting back into the kitchen to inspect the plates returning from the dining room: What were they eating, and what were they turning away? Why? At length, Pierre and Jean caught on: The customer really *was* the king. That wasn't just a saying. Too much time in the disciplined, semimilitary *brigades* of the big kitchens had taught them to perfectly execute a number of gestures that by long-established norms resulted in certain predefined dishes—but those gestures did not really bring them into a personal involvement with their work. They had been following the rules, not thinking. Jean-Baptiste made them think, and he made them taste. After years of assembling dishes by rote, cooks tended to forget the elementary function of actually tasting their own cooking. By teaching his sons to adopt the client's view of their job, Jean-Baptiste turned Jean and Pierre from traditional kitchen workers into modern chefs. Then he went a step further with an utterly incongruous idea: He led them out into the dining room to meet the customers and— what else would they do?—talk about food. Thus began the relaxed, low-key, but still highly professional, relationship of equality between customer and kitchen that a million restaurateurs around the world would soon be copying.

Only a year after the brothers' return to Roanne, the restaurant was rewarded with its first Michelin star. For Pierre Loiseau and his fellow traveling salesmen, it was the golden age of Les Frères Troisgros; the food was improving year by year, and the influx of tourists and gas-tronomes who filled the other tables helped subsidize the *table d'hôte* where the more penurious gentlemen of the road lunched and dined at unbeatable bargain prices. Everyone felt entirely at home in the bosom of the Troisgros family; Jean and Pierre were in the kitchen, their wives at the reception, Aunt Georgette, "La Tata," at the cash register, their mother a skilled backup for any position that needed help, and Jean-Baptiste lorded it over the lot—Rooster Number One in the chicken coop.* As often as not, *le patron* would amble up to the *table d'hôte* with a bottle of cognac and pour the guys a free *pousse-café* at the end of their meal. Gradually, as the years passed and the gastronomic reputation of Les Frères Troisgros assumed international proportions, the simple *table d'hôte* slipped away into history (as, indeed, did the Milleresque VRP trade itself), but for the moment it was heaven for the traveling salesmen. This was what a restaurant should be like.

Of course Pierre Loiseau had no idea at the time of the future glory awaiting Jean and Pierre Troisgros, and even less so of the crucial role their restaurant was destined to play in the life of his first son. For the moment, Roanne was no more than a pleasant stop along his route.

If the life of the VRP lacked the security of a regular salary, it offered Pierre the advantage of being able to set his own schedule, and since much of the *layette* business was seasonal, he had plenty of spare time to spend with his children. His own upbringing had been strict, so quite naturally he followed the same line, even if he later thought of himself as quite the liberal. ("Parents always think they're liberal," the adult Rémy observed wryly. "In fact, they were both quite traditional and severe, especially Papa. You know, he almost became a priest, and he probably would have made a career of the army if he'd been able to, but when he was the right age for it the war had been lost, and there was no more army. He had a very strict side to him.")

"Traditional" for Pierre Loiseau meant obedience and respect for elders, of course, but also long, healthy hikes in the country, exhausting but exhilarating bike rides up and down the steep volcanic hillsides, and church without fail every Sunday and on holy days. There was a radio in the apartment—young Bernard loved the mystery programs—but certainly no TV. A new-fangled gadget like that could never last. Besides, it was expensive.

In summers, the family decamped to the little tile-floored, stone-

---

*Jean-Baptiste died a beautiful death in 1974—struck down at the dinner table, a glass of wine in his hand.

façaded country house that Pierre had built next to his father's *abattoir* in Messeix, an hour's drive from Clermont near the thermal station of La Bourboule and the cattle town of Laqueille, where the locals made (and still make) an excellent blue cheese of cow's milk, smooth and creamy, but with perhaps less bite and character than the fabled cheese that is Roquefort produced a few hundred kilometers due south, from the milk of the thousands of ewes that graze on and around the Larzac plateau.

Settled into the Messeix summer routine, father and sons had plenty of time to go off and do their guy things while Edith tended the house and, later, watched over baby Catherine. Mushroom hunting in the nearby pastures and coppices led to enjoyable rambles, but the really big event in Messeix was the hunt for crayfish — *écrevisses*, the same delicious little brownish black freshwater clawed critters, resembling miniature lobsters, that Fernand Point served *au gratin*, Madame Blanc in a peppery *nage*, and Les Frères Troisgros with eggs in aspic. Thanks to intensive farming and the polluting runoff from pesticides and fertilizers, crayfish, like frogs and snails, have now all but disappeared from the French countryside, but the *pattes rouges*, the largest and tastiest of the species, still abounded in the Auvergne of the fifties and early sixties. Pierre led *écrevisse* expeditions to the Dordogne River, or the Chavanon or the Clidane, with Bernard and Rémy in tow, each proudly carrying a circular, basketlike *balance* crayfish trap that was easy to enter but not to exit. The fishing part required very little expertise apart from locating the potential habitats of their prey. Pierre baited the traps with a bit of scrap meat — beef spleen or such — lowered them into the water, and waited for the right moment to yank them up with the inquisitive visitors trapped inside. On a good day's fishing he and the boys returned to Messeix with eight or ten dozen *pattes rouges*. Then the fun began.

"Bernard was so impatient to get to eating them that half the time, he would spill them out of the traps, and we would have crayfish scampering all over the kitchen floor," Pierre remembered, "but eventually we would get them together and prepare them for cooking."

Edith set a mixture of water, white wine, and aromatics aboil in a pot and attacked the animals one by one, snapping off the tail's middle scale and carefully drawing out the intestine with it, an operation (picturesquely but inaccurately) known in French as castration. It doesn't sound very nice—and doubtless it doesn't feel great for the crayfish, either—but this was an earlier generation and perhaps a more honest one where comestibles were concerned. People were much closer than today to the reality of exactly what they were inflicting upon the animal kingdom for the filling of their bellies. When they bought a chicken or a rabbit for the pot it was usually with the head and the feathers or the fur still *in situ*, and frequently not even gutted. Fish were not filets or breaded cutlets but whole, unscaled, and slimy, with bright little eyes peering accusingly at their purchasers. When nothing else was going on in Messeix, it was little more than casual entertainment for Bernard to drop by the *abattoir* in time to watch his uncle slaughter pigs and sheep and calves, observing how, amid the blood and gore, he broke them down into sellable pieces while commenting professorally on the quality and value of each glistening chunk. (He saved the blood, too, of course, for the *boudin* sausages that go so well with applesauce.) The days were not yet upon France when animal pieces would be so trimmed, sanitized, and wrapped as to resemble Christmas presents.

As for the luckless *écrevisses* caught in Pierre's traps, it was quickly into the pot with them, alive and kicking, and in a mere seven or eight minutes they were glowing bright red and ready for consumption, finger-burning hot but each one more delicious than the last, accompanied by a steaming platterful of boiled potatoes from nearby farms.

Apart from vacation-time treats like this, Edith's day-to-day cooking for normal days in Clermont was strictly local market stuff. The little shops and street markets had not yet begun to feel the deadly pressure of the interloping *supermarchés* and *hypermarchés*, the industrial-sized commercial centers, all plastic, aluminum, steel, and fluorescent lighting, that dominate the French retail food scene today, desecrating vast stretches of previously undefiled farmland. Stuffed cabbage—cabbage from the market, chopped meat stuffing from the family *charcuterie*—was a traditional *auvergnat* specialty that Edith the *ardéchoise* adopted without much of a regional grumble, as was the wonderful, rustic *soupe au chou*: cabbage quarters simply boiled in water with potatoes, carrots, and onions and a large slab of smoked *lard* (a cut similar to unsliced bacon), chockablock with rich, cholesterol-laden fat. Cut thick slices of sourdough peasant bread to serve with it (not forgetting to first whip the knife back and forth over the loaf in a quick sign of the cross) and you have a dish that is the closest thing to the magic potion of Asterix and Obelix. *Soupe au chou* is a true French icon, a peasant curative and *fortifiant* that can go head to head with the world's champion of Jewish penicillins.

Like most other housewives, Edith made her own jellies and jams from fruits bought at the market or brought back from Messeix, sterilizing the freshly filled jars in a washtub of water on her coal-fired stove. The milk that Edith bought was whole and unpasteurized then, and certainly not dispossessed of its fat to resemble the pale blue water that universally greets breakfasters reading their cereal boxes today. Bernard and his brother especially loved to skim off the "skin"* of fat that rose to the surface and spread it on their bread. At Christmas, Edith reverted to her regional roots and cooked a *canard aux marrons*, a duck baked with the huge chestnuts that for centuries have grown wild in the Ardèche. If she was cooking steaks or chops, Bernard was the only family member who insisted on his meat being well-done, a preference he would maintain throughout his life—a rarity for French gastronomes, almost all of whom tend to take their meat "blue," still almost aquiver.

The boy ate like an ogre—anything, anything at all—without complaining, even if later in life he was to discover a previously undetected allergy to raw or undercooked saltwater shellfish. Freshwater *écrevisses* were no problem, but an undercooked scallop or *langoustine* would have him breaking out in red spots and close to suffocation, gasping for breath. The allergy had never been detected during Bernard's childhood because such expensive luxuries did not find their way to the Loiseau table. Scallops, lobsters, and the like were items reserved for the monied classes. As a rule, the French *petite bourgeoisie* has generally been content to stick with the less pretentious, more economical regional specialties that constitute the backbone of the nation's culi-

---

*The brilliant Michel Bras in Laguiole (due south of Clermont, halfway to the Mediterranean, that is to say the middle of nowhere) makes large quantities of milk skin daily, which he incorporates into various dishes as a kind of Proustian madeleine recalling the juvenile gourmandise that he shared with thousands of other French kids. A brash young generation of Spanish and Catalan cooks has rediscovered the trick recently.

nary curriculum. The swells and *nouveaux riches* in the big cities adore flash and novelty, but it is the *petite bourgeoisie* that keeps the pot of tradition alive in France, slowly bubbling on a back burner.

Pierre retained a strikingly clear memory of the omnivorous enthusiasm that marked his firstborn son. "In the early sixties, when Bernard was about ten, I took him and Rémy up north to show them Paris. On the way back I stopped for lunch at a nice place I knew in the Sologne area, about halfway back home. I think it was the first time Bernard had seen a real menu in a real restaurant. When I asked the boys what they wanted, Rémy didn't even have a chance to answer before Bernard piped up. *'Je veux tout!'* he said. [I want everything.] That was his nature—overflowing, excessive, always enthusiastic."

"Bernard was all superlatives, and he could never hide anything," Rémy said. "He wasn't one for nuance. With him, things were either fantastic or lousy. When he became famous and started visiting the restaurants of his *confrères*, he always came back with the same verdict: The food at their places was no good."

Pierre and Edith Loiseau saw from the start that their boy was obviously quick and bright, but his grades in school rarely reflected his innate intelligence. Competitive grading didn't exist *chez les soeurs*, in the religious nursery school run by nuns, but Bernard rapidly fell behind his classmates when he went on to Nestor Perret, the public grade school. The simple fact was that studying always bored Bernard. He couldn't see the interest in learning dates, facts, and figures just because that was what the other kids were doing. Papa and Maman took solace from the fact that he had an excellent memory and good handwriting, and were pleased when one of his teachers remarked on his native facility for mental calculation. No doubt he'll make a good *commerçant* one day, the teacher suggested, as if to excuse himself for the poor grades he was perfectly justified in giving the boy. Meanwhile, Bernard goofed off, rode his bike, and hung out in the parks and squares where grownups were playing *pétanque*. Invited to join in, he became something of a prodigy, a real little ace at throwing the steel balls with great accuracy. He had an odd game, though: he was a righty, but he threw *left-handed*. Bernard never did anything like other people.

When baby Catherine was born the Chamalières apartment began seriously showing its size. Three was a crowd, even if they were just

small children, and Bernard's grades weren't improving—*bien au contraire*. Pierre and Edith decided to send the boy away to Catholic
boarding school. Perhaps the priests might have more success than the
public school teachers in awakening the scholar lying dormant within
their turbulent son. Bernard was eleven when he first crossed the
threshold of the Groupe Scolaire Massillon on rue Bansac, next to the
train station in downtown Clermont. It was to be his home away from
home for the next six years.

Unlike the sterner establishments run by Jesuits, Dominicans, or
other Catholic orders, Massillon was a relatively easygoing kind of
place, allowing kids to return home for weekends and offering them an
up-to-date infrastructure that included a basketball court and a swimming pool. A few lay teachers were even mixed in among the priests
and monks, but that did not mean that matters of discipline in the True
Faith were neglected. A vigorously clanging bell awakened the big dor-
mitory at 6:30 A.M. sharp and it was time get dressed, make the bed,
and shuffle quietly up to the refectory for breakfast. No food was
served, of course, until group prayers had been said. Prayers dominated
the routine at lunch and dinner, too, and a full ceremonial mass—
attendance obligatory—was celebrated every Thursday. Frequently
enough, Bernard served as altar boy, dressed in lace and pious of mien,
passing the vessel of holy oil and holy wine to the officiating priest,
lacking only a vial of holy vinegar for a nicely symbolic prefiguration of
the thousands of salad dressings he would be turning out in his future
career.

In the school's domains that aroused his interest most deeply—the
athletic installations and the refectory—Bernard could allow his extroverted personality freer rein than at the altar. He was one of the fifty or
so boys named *chef de table*, the one who sat at the head of the table of
eight and doled out the food for the others, in his case flooding them
with a machine-gun flow of words and juvenile wit. He was something
of a loudmouth, to tell the truth, and at the activities most cherished by
adolescent boys everywhere—sports and clowning around—he was
among Massillon's finest. On the other hand, he proved to be a
washout at another hallowed pastime of the young male of the species:
fighting. From his earliest youth, he had always avoided aggression and
confrontation.

Peaceableness did nothing to enhance his zeal in studies, though, and his grades showed it. As the years at Massillon passed, Pierre and Edith slowly came around to the realization that their firstborn would never be a doctor, lawyer, or pharmacist. It was a bitter pill for Pierre, whose two brothers had produced polite, studious children who were on their way to extremely respectable careers in teaching. The matter of Bernard's application to studies came seriously to a head in June of 1967 when, at age sixteen, he was confronted with the first serious academic challenge of his life, the BEPC. The Brevet d'Études Premier Cycle does not exist anymore, but in the sixties it was the midpoint between the elementary school *certificat d'études* and the famous *baccalauréat*, the very demanding *lycée* diploma. Taking the BEPC was something of a dramatic event, because it represented the point at which schoolchildren were first culled to determine which ones would go on toward *études supérieures* and which would be shunted off to the more manual studies.

Bernard flunked this test with flying colors. So much so, in fact, that he didn't write anything at all in his copy book. *Feuille blanche*, they call it: He knew he didn't stand a chance of passing, so he turned in a virgin sheet, unsullied by the least pen stroke.

This time Pierre could no longer ignore the reality of his son's academic abjection. Something had to be done. Draping himself in full paternal dignity, he huffed and puffed, did the fatherly thing, and delivered the standard dressing-down—you're a good-for-nothing, you'll never amount to anything and just look at how well your cousins are doing in school.

Bernard hung his head appropriately for the time required. "I want to go to work," he said at length.

"His temperament had always been turned toward what was real and the concrete rather than the theoretical," Pierre says today, putting the best gloss on what was then a terrible situation. "So I asked him what kind of work he wanted to do."

Bernard shrugged. "I don't know."

Long silence. But Pierre had been doing a little thinking on his side. "How about cooking?"

Bernard looked up, reflected for a moment, then made the decision of his life: "*Allons-y pour cuisinier.*"

Let's try cooking, then. Like Jean Ducloux on his thirteenth birthday, young Bernard was about to discover the reality of life in *les métiers de la bouche*, the eating trade.

It began with pastry. Monsieur and Madame Dalzon, friends of the Loiseaus, had a *pâtisserie* in downtown Clermont, and they agreed to take Bernard on as an apprentice. Only a couple of weeks after his BEPC flop, Bernard found himself rising at three or four in the morning, depending on the day, to hop onto his bike and get to work on time. Pastry and baking are essentially for very early risers, because everyone in France expects to be able to buy at least a fresh, warm *baguette*, a basket of *croissants*, or some nice, yeasty-eggy *brioches* by 7 A.M., if not even earlier. Bakers and *pâtissiers* work in the middle of the night, then, and it is the apprentice who needs to get to work first, to create order, sweep up, bring in the fresh milk and take out the empty bottles, scrape the pastry sheets clean—no Teflon in those days— empty the trash cans, and generally make things ready for the arrival of the master. There are always masters in the *métiers de la bouche*, and however even-tempered and friendly they may be, there is one thing and one thing only that they can never tolerate: tardiness. In no profession does the clock dominate more tyrannically than in the business of cooking and eating.

Bernard was on time, then, because if he wasn't, the *baguettes*, *croissants*, and *brioches* would be delayed and he would be swiftly out on the street without a job. Meanwhile, Pierre drove over to Roanne to speak with Jean-Baptiste Troisgros, who offered some good news: The Troisgros' restaurant would have an opening for an apprentice as of March 1, 1968. It was a nice piece of luck and a very good opportunity, because two years earlier Les Frères Troisgros had won a second Michelin star. Now serious gastronomes were viewing the establishment with steadily increasing respect. Over in Lyon, Jean and Pierre's good friend, Paul Bocuse, had already won his third star. Might the Troisgros boys be next in line?

Pierre drove back to Clermont with a real feeling of satisfaction. The matter was settled. His years of frequenting the Troisgros *table d'hôte* and his long acquaintance with Jean-Baptiste had paid off with at least the start of a potential career for his boy. Where he would take it from there was anyone's guess.

Surprisingly enough, he seemed to be making a good start. As lax as he had been with his studies, Bernard took his *pâtisserie* job seriously, even if he was paid only the symbolic apprentice's pittance. He arrived on time, worked the long hours that were required of him, and never complained, even as the autumn of 1967 turned to the frigid blasts of November and December and turned his bike rides into something of an ordeal. He stayed with the Dalzons for six months, then moved into a kitchen helper's job that Pierre found for him in a little neighborhood restaurant called Le Boeuf Api. And at the end of February, six weeks after he turned seventeen, Pierre and Edith drove him to Roanne with his bike tied to the roof of the car.

They arrived in late afternoon. Pierre brought Bernard in through the front door—it was the last time Bernard would be allowed to use that entrance for many years—and met Jean-Baptiste at the reception desk. Jean-Baptiste led the boy into the empty kitchen, showed him the back entrance, through the courtyard, and instructed him to report at eight sharp next morning, March 1. Then he left him with his parents to deposit his suitcase in the room that Pierre had found for him in the house of a lady who lived nearby. After a few perfunctory farewells they said goodbye and drove off. Bernard unpacked the two white cook's blouses and the two pair of gray checker-pattern trousers that his parents had bought for him—his new uniform. What, he wondered, would tomorrow bring?

Coal, mostly. That and Claude Perraudin.

Claude was the previous "new boy," the last-arrived apprentice who by tradition always gets the worst assignments until the next one comes along. He had only just turned sixteen, and he had been on coal duty for more than a year, a longer period than any other apprentice in memory had ever been saddled with. It had been Claude's bad luck to arrive in the Troisgros kitchen at a moment when no new training slots were opening up for a long while, and he was thoroughly sick of the dirty, dusty chore. Now, at last, he could pass it on to the new kid, and even impose upon him a little bit of his newfound authority as a seasoned veteran of the shovel and scuttle. Bernard tied on the big blue apron, donned the old forage cap that went with the job—those two items, plus a bottomless supply of kitchen towels, were the only ones furnished by the house—and followed Claude down into the cellar.

He was tough, this guy Perraudin. Short, stocky, and already well muscled for his age, he had started kitchen work while still only a child, in his parents' small town hotel-restaurant in Bona, just north of the Loire by the cathedral city of Nevers. Charity begins at home; his parents had worked little Claude so hard that the Troisgros gig, even if it was coal duty, seemed like a holiday camp. But he was happy to unload the job on his replacement all the same.

Claude showed Bernard the pile of black oily lumps of high-grade anthracite stored in the coal bin beneath the kitchen, the shovel, the buckets and the garbage cans, and demonstrated how to shake down the ashes from the night before, lug them out into the courtyard, then get a good blaze going in the firebox—paper and wood first, coal after—so the *piano* would be warm and ready for the arrival of the chefs at 8:30 in the morning. The routine would be repeated twice a day, for the lunch and dinner services, as would the ritual scouring, washing, and drying of all the counter tops, ovens, and stove surfaces, until the entire kitchen glowed with a silver sheen. Every two weeks there was a special extra job for the new kid: wire brushing and cleaning the inside of the firebox underneath the removable cast-iron rings on which the chefs set their frying pans and casseroles. Coal delivered heat nicely, but it left masses of soot, and chefs unanimously, universally, hated soot. They hated dirt, too, and disorder, and noise—any noise, that is, except their own. In fact it seemed to young Bernard that they hated just about everything. They were gods, and that was just the way it was with gods.

Magnificent in their towering white *toques*, freshly starched each day, their white blouses and their white aprons, Their Albescent Majesties Jean and Pierre Troisgros stalked into the kitchen at eight thirty sharp, and if you had a brain in your head you stopped the chatter when you saw them coming and shut up until spoken to. Jean—tall, movie-star handsome, his beard trimmed with military precision—was grim and tight-lipped, as severe as a Calvinist preacher. Pierre—shorter, rounder, and bull-strong—sported a neat mustache and just the hint of a glint in the eye that suggested that maybe he was capable of a smile and even a laugh. Jean handled the vegetables, the sauces—he was a world-class *saucier*—and the final assembly of the food on the plates. Pierre was the master of the *garde-manger*—pantry, or cold kitchen—

and knew everything a human being could possibly know about the as-
sessing and cooking of meat and fish.

You referred to them as "Chef Jean" and "Chef Pierre." The former
addressed apprentices as "*gamin*" (kid) and the latter, "*petit.*" Jean-
Baptiste, if he took you into his line of vision at all (which was rare—he
had more important matters to consider, like which year of Puligny
Montrachet to recommend), called you "*petit con.*"

Being in the company of gods—even if their domain was only the
original 20-foot-by-20-foot Troisgros kitchen, where you watched your
step and walked with your elbows in, lest you knock over a pot or, worse,
make physical contact with a god—was an experience so awesome that
it silenced even Bernard, Massillon's former champion of gab.

Then something happened to astound Bernard even more: Exactly
fifteen days after he had arrived in Roanne, both brothers smiled—no,
they grinned! They grinned, and they popped bottles of champagne
and offered a glass to everyone in the kitchen, apprentices included. It
was March 15, 1968. Les Frères Troisgros had just been awarded a
third Michelin star.

The press arrived immediately, of course, and the phone was ringing for forty-eight hours straight, with calls from all over Europe, from
America, from Japan, from every exotic place that a young apprentice
could think of. Telegrams flooded in, and the news was in the Paris papers that very evening. The next morning, the brothers dominated page
one of the local press. For all intents and purposes, the restaurant was
permanently full from that point on until today. The days of the *table
d'hôte* were over for good. Pierre Loiseau's comfortable VRP stopping
point had moved into a new dimension.

Standing in the kitchen in his blue apron with an empty champagne glass in his hand, seventeen-year-old Bernard Loiseau gazed into
space, out beyond the smiling and the backslapping of his fellow workers to where Jean and Pierre stood in earnest conversation with their father. Someday, he vowed, I'm going to be like them. Just like in the
movies.

III

LE GUIDE MICHELIN

(and the others)

"*C'est une catastrophe,*" muttered Pierre Troisgros when he opened the *Guide Michelin* that fate-charged morning of March 15, 1968. At least that's how the legend goes today, and why defy a good legend that makes a good point?

The scene was the sidewalk outside the Roanne train station. Pierre had ambled across the place de la Gare to buy the morning paper and pick up a copy of the latest *Michelin* guide, released to the public that very day. Naturally enough, he had opened the thick little red book at the page for his home town, and there his eyes had fallen upon the very first listing: Les Frères Troisgros—accompanied by three big, fat, beautiful Michelin stars.*

So it had happened. Pierre was seized with a rush of joy and pride, but almost immediately a conflicting emotion surged in to take its place: panic. He was sure they weren't ready for it. True, the funky days of the Hôtel Moderne, the traveling salesmen, and the *table d'hôte* had been winding down over the past few years as he and Jean honed their skills and affirmed a steadily higher degree of gastronomic

---

*The Michelin stars (rather like asterisks in shape), must not be confused with the more classically shaped stars, from one to five, by which the French national tourism authorities classify hotels. Clearly visible on blue plaques affixed to the wall near the front door, these stars designate the hotel's level of comfort, and have nothing to do with food.

sophistication. The second star that *Michelin* had awarded them three years earlier had elevated them from the *petite noblesse* of the trade into the ranks of true gastronomic notables. He and Jean were comfortable on their two-star plateau, and they didn't even feel envious of Paul Bocuse, their longtime friend from the days *chez* Point and the *brigades* in Paris, for the third star that had fallen upon Collonges-au-Mont-d'Or at the same time as the second one had come to Roanne. Paul was the big personality and the big talent, the *chef de file* (leader) that everyone had always known was destined for the top of the heap. Nothing could stop Paul Bocuse.

But Les Frères Troisgros with three stars? That was something else. This category of restaurants, "worth a special journey" in Michelin-speak, was forever associated in his head with the grandees of the trade, Parisian gastronomic cathedrals like the Tour d'Argent, Claude Terrail's high-altitude palace dominating the Seine and Notre Dame; or Maxim's, midway between place de la Concorde and place de la Madeleine, the poshest hashhouse on the face of the earth; or the beautiful, understated Grand Véfour, deep in the somber dignity of the Palais Royal gardens near the Louvre; or Lassere, just off the Champs Elysées, with its host of lackeys and footmen and its spectacular opening roof. There were only a dozen or so three-star restaurants in all of France, and now the former Hôtel Moderne was among them. No, this was folly. The entire kitchen staff of Les Frères Troisgros consisted of just Jean and himself, a *pâtissier*, a *second* to back them up at the old coal-fired stove — and the apprentices, seven snotty, ignorant kids. Hell, the *brigade* at Maxim's in Paris, where he had worked before Jean-Baptiste yanked him back to Roanne, counted forty professionals. Pierre shuddered.

These past few years in Roanne had been enjoyably hectic, but theirs was still a small-town, family-style operation. What with wives and sisters and the aunt, there were ten Troisgros working in the restaurant — "the gypsy caravan," they called themselves — and despite the squabbles that sometimes arose among the women, the years had been both productive and rewarding. Jean and Pierre had timidly borrowed enough from a local bank to make the first kitchen improvements since the Hôtel Moderne became Les Frères Troisgros, but it was still a cubbyhole compared to the "real" three-star places. Certainly the brothers were confident that their finest and most pricey specialties could rival any restaurant in France from the point of view of pure cuisine—their poached turbot with a caviar sauce, their grilled lobster *à la cancalaise*, and their justly famous *escalope de saumon à l'oseille*, the salmon filet with sorrel sauce that was destined to be imitated a million times but still remain forever associated with the name Troisgros the way a tarted-up *tournedos* is inevitably associated with Rossini.

Withal, the relative simplicity of their dining room, the bar where locals still dropped by to drink a *pastis*, the unadorned foie gras terrine and the plate of smoked country ham still listed among the menu's *entrées** were reminders that the simpler old days had not yet entirely disappeared. What insane degrees of sophistication would be expected of them now, and what sort of snobby new clients would they have to cater to? Pierre shook his head. This was definitely worrisome.

"Don't worry," Jean-Baptiste told the brothers when they gathered to confer about the stunning news. He sounded exactly like a football coach giving a pep talk. "Just keep it up and do what you've always been doing. Don't change anything in the way you work. If Michelin gave you three stars, it means you're worth three stars."

Voilà—end of story. The Michelin oracle had spoken, and no one disputed the oracle, not even Jean-Baptiste.

The position that *le Guide Michelin* held, the power it wielded, and the respect it enjoyed were unique in France, and, indeed, in the restaurant world in general. Nothing else came even close in comparison. From its beginning as a pocket-sized compendium of addresses and useful motoring information, the *Michelin* had evolved with the years into a secular symbol of professionalism and rectitude, one of the rare bits of their civilization to which this deeply skeptical and suspicious people willingly accorded their full confidence, untainted by the suggestions of conspiracy that color their regard for almost every other aspect of daily existence. For more than one hundred years now the guide has been sailing through the choppy waters of the hotel-restaurant world at the same stately pace, a constantly reassuring

---

*Signifying starters ("entries") on all French menus but, erroneously, main courses on American ones. Such are the vagaries of one language migrating into another.

presence in an imperfect world where politicians are probably crooked, spouses surely faithless, and labor unions perpetually on the verge of making life impossible by going out on strike.

It is difficult to overstate the importance of the guide, or to understand the pressure that its presence exerts on chefs—and, in particular, how deeply Bernard Loiseau would be feeling that pressure as he scrabbled and fought his way up the ladder—without taking the measure of what it is and how it reached the pinnacle on which it sits so regally today. It is a sobering thought that if this happy-go-lucky, somewhat feckless son of an *auvergnat* traveling salesman turned into a passionately devoted professional almost overnight, plunged into risks that normally constituted persons would have considered foolhardy, indebted himself up to the top of his *toque*, and, undeviatingly following a self-imposed ideal, built an astonishingly successful career out of thin air—it was all for the love of *le Michelin* and the stars that it sprinkles down upon those happy few whom it deems worthy. More poignant yet is a second thought: if he took his life, it was also, fundamentally, because of Michelin. Not that it was Michelin's fault—far from it—but simply because Michelin was there, like Mount Everest, like Papa, like God. And all of this proceeded from something that had begun as a gimmick, a mere marketing ploy for peddling tires.

It is nicely fitting, too, that the Michelin story, like that of Bernard Loiseau, should have begun in Clermont-Ferrand. The saga of the guide sprang from the fertile brain and public relations genius of young André Michelin (1853–1931), scion of a Clermont family that owned a workshop producing rubber balls and miscellaneous agricultural machinery. He was a *polytechnicien*, a Paris-trained engineer, this André, but just as much as his technical skills, it was his faculty for attracting attention and currying customer loyalty that set the little Michelin shop on the road to becoming the colossus that it is today: 120,000 employees worldwide, neck and neck with Goodyear for number one in the manufacture and distribution of tires.

Although it was an Englishman, Robert William Thomson, who invented the pneumatic tire in 1845 (he called it an "aerial wheel") and another one, John Boyd Dunlop, who first applied it to bicycles in 1888 by gluing a rubber tube onto a wheel rim, it remained for André Michelin and his younger brother, Edouard (1859–1940) to find the obvious key for making the damn things practical: a tire and inner tube that could be wrestled off and back onto the rim without all the mess and fuss of the Dunlop gluing process (three hours for repairing a leak and a full night for drying the glue). The Michelin brothers received a patent for their bright idea in 1891, but the public was reluctant to accept the ridiculous idea of rolling on air even after a bike equipped with Michelin tires beat 209 other competitors in the Paris–Brest–Paris race that very year. Determined to get his point across and not overly concerned with the ethics of his method, André organized a Clermont–Paris race the following year, stationed himself ahead of the riders, seeded the road with pointy little nails, and was rewarded with 244 flats. As he had anticipated, the papers reported at length on the ease and rapidity of the repairs that the riders carried out themselves on the roadside. A year later, ten thousand Frenchmen were riding on Michelin tires.

By 1894, Michelin was manufacturing tires for carriages and automobiles—there were two or three hundred of the outlandish contraptions in France by then, and they struck André as a promising development. Year after year he entered cars in various races, winning a few and losing a few, but mostly beating the drum for the excellence of the *pneumatiques Michelin* with which they were equipped. Engaging some of the best-known *affichistes* of the moment, André turned out a glorious series of posters—the *fin de siècle* equivalent of TV spots—that infallibly appealed to the male of the species, who of course did all the buying and driving in those days, by mixing speed with the thrill of danger. "The rail vanquished by Michelin tires!" cried the headline of a breathtaking scene where a begoggled pilot gripping a huge wooden steering wheel careened around a corner in an automotive monster as a locomotive labored over a trestle in the background. Other posters emphasized practicality and thrift (Michelin tires "drank" obstacles) and even a little suggestion of sex, in the person of a gorgeous nymph gracing an allegorical "wheel-of-fortune" poster. With print runs of up to 100,000, the Michelin posters served as interior decorating for countless garages and shops not only in France but throughout Europe, because André had them printed in seventeen languages, including Russian.

It was one of these early drumbeating exercises that created the

Michelin Man (the "Bibendum"), the tubby dummy made of tires who went on to become one of the most famous and successful corporate symbols of all time—one whose corpulence, fittingly enough, suggests an association with gastronomic matters, and who continues today to appear liberally within the pages of the red guide. André and Edouard were visiting a big commercial fair in Lyon in 1911 when, passing by the company's stand, they came upon a stack of tires of different dimensions, bulging out in the middle and tapering upward. "Add arms and legs and you've got a man," remarked Edouard, and quicker than you could say Jacques Robinson, André passed the idea to Marius Rossillon, one of his star illustrators. With that, the Michelin Man was born.

But why the name "Bibendum"? Because Rossillon's first poster in his honor depicted a surrealistic vision of a pneumatic banquet with a hale, unmarked Michelin Man, cigar in one hand and a huge goblet in the other, standing at a dinner table to make a toast. In the goblet lay a selection of the finest tire destroyers, a cocktail of nails, broken glass, and sharp shards of metal, and the Michelin Man was saying *"Nunc est bibendum!"*—pop Latin for "Now is the time to drink"—in the sense of swallowing the bitter pill. On either side of Bibendum cowered the blanched, terrified faces of "Tire X" and "Tire Y," demoralized, scruffed up, and already three-quarters flat, while the accompanying caption cheerily announced that Michelin tires "drank" obstacles. It was perfect, one of those inspired images—funny enough to be sympathetic but clear enough to make the point—that appeal to the public and stick in the memory. Rossillon had created the corporate equivalent of a Snoopy or a Mickey Mouse.

Bibendum evolved with the years, ditching the cigar when it no longer symbolized success and power, his silhouette becoming simpler and more cartoonlike, and the multiple layers of skinny old tires giving way to the dozen or so fatter ones of modern appearance. But he still inspires the consumer loyalty so dear to André's heart. European truckers in particular fiercely identify with Bibendum, with whom they share ample tummies, the badge of their sedentary work, and apparently feel a pride of kinship in his fearless, always-optimistic character. His plastic effigy bolted to the roof of a semi's cab is as much a sign of the brotherhood of the road on this side of the pond as the glistening silver air horns of the truckers' American cousins. The more demonstrative drivers, especially Italians and Spaniards, frequently sport Michelin Men in pairs, lit up from the inside at night. It is unbeatable free advertising, and it must drive Goodyear, Pirelli, Dunlop, and all the other competitors wild with envy. To make matters even more galling, Michelin doesn't even give the Bibendums (Bibenda?) away—the truckers have to *buy* the fetishes with which they advertise the company.

Having proven that it was possible to roll on air, the inventive André turned his energies to ensuring that as many people as possible did this. From the turn of the century on, he promoted not so much the tire as the entire concept of motoring. By helping to make driving ever easier, more attractive, and rewarding, he reasoned, he would encourage the industry to build more cars and, ipso facto, order more tires. Thus was born the idea for the red guide.

André sprang his big surprise at Easter, 1900. Motoring had developed to a very considerable degree over the six years that he had been manufacturing car tires, and the brotherhood of chauffeurs (or engineers, as they were also sometimes known) was ready for a handy and practical promotional stunt like this. Clearly marked "not for sale," the first *Guide Michelin* was filled with ads and offered gratis.* The first two print runs give an idea of how the auto industry was burgeoning: from 35,000 in 1900 to 50,000 in 1901.

"This work appears with the century," André wrote when he released the first edition of the guide. "It will last as long." It sounded vainglorious at the time, but it turned out that he was being too modest. (There's a nice parallel to be made with another similarly colored opus of the same rough dimensions, Chairman Mao's little red book of communistic homilies. Printed in millions—perhaps billions—more copies than the *Michelin*, Machiavellian in intent and murderous in influence, it has already been relegated to the dustbin of history, while André's eminently peaceable inspiration is going stronger than ever.) André's first guide, about the dimensions of a small, fat airmail envelope, was entirely in what has come to be recognized as *Michelin's*

---

*The free ride continued until 1919, when André was visiting a garage and saw one of his cherished guides being used as a shim to level up a bandy-legged table. "People have no respect for what costs them nothing," he concluded. "From now on we'll make the customer pay for our publicity."

style: 575 pages on thin biblelike paper, listing, from A to Z, the towns whose resources in hotels and garages would be of interest to motorists. In the best Cartesian manner of the French educational system, it opened with a didactic 58-page presentation that could be entitled Motoring 1A, covering every subject from the advantages of pretty roads over boring ones, to correspondences of inner tubes and valves for different sizes of hubs, and, of course, the proper method of pumping up a tire, fixing a flat, or checking a leaky valve.

Most of the gas depots *Michelin* listed were not garages but general stores or grocers that sold cans of the stuff, and it did not fail to point out that both saddlers and cobblers were usually skilled at repairing blown tires. Many of the symbols of today's guide were already in use, including the asterisklike stars. In those early days, however, they represented hotels only. There was no listing for restaurants alone, presumably because travelers generally ate in the hotels where they spent their nights. The stars signified hotels offering the room, three meals with wine, plus the service "and the candle" for more than 13 francs (***); 10 to 13 francs (**); and less than 10 francs (*). There were three symbols to indicate which kind of gas the hotel sold and one (a black diamond shape) to indicate that the place was equipped with a darkroom for amateur photographers. In 1901, André added the magic initials "W.C." to his symbol list, indicating that the establishment possessed at least one of those ultramodern apparatuses, the flush toilet. (W.C. stood for that good old French term *water closet*.)

Symbols are Michelin's passion, trademark, and besetting sin. They have grown in number and complication over the years and with changing technology, but there is always a logical explanation for their presence, every last one of them. By using symbols instead of page-consuming texts, *Michelin* is able to stuff an extraordinary amount of information into a workable number of pages that is understandable to any traveler, whatever language he or she speaks. Even so, the 2004 guide counts 1,824 pages, covering some five thousand different towns and cities and, within them, some nine thousand hotels and restaurants.

This is only a small selection of France's total resources in hotels and restaurants, of course, most of which possess no stars at all. But their simple inclusion in the guide means that Michelin has been by

there and approved them as worthy of dispensing beds and nourishment. The more ambitious ones, Michelin reasons, will work hard
enough to raise their standards to starred level and join the trade's aristocracy. With their distance and mileage charts, their regularly updated figures on population, and their useful phone numbers and city
maps, Michelin's coverage of the country* is so extensive and clear that
during the Second World War both German and American armies pi-
rated the guide and issued copies to frontline officers for navigating
through urban areas. (The U.S. version was stamped FOR OFFICIAL USE
ONLY.) Nor is it only military types who pillage the information that the
Michelin people gather so diligently; it is well known that certain competing guides and food writers use the *Michelin* as the best and most reliable data base for mining the names and addresses that they do not
have the staff to gather themselves.

It was in 1933 that the red guide's most spectacular innovation
burst upon the world of gastronomy: countrywide restaurant ratings.
When the previous star system had represented only levels of price, it
was a handy reference for the pocketbook and nothing more. At various times, Michelin had toyed with special ratings for restaurants, but
it was not until 1933, in the depths of the Great Depression, that they
shifted the stars from price indicators to quality judgments of restaurants throughout France: one star, "a very good restaurant in its class";
two stars, "excellent cooking, worth a detour"; and three stars, "exceptional cuisine, worth a special journey."

Worth a special journey—imagine. It was exciting and intriguing,
and it changed everything. Michelin had started something very much
like a revolution. Thenceforward, gourmet motorists would seriously
contemplate firing up the Hispano Suiza or the Clément-Talbot to
drive—and on those old prewar roads, too, before anybody had ever
heard of high-speed throughways—to Bordeaux for Le Chapon Fin, or
down to the Mediterranean at Beaulieu for La Réserve, or across to Alsace for the Hôtel de France, in Moosch. Or, indeed, to Vienne, Valence, or Saulieu, where gastronomy's Holy Trinity thrived. But that

---

*Michelin also publishes red guides now for Benelux, Germany, Italy, Portugal,
Switzerland, and the UK; but the French one is the guiding light, the one with the
most stars and gastronomy's standard reference.

was just the point: Michelin brought masses of people, first from within France and then from all over the world, not only to Parisian palaces but to insignificant little country burgs as well, where gifted chefs had settled for one reason or another and were doing spectacular things with local products.

André was dead and gone by then, but the Service du Tourisme that he had founded was already turning out the wonderfully clear road maps and the green touring guides, heavily pedagogical in tone (convinced, as the French are, that you cannot appreciate the Chartres cathedral if you don't know what an architrave is, or a tympanum or a squinch) that continue today to sell by the millions of profitable units. But the star of the show, the one that got all the press attention, was always the red guide to hotels and restaurants—the public's darling.

How clever were the Michelin brothers? From deep within the volcanic heartland of shabby old Clermont-Ferrand, they had peered straight into the depths of the French psyche. They knew that every Frenchman worth his beret and *baguette* considered himself a world-class expert on just about everything, but especially on cuisine; they knew that every Frenchman was a born talker who loved to expatiate on his universal knowledge; they knew that from his tenderest childhood this same Frenchman had been raised with a reverence for *les belles lettres* and the elegant, egregiously affected forms of expression honed over centuries by the royal courts; and he considers that he manipulates these *belles lettres* rather better than most, if he does say so himself.

In short, André and Edouard knew that the French love to sound off, so they stroked the national ego by turning them into consultants—*collaborateurs*—for the guide: slipped into the back pages of each book they sold was an official Michelin report sheet and an envelope for mailing it in to headquarters. Anyone who felt strongly enough about the meal he had just consumed was encouraged to put pen to paper and tell the Service du Tourisme about it, at any length he wished. "One hundred thousand readers, 100,000 informers," they exulted, and they didn't even pay for the informers' stamps. It was a terrific piece of marketing, and although the numbers never did quite add up as epically as André and Edouard had originally hoped, the Service du Tourisme still sifts through some twenty-five thousand letters a year.

They take them seriously to the extent that several repeated references to the same innovation, change, or failing can indicate something worth watching, but they also know that, professionally speaking, most eaters are gastronomic incompetents—and that letters can be faked, prompted, or even written by the restaurateur himself. Although Michelin will never admit it, the main function of the letter system is to flatter those who buy their guide. The mere suggestion of a guide whose judgments really *are* based upon letters from readers sends the Service du Tourisme into tremors of restrained *auvergnat* hilarity.

Who's in, who's out? With the appearance of the new star system, the ritual question shot through the gastronomic grapevine every year around Easter time. If developments in the one-star and two-star categories were always worthy of interest, the promotions and demotions among the three-stars aroused a continual stream of learned commentary: Which were the best restaurants in all of France (and therefore the world)? How, exactly, did you draw such judgments? Were they always justified? Very rapidly, egged on by media comment, the French were debating Michelin's selections with the same passion that Americans lend to the relative merits of football teams, and English punters to the upcoming racing selections.

Since those early days, the three-star debate has become a national institution, an annual occurrence as predictable as the summer solstice, and a surefire story for every newspaper, magazine, and TV talk show. The lucky chef who is promoted to three stars becomes an instant celebrity, and the economic fallout for his restaurant approximates a big hit on the lottery, with clientele and profits increasing anywhere from 30 percent to 60 percent. It is a tremendous professional honor, the field marshal's baton of the trade, and everybody knows it, too; suddenly the same banks that had been niggling over loans come nuzzling the chef with warm, gushy kisses. No other accolade from any other guide or individual critic has the same rocket-motor effect as three Michelin stars. It is unique. This and this alone was the motivating force that drove Bernard Loiseau for the last thirty-five years of his life as he passed through the professional steps of apprentice to employee to partner to trendsetting *chef de cuisine* and finally to the lofty status of *chef d'entreprise*, the first cook in history to take his business onto the stock market, charging straight into international stardom and the pages of the *Wall Street Journal* and the *Financial Times*.

The pendant to the triumph of winning the third star is, of course, its loss. It is the nightmare of every top chef and restaurateur, because it represents not only a certain plunge in profits but a public reprimand and humiliation that call into question everything that he has lived for professionally, like a respected officer having his rank and insignia ripped off before the troops and being degraded to the rank of ordinary soldier. French newspapers have reported innumerable testimonials over the years of chefs reacting in shock, sorrow, and anger after being blindsided by Michelin's swift sword. None expressed the sentiment more eloquently than Marc Meneau, who soared with the Michelin to the wealth and celebrity of three stars for the personalized cooking he invented in his L'Espérance in Saint-Père de Vézelay. Stunned speechless by the loss of his third star in 1999, he hesitated, searching for the right word. "A bereavement," he finally said.*

When the chef of the grand old Lapérouse in Paris heard similar bitter news, he cried: *"C'est Waterloo!"* Alain Zick went farther. Chef of Le Relais de Porquerolles in Paris, he was demoted from one star to none in March 1966. In October, he shot himself dead. So astonishing was his gesture, and so compounded by other personal and financial problems, that the world of gastronomy in general, and the Michelin brass in particular, wrote it off as a one-time freak event that could never recur. Never.

Michelin's amazing sway over the world of French restaurants took a while to build. Every new undertaking requires a certain breaking-in period, and at the start it looked as if the Service du Tourisme people themselves didn't quite realize what they were getting themselves into. The guide went through a good deal of backing and filling in the early years, the sure sign that no one had quite figured out the standards for the Jovian judgments they were called on to deliver. The somewhat excessive three-star crowning of twenty-three restaurants in 1933, for ex-

---

*After a spiritual and professional crossing of the desert, he finally regained the precious third star in the new 2004 guide. "I went through hell," he said. "I began to think I didn't know how to cook anymore, and didn't even know how to hold a pan right."

ample, was immediately followed in 1934 with the abrupt demotion of nine of them—bloodbath! Later editions would see a restaurant enter one year, be kicked back out the next, only to be reinstated just a year later. Feverish haste of that sort smacked suspiciously of amateurism— a most unseemly contrast with the lofty pretensions of *le style Michelin*. But by the 1939 edition things had settled into a dignified pace and, with it, a more carefully restricted selection of fourteen restaurants at the top level. Then the war came, and everything froze. There would be no new *Guide Michelin* until 1945.

Plucky as ever, the Service du Tourisme did what it could during the war for a society virtually bereft of cars and fuel, by trying to interest bikers in an ephemeral *Guide du Cyclotourisme*, but it was a poor and makeshift thing. Restaurants kept going as best they could, showing a glum official face of rutabaga, cabbage, and potato to the occupying Germans while squirreling away black-market goodies for their regular French customers. Pierre Troisgros retains a clear memory today of steaks and chops hidden in the ceiling and behind wall panels of the Parisian restaurants where he worked in the forties, at about the same time as fifteen-year-old Paul Bocuse was helping to slaughter pigs and calves led down into the dark, subterranean confines of the Lyonnais restaurants where he was learning the basics of the trade.

It was only after the war that the guide's editors found their marks and brought the operation to today's level. Beefing up its editorial staff and hiring new blood, they developed the specialized corps of professional inspectors that are its pride and glory and defining difference from all the others in the guide business. It was slow-going, though, because for several years the country remained on its economic knees. Rationing was still in force and the food supply and distribution network did not return to prewar levels until 1951. Michelin waited, therefore, until that year to crown its first postwar batch of three-star restaurants. They were only seven of them: the Café de Paris, Lapérouse, and the Tour d'Argent in Paris; Le Père Bise in Talloires; La Mère Brazier in Lyon; La Pyramide in Vienne; and La Côte d'Or in Saulieu.

From that point on, the Michelin Machine was in high gear, and it hasn't missed a beat since. The inspectors are at the heart of it. They're a legendary crew, *les inspecteurs*, a tight-lipped bunch of anonymous incorruptibles who eat their way through France every year like cater-pillars doggedly destroying a leaf, munching along the grid lines of a master plan drawn up by their bosses in Paris. Disappearing for a week or two on their *tournées* to hotels and restaurants, they return to the Service du Tourisme in Paris just long enough to file their reports, pick up the next assignment, and trudge back to their cars. (It's always by car, of course—until they start rolling on tires, Michelin will always view trains and planes with sovereign contempt.) Contrary to a common assumption, the inspector's job is neither fun nor easy. They have been hired to work, not to enjoy themselves, and not everybody can stick it out. "The monks of gastronomy," the inspectors are frequently called, and everything about them reflects the industrious, humorless *auvergnat* reserve that has forever been the mark of the Michelin man or woman. Twice a day they must write reports covering lunch and dinner, but that's just the easy part of the grind. There are hotels to visit, rooms to inspect, prices to note—more reports, always more reports. Not just items to tick off: full reports. Clermont-Ferrand expects value for its money.

How many inspectors are there? Nobody knows, and the Service du Tourisme enjoys nothing more than tantalizing journalists with hints, suggestions, and innuendos, while never delivering any real information. Over the years that I have been following the Michelin operation, I have known four editors-in-chief of the guide, and naturally I asked each of them the magic question. The first two—André Trichot and Bernard Naegellen—replied with the same maddening, coquettish phrase: "A certain number." Derek Brown, the Englishman (that was a surprise) who succeeded Naegellen, danced around it with a comely pirouette that rendered further enquiry pointless: "Let's say it's our little secret." Jean-Luc Naret, the latest boss, is rather more communicative, but the question pains him as much as it did his predecessors.

That's Michelin for you—take it or leave it. Such is the power of this deliberately maintained mystery, though, that much speculation goes far astray. Some naïve wire service writers have been led to report as many as a hundred inspectors in France alone, but anyone who does a little basic math about budget consequences will see that this is wildly off base. Still, that magic figure of one hundred does frequently float around the Michelin rumor shop. Derek Brown himself, in the wake of a miniscandal that erupted in February 2004 when an inspector was fired for revealing in-house secrets, spoke publicly of a hundred persons authorized to judge restaurants for all eight of the Europe-wide guides, but his deliberately vague phrasing suggested the possibility that this figure could include office editorial staff filling in as temporary inspectors from time to time. Brown further hinted of a platooning system allowing a certain number of inspectors to be shifted from country to country where and when they might be needed (presumably as publication deadlines approached). Later, in conversation with me, he revised that figure down to seventy, Europe-wide.

"In my time there were seven* of us," René Gerbeau confided. Gerbeau is one of those rarest of animals, a Michelin man—or, rather, an ex-Michelin man—who breaks the company omertà and talks openly about the job. A restaurant inspector in the booming sixties, he retains vivid memories today of long, lonesome days on the road, solitary meals, and endlessly repetitive afternoons tramping up and down hotel stairs checking on rooms. After several years of the routine, an overpowering lassitude set in and finally drove him to quit.

"It was no way to make a living. The salary was pretty poor to begin with, just about what a midlevel office clerk would earn, and they were unbelievably tight with money—we had to justify our expenses down to every last *sou*. We always worked alone. As it happened, I had just been married before I took the job, but there was no question of the company paying for phone calls home. They wouldn't even pay for our laundry. We were supposed to get it done at our own expense when we got home. If you needed a new pencil they wouldn't issue you one unless you turned in the stub of the used one. That's the *auvergnats* for you. That's Michelin."

---

*In 2004 an inspector named Pascal Rémy was fired for threatening to publish a journal describing his sixteen years on the road for Michelin, eating at least two hundred dinners a year all by himself, missing his wife and children, being seized with a serious case of homesickness, and earning what he called a lowly schoolteacher's wages. After his forcible separation from the company, he went ahead and published. His most notable revelation was that there had been a total of eleven inspectors for France when he was hired in 1988, but that by 2003 that number had been pared down to a bare-bones minimum of five—inadequate, he wrote, to carry out a proper number of inspections in full, rigorous Michelin style.

A penny's a penny, as everyone knows, and the tightfisted descendants of André and Edouard Michelin counted them as lovingly as Ebenezer Scrooge ever did. Company old-timers still remember the days when office workers were expected to use envelopes *twice*, turning the used ones inside out for a second life on the other side. Withal, Gerbeau cannot restrain a grudging sense of admiration for his ex-employers, because the famous Michelin probity really was there — it wasn't legend or PR fakery.

"I had graduated from hotel school, so I was qualified for the job, but their main criterion for hiring me was my moral value. I had to give them all sorts of references, of course, and they backed that up by interviewing the people whose names I gave. They even interviewed the concierge of my apartment building to make sure I had a reputation for upstanding morality. I suppose they knew there would be temptations — and there were, too. Sometimes, after I had identified myself, restaurateurs and hoteliers would hint around about maybe rewarding me, one way or another, but they were always frightened to come right out and say it. We would never have gone for it, anyway. We believed in the system — we really were incorruptible."

If Gerbeau finally found the plodding, solitary regimen of the job to be soul-destroying he managed to salvage a few memories of a change of pace that broke up the tedium. The most exciting occurred after he had finished and paid for a meal in a provincial restaurant that had been relieved of its lone star the year before. Flashing his Michelin ID, he asked to see the boss — who arrived on the run from the kitchen with an enormous butcher's knife in his hand. "Ah, *Michelin*, is it?" he growled. "Happy to see you. My *chiffre d'affaires* is down sixty percent since you took away my star."

Inventing some appropriate niceties to mumble, Gerbeau slunk away without further damage, but it was only more evidence that there is no trade where Latin passions run as high as the creative small-business world of cooking. André Trichot, white-haired patriarch of the guide's retired directors, recalled a demoted chef in Lyon who advertised his fury by displaying at his front entrance a Michelin tire with a knife stuck through it.

It was an odd kind of existence, the life of the Michelin monk, a paradoxical mix in which power lay cheek by jowl with submission and luxury, and lobster contrasted with abject thrift. The Michelin hierarchy expected the inspector to be a thoroughgoing organization man, clean shaven, dressed just so, dutifully following his route and writing his reports, Mr. Average, modestly going about his duty. No fashion flairs, no sticking out, no girlfriends, no drawing attention to himself—there's no room for rugged individualists *chez* Michelin. In Gerbeau's day, the standard vehicle for the inspectors was the ridiculous little 2CV, the Citröen *deux-chevaux* with the corrugated tin body and the baby carriage suspension. No swanking it when you arrive in a heap like that.

Ah, but each *inspecteur* had a little bit of Clark Kent in him, a secret lightning bolt hidden behind his namby-pamby demeanor: Superman's power to award or remove stars. To this day, Gerbeau cherishes the memory of chugging up to the grand entrance of the very hoity-toity Hôtel Négresco in Nice and barely getting the time of day from the *chasseurs, voituriers*, and assorted doormen in their Fredonian generals' uniforms as he alighted like Monsieur Hulot from his popping, vibrating little car. He had a swell dinner in the monumental dining room, spent the night, ate his breakfast—and then flashed his Michelin card. This time he had the whole crew, including the hotel manager, standing at attention as he drove away. If they had thought it might help, they would have been blowing kisses at him, too.

For all the submission to behavioral norms that the company expected of him, Gerbeau was pleasantly surprised by the extent of Michelin's loyalty to its men in the field. "Our judgments made the law," he told me. "Once I took away a star from a restaurant whose owner had some very highly placed political friends—all the way up in the president's office. It finally came down to a standoff between the Élysée Palace and me, and the company backed me all the way. The restaurant didn't get its star back."

But whatever happens, Michelin will always be Michelin. One day the company will show magnificent support like that, and the next, it will pull a stunt like the business with the experimental tires. "Clermont-Ferrand had come up with a new design for a tire they wanted to test, so they used the inspectors," said Gerbeau. "The damn things kept coming off the rims, and we had to complain that it wasn't the inspectors' job to be guinea pigs. They never did manufacture those tires."

Gerbeau left the company soon thereafter, relieved to be off the gastronomic treadmill but still happy to have lived the experience of a legendary job, even if its reality did not quite match up with its romantic folklore. Apart from affording him an intimate knowledge of French geography for all the thousands of miles covered in his 2CV, he can flatter himself today as a world-class expert on the cooking and presentation of veal kidneys, a favorite dish that he ordered again and again while on *tournée*. And when he dines at friends' houses, the hostess is always afraid of him.

It was a rare stroke of luck for me to have discovered Gerbeau, and even rarer, I think, that he agreed to reminisce in some detail about the work of the inspectors, because Michelin *hates* having the least bit of information leaking out of the inner sanctum. To say that Michelin has a penchant for secrecy is like saying cormorants have a penchant for fish. With its multitude of inventions and clever manufacturing processes, the company has always lived by the assumption that the entire world is scrambling to get into its corporate pants and steal its secrets.

Michelin defends against industrial espionage by color-coding its work areas and employees' blouses—you work in one color and you stay there—and maintains a perpetual vigilance against transgressors that is just one notch removed from paranoid schizophrenia. Everyone in France has heard the story of how General De Gaulle was quickly shooed from one meaningless vista to another during a presidential visit to Clermont-Ferrand in the sixties, and even an official German delegation, Michelin people swear today, was similarly flimflammed when they had France at their mercy after the 1940 armistice.

Secrecy? "We prefer to say *discretion*," a company spokesman told me a few years ago with that inimitable, ineffable Michelin complacency behind the bland company smile. "Let us say we have our way of doing things."

With manufacturing, so it is with the guide's procedures. Standard routine for the inspectors is to arrive at restaurants unannounced, but if a reservation is required, they call in like any other customer and have a supply of credit cards bearing no company name. They eat, pay—and only then flash their Michelin ID card for a visit to the kitchen and a talk with the terrified chef and proprietor. But restaurateurs can't even count on that. Just as frequently, the Michelin man simply disappears as anonymously as he had arrived, to do his report in the secrecy of his hotel room.

The inspectors are the joy and the sorrow of French restaurateurs, because Michelin gives and Michelin takes away with the same inscrutable despotism. At times their verdicts strike ordinary non-Michelin mortals as unjust and wrongheaded but, like a zealous young traffic cop issuing parking tickets, they have come to their conclusions and they are impervious to whining, charm, or persuasion. So rectitudinously bloody-minded are the inspectors when they flash their cards that restaurateurs instinctively flee from even the thought of maybe offering them a free meal, a nice bottle of wine or, heaven forbid, a bribe—in that way lies dismissal and disgrace.

But when is a bribe a bribe, and when is it mere professional courtesy? That's a big question in France, one that is loaded with tricky ethical nuances. For Michelin, the answer is simple: Anything—anything at all—more than the normal relationship of a paying customer to a provider of a commercial service is out, anathema, verboten. The *Guide Michelin* pays its way, accepts no advertising in its pages, is beholden to no one, and can preen and strut: pure as the driven snow. But of course that's easy, because the Service du Tourisme is backed by the mighty financial muscle of a great multinational corporation with a huge PR budget. Lesser guides or newspapers, with little or no such financial backing, aren't so lucky, and the stark fact of life is that having several employees pay for two meals a day in fine restaurants is ruinously expensive in itself, let alone the costs of salaries, road expenses, and printing and distributing the final product.

The result is this: Almost without exception, foodie journalists can eat for free in French restaurants, and few of them fail to take advantage of the custom and declare their status. On the surface this sounds rotten—to Anglo-Saxon observers, anyway—but there is an implicit trade-off, because everyone knows that a halfway decent article in a newspaper, or a nice paragraph in a guide (even if it isn't the *Michelin*), can fill a restaurant with customers overnight. Invariably, then, journalists and guide critics are not just tolerated by the trade, but actively sought out, pampered, and praised. Professional courtesy, they call it. Theater critics don't pay for their tickets, either. If everyone was bound by the chilly, virginal rules that reign in the *auvergnat* kingdom founded by André and Edouard, *Le Guide Michelin* would be in a position of quasi-monopoly.

The nub of the matter, then, the really slippery part, is the interpretation of the trade-off: one meal against an article or the paragraph in the guide—fine, no sweat. But how about several meals afterward, and maybe with family and friends? Restaurateurs often feel obliged to go along with an ongoing regimen of free chowdowns for hungry journalists who don't have the delicacy to back off. What Fernand Point did out of native generosity, friendship, and a big heart becomes for these restaurateurs a finely calculated business equation.

Worse yet—and here the trade-off slips into downright racketeering—are the guides and semirespectable publications that go much further than free meals, by taking money (either directly or in the form of expensive ads in the publication) to give restaurants a favorable review. Although impossible to prove in a court of law, it is common knowledge that they exist and that it happens. And not only in France.

In short, the Michelin people have it made. Since they never have to get their hands dirty with the kinds of sordid commercial details that govern everybody else, theirs is the only guide that the French trust entirely without afterthoughts of kickback and payola. And now with the Church getting irrelevant, wine getting sugared, and one hundred thousand supermarket Santas chortling a million plastic ho-ho-hos, the Michelin inspector is just about the last symbol of absolute virtue that the French can cling to. Restaurateurs believe in them, anyway—one hundred percent.

"A light to guide us," Alain Chapel told me years ago when I asked him to characterize the guide. "The Michelin spirit means quality in the tiniest details." Coming from a mere mortal this would be impressive enough, but Chapel, who worked himself to death in 1990 at the age of fifty-two, is universally viewed with awe in the profession as one of the greatest culinary magicians ever to hold three stars. His even more famous elder, Paul Bocuse, with a long lifetime of experience behind him, is not afraid to be more categorical still: "*Michelin* is the only guide that counts."

Rich, powerful, and adulated, top chefs enjoy the prestige of true celebrity status, but once a year they shrink to the size of frightened schoolkids when they perform a rite firmly cemented in gastronomic folklore: the traditional pilgrimage to 46 avenue de Breteuil, behind the gold dome of the Invalides in Paris's 7th *arrondissement*. There, in the austere high-windowed, eight-storied headquarters of the Service du Tourisme, they bend a knee and, symbolically, at any rate, kiss the pope's ring.

Rare is the chef who refuses to join the procession, because the single most dreadful event that can befall his business, apart from death or paralysis, is the loss of whatever he possesses in the way of stars. Making the pilgrimage cannot guarantee the stars will remain, but it can't hurt, either. Maybe the oracle will deliver a few hints, point to tendencies, give a wink here and a nudge there. You never know. And the mere fact that you have taken the time and trouble to come in shows how *sérieux* you are. Not even Paul Bocuse, the Emperor himself, a man who has been everywhere, met everyone, done everything—not even he steps out of the line standing in front of the Michelin office.

The oracle likes that. The oracle likes serious chefs. The oracle came to resemble a prep school headmaster when Derek Brown took over the guide in 1998. Many a French eyebrow was raised when Brown got the job, because he was, of all things, an Englishman. On the surface of it, a citizen of *perfide Albion* becoming the top arbiter of Gallic gastronomy seemed little short of heresy, but in fact Brown was just right for the role: he was a graduate of hotel school, a former cook and hotel manager, a former inspector, and a former Michelin spokesman. Perfectly dressed, perfectly manicured, and perfectly coiffed, this son of a naval architect had more than thirty years with the company, during which he grew invulnerably calm, reserved, and practiced in his mission—more *auvergnat* than the *auvergnats*. Bearing a vague resemblance to the former English prime minister John Major, effortlessly articulating the company philosophy in complex phrase upon subsidiary phrase that leaped nimbly between BBC standard English and fluent French, he was a model whom André and Edouard could have taken as one of their very own. How thoroughly did Derek Brown become a Michelin man? When he doodled on the margins of his notebook, he drew not flowers or figures but little Bibendum heads.

Early in 2004 Brown became the center of rather more notoriety than he would have liked because of *l'affaire Rémy*. While no one ever questioned his competence or dedication, it was on his watch that the whole messy business of Pascal Rémy's firing erupted. With threats of lawsuits flying, Rémy went ahead and published his reminiscences of life as an inspector,* the high point of which was the revelation that at the time of his departure, a mere five inspectors were on the job in France. *Bruta figura* for Michelin: the company and the guide seriously lost face. Brown, who by coincidence reached retirement age at about the same time as the publication of Rémy's book, left the guide in the hands of a successor who was clearly facing the need to hire a new, competent bunch of inspectors, and fast. The guide's French inspector corps is now up to fifteen, according to Jean-Luc Naret.

Whoever was in charge, Michelin has always received supplicant chefs at avenue de Breteuil in gray, faceless conference rooms that are like spiritual torture chambers, because the visitors know they will never receive praise, advice, or tips on how to make their places more Michelin-friendly—nothing more than "tendencies," echoes of what people are writing in their letters. The oracle is hermetic, and the impenetrable basilisk gaze that it turns on gastronomic penitents can turn strong legs to jelly. "I was trembling with terror the first time I was led into one of those little rooms," recalled Jean-Paul Lacombe, two-star chef of the wonderful Léon de Lyon. Jean-Paul has been waiting for the third star to fall for more than twenty years now. One of these days it is sure to happen, but the oracle will not be rushed.

So fulsome is the ascendancy of the "Vatican" on avenue de Breteuil that these professional dialogues are for the most part limited to the aristocracy of the trade, those chefs possessing at least a star. Michelin does not have the personnel or time—or, for that matter, the inclination—to receive the teeming thousands of gastronomic hoi polloi who are mentioned in the guide, and there is something like an unstated code of good manners that maintains such individuals at a respectful distance, behind the red velvet ropes, as it were. Guillaume Giblin might be taken as a good example.

Guillaume is a serious and determined chef in his early thirties who broke his and his wife's piggy banks, then supplemented that with a bank loan, to raise enough cash to buy out a cook who was retiring from a village restaurant in a place called Ormoy-la-Rivière, in the Es-

---

L'Inspecteur de Met à Table, by Pascal Rémy, Éditions Équateurs, Paris 2004.

sone countryside south of Paris. Although he is a terrific cook, a skilled professional who was trained under some of the country's best two- and three-star chefs (Passard, Rostang, Martin, Coisel), he would never presume to beard the lion in his den and request a Michelin interview for himself. That would be presumptuous.

Guillaume's restaurant, Le Vieux Chaudron, is merely listed in the guide, starless, and symbolized in the absolute bottom category of one crossed knife and fork ("quite comfortable"). As a yeoman of the trade, he knows his place, and he does not importune or play the grand. But he tries as hard as any young man may to please Papa Michelin. He serves great food at bargain-basement prices, bakes his own bread, washes his own dishes, launders his own napkins and tablecloths, personally cleans his restroom spotless every day, obliges his lone waiter to wear a tuxedo (no jewelry, no flashy watches), even when the hot summer sun is beating down, and sets himself a nonstop work routine that translates to eighty hours a week—all of this just to break even while living on his wife's salary as an accountant.

That, he believes, is only the least he can do. Hell, if Michelin was a light to guide a demigod like Alain Chapel, what could it be for little Guillaume Giblin? You never know when an inspector might show up, and he admitted to living in permanent anxiety of just such a visit. In fact, an inspector *had* shown up just a few months before I spoke with him, and he was still nervous about the verdict, because the man didn't say a word about the food. That's the Michelin way. He discussed prices, supplies, the clients, the terrace, and the furniture, but never the food. Mum's the word—the famous Michelin discretion. One is not an *auvergnat* for nothing.

"But can you remember what he ate that day?" I asked. Guillaume gazed at me with the indulgent smile of Garry Kasparov being asked if he remembered his first game against Karpov. "*Marbré de poireaux et figues en vinaigrette de truffes*," he instantly said. "*Dos de lieu jaune sur tombée de pousses d'épinards, beurre d'oursins; moelleux périgourdin aux noix, figues sèches et crème anglaise. Café.* But I don't think my setting here is good enough to get a star. I'd like to get the place painted, but I can't afford it now. Maybe in four or five years."

Like thousands of his *confrères*, Guillaume is waiting patiently at the red velvet ropes, watching his step, polishing up his silverware and his act. Someday his star will come. For him and all the other professionals who aspire to any sort of quality above that of a neighborhood canteen, the ongoing game of spot-the-inspector is an essential part of the daily routine. A lone man or woman appearing unannounced to ask for a table for one is enough to set the first alarm bells ringing. If the client arrives in an average car and is dressed in a tasteful but average manner—the Michelin man always wears jacket and tie, and you will never see a Michelin woman in jeans and T-shirt—the bell's decibels go up, and if he or she demonstrates the indefinable but instantly recognizable manner of a connoisseur, someone who clearly knows what is going on with food and wine, the noise becomes a deafening clangor and the waiters begin whispering among themselves. Many a lone hairdresser, stockbroker, or guano futures dealer dining alone can thank Michelin's anonymous monks and nuns for the extraordinarily assiduous service they have received.

Of course the company knows very well the strength of the mystique, and happily takes advantage of it to the last degree, notably sponsoring a form of Michelin terrorism that enlists its readers as standard bearers. One line of the guide's introductory text says it all in bold red letters: YOUR RECOMMENDATION IS SELF EVIDENT IF YOU ALWAYS WALK INTO A HOTEL GUIDE IN HAND. Thousands of tourists (especially foreign) religiously follow the instructions, confident that Bibendum, like a voodoo grigri, will protect them from overcharging. They might just be right, too.

In a country where a novel distributed at more than 20,000 copies is considered a best-seller, Michelin's annual sales of between 400,000 and 700,000 guides (the exact figure falls into the domain of "our little secret") make it a megahit. At $25-plus a shot, it is an investment of some consequence, but the best part is that if you really want to follow all the latest developments in gastronomy, hotels, and prices, you need to renew it every year.

So Michelin towers above the competition in France, to be sure— but there is competition. Most famous is the guide now presented under a squished-together double name: *GaultMillau*. It was born as the brainchild of two smart Parisian journalists, Henri Gault and Christian Millau, who in the sixties were laboring together on the city beat for the daily *Paris-Presse l'Intransigeant*, and shared a fondness for good food. They also possessed two qualities notably absent from the *Michelin*: a sense of humor and the ability to write well. Striking off on their own, they founded an irreverent monthly gastronomic magazine entitled with their own names and, to accompany it, an eponymous annual guide in direct competition with the *Michelin*. Both the magazine and the guide did well, too, and the substitution of text—good, funny, colorful text—in place of *Michelin*'s dour symbols* made them extremely popular with a younger, less traditional set of readers.

Gault and Millau's greatest coup was the invention of the gastronomic shot heard 'round the world: the term *la nouvelle cuisine française*. Today it is ancient history, the stuff of dinosaurs, but in the seventies and eighties it was something of a magic formula that transformed attitudes toward cooking—as often for ill as for good, it must be said. But it was one of those rare things that come at exactly the right moment and are enunciated in just the right way. Like a catchy jingle or a skillful advertising slogan, it caught fire and swept the world of cuisine off its feet. (In essence, Gault and Millau were only repeating an earlier marketing masterstroke, the "New Look" that Christian Dior threw out to hungry fashion writers in the fifties. It didn't really mean much, but it was a terrific slogan.) Suddenly everyone wanted to do "new" cooking, whatever that meant. In its best avatars it was just a light lunch by Paul Bocuse: grilled red mullet with a crunchy string bean salad; or Pierre Troisgros's infinitely imitated vegetable terrine; or Michel Guérard's famous *salade folle*, richly larded with *foie gras*. At its worst it was . . . a million things, from turbot with raspberry *coulis* to geranium soufflés. Whatever the inspirations happened to be, though, they were invariably presented as tiny portions served on enormous plates, delicately arranged to demonstrate that the chef was not a mere cook, but an *artiste*. The debate is still on as to whether the nouvelle cuisine movement did more harm than good, but in its more dubious expressions, it was one of the silliest things imaginable.

Nouvelle cuisine eventually led to modern cuisine, then fusion,

---

*Goaded by *GaultMillau*'s insolent success, Michelin struck back at the turn of this century by adding very short texts—one line or two—to describe the hotels and restaurants included in the guide. They are a far cry, though, from *GaultMillau*'s voluminous, wordy essays.

then what became known as *cuisine tendance*, wild inventiveness with
a heavily experimental Spanish accent to it, and fickle Parisian diners,
always avid for novelty, could always be counted on to gallop after
whatever happened to be the latest fashion. For fifteen years or so,
Gault and Millau reigned as the absolute champions of fashionable
eating, but in the early eighties the founding fathers sold out and the
guide began floating aimlessly from buyer to buyer—six or seven
times, at last count—living off the echo of its old reputation and becoming more and more irrelevant with each change of owner.

For several decades of the postwar boom, a rival tire company,
Kléber-Colombes, gamely attempted to match Michelin with its *Guide
Kléber*, similar in style and format but hopelessly outclassed and out-
spent by Clermont-Ferrand. (It was one of the many budget-challenged
that was reduced to accepting the free-meal *largesse* of restaurant owners, thereby losing, hands down, the virginity contest with Big Red.) *Le
Guide Kléber* died when Michelin simply bought the competing company. With a condescending sniff, the Service du Tourisme handed its
hotel and restaurant documentation back to *Kléber*'s surviving edit
staff, for free. In a new format it survives today as *Le Bottin Gourmand*.
It is a handsome, professional effort, but no match for the *Michelin*.

Three or four other guides struggle along with the *Bottin* in the
Michelin's wake, and their efforts combine with the work of several gastronomic critics of daily papers and weekly magazines to form a considerable nexus of food writing. Most of these critics are so well known
that they couldn't pay in restaurants even if they wanted to, but a notable exception to the rule is a dapper, hard-driving *quinquagénaire* of
surprisingly boyish appearance named François Simon, critic for the
daily *Le Figaro*. Working solo, Simon does the full Michelin number,
reserving tables under a fake name, appearing incognito, paying in
cash, sending the bills to his boss, and writing his columns in full independence of spirit. In an effort to maintain his anonymity while promoting his paper, Simon has sometimes appeared masked for TV
interviews, a tactic that drew much raillery and mocking comment
from restaurateurs whom he had savaged in his commentaries. The
mockery had a real edge of resentment to it, because Simon is a man of
strongly disenchanted opinions, little patience, and a famously acid
pen. Better than all his journalistic brothers and sisters, he exemplifies

the tense love–hate relationship that exists in France between critics and chefs—in his case, a relationship rather heavily weighted toward the hate side of the equation for the outrage that his more negative comments can inspire.

As matters evolved in that rainy, muddy, depressing February of 2003, Simon found to his surprise that fate had assigned him a prominent role, along with both the *Michelin* and the *GaultMillau*, in what was to become known as *le drame Loiseau*.

IV

APPRENTICESHIP

"*B*ernard Loiseau, Number One Troisgros Apprentice—one meter eighty, eighty kilos."

Taking his ease in the front alcove of his restaurant—his *Michelin* three-star restaurant—on rue Troyon in Paris, a few hundred yards downhill from the Arc de Triomphe, Guy Savoy harked back to Roanne more than three decades earlier. A broad, affectionate smile of reminiscence lit up his bearded visage as he savored the memory of himself at age seventeen, a newcomer to the crowded, surprisingly exiguous old kitchen of Les Frères Troisgros, gaping at the big guy with the big smile.

"I can still see him as if it was just yesterday. He would take up that favorite position of his, standing by the *timbres*, the kitchen wall that was covered with a series of little square doors to refrigerated compartments. He'd lean back against the wall, hook his thumbs into two of the handles on either side, put one foot forward and make the announcement: '*Bernard Loiseau, premier apprenti chez Troisgros, un mètre quatre-vingt, quatre-vingts kilos.*'

"That was pure Bernard. He was nineteen then and I was seventeen. He was the first and I was the last. I had just arrived—April first, 1970, I'll never forget the date—from my hometown of Bourgouin for my three years of apprenticeship. I was starting my first year and Bernard was already into his third, but we became best friends. At first he was like my big brother. Pretty soon I felt like his twin."

All the boys whom Bernard had met upon his own arrival two years earlier had finished their stints and had gone on to jobs as *commis* in the many restaurants around France that were crying for the skilled, disciplined (and still quite cheap*) young employees that Chef Jean and Chef Pierre molded so well. Now, in his senior term, it was his turn to play the cock of the walk. Bernard had seen tough, hard-working little Claude Perraudin, his first professional "elder"—light-years ahead of him in experience even though he was chronologically two years younger—get a recommendation handsome enough to land the best job of all, the plum post of *commis saucier* at Paul Bocuse's great restaurant by the Saône on the outskirts of Lyon. The others who had shown him the ropes were scattered into kitchens from one end of the country to the other, cooking, learning, and building their nascent careers.

Most of these kids had no idea that they were the reflection of a tradition that was descended straight from the Middle Ages, the system of *compagnonnage* through which French artisans of all sorts had been formed since time beyond memory, moving from master to master over the years in a *tour de France* that ended with the creation of a *chef d'oeuvre* (masterpiece) that, according to the trade, could be anything from a saddle to a pair of shoes to a *pièce montée* of pastry and spun sugar. If the *chef d'oeuvre* was deemed worthy, the young artisan was accepted into the guild,[†] and could soon begin taking on apprentices himself.

In the brotherhood of top French restaurants everyone knows everyone else, and the future of the culinary art is placed in the hands of the young apprentices whom the chefs teach and pass around to one another. Ask any top chef today about his formation and you will hear a litany of two-star and three-star names recited like beads on a rosary. By the early seventies, Les Frères Troisgros was already at or close to the top of the charts of desirable studying addresses for aspiring Ph.D.s of the *piano*. There was clearly something special about the combined pedagogical talents of Jean, Pierre, and Jean-Baptiste that created first-rate young cooks.

---

*Claude Perraudin offered a good example of the apprentice's pay scale. "My first monthly pay at Troisgros was five francs (about one dollar then). I finished at 250 francs a month."

†Today's Freemasons, with their lodges, rituals, philosophizing, and penchant for secrecy, trace their origins back to this medieval "companionship."

Part of it was simple terror. Starting at anywhere from age fourteen to seventeen, homesick and heartsick, yanked from the comforting certitudes of family life when they were barely out of childhood, the kids suddenly found themselves thrust, in a state of near-total ignorance, into a competitive, unforgiving man's world where everything had to be done right now, and had to be done perfectly. Not well—perfectly. The implacable tyranny of those two meals a day—do it right at lunch, then do it right all over again at dinner—meant workdays of at least ten hours, more frequently twelve and sometimes as many as eighteen, with only one day off a week. One day off, that is, unless they were punished for some professional fault or misdemeanor and assigned to clean the inside of the stove, gut fish, or pluck birds.

It was a rough, even harsh environment—no babying, no pats on the back, none of that self-esteem stuff. You did it right or you left—and many of them did leave, too, heaving a sigh of relief and moving on to something easy, like perhaps the salt mines. However many left, though, there was always a waiting list of supplicants to come and suffer in Troisgros University, where a growl from Chef Pierre, or the mere sight of Chef Jean's obsidian gaze turned his way was enough to ruin any adolescent's day. Still, for all the gruffness of the environment, the apprentices had to admit that the brothers worked kitchen hours as long as their own, that they took the three Michelin stars totally onto their shoulders—never, *never* allowing anyone but themselves to finish the preparation of a dish—and that when they were through with the cooking, they joined Papa out in the dining room to jolly up the customers, often late into the night. Sixteen- and eighteen-hour workdays for Jean and Pierre were mere routine. The apprentices had one whole day off every week, but Jean and Pierre allowed themselves only half a day off apiece twice a month—in alternation, of course, there would always be at least one Troisgros at the *piano*. Their annual vacations lasted two weeks rather than the four or five that was the norm in France. That was how you did it if you wanted three stars in a dump like Roanne. With professors of that caliber, it was no surprise that other restaurants eagerly snapped up the young graduates of Troisgros University.

In his boyish naïveté, first apprentice Bernard Loiseau assumed that he would soon be sharing a professional future not unlike that of Claude Perraudin and the others he had seen off over the preceding years. Leaning back against the *timbres*, singing out his number for the other apprentices, he was already imagining his next step along the path to the Michelin stars: some top restaurant in Paris, Lyon, or maybe the Côte d'Azur. But he was wrong, woefully wrong. Things didn't turn out that way at all. There were some big surprises and big disappointments awaiting him, because the plain fact was Chef Jean didn't like him. Chef Pierre, more easygoing, accepted the boy with the equanimity that was his from birth, but Bernard had a genius for rubbing Chef Jean the wrong way. And if you were on the wrong side of Jean Troisgros, a far more choleric character than his brother, you were swimming against a mighty current in the trade.

The problem was that Bernard was a wise guy, or at least appeared to be a wise guy, and that was enough for Jean. Bernard was a talker, too. After the timid caution of the first few weeks of work had worn off, Massillon's champion of gab returned in force, and soon he was entertaining the other *apprentis* with as much chatter and wisecracking as he could possibly get away with—and frequently a lot more that, to his discomfort, he didn't get away with. That first-apprentice bit was another thing. It impressed young Guy Savoy, but there was no such official title as First Apprentice. It was just something he had invented to *craner*, to show off. Naturally Bernard would never have dared take that position by the *timbres* or make that boast (or, indeed, do much chattering at all) when either of the chefs was present, but Jean knew about it—you couldn't hide anything in an incestuous little microsociety like that—and it irritated him mightily.

A braggart, that's what Jean took him for. Now, a joker, or a *farceur*—that was something he could understand, but a braggart, never. Jean's best friend Paul Bocuse was already famous in the trade for the *conneries** he had invented in Paris, with Fernand Point in Vienne, and later in his own restaurant in Collonges-au-Mont-d'Or. As a

---

*The *connerie* is a vital concept for anyone who would understand the French spirit and discourse. The root of the word is unseemly (originally *con* = vagina), but in everyday slang a *con* is a dope or fool, and a *connerie* is an idiocy, a mistake, or some kind of shenanigan. Ill-tempered old men in gilt-trimmed green uniforms, carrying ceremonial swords and expressing themselves in the imperfect of the subjunctive, ardently debate the many permutations of the base word— *conard, conne, conasse, déconner*—in plenary sessions of the Académie Française.

young *commis* at Restaurant Lucas-Carton in Paris, Paul had been responsible for a steady diet of havoc and hilarity at the expense of the chef, Monsieur Richard, a staid, traditional gent of the old school. It was Bocuse who trapped sparrows in the Tuileries Gardens (using stolen caviar as bait) to release them in Monsieur Richard's kitchen; Bocuse who nailed to the cloakroom floor the canvas *espadrilles* that Monsieur Richard habitually slipped into before shuffling up to direct the cooking; Bocuse who lifted a human skull from a visit to the Paris catacombs and slipped it into Monsieur Richard's stockpot.

That was OK—*conneries* and practical jokes were fun, but Jean Troisgros couldn't bear the boastful garrulity of this smartass Loiseau kid. Bernard's job was to shut up and work, not to jabber and entertain the crowd. Jean's irritation was an early predictor of a problem that was to dog Bernard Loiseau all throughout his life—the incomprehension of a personality that was far more complex and subtle than its outward appearance. Fleeting, shifting, and mercurial, young Bernard was growing into the man of many layers who would later confound the doubters by his success but at the same time annoy many critics by his style, while building the Burgundy palace of his Horatio Alger success story in Saulieu. Even as a teenager he seemed to be permanently "up"—enthusiastic and optimistic, but also extravagant, excitable, hyperbolic, and even swaggering—when he was expected to display only the modesty expected of a rank beginner. Few in the Troisgros kitchen could perceive that there was a down side to him, the self-doubt and hypersensitivity expertly concealed by a world-class whistler in the dark. Bernard Chirent, an apprentice who arrived in Roanne in June of 1969 and who went on to a successful career first in France and then in America, was taken in by the same façade that so angered Jean Troisgros.

"Bernard was always slightly unreal," he told me. "When I got to Roanne he was already a *caïd*, a big shot, the central figure among the apprentices—he was the one who stuck out. But it was a strange combination. He was both the *bout en train* and the *souffre-douleur*—the life of the party and the scapegoat at the same time. He was the worst apprentice I ever saw in thirty years of cuisine, possibly the worst that Troisgros ever had. He was the cook who wasn't a cook. He didn't give a damn. The only thing that seemed to interest him was playing *pétanque*. It was no state secret that Jean didn't like him, and never gave

him any support. After he was finished in Roanne, Bernard found himself with no job and no help from Jean. Nothing. I think that was what
gave him such tremendous ambition. He was determined to prove that
he would succeed in spite of the fact that he never got any support after
his apprenticeship."

There you have it. The incomprehension was there from the start,
and Bernard, his own worst enemy, was responsible for most of it. Quite
true: He didn't *seem* to give a damn, but he did, very much—certainly
as much as the others, but their nature, or their better judgment, was to
conform, bend to the task and shut up. Not Bernard. A born noncon-
formist, he was incapable of suppressing the thrust of his incubus, a
personality so forceful and manic that it leaped out in spite of his best
efforts or the concerned advice of his friends.

"Bernard, shut up!" is a phrase you hear reiterated time and again
when you speak with those who knew him intimately, and who endlessly tried to save him from himself. But who among those friends
could have known enough about the symptoms and treatment of bipolar disorder to even begin to figure how to handle him? Certainly not
his employers in Roanne, or his fellow apprentices or, least of all,
Bernard himself.

Otherwise known as manic-depressive syndrome, the bipolar syndrome is a well-documented behavioral illness responsible for serious
distortions of perception and social functioning. It may have genetic
causes that might be hereditary (the point is hotly debated), but in
Bernard's case it is tempting to look back to his maternal grandfather,
the *charcutier* with the vast ambition and terrifying energy, who from
time to time fell into inexplicable pits of depression. Bipolar disorder is
known to be prevalent in about 1 percent of adults, about 15 percent of
whom die by suicide. Its onset generally occurs between fifteen and
thirty years of age. Bernard was seventeen when Chirent met him.

Bernard's extravagant symptoms grew steadily stronger in the decades after he left Roanne but, ironically, they were doubtless as responsible for his tremendous success as they ultimately proved to be for
his crash. He put a near-superhuman energy and drive into the service
of his ambition, but when that energy faltered, it took little more than a
feather of adversity to knock him for the big loop. In those early days, all
Chirent saw was Bernard, the oddball joker, and Chirent was unaware

that there was an observant eye and quick brain behind the ebullience. Bernard was assiduously stocking the lessons he learned in a memory that was nearly photographic. For his part, Chef Jean could not possibly imagine that back in his rented room, Bernard, the insufferable loud-mouth, had pinned a poster on the ceiling above his bed. It displayed neither a view of Clermont-Ferrand nor some unclad beauty of suitably callipygian aspect, but the Troisgros brothers, his first and true masters.

In a manner of speaking, the brothers never left his mental ceiling. As Bernard developed his career and struggled toward his soaring goal in Saulieu, it became apparent that he never quite outgrew the influence of Chef Jean and Chef Pierre, but remained hard on the rails of their classicism and their refusal to tolerate humbug and flash. This undeviating fidelity to a single style was to serve him badly in the last few months of his life. His imagination had always been feverish enough to begin with, but when it began to spin out of control, he fell into a paranoia that convinced him that he was the victim of a vast cabal whose goal was to punish him for his devotion to the purest traditions of French cuisine, as learned from Les Frères Troisgros.

For the moment, though, all that was in the future. Right now in our story, he was only a boy at the start of his great adventure, and who had the good luck to be in Roanne—the Harvard, Oxford, and Sorbonne of cuisine. There was a lot of learning to do. Loudmouth or not, Bernard approached his instruction with perfect seriousness, and his learning curve took exactly the same path as those who had come before him and those who would follow. How they applied it later was their own business.

The general rule for a novice apprentice is logical enough: Start with simple tasks and, as these are mastered, move on to ones of increasing sophistication. The early coal-, cleanup-, and scullery-work is followed by miscellaneous vegetables and potatoes—cleaning and peeling first, then the more complicated operations of cutting them into *julienne* or *mirepoix*, or "turning" them into the almond- and barrel-shaped forms needed for different dishes. ("Turning a mushroom was almost a religion," Pierre Troisgros says today in perfect seriousness.) Over the six months or so of vegetable duty, the aspiring cook learns that most basic of skills: how to handle a knife. Before attaining the admirable, easy competence of the chefs you see on TV, whose flashing blades chop, slice, and sliver in an effortless silver whir, he will have passed through the humiliation of frequent nicks and cuts and trips to the kitchen's first-aid station. Fish comes next—scaling it, gutting it, and later, when he seems to know what he is doing, the painfully careful slicing and lifting from the bone that presents the chef with a perfect filet of sole, John Dory, or turbot. There will be rabbits to gut, and chickens and all manner of smaller fowl to pluck and clean.

Tending the *fonds* and *fumets*—the meat and fish stocks—was a typical chore of apprenticeship: breaking up bones, adding aromatics and meat, fish, or fowl trimmings, depending on the stock, then skimming, degreasing, and adding water—cold water, only, of course, to help congeal and separate out the fats—to the big 30-liter stockpot* as it simmers away, slowly reducing in volume until it has thickened and deepened the tastes that then, as now, constitute the backbone of most of the great sauces of French cuisine.

But no apprentice could go near the meats *chez Troisgros*. This most delicate of products was the exclusive domain of Chef Pierre, emperor of the *garde-manger* (cold kitchen), a man whose appraising eye and keen blade would whip you off a perfect filet of beef or veal or a lamb chop cut just so, and unerringly weighing in at 200 grams every time, give or take a few grams. As for Chef Jean, he could be approached only in an *apprenti*'s last six months of training, when the boy acceded to the redoubtable honor of taking his place next to the master himself at the *piano*, assisting him the way a highly trained nurse assists a surgeon in the operating room, keeping his mouth shut, passing the required instrument or ingredient, and answering every enquiry with the only talking allowed in the presence of such terrifying eminence, the resonant, military bark: *"Oui, chef!"*

Military, indeed. There is an obvious parallel between the hierar-

---

*One of the commonest misconceptions of *nouvelle cuisine* zealots was that modern cooking would (or should) do away with stocks. Nothing could be further from the truth. All the best French restaurants continue to rely on them for sauces—but they are perfectly clean, pure, degreased stocks, made fresh every day. The quick, less complex variant called *jus* (juices) avoids the odium of actually calling them stocks.

chy and discipline of an army and that of a serious professional kitchen—*chef*, remember, doesn't mean cook but chief, boss—and the kids who share an apprenticeship under such authority form a bond that lasts for life. Every leg-trembling stander-at-attention who ever worked at the *piano* next to Chef Jean remembers his ritual gesture when the day's *service* finally drew to a close. His Majesty would throw his *torchon*, the white kitchen towel that every chef always wears under the drawstring at the front of his apron, to the apprentice of the day, with a little grunted admonition: *Tiens, gamin*—catch. And don't say I never gave you anything.

"But the point was," explained Guy Savoy, "that the *torchon* was always *clean*! That was a lesson in itself. They expected us to work well, and good work is neat work. You know, very few people ever get to experience what we experienced in Roanne. The famous army buddies you always hear about, that's peanuts compared to apprenticeship. There's something so special about it. It's like a rugby team. We were the band of brothers, the gang. We loved one another without knowing it."

Of the several youngsters who shared the apprenticeship with Bernard, at least two have died and one, now a professor in a hotel and cooking school, declined to speak with me. But four of them obligingly shared their memories of Roanne and Bernard at his professional debut. Claude Perraudin, Bernard Chirent, Jean Ramet, and Guy Savoy are still neck-deep in the gastronomy scene, each according to his own talents and ambition. Perraudin, with Restaurant le Père Claude, runs one of the best, most popular bistros in Paris, and scorns the idea of even trying for a Michelin star. Why bother? His place, open all year seven days a week, is always full, and there is not a night when he doesn't turn away would-be customers for the unpretentious but faultlessly prepared classics that he learned in the kitchens of the Troisgros brothers, Paul Bocuse, and Michel Guérard. Bernard Chirent worked in some of the finest French and English restaurants, and opened one of his own in Paris before succumbing to the siren song of the greenback and moving to the U.S., where he was paid princely salaries working for luxury hotels, a couple of private clubs, and at least one individual millionaire. Jean Ramet moved to Bordeaux and now owns one of the best restaurants in town (a single Michelin star, but maybe two upcoming one of these days), bearing his own name. And Guy Savoy wears the purple of the gastronomic royalty of Paris, owning one of the city's nine restaurants rated with three Michelin stars.

It is an edifying exercise to jump back in time with these men to Roanne in the late sixties and early seventies. Each of them today is a distinguished, prosperous, and considerably envied pillar of the trade, but as they reminisced, they slid back into the condition of nervous teenagers trying to please the ogres named Chef Jean and Chef Pierre.

They all went through the same steps, but each remembered his part of them, and in his own way. For Claude Perraudin, a laconic, no-nonsense type who still takes the time to personally choose his produce in Rungis—the Paris wholesale market—the mental picture of a workday in Roanne will always be for him the peeling of vegetables side by side with Chef Jean and Chef Pierre, because these were hands-on gods who participated in the lowly chores as well as the exalted, and the kids who stood with them were forever stuck with their obdurate work ethic.

Perraudin reflects: "When that was finished we'd put things in place for the chefs—salt, pepper, oil, vinegar, all the basic stuff—and begin cutting the herbs. Chives, tarragon, garlic and the rest. We would dice shallots—gray shallots, the ones you don't see very much anymore—for the *entrecôtes* [rib steaks], and then we'd prepare the *beurre cancalais*. Whip the butter, salt and pepper it, and add lemon and tarragon. It's still the best sauce there is for seafood. It went on the grilled lobster just before sending it out into the dining room. Then there were the *beurriers*, the butter bowls for the tables: thirty of them, and each one holding five hundred grams of butter. Fresh butter for every *service*.

"When you had the responsibility for the vegetables, you had to store them perfectly, or else you caught hell. The gardener, old man Livet, brought fresh ones every morning at eight—carrots, lettuce, spinach, leeks, turnips, and such, and Chef Jean was always there at the delivery. He never left us alone. That was the way he had learned it. Old school. No boss would clean and peel the vegetables with the apprentices today. I was proud to be in a three-star restaurant in the first place, but when I saw the way they worked, I was especially proud to be with the Troisgros brothers.

"And the fish—fabulous fish! You don't see fish like that anymore. We would gut them, but we had to watch others working for at least a year before they allowed us to fillet them. We pulled snails out of their shells by the thousands, and we killed the live frogs that they delivered to us—took them and bashed them against the edge of the table—then skinned them and prepared the legs. The birds were already dead when we got them—*ortolans*, snipe, thrushes for pâté. Our job was to pluck them clean. When a big bunch came in, it could take us all morning."

The thrush pâté of Les Frères Troisgros was almost as celebrated as their immortal salmon with sorrel, even if it originated as a recipe that Pierre brought from his days with Fernand Point in Vienne. After the apprentices had plucked them clean, Pierre finely ground them up in the *robot*, mixed the meat with chicken livers, juniper berries, and goose fat, and slowly cooked it in the *pâtissier*'s oven, reposing in the gentle luxury of a *bain marie*. When it had softened to the texture of a thick puree, he passed it through a fine sieve to free it of the last bits of bone and beak or any other hard matter likely to distract a client's attention from its enjoyment or tweak his sensibilities by reminding him of all the cute little birdies that had been sacrificed piecemeal for his pleasure.

Bernard Chirent remembered that these same little birdies would occasionally suffer other preliminary indignities before meeting their fate in Pierre's *robot*. "When the brothers were out playing tennis or meeting with suppliers, the atmosphere in the kitchen loosened up. We had these cartons and cartons of thrushes to pluck, and you could always count on Bernard making just the right wisecrack to get things going. Before you knew it the thrushes would be flying back and forth. A couple of times Jean or Pierre came back right in the middle of thrush fights, or when maybe two or three of us were down on the floor wrestling. That was enough to lose our next day off, or an assignment to clean the grease from the exhaust fan over the stove.

"Another time I'll never forget was the afternoon when we were standing around the table by the window to the courtyard, peeling potatoes and tossing them into this big tub in the middle of the table. Michel Bonin, the *sous-chef*, was with us, and of course Bernard. As it happened, Jean had changed over to the meat station behind us,

because Pierre was on vacation. Any loud talking was absolutely for-
bidden when the chefs were around, especially Jean. So there might
have been a few whispered words, but that was all, because we were so
afraid of Chef Jean. Just then Bernard spoke a little bit louder than he
should have, and I guess he forgot about Jean being closer than usual.
He was just joking—he never meant any harm—but the words he said
to Bonin were: 'You don't have the balls on your ass to do that.'

"Jean didn't say anything. He just stayed there like a statue. Didn't
move. We went on peeling. But Bonin was *sous-chef* and Bernard was
just an apprentice, and he had shown lack of respect for a superior. After a couple of minutes Jean came creeping up behind Bernard and
slammed his fist into the base of his neck, like a rabbit punch. *Paf!*
Bernard went flying headfirst into the tub of potatoes. 'That'll teach
you to open your big mouth,' he said. We all broke up laughing."   .

Poor Bernard. He had to shrug it off and make a show of joining in
the laughter, while at the same time demonstrating a suitably appren-
ticelike degree of contrition and trying to save face in spite of the humiliation. But in later years, talking with friends and journalists, he told
of riding his bike alone through Roanne's depressing streets late at
night and bawling like a baby after yet another tongue-lashing in front
of his friends.

This has a certain significance. What was exceptional about it was
not that he wept—Bernard's emotions had always been on hair-trigger
release—but that he forced himself to go off and do it in secret. That
he was even capable of secrecy. There lies the anomaly, because anyone who had more than a passing acquaintance with Bernard Loiseau
as an adolescent, in young manhood, or in middle age knew this about
him: He was constitutionally unable to hide anything. Everything was
up front. It all came out. He was the least dissembling of men. Nice
paradox here: When he was launched into his most wildly extravagant
discourse—and there would be more and more of that later, because
he couldn't shut up any more than he could conceal his feelings—he
could fabulate with the best of men, but his exaggerations and inventions were so transparent and so ingenuous that his listeners always dis-
counted them, anyway. Result: Even when Bernard was lying, he was
honest.

Pierre Troisgros smiled wryly as he tried to sum up the experience of having this curious, unpredictable boy on his hands. "We had no problem with his performance. You could see that he was made for this work. He had the physique for it, he was very agile with his hands, he had the ambition and he wanted to be recognized. But he also had something else. He had this . . . *presence*. He was always there. When something went wrong the others were clever enough to stay out of sight. Savoy or Chirent ducked down into the cellar or hid in the walk-in refrigerator, but Bernard would always be there with that smile of his—and that was even more irritating, because he was supposed to be acting like a beaten dog. So of course he got bawled out for all the others. But even being yelled at, he was still affirming himself. He was present. That gave him a certain importance that the others didn't have."

Bernard didn't run, then, but that was Bernard. The others could hardly be faulted for scattering, because there was really something like terror in the air *chez* Troisgros, a place where one brother growled like a bear, the other ate apprentices alive and spat out the bones, and the patriarch, if he deigned to notice your presence as worthy of planet Earth at all, dismissed you as a *petit con*.

"We all had such inferiority complexes," remembered Jean Ramet, who relieved Bernard of the detested coal duty when he arrived a few months later. "We were just kids! And it got worse, too—the more experience we got with the brothers and really understood who they were and what they represented, the more we feared them. We had so much respect that we were afraid to speak to them, or even look them in the eye. We almost pissed in our pants just being in their presence. I think that's why Bernard dumped the coal in the pan."

Ah, the famous coal in the pan. Every apprentice in every kitchen in the world has screwed up at one time or another, but Bernard's bungle with the coal shovel has become such an integral part of official Troisgros folklore, told and retold so often, that it spins off into a multiplicity of variations. The official version is from Guy Savoy, who was there to witness it.

"We had gone out and celebrated on Friday night, so that Saturday at the lunch *service* we were all under the weather. Michel Bonin, the *sous-chef*, had the day off, and Jean Ramet had been given his position on the stove. He was looking a little bit droopy. Chef Jean said: 'What's the matter, are you asleep? Bernard, come over here!' So Bernard took

Jean's place. All of us were there watching, scared as hell, because we knew it could happen to any one of us any time.

"'Stoke the fire, kid!' Jean said. Bernard worked for a few minutes. Three or four salmon filets were cooking in different pans. Jean told him to put another pan *en plein*, directly over the flames. So Bernard lifted off the cooking ring, and Jean saw the flame was a little low, so he said 'Put in a shovel of coal, kid.'

"That was *le moment pathétique*. Now Bernard had the pan in one hand and the coal shovel in the other. By nervousness or sleepiness or error of coordination or whatever it was, he reached down to the coal scuttle on the floor, scooped up the coal—and dumped it straight into the pan instead of the stove. Luckily there wasn't any salmon in the pan yet. I don't know what Jean would have done if Bernard had destroyed a fresh *saumon à l'oseille*."

Savoy's memory of the incident ended there, but Jean Ramet, who was just as close, recalled Chef Jean's exact words of outrage: *"Tu as la cervelle qui sort par la queue!"*—You've pissed out your brains. He called Jean Ramet back to the stove, and it was one more humiliation, one more Bernard story to make the rounds of French kitchens. It wasn't even the best one, either. The most famous line that ever came out of the Troisgros kitchen was Jean's bellowed prediction after yet another miscue by his favorite scapegoat: "If someday you ever become a cook, I'll be an archbishop!"

The line became famous mostly because Bernard himself, his ultimate goal of three-star chefdom finally achieved, incessantly repeated it to visitors and journalists—especially journalists—who came to Saulieu to contemplate him in his glory. His endless carping on the anecdote only underlined the complexity of his nature and mental processes. It allowed half the journalists to use it in their stories as an illustration of how deeply Bernard's feelings had been hurt by Jean's attitude, and the other half to see it as a gloating cry of triumph. But either way, Bernard knew very well that the journalists would all write it up, because Chef Jean's quote was catnip for hacks, much too good to miss. It was just one more piece of evidence that there was always more to Bernard than what appeared on the immediate surface: beneath the excess and volubility, there could often be a healthy dose of manipulation, too. Things got complicated when you were around Bernard.

So who, finally, ended up manipulating whom? In Saulieu, Bernard taught himself to play the press the way Jascha Heifetz played the fiddle: offering writers unbeatable material for their stories and great eats for their ample tummies. But at the same time he genuinely liked the hacks, and would be miserable if they didn't come down to enjoy his chatter and his magnificent table. He was constantly on the phone, begging them to come down and see him in Saulieu. For their part, journalists knew that it would take only the least hint of a leading question to have Bernard barking colorfully back at them for their papers. So if he was honest when he lied, it can also be said that he was being manipulated even as he was manipulating. Bernard was the prince of paradox and the king of smokescreen.

"He was always a very impressive guy," said Savoy. "Big guy, big, imposing physique, he knew his way around, he had an answer to everything and he had this wonderful air of assurance about him. What fascinated me the most was the number he did when the *service* was heating up and the clients were beginning to arrive. Over against the big window, out onto the courtyard, there was the table where we peeled vegetables, and Bernard kept a lookout from there. He knew the cars of all the regular customers, and he would announce them to Chef Jean and Chef Pierre as they came in: '*Monsieur Preau arrive, Monsieur Marcel arrive,*' and so on. That was useful to the chefs, so they let him do it. Me, I didn't know the clients' cars after three years. But Bernard already had this interest in the culture of the business that extended beyond the strict framework of the kitchen.

"He had a very friendly character—I'd even say joyous. He was very neat, impeccably dressed, and he always had magnificent shoes. He loved shoes. And he always wore the same cologne, Eau Sauvage, by Dior. He made all his pocket money from playing *pétanque* at night in town, or during our lunch break in the courtyard. He was a fabulous player, too, throwing lefty even though he was a righty in everything else. He would squint across the ball in his hand and call his shot: '*J'annonce: carreau en place.*' And then *bing!* He would hit it every damn time. You had the feeling that this guy could do anything he wanted to."

Even if he was the heavyweight champion of the category, Bernard was not the only *apprenti* to bungle, and Chef Jean not the only tyrant. Young Guy Savoy was a serious and dedicated student, far from the *emmerdeur** that Chef Jean persistently saw in Bernard, but he, too, had plenty to learn, and Chef Pierre was not above flexing his disciplinarian muscle when there was a good lesson to be taught. Master and Commander of the *garde-manger*, Pierre was deeply and intolerably affronted by a misplaced turnip or a negligent chive.

"I learned all about that when I had the responsibility for the cold room," Savoy said. "One morning I apparently hadn't stocked the vegetables and herbs the right way, and in less than a minute I had the whole contents passed out to me by Chef Pierre, so fast that I barely had the time to put one crate down before he shoved another one out in my face. 'Now you're going to put it all back and you're going to do it right!' he said, and you can bet I did.

"Another day, Chef Pierre had told me to take care of the beef marrow supply. That was a normal part of our work. We would cut the bones and whack them with a wooden baton to dislodge the marrow and free it from inside the bone. Well, as it turned out, our usual butcher hadn't delivered many marrow bones that day, and there was a big table reserved—twenty-five or thirty clients who were going to take the big steaks we served with marrow. When we were getting the *service* ready, Pierre said '*Petit, la moelle,*' and I showed him what we had.

" 'Is that all?' he said. Like a jerk—and this is why apprenticeship is such a great system—I said that's all the butcher delivered me. I had given him a total idiocy for an answer.

" 'I don't give a goddamn!' he said. 'You take your bike and you go to every butcher shop in town until you've got enough marrow for me.' On that day I learned what responsibility was.

"Troisgros was the best school in the world—it was *the* school. We had the chance of having two great chefs over us—it was as if we had worked in the same restaurant with Paul Bocuse and Alain Chapel. All

---

*"Damned nuisance" is how one French–English dictionary translates this indispensable word. Well, all right, they're being polite. But the root word *merde* is as important, and has as many or even more (and more subtle), permutations in colloquial French than *con*.

we aspired to was to be like them someday. When I took my bike and carried our order for herbs and fresh vegetables to old man Livet at the edge of town, I felt like an important guy."

And, curiously enough, he was, too. Even today, unless you harbor a passionate interest for earthenware crockery of the French Revolutionary period (the Joseph Déchelette Museum), you would be hard-pressed to find a valid reason for visiting Roanne, if it were not for the Restaurant Troisgros,* and the city's inhabitants are very well aware of this fact of life.

"We used to play *pétanque* against local teams at night in the park by city hall," Claude Perraudin recalled. "Bernard never wanted to lose, of course, so sometimes the matches would go on till one in the morning. Eventually the cops shooed us away but they never gave us any trouble, because they knew who we were. OK, you're from Troisgros, they'd say. Now go on home. That shows the prestige we had."

Prestige with the cops was fine, but working in a great restaurant posed some particular problems where girls were concerned. Eager young bloods in the prime of their nascent manhood, the apprentices did what they could to trawl the local supply of *fiancées*, but the problem was that the most propitious moment was Saturday night, and that was precisely the night that the restaurant was the busiest. As a result, the boys could never get to the nightclubs or the popular dances until around midnight, by which time all the best girls had been taken by the early birds. If they rushed directly from the kitchen without taking the time to wash and change, a further complication arose.

"One of them said I smelled of *escargots*," a crestfallen Bernard confided to Savoy one particularly disappointing night.

Occupational hazard. The inimitable Jean Ducloux, the Tournus boy who went as a *commis* to Alexandre Dumaine's kitchen in Saulieu, worked in Roanne for two years during the war in La Taverne Alsacienne, then the best restaurant in town. The Troisgros restaurant did not exist yet, and Bernard and his fellow apprentices had not even been born, but the same hormones were raging in the same manner in 1942 as in 1970, and with approximately the same results. Enterprisingly

---

*Now run by Pierre's son, Michel, the restaurant has adjusted its name in consequence.

pursuing a young beauty who caught his eye in the street, Ducloux tried to impress her by bragging that he was the son of the Taverne's owner. She eventually learned that he was lying, of course, but in fact the subterfuge had proven successful. Less than a year later they were married, and Paulette Ducloux is still his wife today, more than sixty years later.

"I wondered about him," she admits. "It struck me as strange that the owner's son should smell so strongly of onions."

Luckily for the boys in the seventies, there was a nurses' school in Roanne, and nurses are accustomed to hours almost as impossible as kitchen professionals. Leader of gastro-seduction raids, Perraudin and a few others occasionally sneaked pots and pans out of the kitchen to prepare highfalutin midnight snacks for their putative conquests. They made sure to sneak the cooking gear back into the kitchen by early morning, and of course they were far too frightened of the Troisgros brothers to lift any food—that would have been not just dishonest, but suicidal, considering Chef Pierre's gimlet eye over the restaurant's provisions.*

The nurses rarely saw the boy from Clermont-Ferrand, though, and when they did, he usually begged off and went home before the party heated up. Perraudin suggested that Bernard had moral scruples about the evening's potential carnality because of all the years he had spent under the wing of priests at Massillon, but the truth seems to be simpler than that: The life of the party was afraid of girls. Boy and man, Bernard could always be counted on for an overwhelming flow of persuasive talk, and in principle his persuasiveness ought to have worked wonders on the nurses. This was a man whose eloquence in Saulieu could sweep aside the hesitations and objections of bankers and investors when millions of francs and euros were at play, but all through his life he remained a bumbling amateur in the fine French art of flooring women. The big guy was shy.

In his last year of *apprentissage*, Bernard inherited from Perraudin

---

*One notable exception to the rule of never snitching any comestibles from the restaurant was the tempting bottle of port for the melons. A nip or two before going out to a ball or a nightclub would be enough to set a young apprentice into a confident frame of mind, whether or not he smelled of snails.

the job of cooking meals for the personnel, who ritually took their lunch at eleven in the morning and dinner at six. It was a promotion and a professional honor, the only true cooking of entire dishes that an apprentice would have a chance to do in his three years, because the clients remained strictly in the hands of Chef Jean and Chef Pierre. Bernard did himself proud.

"I have a very strong memory of the kitchen and dining room staff telling me how sorry they were to see Bernard go," Pierre told me, "because they ate so well when he was taking care of their meals. He would add his little touch to an ordinary dish like a *blanquette*, and they really appreciated it. I still suspect him of having used rather more of the noble and expensive foodstuffs than he should have—theoretically that was reserved for the clients—but Jean and I winked at it a little bit, even if he cost us money in the long run. A *sou* was a *sou* in those days, and we watched the budget very carefully."

Just because they work in a three-star restaurant definitely does not mean that the staff dines on ambrosia and myrrh. *Au contraire*: noodles, rice, and potatoes are frequent fare for staff in classy restaurants, as are the simpler, cheaper fish like cod, hake, and whiting. For meat dishes, hashes, stews, and ragouts like *estouffade de boeuf* are common, put together with the trimmings and lesser sections of the expensive cuts destined for customers' tables. Even if it is simple food, though, it is still very good simple food, made in a three-star kitchen. All great things have to start somewhere.

In June 1971, Bernard received his CAP (Certificat d'Aptitude Professionnelle) of cuisine, signed by Chef Jean and Chef Pierre. He was now a cook—at the lowest level possible, but still an officially certified cook. As soon as his apprenticeship was finished, the army grabbed him, as it grabbed all healthy young males in those days of the draft. He spent a year hating the classical army basic-training routines of make-work, the discomfort of shabby barracks and long, pointless exercises of marching up hill and down dale—and, after that, cooking. That was rather better—at least he was assured of staying warm over the winter. Assigned to an infantry regiment in the little Alsatian town of Phalsbourg, over by the German border near Strasbourg, he was immediately sent into the enlisted men's kitchen. Such was the power of the Troisgros name that the commanding officer summarily gave him

authority over a *brigade* of twenty-two culinary underlings. It was just
an army mess (the word is well chosen), and the produce was heavy, ordinary, and cheap, but it was his first taste of command.

He liked it. It was in Phalsbourg that he took his first baby steps in
the direction of leading and motivating men. Bernard being Bernard,
he did it his own way, developing an approach that was destined to
come to fruition several years later. Unlike the great historical chefs,
unlike the Troisgros brothers, Bernard could not feel comfortable imposing absolute authority. The only style that agreed with his nature
was to lead with his native enthusiasm—by *selling* himself and his
ideas. Apparently he wasn't his father's boy for nothing. It was a strange,
quirky, and sometimes almost comical system, but it was to work wonders when he finally got to Saulieu.

V

THE GREAT ADVENTURE BEGINS

Paris with Pygmalion,
1972–1975

*S*ummer 1972. His obligatory year of *service militaire* accomplished, Bernard used his free soldier's pass on the French rail system for the last time and stepped off the train at Clermont-Ferrand's main station. Now what?

There was nothing much on the horizon. He moved back in with his parents and started looking for work. It was a bleak, disappointing time. He heard that Claude Perraudin had already gone from Paul Bocuse's restaurant to the tiny Pot au Feu of Michel Guérard's in the Parisian suburb of Asnières; before long, his fellow apprentices Bernard Chirent and Jean Ramet would be taking the same route. That was a very good gig, for prestige as well as for instruction. Guérard was the most exciting chef of the moment, a man who had appeared like a sudden meteorite on the Parisian gastronomic scene. Landing a cooking job in his place was like going for an advanced degree from Berkeley after graduating from Harvard.

But there was none of that for him—not for the wise guy, Chef Jean's *bête noire*. Bernard found himself back home at square one with strictly nothing except memories of the comradeship of his fellow apprentices, a few savory *conneries*, some notable victories in *pétanque*, and a basic knowledge of the cooking techniques of the Troisgros brothers. That and the ambition that still fired him: to somehow reach the level of success that had brought what seemed like half the world's celebrities and beautiful people tramping down to Roanne, slavering for a chance to open their wallets and see what salmon tasted like with sorrel prepared by seven scared kids in floppy *toques*. But how do you get there from here?

For want of anything better, Bernard went to work in the *charcuterie* founded by his grandfather, now run by his uncle. He asked around and wrote a few letters, but nothing interesting came of the effort. He had hung his highest hopes on the Auberge de l'Ill, a *Michelin* three-star establishment in Illhaeusern, not far from where he had done his *service militaire*. With its elegant dining room overlooking a storybook garden shaded by weeping willows on the banks of the little river Ill, the Auberge was an idyllically beautiful restaurant that, like Troisgros, happened to be run by two brothers, Claude and Jean-Pierre Haeberlin. Claude, the shy, soft-spoken one, stayed in his kitchen to cook an exalted panoply of Alsatian specialties while Jean-Pierre, his twinkly-eyed kid brother, did the decoration and ran the *salle*.

In all probability Bernard would have managed to visit the Auberge during his time in Phalsbourg, perhaps dropping by the kitchen and chatting with some of the apprentices and *commis*, even if he never would have dared to approach Chef Claude or Monsieur Jean-Pierre personally. Had he given it some thought at the time, he would have seen that Illhaeusern nicely illustrated the classic formula for a country restaurant's success, and that it was the same old, eternal story: location, location, and location. Half an hour's drive from Strasbourg, the same from Basel, it lay just off the nexus of autoroutes that served France, Germany, and Switzerland, and the high-speeding, high-spending Teutons and Helvetes outnumbered the Haeberlins' French clients two to one. This vexing question of location would follow Bernard for most of his professional life. The 30 or so kilometers that separated Saulieu from the Autoroute du Sud was a weighty albatross just waiting to be hung around his neck when he finally set up on his own and shot for the stars.

Assuming that the magic Troisgros name would be enough to open the door, he wrote Claude Haeberlin to offer his services as *commis*, but his hopes were thoroughly dashed: He never received an answer, not even an acknowledgment. In all probability his letter had somehow gone astray or got lost in a shuffle of papers, because the Haeberlin brothers were too polite and professional to simply ignore a job request from an ex-Troisgros employee, but as far as Bernard could see, it was just another snub. Or was it even worse—might they have called Roanne to check, and received a negative report? He was too mortified and proud to follow up by telephoning Illhaeusern or writing a second letter.

This was the situation, and this was his frame of mind that November when he ran into Bernard Chirent, who had popped down from Paris to visit his parents before leaving for his next job. Bernard was having a smoke in the street outside the *charcuterie* when Chirent appeared out of nowhere: *Deus ex machina*, just like in the movies. And, also just like in the movies, it proved to be the turning point of his life.

Chirent explained that he was about to quit his job in Paris and go to work for the famous Roux brothers in London. The boss is looking for someone to take over from me, he explained. Why don't you give him a call? His name is Claude Verger. Bernard made the call. Verger sounded interested. Come on up and see me. We'll talk.

A few days later Bernard hopped back on the train, this time bound for Paris. He was twenty-one years old, and he had never been in the big city. He felt like a hayseed, and he rather looked like one, too, as he fumbled and wandered around the Paris metro system in his shiny new shoes, smelling of Eau Sauvage and trying to locate a place called Porte de Clichy. He finally got there, but what he saw was hardly a reflection of the professional glory he had in mind. Clichy was an undistinguished proletarian suburb in the northwestern corner of Paris out beyond Montmartre and Pigalle, squeezed between a crook of the river Seine, the railroad tracks leading to the St. Lazare station, the *boulevard périphérique* ring road, and a factory sprawl of the Citröen autoworks. His rendezvous was in a place called Le Bistrot de Lyon, at number 1, rue de Paris, almost astraddle the administrative boundary where Clichy met the Paris city limits.

Standing under the roar of the traffic on the *périph'*, Bernard found himself before a typically modest turn-of-the-century bistro on the ground floor level of a five-story apartment block: big awning in front, the inevitable bar on the right and the kitchen behind, and seating room for thirty or forty clients. He entered and asked for Claude Verger. A skinny, businesslike man of fifty or so approached, wearing a cook's apron and a sardonic smile. His face bore the characteristic flush of the wine-drinking bon vivant, and when he spoke, his voice had a curiously thin, high-pitched timbre to it. Bernard-Galatea was about to have his first experience with his very own Pygmalion.

Claude Verger was quite a case. All the important French chefs knew him well, and the mere mention of his name, then as now, was enough to elicit a smile and probably a burst of laughter, too, because he was one of gastronomy's true characters. Like Bernard's friend Guy Savoy, but one generation earlier, he was born and raised in Bourgouin, east of Lyon by the border with Switzerland. He reached manhood just in time for the disaster of the Second World War, and his experience as a bombardier in the hopelessly outclassed French air force—first trying to drop bombs on Germans, then getting bombed twice as hard in return and finally limping off with the remnants of his unit into French North Africa, where he nearly died of yellow fever— forged an attitude toward life that never varied from then on.

Claude Verger didn't give a damn. He was not exactly a nihilist, because he wasn't a philosopher, but rather a man who had decided once and for all that since human existence was some kind of cosmic joke, you might as well do your best to enjoy your brief moment of participation in it. He tried a number of different trades and a couple of marriages, but what set him on the road to meeting Bernard was the Robot-Coupe. This clever French invention, the ancestor of all the millions of food processors that now take up space in households around the world, was originally designed for professional kitchens, as a quick and handy labor-saving device to perform the slicing, dicing, shredding, and grating operations that from time immemorial had been done by hand.

Soon every chef wanted one, and Claude Verger, a friend of the company's boss, was the guy selling them and picking up a 15 percent commission on each one. For the best part of a decade he haunted all the top restaurants in France, invading their kitchens to demonstrate and explain his gear. He was good at it, too, surprisingly good, because his manner was a complete break with the usual honeyed, ingratiating tone of traveling salesmen of the traditional school. Quick, nervous, bright of eye and sarcastic of tongue, Verger entered a kitchen like a bantamweight boxer spoiling for a fight, challenging any chef to not appreciate his visit and buy his equipment. Joshing and chivvying instead of flattering, he made a few enemies, but mostly friends, among the chefs, because he knew his business and he knew cooking, too, from the years he had spent running a little restaurant with his sister in Bourgouin. In the sixties, there wasn't a two-star or three-star chef who wasn't familiar with Verger's rubescent face, his crooked smile, his plentiful wisecracks and his criticisms.

Verger was a virtuoso of criticisms. As a professional frequenter of cooks and kitchens, he became, by the simple logic of his work, something like a professional eater, too, and it did not take long for him to feel the dilemma common to all full-time gastronomic critics: Most of the time he wasn't hungry. Great French food day after day after day was too much to take. He yearned for cooking that was simpler, lighter, and less abundant.

"When I saw the way chefs worked," he told me, "I figured I wasn't any dumber [*pas plus con*] than they were, and I could do at least as well. Since I had no formal training as a cook, I had my own special techniques. Most of the time, I didn't understand their cooking. Or rather, they didn't understand mine. When I asked them why they did a dish this way or that way, they told me that was how it had been done for the last hundred or two hundred years, so that was the way it should always be done. I didn't agree with them. Ninety-nine percent of what I was eating in their places was *de la merde.*"

Singular type, this Verger—somehow he got away with his outrageous rants without being conked on the head with a potato masher, because chefs generally liked him. Not only was he funny and entertaining, but it was also clear that behind his provocative exaggerations there lay an undeniable germ of truth. Just as Henri Gault and Christian Millau had seen, much of French cooking had become too heavy for modern tastes. After the deprivations of the gray, hungry war days, when fear of the occupying Germans had been compounded by an almost total lack of decent food, it had only been natural for a famished population to dive joyously into rich feasts of sugar, cream, butter, milk, and all the other luxuries they had been dreaming of for six long years. By the seventies, though, the orgy had begun to pall. It was time for a change. Claude Verger was one of the point men of the movement to make that change a radical one.

His greatest ally in this gastronomic *jacobinisme* was Michel

Guérard. By the time Verger met Guérard in his minuscule Pot au Feu, on the other side of the Seine from Clichy, he had sold so many Robot-Coupes that he had a wad of cash just waiting to be spent. Although they were entirely different in character—Guérard was a visionary, one of the rare cooks who deserved to be called an *artiste*, while Verger was an opportunist, a clear-eyed businessman who knew how to count—the two men became fast friends. Guérard appreciated Verger's humor and blunt honesty; Verger recognized a true genius in Guérard. You know, you ought to open a bistro, Guérard idly told him one afternoon as they were exchanging ideas. Verger did some quick mental calculations, took a second look at Michel's situation, and came to a quick conclusion: The guy was right.

Michel had bought his doll's house restaurant in 1962, not long after his thirtieth birthday, at what the French call a *vente à la chandelle*—a colorful but nerve-racking style of property auction dating all the way back to the fifteenth century. The auctioneer opens bids by ceremoniously lighting two small candles—or rather tallowed wicks—one slightly longer than the other. The bidding briskly follows, because the wicks last no longer than fifteen or thirty seconds. The first candle goes out (the tallow's greasy smoke the undisputable sign of its extinction), and then the second, giving bidders one last chance, because at this moment the auctioneer lights the third and final wick, and the suspense mounts as the bids fly. The last one to shout or make a sign before the third candle winks out and the black smoke rises is declared the winner. The Pot au Feu, situated on an impasse next to some old factories in an undesirable corner of Asnières, wasn't exactly a prime piece of real estate. Michel got it with a princely bid of 18,000 francs— about $3,600 at the time.

It was the gastronomic deal of the century. Soon word went round the foodie grapevine that extraordinary things were happening in Asnières, and the Pot au Feu morphed into the most coveted eating address in France—getting a table reservation there became the gold standard of challenges for the concierges of every ritzy hotel in Paris. By jamming one table behind the bar and another against the door to the toilet, Michel was just able to squeeze in thirty clients, both lunch and dinner. That was it, and anyone who wanted to pee during chow time would have to go outside and find some other solution.

Who, everyone wondered—as they swooned over his *salade gourmande* (mixed greens, asparagus tips, string beans, shallots, truffles, and foie gras), his *feuilletés* of asparagus tips, prawns, and truffles, his John Dory with a pepper *sabayon* or *justement*, the peasant *pot au feu* that he dressed in formal clothes—was this guy Guérard? Very interesting case. Short, puckish, bright of eye, and quick to smile, he was cute as a button, but he was also devilishly smart and reeking of creativity. Son of a modest family of butchers in the riverside town of Mantes la Jolie, 30 miles west of Paris, he had been apprenticed at a tender age to a *pâtissier-traiteur* of the old school, working impossible hours for next to no pay but learning a thousand tricks of the trade, everything from making a perfect, and perfectly delicate, *pâte feuilletée* (puff pastry) by laborious hand-rolling, to vinifying the pressings of his boss's grapes into drinkable wine, to slaughtering a calf when *quenelles de veau* were required for a *vol au vent*.

"It was a fabulous experience for opening the mind," he says today. "I had the luck to see every side of the business. My apprenticeship was unbelievably rigorous, but good God—after you've gone through that, you're at ease anywhere."

After the army, young Michel soared through the triennial Meilleur Ouvrier de France—Best French Artisan—competition, easily winning his diploma in the pastry chef category, and went to work at a couple of the most prestigious addresses in Paris, the Hôtel Crillon and the famous Lido music hall. It was enjoyable work, and the pay was good, but his extraordinary talents were eclipsed as pastry chef in what was a large, anonymous *brigade*. It was only when he struck out on his own, abandoned pastry, and turned full-time to general cuisine that the French came to the sudden realization that they had a monstrous talent out there in a musty little corner of Asnières. More than Paul Bocuse, more than even the Troisgros brothers, it was Michel who became identified as the pope of the cuisine called *"nouvelle."*

Michel the magician invented the way Mozart composed, the way a bird sings, seemingly without effort. Endlessly spinning new ideas from what he happened to find in his local markets, he never felt the need to reach for the exotic spices, chemical stunts, or foreign ingredients that a clutch of lesser chefs were to brandish a generation later. Any follower of his career in Asnières and then later in Eugénie-les-

Bains (500 miles to the south, where he continues a no less dazzling career today) could cite dozens of remarkable creations that Michel pulled out of his *toque* in Asnières, but the cleverest one of all has to be the *ailerons de volaille aux concombres* that for years held pride of place on his menu.

It was elegant, it was original, and it was cheap—exactly the kind of *haute cuisine* that any entrepreneurial chef dreams of. From his days at the Lido, Michel knew that the easy-eating legs and filets removed from the chickens and served up to tourists who came for the music hall's lush spectacle, the winsome bare breasts and the *oh, là là*, but only incidentally for the food, left hundreds of orphaned wings to be thrown into the garbage every day. Moving into high finance, he negotiated a deal to officially purchase the wings for one symbolic franc (twenty cents), laid out a bit more for a few cucumbers, shallots, mushrooms, and tomatoes and, with that, had the makings for a little masterpiece. He blanched the wings, removed the central bone and pushed the meat forward to make a kind of chicken lollipop that he sautéed to a lovely golden color. He did the same for the cucumbers, which were turned into little olive shapes and blanched before taking their place in the pan of hot butter. Make a quick little sauce of diced mushrooms, shallots, tomatoes, and herbs mingled with white wine* and a bit of cream, and you have a dish to tickle a millionaire's fancy at a cost to you of peanuts. No business school can teach masterstrokes like that.

Claude Verger was no fool. He spotted Guérard immediately as a culinary grand master, but saw something else: He was also a capitalistic wunderkind. Completely apart from the great food, the relaxed, low-key atmosphere that he created in the Pot au Feu at minimal cost rapidly became an obligatory part of the city's *chic*, the place where the Parisians, eternal slaves to fashion as they are, had to go see and be seen—*le must*. Verger saw a gold mine and was determined to go out and dig into the lode for himself.

---

*Because his little restaurant was soon equal in prestige to the Tour d'Argent or any other sanctified temple of Parisian gastronomy, Michel used a Meursault, a pirouette that gave the swells the impression that the Lido's hand-me-down chicken wings were worth the outrageous price they were paying for them. A less aristocratic wine would doubtless have worked just as well.

The times were propitious for it. With *les trente glorieuses* well under way, the French economy was booming, and a new class of prosperous young professionals had money to spend on *la belle vie*, but for the most part felt uncomfortable in the grandiose three-star places. (Guérard at the time had two Michelin stars, even if his cooking was easily worth three. But the guide's *Nomenklatura* hesitated to give the ultimate accolade to Asnières. How could you rate a restaurant at three stars when clients had to wander outside to go to the bathroom?) Paris was wearing miniskirts and long hair now, and the kids were dancing to an exciting new *zeitgeist*. Rock and discos had left the fox-trot and the *paso doble* irretrievably in the dust, and if you could serve innovative cuisine—all the better if someone qualified it as *nouvelle*—customers would appear out of nowhere to gobble it up, even in crummy surroundings. *Especially* in crummy surroundings: Slumming it was fun, *mon cher*. The Parisian *beau monde* was learning to revel in refined simplicity—smart new bistros, the chewy sourdough loaf of Lionel Poilâne, the pungent raspberry-and-banana nose of Georges Duboeuf's Beaujolais Nouveau.

And the Barrière de Clichy of Claude Verger. Claude followed Michel Guérard's lead to the letter, avoiding the stratospheric prices of Paris *intra-muros* and snooping around the seedy suburbs until he found a bistro in Clichy so cheap that even if it didn't work, he would not be too seriously out of pocket. He signed for it in October of 1972, named it Le Bistrot de Lyon, and called Roanne for help. Jean-Baptiste told him that an ex-apprentice named Bernard Chirent was doing some extras at Castel's, the most fashionable disco in town, located on the pleasantly named rue des Canettes (Duckling Street). Chirent was happy to take the job, but he warned that he was just marking time before he left for London to go to work for the Roux brothers. Find me someone to take your place, then, Verger asked. And that was how Massillon's ex-king of gab, the best *pétanque* player ever to work in the Troisgros kitchen, landed in Clichy on a typically lousy November day, talking with this improbable character named Claude Verger.

No sense in beating around the bush. "I want three stars," Bernard announced.

"You start January first," Verger shot back.

That was the gist of it, anyway. In truth, both of them were improbable characters, and this intersecting of orbits was so right that it was as if it had been preordained, because each one's strength played to the other's. Behind both their hyperbolic natures there also lay a good measure of purely rational calculation. Verger was willing to hire Bernard without having seen him work because he knew Troisgros University and the quality of its instruction. Even its lowliest apprentice would be better (and cheaper—that was part of the equation, too) than some weary old journeyman from a placement bureau. Bernard, for his part, had heard plenty about Verger from Chirent, notably his friendship with Michel Guérard. And of course he was very well aware of Guérard's meteoric rise in the culinary world. Announcing a three-star ambition may have been something of a youthful fanfaronade, but it was not entirely out of place within the context.

Most restaurant owners would have laughed in his presumptuous face, but Verger neither mocked nor criticized Bernard for this outlandish naïveté. He was intelligent enough to know that some personalities flower through rigor and discipline, others by suggestion and encouragement. Instinct told him that this kid, with his ingenuous enthusiasm and illusions of glory around the corner, was definitely the second kind. Not having undergone the caste system of traditional kitchen *brigades* himself, Verger had no prejudices or preconceived notions about seniority on the professional ladder. All he cared about was the result. If the kid could work hard and cook the way he wanted him to, he could imagine himself as Escoffier reincarnated, for all he cared.

"His ambition was there right from the start," Verger told me, "and I never put him down. He was the kind of guy who would be destroyed if you discouraged him."

Verger's intuition proved to be tragically prescient, but it was also perfectly apt. From the very start there seemed to be a chord vibrating between these two men that made the fit exactly appropriate for each one's purpose. Destiny is a big, heavy word, but there was something like it there. By whatever chemistry that courses between human beings, Bernard decided almost instantly to hitch his wagon to Verger's star, and Verger's habitual filter of world-weary cynicism softened up enough to perceive more in this big puppy dog from Clermont than just another rawboned *auvergnat* hick. Over the next decade he would evolve from Bernard's boss to his adviser and guru until finally—as awful as the platitude sounds—he was very much like Bernard's spiritual father. An often tyrannical father, to be sure (those flinty opinions of his didn't go away), but a father figure nonetheless.

Bernard's class at Troisgros University was a rich vein that Verger mined assiduously as he built the success that was to see him multiply his restaurants into a minichain, building on the success of one to create another until, at the high point, he had seven bistros scattered around Paris. The gold mine that he dug proved to be even richer than Guérard's, and to keep it turning over at a good clip he hired not only the two Bernards, Loiseau and Chirent, but, later, Claude Perraudin and Guy Savoy, too, as the empire expanded. He also made a firm offer to Jean Ramet, but Jean was not a gambler. After passing a few months learning magic at Michel Guérard's place, he opted for the prestige of René Lasserre's three-star kitchen on avenue Montaigne. Of all the Troisgros crowd, though, it was Bernard who felt the deepest affinity with Verger, adopted his style most closely, stayed with him the longest, and learned the most.

It was quite a ride. The first thing Bernard noticed when he reported for work two weeks before his twenty-second birthday was that his new boss had changed the name of his place. What he had seen as the Bistrot de Lyon was now La Barrière de Clichy. This was further evidence of the salutary influence of Michel Guérard—or rather, of his girlfriend and future wife, Christine, a cool, brainy woman of strong opinions strongly expressed. "Bistrot de Lyon is a ridiculous name," she snorted. "Call it La Barrière."

She was right—her suggestion was a much better, more original, and appropriate name, harking back to the medieval days before France was entirely unified into a single modern capitalist state and trade became free, when customs barriers stood at the gates to all large cities—one of them hard by the address of Verger's new restaurant. So Barrière de Clichy it was. Bernard's job was to build on its remarkable start and keep it turning over smoothly. Claude had already made a successful launch, with a little help from his friends.

He had opened the restaurant a few days after signing for it that same October. With Guérard behind him for advice and recipe ideas and Bernard Chirent in the kitchen, he had felt reasonably optimistic. "I was the boss, the chef, the waiter, the sommelier, and the dishwasher," he told me ruefully as he recalled his first few precarious weeks. "For the first two months there were strictly no clients—empty, nothing. Do you know what it's like to go four days in a restaurant without a single client, when you've got fresh food on hand that will spoil if you don't use it up? My only clients in those days were Michel Guérard and our friend Jean Delaveyne,* who had the Camélia in Bougival. I had always gone to their places to eat, so now they came to mine to cheer me up and help me with all that surplus food. That was nice of them, but what I needed was paying customers.

"Then one day in December, I saw two pilgrims come through the door asking if they could have lunch—it was Robert Courtine of *Le Monde* and Jean Didier of *Le Guide Kléber*. No sooner had they started eating than an inspector from the *Michelin* showed up! What a day."

The two pilgrims had been sent by Michel Guérard. Obviously, Michelin had been snooping around his place, too, even if the inspector's arrival at the same time as the competition was purely fortuitous. In any case, if ever Verger had doubted the importance of the press, his doubts vanished after Courtine published an article describing the rabbit with sautéed turnips that he had enjoyed at La Barrière de Clichy. The pump was primed: Next day at lunch every table was filled, and the restaurant prospered continuously thereafter.

When Bernard arrived in Clichy, the first instruction he received from Verger covered, naturally enough, the kind of cooking he wanted: top-quality ingredients treated quickly, lightly, and at the last minute. In sum, the cooking program he outlined for Bernard on his first day was a simplified, stripped-down version of the Asnières style—*Michel Guérard for Dummies*, as it were.

But Verger's Second Commandment, constantly reiterated over the months that followed, was one of basic PR: always, *always*, court the

---

*If Michel Guérard is generally accepted as the pope of the cooking called *nouvelle*, Jean Delaveyne would be in the position of the prophet Abraham, because he was the only chef who might be referred to as Guérard's master. Camélia, the restaurant of this brilliant and totally original creator, lay 20 kilometers to the west of Paris.

press. Gastronomic critics were the best clients to get into the restaurant, of course, but any journalist at all was important, because journalists always know other journalists, and word gets around. Journalists are hungry but their pay is lousy, so be nice to them. Bernard never forgot the lesson.

Journalists followed journalists to La Barrière, then, and the crowds followed them, sure as night follows day. Suddenly the place was booming like the Pot au Feu, and the complicity between Verger and Guérard made for the most potent one-two punch on the Parisian gastronomic scene. When Guérard needed an extra hand, Verger sent him Chirent to work out the last few weeks before he left for London; Guérard paid back the debt in person, often coming by Clichy on his day off, or after closing his place for the evening, to assist Bernard in the kitchen during the long late-night hours. As long as the customers kept coming Verger liked to keep serving, and La Barrière catered so thoroughly to the after-theater crowd that it seemed to be almost perpetually open. Cuisine specialists would have viewed the spectacle of Guérard assisting Bernard as approximately equivalent to Vladimir Horowitz coming by to turn the pages for a Juilliard student's recital, but that was the time, that was the friendship between the two men, and that was the atmosphere. It was groundbreaking, it was fun, it was exciting, everyone was making buckets of money, and Bernard was in the thick of it.

He shared a cheap, remarkably unkempt room in Clichy with Chirent, but neither used it for much more than to collapse on his bed late at night, because they were both going flat-out. "We slept, showered, and then went off to the restaurants," Chirent said. "We practically lived in them, because we were working like donkeys— fourteen, fifteen hours a day. Bosses would never be allowed to work employees like that today. Even on our days off we worked, because there was always something that needed to be done. We held up by drinking espressos."

No sweat. Bernard loved every minute of it. He would have been happy to put in twenty-hour days if he had to, because his world had gone topsy-turvy overnight. The laughingstock who had dumped the coal into his frying pan, the incompetent who got knocked headfirst into a tub of potatoes, the guy whose letters didn't even get answered, was suddenly *chef de cuisine* in one of the most fashionable restaurants in Paris at age twenty-two. Everything was go, go, go—they were already writing about him in the press! Well, about his work, anyway.

"Barrière de Clichy (Bistrot de Lyon)," wrote the *GaultMillau* magazine in March, still not entirely comfortable with the restaurant's change of name, "made known by Michel Guérard, Claude Verger's friend, who sends the overflow of the Pot au Feu to Clichy. Cuisine very much derived from Guérard. Sublime salads. *Délice de foie gras*, artichoke hearts, green beans, vinegary *frisée* lettuce—and (audacious!) a variant with lobster and olive oil. Rabbit with finely sliced turnips. Veal sweetbreads with truffle sauce. Pears poached in Brouilly."

"Verger had a real flair for discovering talent," Pierre Troisgros said, reminiscing about the old days over a lunch of roast lamb at his house in Roanne. "He gave cooks responsibility very young, and with Loiseau and Savoy he hit the bull's-eye. Jean and I were of the generation of cooks who had to work their way up, and you could never get to the position of chef before you had a certain maturity. *Chef de cuisine* at twenty-one or twenty-two struck us as an aberration. But Verger knew exactly the style of restaurant he wanted and the kind of modern cuisine he intended to serve in it. And he came on the scene at a time when gastronomic journalism was evolving, and Gault and Millau were looking for young chefs to make into stars. Just a few years earlier a success like that would have been unthinkable. Bernard and the Barrière would have remained completely anonymous."

Napoleon, it is said, had a single overriding criterion for choosing the men whom he would name as his generals: They had to be lucky. So it was that Bernard began to savor the sweet taste of fame when he was barely past age twenty-one. He was lucky and he always had been. It was something that followed him almost unfailingly through life. Whenever he was faced with disaster, he somehow managed to squirm away at the last minute; if he did fall into trouble and woe, he always bounced back with that big, ingenuous grin that so aggravated Chef Jean. It was Bernard Chirent who opened the Barrière with Verger, and who did the cooking on the famous December day when Robert Courtine, Jean Didier, and a Michelin inspector arrived at almost the same minute—but since he was going off to London, it was Bernard who inherited a restaurant that was going well and heading higher.*

He was lucky and he was a fast learner. Troisgros is good, very good, Verger told him, but what you're going to do here is Troisgros cuisine in my style. "I gave him specific illustrations," he explained. "Spinach, for example. In those days the Troisgros cooked a kilo of spinach in five liters of water. I taught Bernard to just wash it and then sauté it in butter with the water that remained on it from the washing. Same thing with mushrooms—everything done at the last minute in butter or olive oil, and cooked as little as possible. I never stewed veal sweetbreads or kidneys—I sautéed them quick, over high heat, just for a few minutes.† I cooked my fish mostly à l'unilatéral—on one side only, and served them rose à l'arête, still a little pink at the bone."

The matter of fish rose à l'arête is something of a minisaga of modern French cuisine. Good fish is expensive, and it is rapidly ruined when overcooked, of course, but it is equally inedible when it is not cooked enough. Verger was a leading prophet of the new school of walking the razor edge of almost-not-enough, searing the little critter on one side, tossing in a lump of fresh butter, and covering the pan for the hot steam from the butter to rise and cook the top, just barely enough.

"It was an idea that Henri Gault had at the same time as me," he told me. "I always tended to undercook things. When people saw me making fish rose à l'arête, they said quel con, you don't know what you're doing, but then when they read in the magazine that Gault and Millau liked it that way, everyone started doing it. Of course that's the way I taught Bernard to do it.

"There were just three of us in the kitchen—me, a helper, and

---

*In 1976, a year after Bernard had left Paris, Michelin finally awarded a star to the Barrière de Clichy. By then Guy Savoy, a future three-star god of the trade, was at the piano that Bernard had left behind. The restaurant never climbed higher in the Michelin ratings, but that was fine with Verger. He had never meant it to be anything more than friendly bistro with fine food. Haute cuisine was an entirely different gig.

†Without realizing it, Verger was at least partially anticipating here the Asiatic cooking techniques that many chefs would be adopting a generation after him. Much of his cuisine was like a cousin of the Chinese stir-fry in a hot wok.

Bernard. At first he was a little bit mystified by the different approach I expected of him, but after three or four days he got the picture. He was a lively guy. He caught on quick."

Verger was opinionated and often impossible, but he was no dilettante. He knew his stuff, and at the start of his new boy's incumbency in the kitchen he was at the *piano* almost as much as Bernard, watching and directing. Gradually, as Bernard assimilated his lessons and grew in confidence, he backed off, spent more time in the *salle* among the guests, and assumed the classical role of director rather than executor of the cooking—exactly as Bernard would do in later years at Saulieu. By the middle of 1973 the roles were well established: Verger was Chef, Bernard, chef.

Guy Savoy, who came to the Barrière as chef in 1976, and who had the pleasure of mentally pinning the Michelin star on his blouse when it arrived, was by then an experienced cook, but even with all his professional baggage he was impressed with his new boss's skills. "He spent a lot of time in Rungis [the Paris wholesale market] and brought back only first-rate produce. He was quite knowledgeable about cooking, and he had certain basic principles—*'pas de cuisine de pédé,'* he repeated all the time. *'Pas de cuisine de puceau'*—no cooking for fairies or virgins—cooking that had balls, he said. Best produce, nothing set up beforehand, everything at the last minute, quick cooking, very exact seasoning. No stocks, no classical sauces, just deglazings and little short *jus*—juices. Food had to be chewy, and above all have taste—real, firm, strong taste. He was a good cook, less of a technician than we were, but his instincts about cuisine in general were excellent. And once he saw that we understood his style, he gave us almost total liberty to make what we wanted."

By then Claude had perfected a winning formula for his minichain of Barrières: eager young cooks hired after formation by respected masters; careful preliminary instruction in the style of cooking he demanded, followed by independence of execution, once they got it right; only top-quality ingredients—all the money for food, nothing for the décor. Verger himself chose the produce for his burgeoning little empire. Three times a week he rose at 2 A.M. to hustle out to Rungis an hour later to snap up the best fish in from Brittany and the finest and freshest fruits and vegetables. He was a careful buyer and a sharp bargainer. He knew what he was about, and he commanded respect among the wholesalers.

The theoretical underpinnings of the cuisine that Bernard would be developing in Saulieu were already established at Poquelin: a straight line from his mother's home cooking—those simple deglazings for sauces—to Troisgros to Verger, with homeopathic doses of Guérard thrown in. Not too much of this last, though—attempting to copy Guérard has always been a perilous enterprise. Bernard knew it, too.

"Bernard was a good cook," Guérard told me, "and he was clever enough not to try to make dishes that were over his head. He mastered certain things and he did them well. They were quite a couple, he and Claude. The restaurant made a hit because Claude was an exceptional composer and Bernard executed his recipes well. Verger did his lobsters *à la minute*, and served them out of the shell on a puree of watercress. It was very good that way, too. With his rabbit, he sautéed his turnips raw. That was something you would never have seen in classic cuisine, where the routine was always to cook the turnips first in boiling water."

Among all the new dishes and combinations that Verger threw out to his Parisian fans, it is his rabbit—the *lapin sauté aux navets crus*— that became identified as his signature dish, the one that sticks in everyone's memory thirty-plus years later. As luck had it, it was this same creation that broke Bernard's anonymity and brought him his first bit of personal fame. It came via the pen of Michel Piot, then gastronomic critic of the daily *Le Figaro*.

"The first time I went to the Barrière it was Jean Didier who brought me," Piot recalled. "Everyone was talking about this guy Verger who had come up from the provinces and opened a bistro where the food was as good as a starred place. We went without declaring ourselves, and ate incognito. It was very good—rabbit with turnips. After we had finished we told the waitress who we were and asked if we could see Monsieur Verger. She kind of blushed. He was away, she said. It was his cuisine, but he wasn't the one who had made it. Oh, really? Well, we'd like to see the person who did it, because we really liked it a lot. The waitress said, I'll go see.

"Five minutes later this boy arrived from the kitchen, covered with sweat and trembling like a leaf. So that was how I met Bernard Loiseau.

It was obvious to us that this was an immense cook, and I wrote him up that way in the paper, saying we had eaten admirably well in a bistro style that was profoundly in the French tradition, but with food that was classical and modern at the same time. 'We did not have the chance to meet Claude Verger,' I wrote, 'but we had the great good luck to meet the one who does his cooking for him—Bernard Loiseau. Remember this name. You'll be hearing it again.'"

Although Piot said nothing about his dessert in the article, the chances are good that he and Didier enjoyed another Barrière specialty that was headed straight for the same kind of international celebrity as the now-ubiquitous *tiramisù* and *crème brûlée*: the *tarte fine aux pommes*. Like so much else, this brilliant little inspiration had originated in the well-made noggin of Michel Guérard. Abandoning the *pâte brisée* and almond cream of the classical French apple tart, Michel set thinly sliced apple sections onto a disk of puff pastry, brushed them with butter and sugar, and slid the finished product into a gentle oven for an hour, just long enough for it to cook to a beautiful uniform gold. Verger adopted the *tarte fine* outright with Guérard's blessing, and it conquered the world. Bernard didn't forget that, either.

Now that the press had another identity to chew on in addition to Claude Verger's already arresting personality, Bernard's name began appearing in articles next to his mentor's, and sometimes even separately, on his own merits. His love story with notoriety was off to a good start. But just then, toward the end of 1973, Bernard made a disastrously ill-advised decision: He impulsively bolted from Clichy to take a job as cook in the Hôtel de la Poste, a very classical restaurant with two Michelin stars in Avallon, a sleepy old fortified town 150 miles south of Paris, at the gateway to Burgundy. Exactly why he did it is a matter of some disagreement. Bill Echikson, whose book *Burgundy Stars* recounts a year spent in the presence of Loiseau in the early nineties, psychoanalyzed this departure as a fit of adolescent rebellion against an overbearing father figure. Dominique, Bernard's future wife, wrote in *Bernard Loiseau, Mon Mari*—Bernard Loiseau, My Husband—a memoir that she published in France seven months after his death, that the young cook felt he wasn't progressing at Clichy anymore.

"He wanted to redefine the menu according to his own ideas," Do-

minique wrote, "but Verger refused. The proprietor was wary of his protégé's immoderate taste for the most expensive produce. He wanted to
continue controlling the buying himself, and the best way to do it was
to keep the upper hand on the menu."

Balls, Verger replied, in essence. He, Claude Verger, was the boss,
the one who paid the bills and the salaries; he was the one who did the
buying and he always bought only the best and most expensive ingredients, in any case—he didn't need Bernard to tell him to do it. And
there could never have been even the hint of a debate about handing
over his prerogatives to his employee. "Bernard left because he saw
those stars," he said with a shrug. "There were two in Avallon and none
in Clichy. It was as simple as that."

Given the avowed, lifelong, and undeviating goal that Bernard was
chasing, coupled with his excessive hurry-up nature, it is Verger's explanation that rings truest. But all parties agree on one thing: Bernard's
bailout was a vast *connerie*. "They had him gutting chickens by the ass-
hole," Verger snorted.

That was a typical Verger kind of imagery, but it was also accurate.
The job Bernard had landed in Avallon was to run the *garde-manger*,
and preparing poultry would be one of his main responsibilities. He
didn't like it. What he had been expecting was the big-league stuff. He
wanted to be at the *piano*, like Chef Jean. The hotel's boss looked at his
meager CV, looked again at his twenty-two-year-old face, and decided
that the boy was trying to *peter plus haut que son cul*, as the sanctified
French expression has it—to fart higher than his ass. He fired him
three weeks later.

Oh, dear. Now it was back to Clermont and back in with his parents again. Bernard swallowed his pride and lowered his sights. There
was always the Frantel. He heard they were looking for a cook. Frantel
was a modern operation, one of those cookie-cutter chain hotels that
by the seventies was rapidly supplanting the mom-and-pop Hôtels
Moderne throughout France. Although totally lacking in charm,
beauty, and character—they were typical products of modern engi-
neering and the business school mentality that could just as well be set
up in Indianapolis, Lagos, or Stuttgart—they were at least efficient and
not too expensive.

Bernard got the job and lasted exactly a week before getting fired from there, too. His Troisgros–Verger cooking style and his extravagant personality were exactly right for scandalizing the B-school–trained, rule-following administrator in charge of what passed for gastronomy at Frantel.

"He found himself up to his neck in what they call *le ratio*," Verger said. "Everything was calculated, every slice of meat had to be exactly 150 grams—and in Clichy he had gotten in the habit of cutting generously."

It was one more flop for him to digest, but it also offered another lesson: everything in its time. Bernard had to learn at least a few preliminary atoms of patience. He gulped, picked up the phone, and called Verger.

It was a good thing he did, because, *justement*, Claude was about to open his second Barrière, on the little rue Molière, smack in the middle of Paris next to the Palais Royal and a brisk five-minute walk from the Opéra. Barrière Poquelin, this one would be called. Here, too, the name was a bright idea bearing the shadow of Christine's influence. It would have been perfectly logical to call the place Barrière Molière, but that was obvious and boring. Jogging clients to think twice by reminding them that the playwright was born Jean-Baptiste Poquelin (Molière was his professional pseudonym) was like a little wink that lent it a smart, theatrical cachet.

The name clicked, and everything else with it. Poquelin was so close to the center of everything that journalists, jet setters, actors, actresses, and the world's most skillful collection of ancillary showbiz freeloaders were no longer obliged to get their feet muddy by trekking all the way out to Clichy. Verger held what amounted to a permanent open house in his new Barrière, and nothing pleased him more than to lead his clients down the steep stairs into the little kitchen in the cellar to watch his eager young star in action. When, late at night, the last kidney had been sautéed and the last crayfish shucked, Verger exactly replicated the *modus operandi* of Jean-Baptiste Troisgros in Roanne with his two sons, and brought Bernard up into the dining room to mingle with the beautiful people. Instantly and unanimously, Bernard charmed them. When that signature smile of his, a huge, face-splitting jack-o'-lantern grin, combined with the effusive chatter that came as easily to him as meow to a cat, Bernard exuded a warmth and humanity that effortlessly melted the stoniest Cartesian reserve.

Poquelin was a theater, and every night was a different play within a play. Host and impresario, Verger chivvied and wisecracked, insolently flattered the showbiz types, and yelled at the journalists for not giving his boy Bernard more and better press, while everyone was giving everyone else two* Gallic kisses on the cheeks, one for each side, saying darling and *cher ami*, and sometimes even paying the bill. That was fine with Verger—among the role players there were plenty of normally paying customers to keep the place going nicely, and he and Bernard were fast becoming an integral part of *le tout Paris*.

Early in 1974, Gault and Millau reflected the generalized infatuation with the latest Barrière by awarding it the very respectable grade of 15 in its merit scale of 1 to 20. "A remarkable chef, Bernard Loiseau, who flew the coop[†] from Troisgros, [offers] a menu full of invention, a cuisine that is simply admirable, including marvelous salads and sublime braised sweetbreads with spinach." (It was in February of the same year that I first met Bernard, down in his kitchen in Verger's catacombs, as he hyperactively cooked for a full dining room while grinning the huge, irresistible grin that was his eternal trademark. The lunch menu he fired up for me was fast, intelligent, and as close to perfection as I could have imagined any solo cook managing when he had thirty or forty other clients to take care of at the same time: *frisée* salad with truffles; chicken sautéed with crayfish; *tarte fine aux pommes*.)

According to Dominique Loiseau, Verger's insistent promotion of Bernard as a personality among the personalities who haunted Poquelin enabled her future husband to gain ten years of professional life by establishing his credentials once and for all as not just a legitimate

---

*Never four—that's for schoolchildren or plebeians. The delivery of four cheek kisses is a sure sign of working-class culture. In a similar vein, the swells who still practice the *baise-main* (kissing ladies' hands) would never dream of actually making lip contact with the proferred extremity—how vulgar. One bows slightly (optionally clicking one's heels) and *makes the motions* of kissing the hand, as in a charade.

[†]No writers, in any language, have ever been able to refrain from making the most outrageously corny puns on his name. Literally, Bernard Loiseau means "Bernard the Bird."

chef de cuisine in spite of his young age, but by making him a famous one, too. At age twenty-three he was kissing starlets' cheeks, backslapping big-name TV producers and presenters, and saying *"tu"* to every journalist who came along. Bernard took to the celebrity game as if he had been born to it. Boisterous, vociferous, and optimistic, he let fly with the same skills that had made him Massillon's king of gab. And the Parisians *liked* it. They always look for someone to erect into stardom, someone to talk about in the endless talking that characterizes the Parisian scene, and for talking about cuisine, Bernard was perfect: He was young, handsome, overpoweringly energetic, and unfailingly friendly. For his part, he was discovering something about himself, an unshakeable character trait every successful chef seems to be born with: He loved to receive people and he loved to please them. For the moment his cooking was mostly Verger's, but his personality was his own, and it was so strong and so persuasive that suddenly he was leapfrogging all the other kids of the Troisgros kitchen.

Chef Jean's *bête noire* was going places. Little could Bernard suspect, as he rattled his pots and pans or later, after the *service*, as he swam in the cigarette smoke, the noise, the japes, and the jabberings of his Parisian clientele, that his next stop was to be a silent, godforsaken little town in the middle of the windswept Morvan plateau. And even less, of course, that it was to be for the rest of his life.

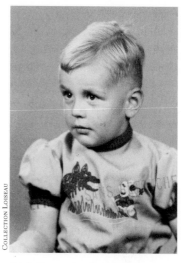

Little Bernard as he moves from
babyhood to little-boyhood

Little Bernard, bundled up for
winter in Clermont

Edith Loiseau on the street near the family
charcuterie in Clermont-Ferrand. Rémy in
baby carriage, Bernard walking. The little
girl is a cousin.

The old Hôtel-Restaurant Les Frères Troisgros, shortly after it got renamed from Hôtel Moderne. It was this very modest establishment that set the world of gastronomy afire by serving a cuisine equal to or better than the great palaces of Paris.

Jean, *left*, and Pierre Troisgros (seated) with their apprentices in Roanne. *From left to right*: Bernard, two unknowns, the patissier Andre Delorme, Daniel Metery, Jean Ramet, and Claude Perraudin

The backside of the Côte d'Or that guests rarely saw but which Bernard had to live with, hated, and was determined to change. The flat surface is the old garage, and the sloping roof behind with the two smokestacks is Dumaine's rotten old kitchen. The "L" angle where the two wings join is where the monumental staircase now stands.

Bernard and Chantal stand by the entry to the Dumaine dining room, on right. Picture dates from about 1982.

~ Bernard Loi

Vous Propose :

La Salade 'Côte d'or, Foie frais, haricots Verts salade	42
La Salade de Queues d'Écrevisses	36
La Salade de Homard frais aux petites asperges	70
La Salade de truffes fraîches	
La Salade de Haricots Verts à la Crème	16
Le Foie Gras frais de Canard des Landes, préparé à la maison	44
La terrine de Homard aux petits légumes de Printemps	45
La Bisque de Homard Frais	23
La Soupe de moules au Safran	15
Le Jambon de Parme	25
Des Œufs Brouillés aux Truffes	33
Des Escargots de Bourgogne en Cassolette	29
Des Asperges Sauce aux herbes	42
La Cassolette de Queues d'Écrevisses à la nage	50
Des Filets de Sole sur lit d'Épinards	39
Le Navarin de St Jacques aux Poivrons rouges doux	39
L' Escalope de Saumon frais Sauce à l'oseille	47
Des Écrevisses pattes rouges sautées à l'Estragon	43
Des Coquilles St Jacques sur mousse de Cresson	39
Des Huitres chaudes (dans leur Coquille)	39
Le Pigeonneau Fermier rôti dans son jus	46
La Poularde de Bresse à la Crème d'Estragon	36
Des Aiguillettes de Canard aux Pêches jaunes	41

Soupe d'Huitres et
St Jacques 55

Ris de Veau aux
Pointes d'Asperges 58F

Menu from 1977

Taxes Comprises
. Service 15% au sus .

Le Ris de Veau Périgourdine — 47
Les Rognons de Veau, Sautés au Xérès — 39
Le Ris et Rognon de Veau, aux Ecrevisses — 52
Le Filet de Boeuf, Sauce Bourguignonne au Poivre vert — 47
La Noisette d'Agneau aux Petits Légumes — 39

Le Plateau des Fromages, Selectionnés par "Androuet" — 14F

— Les Desserts —

Le Chaud des Desserts — 20
Les Pruneaux au Thé — 12
Les Oeufs à la neige — 12
Le "Sphinx" Gâteau fondu d'amandes et Chocolat — 15
La Glace Vanille, ou les Sorbets "Maison" — 15
Le Pamplemousse Confit — 12
La Salade d'oranges et pamplemousse aux Zestes confits — 12
La tarte Chaude, et tiède aux Pommes — 12
(à céder au début du repas)

Ragoût du Pêcheur 75F

Filet de St Pierre aux Concombres 45F

Bernard in Saulieu, circa 1980–82,
posing before a dish of partridge
with figs

Bernard on a wine-tasting trip in Burgundy. Behind him is Henri Jaillet, one of the most knowledgeable winemakers in all of Burgundy

Bernard at work in the kitchen of the Côte d'Or. Bernard and Hubert at left, and Patrick Bertron second from right

Bernard in the Côte d'Or wine cellar, with Pierre Troisgros on the left and Claude Verger on the right

Bernard out hunting for mushrooms

MARIANNE ROSENSTIEHL

COLLECTION LOISEAU

Bernard out hunting with his buddies. This is the sacred moment of the *casse croute* (breaking of the bread) when they tuck into the white wine and snacks that Bernard has brought for them.

Bernard's parents, Pierre and Edith, standing in the garden behind their little country house in Messeix, an hour's drive from Clermont-Ferrand. It was from here that Bernard and brother Rémy went out hunting for frogs, mushrooms, and *ecrevisses*.

Bernard holding little Bastien by the hotel's front entrance

R. CHELMINSKI

COLLECTION LOISEAU

VI

LET'S DO IT:

A Rocky Start in Saulieu,
1975–1976

*E*arly in February 1975, driving back to Paris after visiting his sister in Bourgouin, Claude Verger decided to stop for lunch at the Côte d'Or in Saulieu. After passing by Beaune and Dijon, he quit the autoroute at Bierre-les-Semur and, following twisty little country roads through the villages of Précy-sous-Thil and Montlay-en-Auxois, arrived at the northern edge of town. It hadn't changed a bit since the last time he had been there. Saulieu never seemed to change anymore, now that the superhighway had drained the traffic that used to flow down the Route Nationale 6. February was a lousy time to come visiting, too. It was cold, dismal, and rainy, and the fourteen or fifteen hotels that had fed off the R.N. 6 in the glory days—an absurdly large number for a town of less than three thousand souls—loomed empty and somber, several of them shuttered tight, awaiting a hypothetical return of clientele with the spring sun. The life-sized bronze statue of a bull, honoring the cattle-raising tradition of the Morvan Plateau (the soil was good for little else), stood as stolidly as ever at a grassy square near the town hall, but none of the rare passersby, hunched down against the weather, would have granted it even so much as a glance. The statue, the work of a moderately esteemed *sculpteur animalier* born in Saulieu with the slightly ridiculous name of François Pompon (1855–1933), was about all that the town could claim by way of distinction. That and the hotel-restaurant La Côte d'Or.

More than a decade had passed since Alexandre Dumaine had

taken his retirement—coincidentally, both he and Jean-Baptiste Troisgros had died just the year before—and the time since had not been altogether kind to the grand old barn. Dumaine's successor, an equally
traditional if somewhat less illustrious cook named François Minot,
had maintained a culinary offering—thick slices of Morvan ham in
cream sauce, inevitably served on a bed of spinach, steaks from the
white Charolais cattle that grazed on every local hillside, lamb chops
with green peppercorns, and his own version of Dumaine's classic *pâté
en croûte*—of high enough standard for Michelin to award him two
stars. That was the plus side. On the minus side, the autoroute bypass
had so dramatically diminished clientele that Minot had been able to
do little more than simply keep his head above water, putting off repairs and redecoration of the hotel and hanging on to Dumaine's old
kitchen as it was. His single investment of consequence had been to replace Dumaine's antique coal stove with a more modern one that
burned heating fuel. (Dumaine's stove had shared a hot-water reserve
with the hotel's clients; when too many of them took baths at the same
time, the stove began to lose heat.) Even the new installation was showing signs of fatigue, though, and day by passing day, slowly and almost
imperceptibly, the whole establishment was taking on that indefinable
but clearly recognizable air of genteel shabbiness that marks places
and people that had known better days and were reduced to the edge of
penury. Minot was ready to throw in the towel.

"You know a lot of people in the business," he said to Verger in the
dining room. "Can you find me a buyer?"

"No problem," Verger shot back automatically, almost without reflection. It was true: He did know a lot of people, his business was going very well, and he was brimming with confidence. He was sure he
would run into someone who was interested. After all, the Côte d'Or
was still a very big name. He drove off turning the idea over in his head.

A week or so later he was back in Saulieu. "Have you found me
your guy?" Minot asked. "Yeah," said Verger, "but I forgot to ask you
the price you wanted."

When Minot named the sum, Verger realized he had guessed right:
the price was surprisingly low, even cheap. It looked like Minot just
wanted to get the hell out of there. "OK, it's agreed then," he said.

"You've got power of attorney for the guy?"

"No," said Verger. "I'm taking it for myself." He drew out his check-book and wrote out a 10 percent deposit on the spot. Before the month was out he was back in Saulieu again, this time to sign the documents making the sale official and to hand over final payment. It was quite a moment for him. The former Robot-Coupe salesman, former part-time cook in an insignificant Bourgouin bistro, was now owner, master, and commander of one of the consecrated temples of French gastronomy. It was not unlike a tugboat captain taking over the *Queen Elizabeth*.

But Claude Verger was a tugboat captain with a mattress—several mattresses—full of money, a fast-expanding business in Paris, and the clear head of a successful entrepreneur who was exploiting a going thing. So if there was emotion at the signing ceremony, there was also some solid reasoning, built around a single overriding idea: *Put Bernard in here*. With his energy and enthusiasm—or his rashness, or whatever you could call the fire in him—he might just pull this thing off. It was worth a try.

Things were going very nicely for Bernard in Paris just then, thank you very much. The *GaultMillau* guide for 1975 had already qualified Barrière Poquelin as "one of the best little restaurants in Paris," citing specialties of chicken with crayfish, and green bean salad with foie gras, and identifying Bernard by name. His glory was abuilding, as was a lasting friendship with Henri Gault, a jovial, discerning gourmet who loved the light, fresh, last-minute style of cuisine that had filtered down to Bernard by way of Troisgros, Guérard, and Verger. Gault and Christian Millau were already gained to Bernard's cause and proved to be faithful and enthusiastic supporters of the Côte d'Or under his stewardship. But even if they, along with Michel Piot, Robert Courtine, and a few other Parisian restaurant critics, were the most important for professional fallout (that is, on this mortal side of the empyrean where Michelin reigned), Bernard continued to sedulously cultivate journalists of all ilk, exactly as Verger had told him to.

"I used to call Verger 'Chef Pipeau,'" said François Roboth, a photographer and food specialist for *Le Figaro* who later went on to edit a short-lived restaurant guide. "Then when I met Bernard and saw him doing his number, I named him 'Chef Super-Pipeau.'"

Roughly translated: "Chef Bullshit" and "Chef Super-Bullshit." Roboth spoke the term affectionately, but, in view of their relentless campaigns of PR and jollying up the press, there was more than a grain of truth in these titles for Verger and Loiseau. "Bernard was a very engaging guy, really an exceptional person," Roboth remembered. "He had a way of drawing you out—*prêcher le faux pour savoir le vrai*—saying one thing while actually meaning something else, to find out what you really thought. He had a kind of peasant shrewdness to him, and he deliberately played on ambiguity. 'I've got to go now and take care of the *pipeau*,' he used to say. He was a lot less naïve than he appeared."

So who was manipulating whom? The eternal question about Bernard's psyche was there from the start, and a lot of those clever, nimble-minded Parisians who patronizingly took him for just a charming, ingenuous kid were being assessed much more coolly than they ever realized by those big brown *auvergnat* eyes.

It was around this time, if Verger is to be believed, that Bernard's relations with the press moved to an altogether different plane and took a rather more direct form of contact: He lost his virginity. Claude Perraudin and the other Troisgros apprentices had already noted back in the Roanne days that their swaggering friend, the motormouth who could trade repartee at the drop of a wisecrack, was painfully shy with girls. Logically enough, they attributed it to his formative adolescent years at Massillon, living under the thumb of the priests.*

"Bernard was always very introverted where girls were concerned," Bernard Chirent remembered. "Come to think of it now, in Roanne we never got into ass talk [*parler cul*] with him the way we did with the other guys. Never. It was a mixture of several things in him, I think— Boy Scout mentality, religion, timidity."

Whatever the profound psychological foundations for Bernard's sexual Sahara, it lasted all the way to age twenty-four, according to Verger's version of events. It was then, according to this same account, that a female journalist from TF1—the biggest and most popular na-

---

*Comically enough, and for what it might be worth to fanatics of extreme psychological analysis of the impact of gender confusion, many priests in those days still wore the traditional *soutane*—the black, multibuttoned dresslike cassock. For them, bicycle manufacturers continued to sell the *modèle ecclésiastique*, basically a woman's bike but heftier, and diplomatically shorn of the high central bar that would raise skirts to shockingly immodest heights above the priests' knees.

tional television chain—radically resolved the matter, with not a little encouragement from Verger and Roboth, by seizing the lad by the ear and dragging him into her boudoir. Whether he went whimpering and protesting or whether he took his punishment like a man is not recorded.

It was not long after his boudoir traumatism that a sadder and wiser Bernard received an exciting piece of news to lift his morale. "I've found something for you," Verger announced. "You want three stars, but you'll never get them in Paris. The investment's just too big, and with the prices here, you'll never make it. But in Saulieu you'll have a chance."

Verger's offer was not pure charity. He knew that in spite of Bernard's extreme youth and inexperience, he had the drive and charisma of a potential star of the trade. Already a fellow entrepreneur—an author and food critic who moonlighted as an agent—had been circling around him at the Barrière Poquelin with a flattering argument: I can set you up. A guy with your talent could make money cooking in a rabbit hutch in Paris. "The only rabbit hutch I want is three stars," Bernard shot back memorably.

So Verger's offer of Saulieu looked tempting. Bernard hitched a ride with François Roboth and drove down with him for lunch at the Côte d'Or. Unsurprisingly, considering his own very Manichean tendencies and the years he had spent at Verger's side, he decided on the spot that Minot's Dumaine-derived cooking was *de la merde*. He must have shown his disdain—Bernard was never able to hide anything—because he and Minot cordially detested each other from the first moment they met. Unfortunately, the animus that developed that afternoon was to weigh heavily against Bernard after Minot signed for the sale, when he liberally spread the word around the profession that the Côte d'Or was headed for disaster under its new leadership.

"What do you think?" Bernard asked Roboth as they looked around after lunch.

"You're going to need plenty of courage and determination," he mused. Roboth was right. Dumaine's little dining room, fairly glowing with the patina imparted by decades of intimate contact with *foie gras*, truffles, aged cognac, and thousands of deliciously perfumed *décolletés*, was an elegant piece of history, but the kitchen was antediluvian,

the hallways drafty, and the hotel run down and neglected. The imposing Hôtel de la Poste, just across the street, looked much more impressive: bigger, better, cleaner. Roboth remembers his friend falling into
uncustomary quiet and contemplation on the drive back to Paris. The
prospect of moving down to the middle of nowhere to take over this
white elephant was enough to make even Bernard hesitate, but still
it was the Côte d'Or, a monument, in its own way, as prestigious
and history-charged as, in lesser fields of endeavor, Yankee Stadium,
La Scala, or Lords cricket grounds. Dumaine's place had been revered,
Bernard knew, in every corner of the globe when Troisgros was nothing
more than a little bistro across the way from the railroad station in
Roanne. Now it was being offered to him on a silver platter. It made his
head spin. Courage and determination? Hell, yes! When he got back to
Paris he told Verger, let's do it.

It wasn't a reasonable decision, of course, but reasonable decisions
are what create anonymous careers in international banking, hairdress-
ing, and arbitrage negotiating. Young Bernard was rapidly growing into
a make-or-break kind of guy.

"He had to have guts," commented Pierre Troisgros, half in admiration and half in wonder. "Not many would have dared to take that
place on. It was really a big chunk to chew on. I always thought
Bernard had a dose of *inconscience*—unthinking recklessness. If he
had reasoned it out and analyzed things, he wouldn't have accepted
the challenge, but he had this daredevil quality in him, and he made it,
too, didn't he? It's amazing to have succeeded the way he did, starting
from nothing."

On February 28, 1875, Minot took his departure with his wife, his
dog, and his suitcases. Bernard arrived with one bag to take over the
Côte d'Or for good, and the restaurant didn't miss a single meal with
the changeover. The breathless pace of the whole operation—from
first informal conversation to sale to installation of a new chef—was
typical of Verger's get-with-it, hubba-hubba style. Now it was up to
Bernard to see what he could do with it. From Minot's administration
he inherited a staff of seven in the kitchen, six in the *salle*, one laundress, an old receptionist, and a porter. The kitchen was organized in
the familiar Troisgros pattern: one *second*, a *pâtissier*, and five young
apprentices who would soon be moving on, as apprentices always do.

The dining room staff, though, was something else. They had been there for so long that they constituted something of a monument by themselves—the oldest *maître d'hôtel* totaled forty-eight years of service, reaching all the way back to the prehistoric days before Alexandre Dumaine.

Truculent old salts, they had all been formed in the grand manner of the *oreiller de la belle Aurore*, of headwaiters in tails and the ocean-liner style that Dumaine had brought to Saulieu and Minot had hardly altered. They were economical of smiles, but beneath their gruff exterior they proved that their hearts were in the right place when their new chef, only twenty-four years old, arrived from Paris: They hated him.

"*Cuisine moderne,*" they said to one another as they inspected Bernard's dishes, drawing out the *modeeeerne* in a long, contemptuous drawl. The old receptionist, Madame Rancin, took a positive pleasure in clucking, shaking her head, and telling clients that everyone was very, very worried. Someone—the culprit never owned up—started a rumor that the new Côte d'Or was intended as the first link of a fast-food style restaurant chain that Verger was contemplating.

At his lunch with Roboth, Bernard's dismissive reaction to Minot's cooking came back to haunt him almost immediately; the new *Michelin* guide not only removed both of the Côte d'Or's stars, but dropped it from the restaurant category altogether, listing it as a hotel only, and not a very distinguished one at that. For all any passing motorist could tell, Bernard's new command didn't serve any meals at all. To this day, Verger is convinced that Minot called every guide and gastronomic critic on his list and advised them to blacklist Saulieu. Particularly telling had been his haste in notifying Michelin that he was pulling out and leaving his place to a green youngster from Paris. His warning came just in time for the guide's editors to remove the two stars and the restaurant symbol before bringing out the 1975 edition at the traditional Easter time release date.

It was a painful blow. "Sometimes I would see big, expensive cars pull up in front of the place," Verger remembered, "then drive off after the people looked it up in the *Michelin*."

Verger had hoped to retain one of Minot's two stars, and at the very least a respectable restaurant symbol like the crossed red forks and spoons that denoted a classy, pleasant place for a meal. But no. Michelin clobbered him with a gastronomic haymaker. Why? Verger could only assume that, in addition to Minot's abuse, the *grande dame* of avenue de Breteuil disapproved of him and his trendy Barrières because they were the darlings of those vulgar interlopers from *GaultMillau* and the food critics of the Paris daily press. Everyone knew that it was standard Michelin practice to demote a restaurant a notch or two when its chef retired or left for another place, but this total wipeout smacked suspiciously of spite. (*Grandes dames* can get prissy and vengeful when they feel offended, especially by the competition.)

Now young Bernard found himself up against a double challenge: no listing in the guide and defiance from his staff. It was a distressing new experience. Working almost alone in the Barrières—he had never had more than a single assistant—he had not been faced with the need to command and motivate a staff, and even less, a staff of recalcitrant professionals who were without exception older and more experienced than he was himself. After the warmth and acclaim that had washed over him in Paris, he suddenly found himself the butt of provincial hostility in Saulieu. Disoriented, lonesome, and unsure of himself, he suffered cruelly.

"I used to work my ass off all day long," he told me several years afterward, as he recalled his debut in Dumaine's old barn, "then go up to my room and cry for most of the night, I was so miserable and frustrated."

The problem was that at age twenty-four he was still a boy, only on the verge of becoming a man. Like a dog pack, his theoretical subalterns sensed his insecurity, took advantage of it, mocked him behind his back, and spoke openly of their doubts. How could they fail to when they saw the way he wore his emotions on his sleeve, when his salary was less than that of the head *maître d'hôtel*, and his entire living quarters consisted of a single room upstairs that looked like a student's pad, with the toilet and shower down the hall? The boy did not exactly exude an aura of authority.

"He was like Rastignac [the ambitious *arriviste* of Balzac's *Comédie Humaine*]," said Gilles Pudlowski, editor and publisher of the Paris-based restaurant guide bearing his own name. "But he lived like a migrant worker in one miserable little room. He had his clothes hanging all over the place and his precious press clippings in a big pile up on top of the wardrobe. He had already dedicated his life to his work, but I couldn't understand why, if he was the boss, he lived in that lousy room. 'Because Monsieur Verger put me here,' he told me. It took him three years to ask Verger if he could change it to something bigger. He was really like a big kid."

There it was, the cruel truth: Bernard wasn't the boss, after all. Everyone knew that it was Verger who wrote the checks, who owned the place, and who paid everyone's salary, including the chef's. Certainly he gave Bernard carte blanche to create his own personalized cuisine, but when Verger and his wife came down Friday evenings to spend a long weekend like country squires in Dumaine's old apartment, there was no doubt about who was in charge. It was only gradually that Bernard's shoulders broadened and he began asserting his authority as the one giving the orders, whoever the titular owner happened to be.

For the moment, the kid was in Verger's service—and at his service, too, because he cooked for him and his wife, as well as for the paying customers, over those long weekends. For Claude, the Côte d'Or was like a *résidence secondaire* where he could take it easy and regain some of the nights of sleep he had missed by his thrice-weekly nocturnal treks out to the Rungis wholesale market buying produce for his burgeoning chain of Barrières and for the rather more grandiose folly he had acquired through his bargain-hunting in Saulieu.

Juggling the management of his little empire, Verger established a routine that varied little in the first few years: he bought the foodstuffs for the Côte d'Or; Alfred, the porter, drove up to Rungis two or three times a week to pick them up; Bernard stayed in Saulieu to cook the purchases; and the profits from the Barrières kept the big old place afloat until the customers started to come back.

And Verger was sure they would come back, because Bernard could make things happen. Verger had been around the restaurant business long enough to sense that Bernard's combination of charm, charisma, and vision would bring the journalists scampering down to Saulieu to see what was going on with their buddy Bernard, and that after them the regular customers would be sure to follow. He encouraged Bernard to be Bernard, then, to develop his cuisine and his personality as fast and as strongly as he could.

Nor was his approach purely mercantile. Although Verger was undeniably a hard-nosed businessman with profits to make from the people he hired, he was not immune to personal feelings, and he had a genuine liking for this surprising, cheerfully overwrought kid from Clermont. For Savoy, Perraudin, Chirent, and Bernard's other companions from the Troisgros days, the relationship between the older and younger man was clearly that of father to surrogate son, even if it was marked for years by a curious kind of formalism: as long as he was Verger's employee, Bernard addressed him in the respectful *vous* form, while Verger responded with the *tu* generally reserved for children or social and professional subordinates. (Like so much else that he learned from Verger, Bernard continued this practice with his own staff in later years.)

"You can say *tu* to me when you become owner of the place," Verger told him. Meanwhile, as the ambiguous situation of one boss and one not-quite-boss continued, the air in the Côte d'Or grew less and less breathable until finally, after long, anguished hesitation, Bernard lanced the boil.

"One morning," he told me some years later, "I came down from my room and called them all together. 'Take a good look at my face,' I told them, 'because I'm here to stay, so you'd better get used to it. Now either do that or get out.' And you know what? They got out. None of them is here anymore."

He must have spent days, if not weeks, rehearsing his speech and pumping up his courage to face down the mutinous crew, because if ever there was a constant in Bernard's life, it was this: He was big and strong, but he hated violence and he fled from confrontation. There would be several other critical moments in the following years when he pulled himself together, only at the very last moment, to avert disaster that was looming in his face. But the showdown in the dining room was the best move he could have made, because with the departure of the Côte d'Or's graybeards he began building a youthful new staff, in both kitchen and *salle*, whose competence and easy, unfeigned amiability was to become the envy of the profession.

Nevertheless, the first few years in Saulieu were dreadful. If Minot left town a discouraged man, he at least had enjoyed the steady drawing power of two Michelin stars. With zero stars in 1975, the Côte d'Or clientele dropped off sharply, especially after the predictable summer migration of hungry motorists and foreign tourists had run its course. In those early days, Bernard could not suspect how dramatic the difference would be in Saulieu between the summer and the winter seasons. In Paris and other important cities, restaurants always boom in the winter, because they are havens of warmth and conviviality. Everyone is working hard, everyone is making money, everyone has to go to lunch, and everyone is hungry—a perfect situation for restaurateurs. Making money with a classy restaurant in Paris is like shooting fish in a barrel. In the provinces, winter is like being suddenly shoved behind the Iron Curtain.

As the last vacationers of September sped north, and as October gave way to November, Bernard discovered that he was living and working in Moldavia. Like Verger in the first two months of his tenancy at the Barrière de Clichy, he would see a handful of clients now and then during the week, and a few more on weekends, but some days would pass with only two or three, and some with none at all. The town was barren and there was nothing to do. No movie house, no girls, no action, nothing. In those days, people used to say, the crows flew backward over Saulieu, so they wouldn't see the misery.

It was after another typically depressing day—on a Saturday evening, as it happened—that Bernard abruptly decided to arrange a little morale-boosting outing for himself and four of his kitchen staff. He piled them all into his little Renault and drove to the White Horse, a rustic nightclub 30 kilometers away in Semur-en-Auxois. Rushing back to Saulieu after midnight he missed a corner, totaled his car, and smashed his head so severely against the windshield that he remained unconscious for several hours.

He wasn't even drunk (Bernard was always extremely abstemious with alcohol), just a bad driver and a sleepy one, going too fast as he always did. No one else was hurt in the accident, but his injury was severe enough to knock him out of action for a couple of days. This was bad news for everyone, but especially Claude Verger, because the regional association of druggists had scheduled their annual lunch for Sunday in the Côte d'Or, and he had no choice but to stand in for Bernard at the *piano*.

Roast beef was on the menu that Sunday, and Verger decided to cook it in presliced portions, but he was unfamiliar with the caprices and the irregular heat distribution of the Minot's goofy oil-burning oven. The result was a disaster: Hungry Frenchies are as picky as Goldilocks about the exact cooking of beef—well done, just right, bloody or blue—but at that lunch, half of the *pharmaciens* complained that their meat was burnt to a crisp and the other half grumped that theirs was raw. An uncustomarily contrite Verger came into the dining room to apologize and explain that the chef had been injured in a car crash. The pouty faces immediately softened. Car crashes were one thing that everyone in France could understand and sympathize with, because in those days before traffic radar and speed limits that were actually enforced, they all drove like fiends. The druggists showed appropriate sympathy for Bernard, then, but also let it be known that ill-cooked beef had better not happen again.

It didn't. For all intents and purposes, Bernard tied himself to Saulieu for the rest of his life, surrounding his absences with such a wealth of precautions that no client, unless he barged into the kitchen and looked, could tell that the chef was not there. Besides, even when he was there, he would rarely be doing the cooking himself. In the first few heroic years, when Bernard was indeed involved with the hands-on work, he had transferred Verger's cuisine of the Barrières more or less intact to Saulieu, and did much of the actual cooking himself. As he began developing his own personal style, though, he gradually shifted the cooking duties over to his new kitchen staff, promoting one of his apprentices to *commis* and, when he saw that he could handle the challenge of greater responsibility, elevating him all the way to *second*: in practice, the one who actually did the cooking.

Bernard's move exemplified an old debate and a common misunderstanding: Who is a cook and who is a chef? The situation that he had known in Roanne, where the Troisgros brothers were actually at the stove wielding pots and pans themselves every day, twice a day, was in fact unusual in the world of *haute cuisine*. It happened because the genius of Jean, Pierre, and their father had unexpectedly rocketed their family restaurant into three-star orbit while it was still an artisanal operation in the hands of two remarkable professionals seconded by teenage apprentices. Far more common at the three-star level are the larger, military-style *brigades* of seasoned specialists, each working a specific task under the absolute authority of a chef who stands at the *passe*, taking orders from the waiters, inspecting and adjusting the finished products before passing them back out to the waiters, and generally coordinating the complex clockwork of men, machines, and foodstuffs lying behind a successful dish.

It is a full-time, crucial, and devilishly tricky job, because the chef has to be intimately familiar with all the details of every post in the *brigade*, and only his eye and his perfectionism stand between a flop and a dazzle. Jean and Pierre Troisgros had a staff of eight behind them in 1968, but today young Michel Troisgros, at the *passe* of the same restaurant, watches over the work of twenty-two seasoned professionals. In short, the chef directs and the cooks cook. Three-star luminaries of the trade like Pierre Gagnaire and Bernard Pacaud in Paris and Michel Bras in Laguiole, who both direct *and* cook, are admirable beyond words, but they are relatively rare.

"I must be the world's dumbest chef, because after all these years I'm still cooking," says Gagnaire ruefully, but he wouldn't have it any other way. Anyone who has ever seen him scanning an entire kitchen with his bright blue eye to discover precisely the one dish where the wrong amount of parsley lies on a tiny portion in a tiny ramekin, then shortstopping it and making the readjustment before allowing it to go can get a small idea of the mad perfectionism that drives these characters, and sense the decades of experience that brought them to the almost spooky level of mastery that they demonstrate twice a day.

"*Pacaud est un chien!*" Bernard Naegellen, retired director of the *Guide Michelin*, cried the other day with unconcealed admiration. Chef and presiding genius of the classically elegant Ambroisie on the place des Vosges in Paris, Bernard Pacaud could not dream of a greater compliment than to have Michelin compare him to a dog—*sous-entendu*, a mad dog, of course.

At the other end of the spectrum from these Stakhanovites of the casserole are the CEOs of cooking enterprises, big-picture overseers like Paul Bocuse in Lyon or Alain Ducasse, just about everywhere in the world. These chefs create the style and dictate the cuisine of their restaurants, but may not spend much time at all in the heat of the kitchen, because they have trained people to do that for them. They'd better do it right, too, because these chefs expect very precise, flawless results, and they know everything there is to know about every last detail of their kitchens and the dishes on their menus: That's how they became chefs. I once asked Bocuse if he was capable, himself, of doing every task that he asked his kitchen staff to do.

"And twice as fast," he barked back without hesitation. (That was some years back. He now allows that age might have slowed him down to a mere mortal level of speed.) The same Bocuse is not in the least ashamed to admit that long ago he delegated the execution of his cooking, just as Fernand Point did in Vienne. "Who does the cooking in my restaurant when I'm away?" he asks rhetorically, before delivering the prepackaged punch line: "The same one who does it when I'm here."

That's fine with Michelin, and in fact Derek Brown, who succeeded Naegellen at the guide's directorship, frequently repeated Bocuse's *bon mot* when he described the different styles and approaches to the restaurant business that he and his inspectors encountered every day. It takes all kinds to make a great restaurant, and as long as the style, the personality, and the quality—the *niac*, as they say in the trade (probably stolen from the English "knack")—are present, he wouldn't care if the cuisine he is judging had been executed by martians.

And, indeed, there is a martian in the trade—an intense, articulate, and perspicacious international businessman named Alain Ducasse, who also happens to be a first-rate cook. (He began the other way around, a three-star cook who turned to the world of business, but his success has been so tremendous that he cannot be viewed now as anything other than a captain of industry who also knows how to cook.) Ducasse has transcended the stereotypical model of the chef so thoroughly that he doesn't even have a kitchen anymore—or, rather, he has dozens of them around the planet, each one another link in the chain of Groupe Alain Ducasse. Apart from a small Provençal inn that sits prettily in the wilds north of Cannes, he does not actually own the dizzying and apparently ever-expanding list of luxury establishments that comprise the group, but rather lends his name and expertise to a gaggle of financiers eager to reap profits from his fertile brain and the unbeatably strong public image of the first man in history to have won six simultaneous Michelin stars—three in Paris and three in Monte Carlo. Formulating the style and décor of each new restaurant, developing the menu, laying down precise procedures for making each dish to be served there, exercising strict quality control, and training the personnel according to his own exacting standards, he resembles nothing so much as the Ray Kroc of *haute cuisine*, the pendant at the exclusive, expensive upper end of eating to the prophet of the cheap, mass-produced burger at the lower end. He is the McDonald's of gastronomy.

"McDu," he said, with a quick little smile. "I like that."

There are plenty of different routes, then, that lead to great cooking, but common to them all is this: The end result bears the unmistakable mark of the chef's personality, whether or not he is the one who actually executes the dishes. Bernard's route in Saulieu was halfway between the obsessive hands-on approach of Gagnaire and Pacaud, and the virtual kitchens where Ducasse cooks with his brains. As his *second* grew in skill and confidence, Bernard progressively withdrew from the *piano* himself to adopt the role that fitted him best: the idea man, the inventor, the tester, the taster, and the motivator. He was smart enough to realize that with the limited technical skills he had gained in two and a half years of apprenticeship in Roanne, he could never hope to rival monsters of technique like Bocuse, Guérard, Ducloux, or the Troisgros brothers—men who had been everywhere and learned everything. On the other hand, he had ambition, energy, and vision to spare, along with a finely discerning palate that with the years was to develop into one of the best in the business.

This proved to be one of the great surprises within the rarified atmosphere of the highest echelons of French *haute cuisine*. Neither Chef Jean nor Chef Pierre, as they lorded it over their terrified band of bungling *apprentis*, could suspect that Bernard, their bungler-in-chief, was something of a natural-born genius of taste, a young man whose talent was only awaiting the right moment and the right environment to grow and blossom. As he slogged through his first years in Saulieu, he began discovering that talent himself, then expanding it and perfecting it until it became the leitmotif around which he built his entire career, from zero to three stars. Taste: straight, pure, unadulterated, undisguised taste.

VII

BUILDING LE STYLE LOISEAU,

1977–1982

"*C*ôte de'Or, Saulieu 15/20. Their success is almost assured. Ragout of scallops, sweetbreads, and veal kidneys with crayfish; filet of sole on a bed of spinach; Bresse chicken with tarragon."

Devoted as ever to Bernard and to the cooking to which Claude Verger had guided him, the *GaultMillau* guide for the year 1976 had faithfully followed to Saulieu the man they considered to be one of their most promising discoveries,* and they liked what they found there. Promising he surely was, but the discovery was only twenty-five years old, and he had not yet found his footing. Bernard's cuisine was still basically the same as the Barrières, and the mere fact that *Gault-Millau* employed that plural "their" indicated that the Côte d'Or was still being viewed as one more of Claude Verger's multiple enterprises,

---

*From the very start of their adventure in the food guide business, Henri Gault and Christian Millau made a great specialty of nosing around the French restaurant scene to find talented and still relatively little-known young chefs, and then promoting them hard and fast. Infinitely more conservative, Michelin made these same aspirants go through a long period of purgatory, sometimes lasting many years, before rewarding them with a star or two or, of course, all the way to three. Guy Savoy, for instance, waited twenty-seven years to climb from the level of one star to all the way up to three. The *grande dame* had learned hard lessons in her early years about looking silly by promoting and demoting too hastily. Thenceforward, she refused to be rushed.

or at best a team effort between Verger and his hired cook. But Bernard was already pondering a plan to begin the climb toward his three-star ambition.

On the face of it, he was wildly, extravagantly out of line to even entertain such a lofty notion. Certainly he had enjoyed a nice flash of celebrity in Paris, but how much of that was owed to Claude Verger's powerful personality and how much to Bernard's own culinary talents? And anyway, the incestuous little world of Parisian star makers was a notoriously fickle thing that could get bored with terrifying speed, dumping overnight what it had adored the day before. *Pipeau*, that was the problem—the kissy-kissy world of what was fashionable in Paris was a lot of fun, but you can't keep a fad going by bullshit alone when you're sitting on a gloomy, windswept plateau 250 kilometers away from the big city.

Bernard was certainly aware that he would have to continue, and in fact expand, his campaign of caressing the media and the showbiz types who had contributed so much to his notoriety in Paris, but that wouldn't be enough. If he was to force his entry into the kingdom where the big boys of the restaurant trade played, he would have to make a reputation and an image independent of Verger by developing a personal style of cooking identified with himself alone—a *cuisine Loiseau*. He had been in the business long enough and spoken with enough of his *confrères* to conclude there were three fundamental criteria that Michelin cherished most in judging a chef: quality, regularity, and personality.

He reasoned it out. Quality was the most obvious. Your stuff had to be good. No need explaining that any further. Regularity had always been a particular Michelin fret: chefs who get it right not only twice a day but day after day, and year after year. That required the kind of obsessive perfectionism that could make a Michelin boss beam and be prepared to sign a medical certificate attesting that an admired chef was a mad dog. Michelin hates, absolutely *hates*, flashes in the pan. This is a theme that recurs constantly whenever anyone even remotely connected with the guide speaks of its work.

"We're trying to make a guide that is reliable," Derek Brown insisted, with that inflexible, inexorable earnestness of the true Michelin arbiter.* "We want to be sure that something that looks like a trend doesn't turn out to be just something that's trendy. There's a certain impression that we only look for what was good and old and classic in grandmother's time. That is not true. We've got the modern, *branché* ["in"; fashionable] restaurants in the guide, but we want to be sure that they'll be there as long as that guide lasts. We did a little exercise in Paris not long ago. We went to a lot of the trendy restaurants, and particularly followed about twenty-five of them. At the end of the year, three-quarters of them didn't exist anymore."

So there. Unspoken but understood: Buy *other* guides and you'll be knocking on restaurant doors that had been shut for months. All right, then, Bernard could have reasoned with this in mind, I'll try harder and be more regular, more *constant*, than everyone else—but anyone, even a mediocre cook, can work hard. Regularity wasn't enough, then. There was something more that Michelin expected to find up in the rarified atmosphere of top restaurants: personality, real personality. Chefs turning out a singular, clearly recognizable cuisine that reflected their character and their ideas. And those ideas had better be good, too, because there was always a delicate question hanging in the air. It concerned the nuance between personality and that thing called creativity. Since time immemorial, everyone has insistently paid lip service to creativity in cooking, but creativity runs wild leads straight into the shoals of trendiness and precious *nouvelle kiwisine* horrors like those geranium soufflés and that turbot with raspberry *coulis*. It is great to tinker and invent and experiment, but never forget that cooking is a manual act: Beware the cook atremble with the aspiration to be considered a poet.

As he wandered around Dumaine's musty hallways during those first long, lonesome winter months, Bernard had plenty of time to reflect on how to construct *le style Loiseau* and build the personal image that would set him apart from others and catch Michelin's eye. He had lots of company in this reasoning process, of course: By design or by instinct—but never by accident—it was something every great chef had gone through before him, each one bending the enormous syllabus of

---

*Having turned sixty, the official Michelin age for calling it a day, Brown retired after producing the 2004 guide.

French cuisine in his own manner into his own coherent whole—his *oeuvre*. If, for instance, you go to Alain Senderens's Lucas-Carton in Paris, you'll choose your wines first and Alain will make you a dynamite dinner around that. Pierre Gagnaire will pull one rabbit after another out of his hat, showering you with such a dizzying procession of dishes and accompanying dishes—the plots, subplots, pirouettes, false dénouements, and ultimate resolutions of his culinary detective story—that your head will spin and your mouth will water at the same time. Down in Lyon, Paul Bocuse, lord of the gas rings and emperor of the trade, will play Von Suppé for you on the world's largest fairground organ and set a culinary "Ode to Joy" on your plate, a classically flawless symphony of taste and presentation that irresistibly makes you think: Best-of-Beethoven. In Cancale, Olivier Roellinger takes his clients on a cruise around the globe with a restless, macrocosmic gastronomy perfumed by exogenous spices and combinations universally considered "exotic," until he came along, while deep in the southern reaches of Auvergne his brilliant, ascetic friend Michel Bras does precisely the opposite, roaming the rocky confines of his native Aubrac plateau to discover the world in a grain of sand and heaven in a local wildflower. Bras creates a stunning universality from the lowly microcosm of the wild herbs, roots, and plants that lie within walking distance of Laguiole, the little town of his birth.

And so it goes, each one digging according to his or her* talents and inclinations into this country's unparalleled inventory of produce, tradition, and expertise, to put forward yet another personal interpretation of the vast epicurean tableau. Each one is different from the others, and they're always shifting, adjusting, evolving. Taken as a whole, these men and women represent a wealth of expertise, originality, and variety in great food that has no equal anywhere in the world.

But what would Bernard's interpretation of the tableau be? How could an unrated and still largely untested twenty-five-year-old new-

---

*To date, only four women chefs have ever won three stars: Eugénie Brazier in Lyon, Marie Bourgeois in Priay, 50 kilometers north of Lyon, and Marguerite and Charlyne Bise in Talloires, near Annecy. Mado Point, Fernand's widow, held on to three stars until her death in 1986, maintaining her husband's cuisine and intransigence for quality but staying resolutely out of the kitchen.

comer distinguish himself among the swarm of notables older, wiser, and more experienced than he? He was convinced that Verger's approach of last-minute manipulation of top-quality ingredients was the right way to go, but that only got him to Square One. Bernard was clear-eyed enough to realize that he did not possess the professional baggage to rival in cooking technique the men with whom he aspired to rub shoulders at the top of the trade. What he *could* do, though, was to go even farther than them in the mad, manic game of perfectionism. From the moment he assumed leadership, there would be nothing but the best for Saulieu: best ingredients, best wines, best service.

His obsessive pursuit of the very best was aimed at seducing Michelin, of course, but he did not have to force himself: It came naturally to his excessive, Manichean nature. Anyone who worked with him can recount dozens of examples—droll, touching, sometimes infuriating—of Bernard's devotion to hyperbole and excess. Verger astutely concluded that it was precisely this maddeningly unreasonable nature that could allow his protégé to climb toward the summit of the trade, but the prime example of Bernard's immoderation that sticks in Verger's mind today concerns not cuisine but sport. "One day we got to talking about tennis, and I found he was fascinated with Björn Borg— he was the only one Bernard would say anything good about, because that was the time when Borg was winning everything. Everyone else was *de la merde*. The only thing that interested him was the first. Second place didn't count for him."

A little vignette that became part of the established folklore of La Côte d'Or some years later concerned Bernard and a *sous-chef* who mistakenly thought he was defending his boss's best interests when he began bargaining over the phone with a supplier for some expensive ingredients. Overhearing him, Bernard held his patience for a few minutes, then grabbed the phone from his hand. "*Allô!*" he shouted. "Just give me the best you've got. I don't care about the price."

As he began his Michelin-seducing campaign, there was only one aspect of the best he could afford: the food. The best rooms for the hotel, the best silverware, the best china—all that could come later. For the moment, he was concentrating only on the plate.

Intentionally or not, this was very much like throwing down a gauntlet to Michelin. The guide's editors never tired of insisting that it was the plate alone that determined the attribution of stars, regardless of the décor. Now, stranded in the empty shell of Dumaine's prestige and working with hand-me-down china, silverware, and cooking gear from his predecessor, he undertook to bring a restaurant totally stripped of three stars back up from point zero to the Michelin summit. It had never been done before.

For its part, Michelin unbent enough by 1976 to allow that Bernard's place really was a restaurant, after all. That had taken some doing. Verger's wife, Martine, took time off from her busy dental practice in Paris to charge into Michelin headquarters and beard the lion in his den, buttonholing André Trichot, then editor-in-chief, to complain about the injustice of removing the Côte d'Or's restaurant from his guide's august pages. Trichot relented, and the crossed forks and spoons reappeared in the new guide. That was a start—better than nothing—but Bernard could only gaze with wistful eyes at the listing for the Barrière de Clichy, now emblazoned in the very same guide with a bright shiny star under chef Guy Savoy, his sidekick and "little brother" from Roanne. Guy was a terrific cook, but it was clear that much of the glory he was harvesting had been built up under Bernard during the Barrière's waiting period in Michelin's gastronomic anteroom. Never mind. Guy was his best friend. Bernard didn't begrudge him the pleasure of his newfound laurels.

Some big things were happening down in his area, too. In three consecutive years, 1974, 1975, and 1976, three Burgundy restaurants made the jump from one to two Michelin stars. First there was Jacques Lameloise (a wunderkind only five years older than Bernard) down south in Chagny, near Beaune; then, in St. Père de Vézelay, 30 miles across the hills, the Espérance of Marc Meneau, the self-taught son of a village saddle maker; and finally Michel Lorain with his Côte St. Jacques, on the same R.N. 6 by the River Yonne in Joigny, at the northern edge of Burgundy. All three would eventually make it to the summit of three stars, and in the same order of precedence: Lameloise, then Meneau, and finally Lorain.* Michelin, it seemed, was making a

---

*Lord Michelin giveth and Lord Michelin taketh away. Meneau (in 1999) and Lorain (in 2001) were rather mystifyingly demoted back down to two stars, but both regained the top rating in the 2004 guide.

deliberate effort to encourage young chefs in the provinces. Bernard fairly quivered with anticipation at the thought of joining these regional eminences.

There was another important event in 1976, one that had a considerably greater impact on the world of gastronomy—and in particular, on the cooking style that Bernard was seeking to develop—than these two-star awards: Michel Guérard published *La Grande Cuisine Minceur*.

The Mozart of French cooking had been thunderstruck by the condemnation for demolition of his little restaurant in Asnières for an urban renewal project. Shortly thereafter, he got married. Christine, his new wife, plunked him down in the middle of nowhere—a place called Eugénie-les-Bains, in the Landes, the foie gras and armagnac country of the deep southwest, where the foothills of the Pyrenees rise—because Papa owned some properties there: a little chain of spas that he had picked up for cheap because spas were essentially a nineteenth-century fashion, and nobody was doing that trip anymore. Wouldn't it be nice, Christine said in essence, to settle here and get people to come back to Eugénie? Yes, dear, said Michel, and began thinking about how to find a gimmick that would persuade Parisians, and maybe foreigners, too, to make the 500-mile trek down from the big city and join him and Christine in the sticks.

The gimmick he came up with was *cuisine minceur*: cooking to lose weight by, also known in one of its later commercialized avatars as Lean Cuisine. It was a stroke of pure genius, and it worked like a charm. Michel completely rethought the cooking from the Pot au Feu and produced an entire range of recipes that were ingeniously low in fats and calories but still looked and tasted great. Taste: That was the hard part. Anyone, even a doctor, can make harmless dietary food by boiling carrots and beef and serving them up with a leaf or two of lettuce, but Michel's challenge was to make gastronomic dietary food: *haute cuisine* for the ponderously challenged. He steamed a chicken leg, stuffed it with nonfattening sweetbreads, mushrooms, and truffles, and served it with a bright, optimistically green sauce composed of watercress, spinach, mushrooms, and marjoram cooked together in a *bouillon*, emulsified in a blender, and then reduced over a direct flame. With his near calorie-free recipes, he achieved a character and depth of flavor nearly equal to classical dishes prepared with butter, cream, and rich meat reductions.

Dozens—hundreds—of combinations of this sort sprang from his agile brain, from grilled pigeons with garlic puree to veal kidneys with a sauce of zero percent *fromage blanc* and mustard thickened with mushroom puree, to luxury items like roast lobster with aromatics and herbs. For sea bass, he invented an accompaniment so peaceable and inoffensive to the health that he named it *sauce vierge*—"virgin sauce"—a concoction of tomato, garlic, chervil, parsley, tarragon, coriander, and olive oil. Michel went so far as to incorporate mineral oil into sauces and vinaigrettes for his salads, but after he decided it was perhaps not ideal for the human digestive system (*huile de paraffine* is a derivative of petroleum, like kerosene), he invented a nearly fat-free oil substitute made of vegetable *bouillon* lightly gelatinized with chicken bones and finished off with just a touch of olive oil for taste.

It was major groundbreaking wizardry that was going on in Eugénie in those early days, as Michel and Christine built up their clientele, and within a few years, *cuisine minceur* rocketed both the cook and his newly renovated spa into the orbit of worldwide celebrity. Eugénie-les-Bains now officially styles itself Premier Village Minceur de France. Michel has an unejectable seat on the town council—his fellow citizens would gladly name him mayor if he ever took the time to stand for office—and the massive influx of tourists and *curistes*—chubs taking the cure—has turned what was formerly a forgotten little backwater burg into a prosperous, artfully decorated, and beautifully equipped model town, thanks to the shower of cash that Michel conjured up.

"I had to do something dramatic and different to draw attention to Eugénie," he explained to me some years later. "*Cuisine minceur* was just the thing."* A gimmick it was, then, but it was an inspired gim-

---

*Two years after his forerunning *Cuisine Minceur*, Michel published another book—the guy had been working like a madman—his now classic *Cuisine Gourmande*, a compendium of his original recipes freed of the shackles of weight loss, and luxuriating in all things rich, caloric, and delicious. "I never said *cuisine minceur* and *nouvelle cuisine* were the same thing," he said. "Butter, cream, and egg yolks are central to French cooking. It strikes me as difficult to do without them." It could have been Paul Bocuse speaking.

mick and a true act of creation. *Cuisine minceur*, like *nouvelle cuisine*, was a shot heard 'round the world. Knowingly or not, thousands of cooks on every continent benefit today from tricks and techniques developed by Michel Guérard down in his spa, lightening up and freshening up the cooking they put on the plates of an increasingly diet-conscious and weight-conscious clientele.

In Saulieu, Bernard heard Michel's shot loud and clear. He was in the sticks, too, and he needed a gimmick every bit as much as his more celebrated elder in Eugénie. Throughout his career, Bernard took great pride in his originality, frequently averring that he had never opened a cookbook in his life, and that all his recipes had sprung sui generis from his head. Even so, it is clear that he knew all about the many wonders that Michel was producing down in Eugénie—they were the talk of the trade. He would have been foolish to ignore them as he sought to distinguish himself by building the grammar of what he would eventually present to the world, and to all those Michelin inspectors he was hoping to feed, as *le style Loiseau*.

So Bernard learned, and as he learned he borrowed. From Mama's home cooking (honest regional dishes, sauces from simple deglazings with water) to Troisgros (great French classics relieved of much of their heaviness) to Verger (best products simply treated at the last minute) to Guérard and the magical lightness of his *cuisine minceur*, the intellectual development of his culinary thinking followed an arrow-straight line. It would be several years before he amalgamated it all into a coherent proposition, but even in the early days the rough ideas were in place: He was in Burgundy, so his cuisine would lean heavily on some classics of the region, but reinterpreted in his fashion; it would be light, as fat-free as possible, and easily digestible; and above all it would emphasize the purity of taste—things would taste exactly like what they were. It would be a cuisine of *essences*.

It was flattering to the young, inexperienced chef of 1976 that the *GaultMillau* had praised the ragout of scallops, sweetbreads, veal kidneys, and crayfish that he presented to them, but the mature Chef Bernard turned his back on such a profligate mix of tastes, colors, and textures. The ragout was surely delicious, but it smacked suspiciously of mishmash. It was not *pure*. As the years passed and he honed *le style Loiseau* into a disciplined syllabus with defining rules and taboos,

Bernard grew far more sectarian about what was right and what was wrong, and his rules hardened into something like a party line. There were to be no more than three *saveurs* on the client's plate: the main ingredient, pure in its true, unadorned flavor; a simple but vigorous sauce that recalled and reinforced that flavor; and two accompanying sub-dishes, each one designed for that ingredient alone and not for any other. Unsurprisingly, this cuisine reflected his character. Like the theorizing Parisian intellectuals who continued to cling to their uncompromising Marxist–Leninist weltanschauung, even as the world of communism was falling into shambles everywhere, Bernard's insistence on purity of taste had an absolutist ring to it that was strangely reminiscent of Maoism.

Claude Le Gall, a young *maître d'hôtel* who came to the Côte d'Or in 1978, remembered a telling scene that occurred next to the hotel's reception desk, where Bernard habitually stood to speak with clients as they filed out after their meals. The chef wore that huge, winning smile, as he always did, while harvesting the chorus of praise that inevitably washed over him after every lunch and dinner. This time, though, there was a customer who was only 99 percent ecstatic, and that was like a handful of sand in the skin balm.

"*Monsieur Loiseau*," he said, "our lunch was wonderful, but could I perhaps make one small suggestion?"

The smile continued to hang on, but his face clouded ever so briefly. The chef nodded.

"The *purée de celeri* was very good, but perhaps a bit strong in flavor for some people. Perhaps you could mix some mashed potato in with it?"

"If you don't like celery root, don't eat it," Bernard snapped. End of conversation. There was a right way and a wrong way for everything in *le style Loiseau*. He always asked for criticism—he truly did want to make everything about his place perfect—but he rarely liked it when he got it, and he tended to go into a funk.

In 1977 the Côte d'Or won its first Michelin star at the same moment that Michel Guérard won his third. (After moving to Eugénie-les-Bains, Michel got his first star in 1974, his second in 1975, and his third in 1977, the fastest promotion from zero to three in Michelin history. But it wasn't really quite zero, because everyone knew that he was already worth three stars before he left Paris. Even so, Michelin had to abide by tradition and propriety: Stars are to be delivered singly, not severally.) Bernard's single star, while less brilliant than Michel's triple, was not bad for a chef who, at twenty-six, was only six years out of apprenticeship. Not bad at all, but his menu still reflected his youth and inexperience, and was derived heavily from his masters. There was nothing reprehensible about this—chefs constantly crib one another's ideas, and the good ones tend to be reproduced thousands of times, with slight variations, as they make the esculent circuit. The green peppercorns, the little raviolis, the salads with warm goat cheese,* and the *crèmes brûlées* all began somewhere with someone, to be picked up and cloned more or less faithfully throughout the world. More recently than these, Michel Bras's extensive use of wild herbs and roots in his cookery has been liberally plagiarized without the least attribution. (But that's all right. No one can do it like him.)

Barely six weeks after Bernard won his first star, I had the occasion to see him again up close in Saulieu. I was in company with Jean Didier, editor of the *Guide Kléber*, Michelin's lesser rival from the lesser tire company that the Clermont-Ferrand giant gobbled up a few years afterward, spitting out the *Guide Kléber* like so many chicken bones. As it happened, the Côte d'Or was the last stop on a grueling week-long inspection trip that Didier had undertaken in the Burgundy area, one of the many *tournées* through which he courageously attempted to personally take the place of Michelin's cohort of inspectors.

---

*The *salad au crottin chaud* is one of these rare specialties to which it is possible to assign a plausible paternity (or, rather, maternity). It first appeared in the early sixties on the menu of Les Belles Gourmandes, the terrific restaurant of chef Henri Faugeron, located on a little side street off the rue du Bac in Paris. Faugeron, who later moved to the hoity-toity 16th *arrondissement*, went as high as two Michelin stars, but never to three. He told me it was a little old Parisian lady, a passerby who stopped to inspect the menu posted by the front door—a favorite pastime for pedestrians everywhere in Paris—and came into his restaurant one morning to suggest he add a dish she enjoyed making herself: heating a goat cheese to nearly melting and serving it on salad with a good, strong vinaigrette. He was so impressed that he wanted to offer her a free meal for it. She refused and disappeared like an aged fairy godmother into the carbon monoxide haze of boulevard St. Germain, never to be seen again.

As editor-in-chief, the guide's primary writer, and only salaried inspector, Jean could not possibly hope to remain anonymous, so he chose the opposite tack—brazenly advertising his presence by driving from restaurant to restaurant in his fire-engine red Lancia convertible, bursting into restaurants and jovially greeting the chefs as soon as he arrived. After all, he reasoned, how much better can they make their stuff for me than for the ordinary client? After the first day of each *tournée*, the entire region knew that the *Guide Kléber* was on the prowl, and Jean became the turkey to be more and more deliciously stuffed with each passing meal.

It was on April 30 that Didier arrived for lunch in Saulieu, and Bernard had been warned that he was on his way. How far had Bernard pushed his perfectionism, and how hard was he trying? I'll tell you. Jean had visited all of the greatest eating places in Burgundy on that trip, from Blanc to Bocuse to Troisgros, the Tinkers-to-Evers-to-Chance of the gastronomic circuit, plus all the others in between, but it was only in Saulieu that the chef was waiting to greet us in person. Literally waiting: as Jean wheeled up the steep little rise at the side of the Hôtel de la Poste and the Côte d'Or came into view, what should we see but Bernard himself, standing halfway out into the roadway, unmistakable in his immaculate white regalia, peering down rue Argentine, smiling enormously, making traffic cop gestures and waving us straight into the hotel's garage.

Within milliseconds we somehow had *kirs** in our hands and Bernard was shooing us into Dumaine's famous dining room. Hell-

---

*Chanoine (Canon) Felix Kir (1870–1968) represented everything that was best in the French nation: native Burgundian, gourmet among gourmets, and spiritual advisor to thousands, this Catholic priest of great longevity was a resistance fighter during the war who was saved from a Gestapo firing squad only because hostilities ended before they could carry out the sentence. Elected mayor of Dijon and deputy in the national parliament, he systematically offered visitors to his office a cocktail of two-thirds Aligoté white wine and one-third cassis (black currant) syrup. Today the proportions have shifted toward much more wine and much less syrup (the same kind of route taken by the dry martini, originally two parts gin to one of vermouth), but the good father's drink, the *kir*, lingers on in just about every corner of the world.

bent for seduction, he immediately went into action and sent out first a lobster *terrine* with little spring vegetables, then poached oysters, sauced and laid lovingly back in their shells, and a ragout of rockfish with sweet red peppers, all of which we managed to choke down with the help of a prodigiously good 1971 Puligny-Montrachet, bright yellow, fat, and full of flowers and honey.

Hardly able to get a word in edgewise upon his arrival, and then submitted to the onslaught of Bernard's hyperbolically warm welcome and the ensuing food that appeared without bidding, Didier had scarcely had a chance to study the menu. Now, almost furtively, casting his eye to the side during breaks between the avalanche of Bernard's offerings, he gave it a quick, expert perusal.

In presentation and layout, it nicely reflected Verger's number-one Barrière rule: everything for the food and to hell with the décor. The card was large but simple and clearly not expensive to produce, two handwritten pages inside a heavy, unglazed faux parchment folder featuring a rather amateurish charcoal drawing of the Côte d'Or with a festive table set up before it: a ham, a chicken, a stockpot, a bottle of wine, a tart, a cheese, and a fruit bowl. The carefully disciplined script of the two interior pages showed a selection of specialties that was extremely generous for a country restaurant that, unlike urban places of similar size, had no reliable customer base to count on, and by professional ideology, refused to countenance frozen or canned foods. There were thirteen *entrées*, seven seafood dishes, three fowl, five meat, and eight desserts, with the addition of four little extra tags for the day's specials, affixed to the bottom of the card with paper clips. But if Verger was being economical with printing expenses, his chef had already become profligate where image was concerned. The entire top of the menu was occupied by a single line:

Bernard Loiseau proposes

What he proposed was very interesting, because it bespoke a young chef in transition, determined to make a name for himself but still not quite sure of how to do it. Many of the dishes on offer were classics that could have appeared on any menu in the region: lobster bisque, smoked ham, Burgundy snails, Bresse chicken in a tarragon cream sauce, sweetbreads with the truffles and Madeira accents of a *sauce* *périgourdine*, steak with the green peppercorn sauce* so popular in those days. Other dishes were straight borrowings from his distinguished elders. The mussel soup with saffron was a reprise of a staple on the cards of Paul Bocuse and the Troisgros brothers, and harked back beyond them to Fernand Point. The candied grapefruit recalled a similar dessert specialty at Jean Ducloux's Restaurant Greuze in Tournus, and the tea-infused prunes that Bernard served with it owed a debt to Alain Senderens in Paris, who had been making tea ice creams and sherbets for several years. What he called the *salade Côte d'Or* (based on lettuce, foie gras, and green beans) was Guérard's *salade folle* by another name, and Bernard could have made the salmon in sorrel sauce in his sleep after participating in its preparation for nearly three years in Roanne. The light apple tart served hot (ritually marked on every menu as an item to be ordered at the beginning of the meal) was nothing but Michel Guérard's *tarte fine aux pommes*, an emigrant from Asnières to Clichy to rue Molière to Saulieu. On the other hand, several other dishes bore the imprint of Bernard's thinking about a *style Loiseau* that emphasized the lightness of last-minute legerdemain: asparagus with a simple herb sauce; scallops on watercress mousse; sweetbreads with asparagus tips; filet of John Dory with sautéed cucumbers (prepared like Guérard's one-franc chicken wings from the Lido); tiny lamb chops with spring vegetables.

The kid was thinking. The ideas were coming. Even if the hotel was dilapidated and his kitchen a wreck, the mere act of bringing his *cuisine moderne* to Dumaine's august address was creating the kind of favorable comment that had brought Jean Didier and a host of other critics and journalists down to Saulieu. Nor was everything about the place rotten, because down under his feet in the basement he had a secret weapon: a first-rate *cave à vin*. That was a godsend. As he watched Didier sipping and slurping that magnificent 1971 Puligny-Montrachet Le Cailleret, Bernard must have been thanking Bacchus and the perspicacity of his predecessors, because the Côte d'Or's wine list was a

---

*First sprung on Parisian gourmets in the late sixties by young Alain Senderens in his Archestrate on rue de Varenne. When Senderens broke camp and moved to the monumental Lucas-Carton at place de la Madeleine, Alain Passard moved in, eventually bringing his own Arpège up to three Michelin stars.

wonderfully effective part of his best-of-everything campaign. No fool, Verger had known before he signed any checks that the successive proprietorships of Dumaine and Minot had endowed the old barn with one of the region's richest wine cellars—one that was, curiously enough, especially deep in reserves of fine Bordeaux. The heavy stock of Bordeaux may have simply been a reflection of a longstanding customer preference for the local Burgundies, but they offered the added advantage of being virtually impermeable to the passage of time: for the most part they simply got better as they aged. On the value of the *cave* alone, Verger had got himself a bargain when he took the place off Minot's hands.*

Bordeaux be damned, though—Bernard wasn't going to serve *le Kléber* anything but Burgundy at that memorable lunch, not in a restaurant named La Côte d'Or, situated at the heavenly gates to the golden slopes where the grapes of Chardonnay and Pinot Noir even then were sucking up the goodness from the rocky soil that would turn their juices into the makings of the world's most magnificent wines. After he had wolfed down the last scrap of his rockfish, Didier got a muscular Latricières-Chambertin to accompany thin cutlets of duck breast that Bernard had briefly seized in a scalding pan on both sides, leaving them nearly raw in the middle, and artfully supporting them with a half-moon formation of peach slices, browned in butter on the outside and canary yellow within. From beginning to end, the whole lunch had been light, imaginative, and easy to eat, and Jean told him so. For those few minutes, at any rate, Bernard didn't give a damn that there were no girls and there was nothing to do in Saulieu.

It was time to look at the kitchen. In those days, Bernard brought professional visitors into his kitchen the way an anatomy professor might bring fellow doctors to contemplate his collection of two-headed fetuses preserved in formaldehyde. Dumaine's famous old workplace was already tired when he left it but now, thirteen years later, it was a

---

*I had been to the Côte d'Or under Minot's administration only once, in 1974, and had been struck by the extraordinary wealth of the wine cellar. The food on that occasion did nothing in particular to stick in my memory, but the *cave* was another matter. I am not about to forget the two bottles that accompanied my meal: a 1966 Chambolle-Musigny and a 1957 Richebourg.

two-level ruin long past amortization, with holes in the ceiling, wob-bly, rusting equipment held together with wire and glue (including that famously idiosyncratic oil-fed *piano*), an untreated concrete floor, a direct view into the grease-splattered garage, and, down below, a pas-try section masquerading as the Black Hole of Calcutta.

"Pretty good, huh?" said Bernard, for once abandoning his gushing spontaneity to lapse into irony. Didier shook his head and made a men-tal note to be kind to the boy in his next guide. Just as we returned to the now-empty dining room, Claude Verger himself appeared, down from Paris for the weekend at an average speed of 100 mph (traffic cops were rare then, and road radar nonexistent). Sharp and aggressive as a game-cock, and as outrageous as Lenny Bruce, he enjoyed nothing more than shocking listeners with hyperbolic generalizations expressly designed to provoke. He called for a bottle of champagne (Perrier-Jouët) and railed on in that thin, reedy voice of his, denouncing just about everything and everyone in the profession. Ninety-five percent of cooks in France were lousy, he shouted, and he knew of only two or three who could put together a decent *steak marchand de vin*. The only guy in the world who knew how to make sauces was Jean Troisgros, but then most sauces were no damn good, anyway. When Didier—a good-natured bloke—failed to rise to the bait and argue, Verger put up his dukes like Mohammed Ali and poured calumny over the gastronomic guides and food critics in general. "You're all whores," he shouted, but Jean was too full of good food, good Burgundy, and good champagne to do anything but smile indulgently. Bernard was grinning, too, but as Verger's diatribe flowed on, the smile began to look more and more forced. *Don't overdo it, boss, don't get me in trouble just when things are starting to look up.*

VIII

BACHELOR DAYS IN SAULIEU,
1977–1982

After the milestone of his first Michelin star, Bernard had five years remaining as Verger's employee. They coincided exactly with the last five years of his bachelorhood. With the Vergers bankrolling the restaurant like surrogate parents, as he matured into a fully fledged chef and leader, there was a plausible analogy to be drawn between those five years and the situation of a teenager growing into manhood—except that in this case it was the "parents" who eventually left the house. At the start of the Saulieu adventure, Claude and Martine Verger arrived religiously every Friday evening and stayed until Sunday night, sometimes helping out with the reception, planning, and personnel, but mostly unwinding from the hard week's work in Paris. Little by little, as the months and years passed, they began arriving later and leaving earlier, and frequently it was just Claude himself who rocketed down in his big gray Citroën BX while Martine stayed behind in Paris—as indeed happened on that memorable Saturday afternoon of Jean Didier's lunch. Over those years, the Côte d'Or gradually came to be identified with Bernard alone: his cuisine, his authority, his personality as the mark of the house.

Supplanting the father figure is, of course, the normal role for any young striver in most human endeavors, especially one of competitive excellence, but in Saulieu it was a supplanting that Verger actively encouraged. "He had the ambition and he had the drive. I put the place in his hands and gave him a free rein. After a while I came around to believing that he really was going to make it. You see, the thing about Bernard was that he never admitted defeat."

From the start, both men agreed to a fundamental premise: since they had a monument on their hands, they would not debase it with anything but gastronomic fare: top-level for everything and no corner-cutting. "We couldn't serve *bifteck-frites*, not in the Côte d'Or," said Verger. "But that didn't mean we would just reproduce Dumaine's cooking. We did our cuisine—my cuisine. That turned everything up-side down. A lot of the old farts of the traditional clientele didn't like that, and they came at us with their shotguns, but things worked out af-ter a while and a new clientele built up."

At length, the "my" label on the cuisine changed from Verger to Bernard through the normal course of development, but either way it was risky to chuck tradition out the window at a house that had prospered on tradition ever since the eighteenth-century days of horse-drawn car-riages on the north–south route. But Verger was a gambler and Bernard was a true believer, so they shot for the moon. Curiously enough, their hell-for-leather approach probably pleased the high priests in the temple on avenue de Breteuil, because as much as Michelin deeply mistrusts fads and trends, the guide tends to look benevolently upon chefs who take risks—but only within bounds. Intelligent risks. Reasonable risks. Coherent, productive risks. Risks that please a Michelin inspector.

But which ones are these?

There lies the whole mystery of Michelin's dominant but sibylline presence in the world of gastronomy, and the maddening difficulty of at-tempting to anticipate or influence their judgments—most especially where the magical three-star summit is concerned. Nobody really knows. Judging restaurants, like judging a landscape, a beautiful woman, or a pleasant melody, is subjective and largely indefinable. Who touches the heart most deeply, Schubert or Mozart? Who's your ideal of feminine beauty—Monroe? Deneuve? Cleopatra? Is Manet a better painter than Monet? Every such act of judging is riddled with imponderables. There are a great number of wonderful restaurants that almost made it to the top, but not quite, and no one, either within Michelin or without, can clearly articulate the difference between a two- and a three-star place, when the food is often equally stunning in both. In the end, it probably comes down to the personality of the individual who runs the show. A most pertinent example is La Pyramide in Vienne. When Fernand Point died, not even *Michelin*, the Godzilla of guides, had the guts to remove any stars at all, because Mado Point was a formidable, intimidating personality who knew her business inside out, tasted her food better than any inspector, and judged wine more accurately and severely than 90 percent of the males in the trade. (I have watched grown men tremble as she arrived on the scene of a *dégustation* of Côtes du Rhône.) As a result, La Pyramide sailed tranquilly along with three stars until Mado expired in 1986. On the other hand, when the very great Alain Chapel checked out in 1990, the guide instantly demoted his restaurant to the two stars that it still holds today under the direction of his widow, Suzanne, and his longtime chef, the faultless professional Philippe Jousse.

"I did that," Bernard Naegellen told me without the least hesitation. Director of the guide until the advent of Derek Brown, Naegellen had run a tight ship, sticking unwaveringly to the ancient Michelin principle that when a chef departs—feet forward or otherwise—his restaurant will be *déclassé*. "Leaving the three stars would have been a lack of respect for Chapel. It would have indicated that Michelin thought he had counted for nothing in the excellence of his restaurant, and it would be just as good without him."

Misguided multitudes of two-star chefs, reasoning that décor and luxury can make the difference, have broken their wings trying to buy their way to the top by launching ruinously costly building programs. Many more have wandered off into the swamps of unbridled creativity and ended up just looking foolish, with wasabi, coconut milk, and agar-agar all over their faces.

And yet they keep coming back to the fray, because the three-star rating is the Oscar, the *légion d'honneur*, and the Pulitzer Prize all in one, where cooking is concerned. There's an interesting psychological point here: Who are these people, and what is the nature of the demon inside them? Among all the tens of thousands who make their living as chefs, there is a tiny minority that deliberately sets out to be the best among the best (or at least perceived as such), itching for those three stars and nothing else. But only twenty-five or so of them finally make it to the top of the heap. Call them what you will—aristocracy, all-stars, mad dogs, whatever—but they are all exceptional people who would surely have been equally successful in any other work they undertook. What they accomplish along their route is an extraordinary act of will, intelligence, and perseverance, because reaching that professional summit is as exhausting as it is fraught with obstacles, and is frustrating and frighteningly expensive to boot. Most normally constituted persons, sound of mind and reasonably aware of the body's need for occasional rest, wouldn't bother trying. Why bother, indeed, when a well-placed pizza parlor can bring in bigger and faster profits than a three-star palace?

Because any M.B.A. can run a pizza joint, a bank, or the International Monetary Fund, that's why. Obstinate chasers after the big brass ring, these characters are all obsessive perfectionists who want more than money. As much as fluttery terminology tends to be overused in relation to cooking, there is an aspect of art in their endeavors, a seeking of something more estimable and transcendent than the famous bottom line that rules our advanced Judeo-Christian societies. Such quixotics are rare, though. Of Bernard's fellow apprentices in Roanne, only he and Guy Savoy chose to run the body-strewn obstacle course. More reasonable, the others settled for less. Jacques Cète became a teacher in a cooking school, and is alive and well in sunny Menton with an untrammeled view over the Mediterranean. Bernard Chirent went to work for others, where the money was, mostly in the U.S. Jean Ramet limited his ambitions to the single star of the excellent little restaurant that bears his name in Bordeaux. Claude Perraudin was perhaps the most lucid of all. This is a man who learned *la grande gastronomie* at the feet of four of the trade's greatest masters—Jean and Pierre Troisgros, Michel Guérard, and Paul Bocuse (not even to mention Claude Verger, because Perraudin had cooked in one of the Barrières, too), but he resolutely turned his back on the search for any stars at all—too damn much trouble. Instead, he created Le Père Claude, the kind of unpretentious Parisian *bistrot* that everybody loves.* The place is not even mentioned in the

---

*Perraudin, a man capable of cooking up the entire gamut of exquisite *nouvelle cuisine* creations, unapologetically unleashes upon his blasé Parisian customers a down-home barrage of sausages, pâté, bouillabaisse, frogs' legs, steaks, and roast chicken, pushing his temerity to the point of serving the latter with mashed potatoes, if you can imagine anything as *démodé* as that. But the place is packed, and the *président de la république* has to elbow his way in to get to his favorite, the peasant specialty called *tête de veau:* calf's head, containing every unspeakable element except the eyeballs.

Michelin at all, but Perraudin was well rewarded for his perspicacity. The restaurant is full, lunch and dinner, every day of the year.

"I always kept my feet on the ground," he explained. "Bernard was more of a dreamer. But Saulieu turned out to be something of a poisoned gift for him."

Down in Saulieu, the dreamer could have had a much easier ride by taking the same tack as Perraudin, sticking with the great regional specialties of Burgundian cooking and contenting himself with one or two stars. But he couldn't do that. He couldn't make the itch go away. He had to go for the big prize: three stars or bust. It very nearly was bust, too, because the risks he took in later years were greater than any of his contemporaries would have contemplated. But even in the days when he was just Verger's employee, and hardly concerned with the financial side, he was already monomaniacally intent on tracking down Michelin, seizing it by the scruff of the neck, and loving it to death.

"When a nicely dressed gentleman would come for lunch alone," remembered Claude Le Gall, "he told us to go out and check his car to see if the tires were Michelins. That wouldn't be proof, but it could be an indication, anyway. Sometimes, when we weren't sure which car he had come in, he would have us going through his coat pockets in the *vestiare*, to see if the keys might identify the car."

Le Gall was an important element of Bernard's early career at the Côte d'Or. Hired as waiter in March of 1978, exactly a year after Michelin awarded the first star, this Breton was a stripling of twenty-three when he arrived in Saulieu, the first of the young dream team of dining room personnel that was soon to become the envy of all of Bernard's *confrères*. Both within and outside the restaurant, Le Gall shared the experience of growing to professional maturity under a boss who was a mere four years older than himself. (With that slightly anachronistic but still elegant formalism that characterizes so much of French society, he never would have dared to address his boss with any term but "*Monsieur Loiseau*," in spite of the proximity of their ages, and in spite of *Monsieur Loiseau*'s often childish behavior.) Like the rest of the staff that would be coming in over the following years, he rapidly succumbed to the unique and disconcerting new style of captaincy that Bernard had invented: leadership by wild, unbridled enthusiasm. Never had the *méthode Coué*—"Every day, and in every way, I am becoming better and better"—been applied as indefatigably and effectively as at the Côte d'Or under Bernard Loiseau.

"On est les meilleurs!"—"We're the best"—was the house mantra under Bernard, and anyone who didn't come to sincerely believe it soon realized that there was no place for him in Saulieu. Bernard's incessant cheerleading was totally successful, too. There were two reasons for that: first, the staff he hired after the departure of Dumaine's and Minot's grizzled veterans was young and impressionable, with an innate idealism that was just waiting for the chance to vibrate to the call of a charismatic leader; and secondly, he really meant it—the guy was utterly sincere.

And then there was the flip side of the mantra, the only other one that existed within the hallowed walls of the Côte d'Or: *"Vous êtes les meilleurs"*—You're the best. When Bernard turned it around like that and directed it at his kitchen crew or dining room staff, there was not a one who did not soak up the ardor of his enthusiasm and the positive reinforcement that he lavished on them. No one, whether employee, guest, or passing observer, who ever spent more than a few minutes under the Niagara flow of Bernard's volubility—punctuated by those characteristically sweeping gestures, those big, glistening brown eyes, and that enormous Halloween smile—can forget the charm that the man exuded: direct, primary, muscular, right-now charm, impossible to escape and phenomenally persuasive. When Bernard was "up," he could wring a grin from an ayatollah, or make a Puritan elder dance a jig. And he was "up" 99 percent of the time.

This, then, was the new personality that he imposed on the staid old barn in Saulieu, the force that motivated his staff far more effectively than the rigid hierarchies and military-style rule-by-terror that traditionally obtained within the French restaurant establishment. And it worked beautifully. Banks lent him great sums of money against all reasonable expectations of return, and not even Fortress Michelin could resist the incessant assaults of his enthusiasm. In 1981, only five years after Monsieur Trichot had grudgingly admitted that his place was a restaurant after all, Bernard was rewarded with his second star. The third would come, too, sure as the earth turned and the sun rose. It was written, and that was all there was to it.

With the second star, the media leaped onto the Bernard Loiseau story with even greater passion. The talented kid whom Verger had led out of the kitchens of the Barrières was now receiving journalists in Saulieu like the lord and master of the house. The press came for the free meals, of course, and, for many of them, entire weekends of sybaritic rustication, accompanied by their girlfriends/boyfriends/mistresses/dogs, or whatever. It was all on the house, but the arrangement was far from being a one-way street. Like all great *aubergistes*, Bernard truly loved receiving people and loved seeing them enjoying the microcosm of pleasure that he was able to wrap around them. For the time being it was Verger who was footing the bill for all those nonpaying guests, but Verger was a canny old fox who knew all about Bernard's powers of persuasion. Never mind about a few rooms, a few bottles of wine, and a few slices of foie gras: The press would cough up nice articles about Saulieu, and that was worth a fortune in free publicity.

And cough up they did, too, because Bernard Loiseau was a terrific story. He was bright, funny, energetic, and astoundingly articulate. He had started from nothing and come from nowhere to earn his place among gastronomy's budding elite. He could always be counted on for the striking quotes and colorful analogies that all reporters love, and just in case they hadn't heard, he repeated for them the story about Jean Troisgros swearing to become an archbishop. Great stuff.

"It was a regular procession of journalists," Le Gall remembered. "A lot of them came down on Friday evening at ten P.M. and didn't leave until after breakfast on Monday. Once we had a guy from the radio station Europe 1. They had this promotion where he drove around in his Renault R16 painted in the orange and black Europe 1 colors, broadcasting live from the car. He would drive up behind cars and announce their license plate number. If they were tuned in to Europe 1 they would hear him, pull over, and win an envelope full of money. Europe Stop, they called it.

"Over lunch he told Monsieur Loiseau he could set up a Europe Stop for his chef, Dominique Hensch. 'You take your car and head off on the A6 toward Paris, and I'll come up on you,' he told Hensch. 'When I interview you I'll ask you where you work, and then you can say Bernard Loiseau and the Côte d'Or. Make sure you say it loud and clear.' They went off and we all gathered in the kitchen with our transistors. In a few minutes the Europe Stop came on. 'I'm just leaving a village called Saulieu,' he said, 'and I'm following a car with the license number so and so. Does he hear me? Ah! He's got his turn signal on, and he's pulling over. Now, be careful, *monsieur*, just park your car and come right up to our radio car.

"'Congratulations, monsieur, for staying tuned to Europe 1 and winning our Europe Stop. Could you tell us your name, and where you're coming from?'

"'Dominique Hensch. I'm coming from Saulieu.'

"'I see, and what is your line of business?'

"'I'm a cook at the Côte d'Or, the restaurant of *Bernard Loiseau*.'

"The guy kept the interview going for a few minutes just to be sure, and Hensch must have said *Bernard Loiseau* ten times. Monsieur Loiseau was ecstatic. 'Hey, can you believe it, guys,' he kept repeating— 'we're live on Europe 1!' When Hensch came back, Monsieur Loiseau told him to make sure to share the money out with all the kitchen staff. That's the kind of guy he was."

In a situation like that, who was using whom? Certainly the media freeloaders never had to crack their wallets, but as long as Bernard had them under his thumb in the dining room they were a captive audience, trussed up like a *poulet de Bresse*, ready to be overwhelmed by his food, his gab, and his charm. The situation might have made an interesting conundrum for moralists to debate, but on site, nobody gave a damn—both sides were enjoying the free ride, the great cause of gastronomy was being served, and Bernard was discovering that he rather enjoyed the twentieth-century invention of image building.

"Image is everything," cried the young André Agassi as he bounded around the world's great tennis tournaments in his flowing bleached hair and psychedelic outfits, and Bernard had concluded the same thing even earlier. Agassi was not a star yet, though, so the one Bernard imitated was the Swede, Björn Borg. Le Gall recalled the afternoon when he casually mentioned that he was going to play a little tennis on the Saulieu municipal courts with some of the guys, and perhaps Monsieur Loiseau would like to join them. Sure, said Bernard. I'll see you down there.

"We were still warming up when he arrived. He had two new sport bags, four of the latest rackets, five pairs of shorts, maybe ten or fifteen T-shirts, three pairs of shoes and one hundred balls—he didn't know how to play, but he had emptied the Saulieu sporting goods store! He played maybe three times, then dropped it and gave the equipment to the guys. That's the way he was—he had constructed in his head this image that he wanted to become. He wasn't there yet, but Bernard Loiseau had to be *someone*, and that required some adjustments. So if he played tennis, he had to be outfitted like a star. Other times, he would send me to Autun to buy his socks and underwear, because it didn't fit his image to do it himself. Chef Bernard Loiseau didn't walk into a local store and ask for underpants. That just wasn't done."

The underpants-and-socks chore is a classic of Côte d'Or lore, and others after Le Gall were charged with the same mission. When he put their purchases on his person, along with all the rest of the clothing that went with them, he was fastidiously neat, with every pleat or crease pressed razor-sharp and shoes as shiny as the day they had been bought. Whenever a waiter or *maître d'hôtel* accompanied him to Paris for some business meeting or professional function, he underwent a preliminary inspection—shirt freshly pressed, tie in place, shoes glistening—by the boss before being permitted to join the expedition. In the kitchen, Bernard changed his tunic and apron several times a day if the least spot troubled their brilliant white surface.

Like everyone else who worked under him, Le Gall looks back at his Saulieu days with a curious combination of nostalgia, disbelief, and affection, suffused with the kind of feeling that makes a man smile and shake his head at the same time. "His self-image was out of all proportion, but he was the nicest guy in the world. Out of the blue he would throw us the keys and say, take my car to Dijon and go see a movie. He was incredible—we could ask him for anything, he was so generous. He genuinely liked to please people and make them happy—not just the guests, but us, too. But at the same time he had this grossly inflated self-image. We would look at him and say, this guy's nuts, but then when we saw what he managed to accomplish, and how he had all these journalists and photographers and showbiz people following him around like puppies, we had to admit he wasn't as crazy as all that. You always take geniuses for nuts, don't you?"

Bit by bit, brick by brick, encouraged by his showbiz friends and abetted by the stream of flattering articles in the press, the image of Bernard Loiseau the innovative genius and *grand chef* took on detail and shape until it became unassailable, waterproof, and fire resistant.

Le Gall was on duty one quiet afternoon after lunch when he was startled by an engine roar and a squeal of brakes as a flashy Porsche drew up at the front entrance and a stranger burst in, shouted *bonjour*, strode straight into the kitchen, and began cooking himself lunch.

"I had no idea who that excitable little character was, but he seemed to know what he was doing. I went upstairs and woke up Monsieur Loiseau from his nap. It turned out the guy was Jacques Maximin,* who had two stars at the Négresco Hotel in Nice in those days. A little later, when the kitchen staff was getting ready for the dinner service, he was kidding around with Monsieur Loiseau and he shouted out to the whole brigade: 'Hey, guys, doesn't it bother you to work for a chef who doesn't even know how to make a béarnaise or whip up a mayonnaise? Come on, Bernard—make us a béarnaise!'

"That didn't faze him a bit. '*Je t'emmerde*' [roughly: Screw you], he said. 'I don't know how to make a béarnaise or whip up a mayonnaise, but I'm still the greatest!'"

There it was. The image was in cast-iron—a great chef can always hire a technician to make a mayonnaise. Don't bother me with details. The comparison with Mohammed Ali springs inescapably to mind. No one will ever know for sure how much of the bluster in each of the men was real and how much was whistling in the dark—but Ali did knock out George Foreman, and Bernard did win three stars. Also like Ali, Bernard never hid his thoughts or his purposes—or anything else, for that matter. The man was an open book. Bernard would have been the world's worst spy, because he couldn't keep a damn thing secret, neither his chagrins nor his joys. From the day he first met Claude Verger he laid himself wide open to snickering by announcing his three-star ambition, and he shared that ambition every day with his staff in Saulieu, never tiring of reminding them of the goal they were chasing together. Withal, in winter, the cruel season, when the angling rains turned to sleet on the Morvan plateau, and the sleet to mushy snow, it must have been excruciatingly hard to maintain the fire of that relentless optimism.

---

*A daring and intensely creative chef, Maximin now has a two-star restaurant, bearing his own name, in the pretty Provençal town of Vence, 23 kilometers above Nice.

"He would pep-talk us about those three stars even as he was gnawing at his nails and looking out over the lace curtains at the empty street," said Le Gall. "I remember one winter day when we had no clients at all for lunch and only one for dinner. And do you know who it was? Guy Savoy, who had come through Saulieu to pick up his son from a skiing vacation. On days like that, even the most solid of men must get depressed and wonder what in hell he's doing in a place like that."

When he was feeling the stress of overwork, Claude Perraudin had an infallible remedy for the big-city blues: He would hop onto his Harley hog and rumble peaceably on down to Saulieu, where Bernard was sure to greet him with an icy bottle of champagne, feed him his best creations, put him up for the night, and generally treat him like royalty for as long as he cared to stay. It was rarely for more than twenty-four hours—Perraudin's own place needed attention, too—but reciprocating properly was almost impossible, because Bernard's visits to Paris were always rushed, nervous, and filled with one appointment after another. But still he made a point of visiting Le Père Claude, shaking the hands of his kitchen personnel, grabbing a quick bite, and leaving a big tip.

"He would look around the place and ask me, '*Combien de couverts?*,'" said Perraudin—How many customers today?—"He had that wistful look, because it was obvious that my place was full while his was empty. But then he would cheer up when the clients smiled at him. 'You see that? They recognize me! Don't they?'"

To a certain extent, that recognition, the fruit of his love affair with the press, compensated for his own lack of customers: That always boosted his morale. The certainty, even as he was gnawing his fingernails, that his image was one of glory and triumph helped soothe him through those miserable winter months. Strength and joy returned with the leaves and the sun of springtime.

"We just waited for summer to come around," said Le Gall. "When it did, we took advantage of it as much as we could. After the famine, it was the feast. We never turned away a client, and we put them everywhere—in Dumaine's dining room, in the entryway, in the halls, in the winter garden. Sometimes, when there had been an accident and the autoroute was closed, the A6 became like the old A6, and they detoured traffic through Saulieu. Then there were plenty of customers.

"Monsieur Loiseau was incredible, super generous. I saw him take in these young couples—kids who didn't know anything about the sorts of prices we charged—and give them lunch for nothing. 'I'm proud to see young people interested in French gastronomy,' he told them. 'You are my guests.' Sometimes this generosity could make problems, though. Once he told me to lend my car to a journalist from Channel Two, because his wasn't free. She ran it off the road and ended up in a field. Monsieur Loiseau was embarrassed about that and apologized to me."

What were the guests eating in those days? As the seventies turned to the eighties, Bernard's cuisine was still in transition, but he was beginning to sing a lot of his own songs. His roast lobster on a watercress puree was straight Verger from the Barrières, his vegetable terrine recalled the famous *terrine de légumes "Olympe"* of Pierre Troisgros, and both the *feuilleté d'asperges aux écrevisses* and the *tarte légère aux pommes* harked straight back to the *pâtissier*'s legerdemain of Michel Guérard—even if, in occasional moments of rhetorical transport, Bernard would claim unwarranted fatherhood of that celebrated little masterpiece. There were interesting adaptations, too, taking a fellow chef's idea for a certain ingredient and shifting it to another. In Roanne he had watched Chef Jean and Chef Pierre go through the delicate steps of their *tomate à la tomate*, a surprising, quirky little dish in which tomatoes were sautéed, then cooked in the oven, and finally stuffed with cream and a mixture of chopped tomato, garlic, onions, and aromatics. Bernard conceived of a dessert based on the same principle of redundancy: *orange à l'orange*, the fruit slowly cooked in syrup and served with slivers of its own candied skin over a sharply flavored orange *coulis*. For the classics, he continued to offer items like Bressane chicken in a tarragon cream sauce, foie gras terrine, and the banal but eternally popular sliced Morvan ham.

But Bernard was thinking, and *le style Loiseau* was peeping up from under the layers of the classics and the borrowings: perfect preparation of perfect ingredients, light, fast, undisguised, recognizable for what they were and easily digestible. His warm salad of mixed greens and sweetbreads went with a vinaigrette redolent of nut oil; he served fat turbot slices with quickly sautéed *cèpes*—mushrooms; river trout cooked in a *court bouillon* and stuffed with a vegetable *julienne*; and there was his old favorite, the *gibelotte*—fricassee—of rabbit, but now accompanied by buttery cabbage leaves rather than the turnips that had the gourmets salivating all over Clichy. His *bavaroise* of artichokes with a puree of fresh tomatoes was as light and attractive as his fricassee of vegetables with lemon grass—*citronelle*—and *GaultMillau* labeled his varieties on the theme of crayfish "phenomenal." (His devotion to the little critter that he had so enthusiastically trapped with Rémy and his father during summer vacations in Messeix was a Proustian reflex that never left him.)

But Le Gall recalled most particularly three other dishes, because each one in its own way was a precursor of the full-blown symphony of *le grand style Loiseau* that would be coming in later years: *soupe d'escargots aux orties; bar au jus de truffe*; and *sandre au vin rouge à la moelle*—snails in nettle soup; sea bass with truffle juice; and pike perch with beef marrow in a red wine sauce.

The first dish—*soupe d'escargots aux orties*—is probably the most significant, because it tells volumes about Bernard as a person, a cook, and an entrepreneur. Ardently determined to make a name for himself but still under the influence of the thrifty traditions of his native Auvergne, he decided to reinvent nettle soup, an old peasant classic that his mother had occasionally made at home, as did thousands of other penny-pinching housewives. Young nettle shoots from the top of the plant can be treated exactly like sorrel, softened in butter to make a vegetable dish accompanying meat or, if meat is lacking, simply with potatoes. More commonly, though, the shoots are cooked in water or *bouillon* to make a cheap, healthy soup. (No need to worry—cooking destroys the formic acid that gives nettles their sting.)

Bernard was thinking. Pirouettes were turning in his head—creators love jokes, puns, plays on words, winks and nudges. To begin with there was the ancient regional specialty of *escargots de Bourgogne*, the fat snails that are perpetually enshrined in the pantheon of Burgundy cooking along with *boeuf bourguignon* and *coq au vin*. It would be right and proper to have snails on his menu, then, but how could he do them differently, in a way that would jump out and say hi to a Michelin inspector? He winked at tradition by making humble snails even humbler, presenting them in a peasant pauper's soup. He began by shelling fresh snails and cooking them on low heat very slowly (four or five hours) in a strong *court bouillon*. Set aside, they awaited the two-step confection of their bath: tender nettle leaves cooked *à l'anglaise* in boiling water, then quickly chilled to maintain their brilliant green chlorophyll. Puréed in a mixer and thinned out with *bouillon*, the soup was thickened to a velvety consistency with a mash of leaves cooked in butter and puréed. The final presentation had the snails reposing in an intensely green bath of concentrated essence of nettles, greener even than the buttery *persillade* of the traditional Burgundy recipe. It was a daring stunt for a restaurant that aspired to three stars, but it was funny and surprising—"I rehabilitated nettles!" he cried—and it became an instant hit. Within only a few months, all of France knew that Loiseau was the guy who went out into the Morvan fields and meadows with a begloved crew of waiters and *maîtres d'hôtel* to handpick nettles for gourmets.

With that little dish, Bernard may have been responsible for a great deal more than he could have suspected. After a few more years had passed it became apparent that with this little inspiration he had lobbed into the tranquil waters of high-level cookery a stone whose ripples would continue outward far beyond Saulieu. His nettle stunt set colleagues to thinking about the advantages—both in the kitchen and in the media—of hunting and gathering. One of the most widely publicized offshoots of contemporary French cooking, clamored with voice stentorian by the self-celebrating mountain maestro Marc Veyrat in Megève and Veyrier-du-Lac,* is the use of wild plants and herbs to astonish clients with flavors and combinations never heard of before. Married to a public relations professional, Veyrat built an extremely effective media campaign, complete with regional costumes and Disneyland-style accessories (notably a floppy black mountaineer's hat which never leaves his head, indoors or out), to advertise his system *urbi et orbi* as a fulsome new creed of natural cooking unique to him-

---

*Like Alain Ducasse with one restaurant in Paris and another in Monaco, Veyrat is a six-star chef. But whereas both of Ducasse's three-star places are open the year round, Veyrat closes his place in Veyrier-du-Lac when he opens up for the winter sports season in Megève. In essence, then, he is operating one restaurant that changes locale with the seasons. Ducasse is the only chef in history to run a pair of three-star restaurants simultaneously.

self, while scornfully dismissing the entire corpus of French classical cuisine as "has-been." Veyrat now has established a firm lock on the plants-and-herbs image, but there is another colleague who was there long before him, and with considerably less noise: the great Michel Bras. Son of a blacksmith in the little *aveyronnais* city of Laguiole, famous for its goat-horn knives, Bras is as genuine as Veyrat is hokey, a marathon runner and fanatic of nature and organic foods who spends long, contemplative outings roaming the lunar landscape of his Aubrac plateau in search of new surprises for himself and the customers of his wonderful restaurant, crowned by Michelin with three stars in 1999. He pioneered the use in cuisine of the local wild plants that thitherto had been known only for their medicinal and curative qualities— things like wild sorrel, meadowsweet, broom, purslane, and amaranth. Veyrat saw what Bras was doing, liked the idea, and ran with it, banging the drum as he went. But with his nettle soup, Bernard was the initiator, the first to bring the fields and meadows into *haute gastronomie*.

The second of Le Gall's list of Bernard's memorable dishes—sea bass with truffle juice—was typical of his mature cuisine. Truffles are ruinously expensive, and any restaurant's supply of the odoriferous little black tubers must be husbanded with great care. Profligate dishes like Paul Bocuse's *soupe aux truffes*, featuring big, luxurious slices of them, are relatively rare. But truffle trimmings, mere specks infused in water or *bouillon*, can give a depth of flavor that otherwise would be impossible without recourse to classical wine reductions, *fumets*, *fonds*, and the liberal use of butter, all of which Bernard chose to eschew (or at least limit) in his later years.

As for the *sandre au vin rouge*, it may have caused less of a stir at first than his little food joke with nettles, but it finally turned out to be a dish like Guy Savoy's truffled artichoke soup, the Troisgros brothers' salmon with sorrel, and Bocuse's sea bass stuffed with lobster mousse— an irreplaceable, ineradicable icon that he could never remove from his menu, even if he wanted to, lest gourmets denounce him for criminal behavior. Today, still, it is one of the two or three dishes most frequently ordered, an exemplary archetype of *le style Loiseau*.

And a beauty of a creation it is, too, as light and delicious as it is intelligently conceived and pleasing to the eyes: a blaze of gold and white on a background of deep crimson. Gold: the pike perch, a delicate

freshwater fish native to French rivers and lakes, is cut in generous un-
skinned filets and quickly seized in a hot pan on the skin side, turning
the surface to a luscious mahogany-gold color, then covered and finished over low heat. White: the pure, virginal flesh of the fish beneath
the skin. Crimson: the sauce—Bernard's famous *sauce au vin rouge*. By
itself, something of a little masterpiece, the sauce is a potent reduction
of red wine—strong, sun-baked wine from the south of France—seven
liters of the stuff boiled down to a single liter, tart, tangy, and thickened
to the consistency of blood. Too tart and tangy, in fact, obliging the
chef to finish it with a large, plump lump of fresh sweet butter, a last-
minute adjunction that balances the tastes just right. (Not even
Loiseau, the high priest of antifats, could entirely and always do without the magic of butter.)

He made an elegant variation on another great Burgundian classic,
oeufs en meurette, setting poached eggs on a bed of puréed onions and
slivers of smoked *lard* (the French cousin of American bacon), all of
which reposed on a glistening puddle of the same pungent red wine
sauce, ringed by tiny *tête de clou* mushrooms sautéed at the last
minute. And what might a young cook in Burgundy do with appetizers
to stand out from the crowd? Bernard constructed tiny bite-sized delicacies to send out with *flûtes* of the finest champagnes. Those guests
who looked closely enough discovered that what they were eating
was . . . pizzas! *Ah, mon cher, que c'est drôle! Que c'est exotique!*

Bernard was having fun. The French economy was doing well in
the eighties, and the restaurant trade prospered along with the rest of
the nation. Even with the gloom of the barren winter season, the Côte
d'Or was turning a good profit, because Verger was already charging
nearly as much as many three-star restaurants. Once again, his Barrière
formula was proving successful: everything for the food, the service,
and the staff, and to hell with the décor and the rooms—that was just
needless expense. But Bernard was beginning to see things differently.

Having passed his thirtieth birthday, he had matured as a cook and
a man; now the entrepreneur inside him awakened, as he tramped
around Dumaine's domain and imagined what he could do with it. It
was obvious that something *would* have to be done, and sooner rather
than later, because the Côte d'Or environment was on its last legs.
Henri Gault had famously described Bernard's kitchen as worthy of the

cargo hold of a Panama tramp steamer, while speculating that Loiseau would soon be moving to Beaune, Dijon, or Paris, where he could find an installation worthier of his talents. There was no garden, the façade giving out onto the main road was cracked, the halls mildewed and creaky, and the rooms cramped, ugly, and totally outdated for the last quarter of the twentieth century. Nor were there enough of them; during the well-frequented summer season Bernard was frequently obliged to send potential guests across the street to the bigger Hôtel de la Poste, instead of taking their money himself. Verger's formula of indifference to décor had reached the absolute limit.

There was no way, Bernard was certain, that the Côte d'Or could hope for three stars in its present condition. Ah, but he envisioned it vastly expanded, with a big new dining room, a new kitchen, and new rooms—no, *suites*—for the hotel, he could see in his mind's eye the silk purse he could make of it, a piece of paradise comparable to Troisgros or Bocuse—or, better yet, like Georges Blanc's place in Vonnas (which was rapidly mutating from Blanc's mother's little country inn Chez la Mère Blanc into the luxurious caravansary now proudly renamed Georges Blanc) and favored with a gratifyingly dispendious international clientele. Bernard ached for something like that. With his name in big fat letters up on the front of the building. He began pestering Verger to sell it to him. Later, Verger said. When you get married. You've got to settle down first.

There didn't seem to be much chance of that. Neither Saulieu nor the neighboring farm villages had produced any available women who attracted him and, being anchored to his kitchen by those imperious twice-daily services, he hardly had the chance to move in the Parisian circles where lightning might strike. And besides, there was that old thing of his shyness with the opposite sex.

"He was such a surprising guy," Le Gall said. "I remember a time when there was a lone woman among the guests at the hotel who Monsieur Loiseau liked the looks of. He asked us to go talk to her for him. We thought that was great—maybe the *patron* was going to get laid. We set her up for a date and she said OK, so he took her to a nightclub after dinner that night. Some of us went to the same club later and we found the girl all by herself, while Monsieur Loiseau was playing 421 [a dice game] at the bar. He never touched her. We finally took her back ourselves. He was very uptight with girls. He just didn't dare. That sort of thing happened two or three times."

But was it simply shyness? There's something more than academic hair splitting to the question, because the matter of a deep-seated, fundamental insecurity is something that all those who knew Bernard well, and were able to see through his smokescreen of optimistic bluster, wondered about all the time. Especially now in retrospect, when they reflect on the last six months or so of his life, those fatal months when whistling in the dark no longer worked, and he lost it.

There was not a trace of shyness when it came to promoting the restaurant and himself. Even before age thirty he was a boffo media hit, and in later life he became a true national celebrity, actively sought out by radio and TV producers when they needed a colorful character to liven up shows and broadcasts. No: there was something else, something more. Plenty of people more qualified than I have seen evidence of a fundamental, longstanding self-doubt in the mere fact that he felt the need for such endless self-promotion. Even mighty Michelin saw it.

"I was worried about him," said Bernard Naegellen, the *Michelin* guide's director before Derek Brown. "He was just too excessive."

As early as 1979 *GaultMillau* had been rating Bernard among the ten or twelve best cooks in France, and in that same year his Burgundian neighbor Jacques Lameloise won his third star in the town of Chagny, south of Beaune. The regional restaurant scene was beginning to look very encouraging, but it was neither toward Lameloise nor toward Marc Meneau in nearby Vézelay that Bernard turned for inspiration. His eyes were fixed on Collonges-au-Mont-d'Or, a little village just this side of the Lyon city limits on the River Saône, home of Restaurant Paul Bocuse. He had already decided that Bocuse and no one else was to be his professional and personal model.

In itself, this was a sign of excess, because Bocuse was—still is—an enormously important individual, the great national father figure of the French culinary scene, a presence that dominates the business like the Commandatore in *Don Giovanni*. With the passing years it became apparent that Bernard had fixated on Bocuse as both his idol and, in a curious way, his deathly rival. If ever he was to reach the summit toward which his soaring ambition was carrying him, sooner or later he would inherit—or take over—Bocuse's position as *chef de file*, symbolically killing him to become leader of the pack in a battle of personalities, like the famous battling kings imagined by Frazer in *The Golden Bough*. Farfetched? Perhaps, but Bernard was stubborn beyond belief once an ambition became an *idée fixe*, and even if he didn't reason it out in detail, the end result was this: He aspired to become Paul Bocuse.

Verger had heard his young *commis* announce a ridiculously cheeky three-star ambition, and trace a comparison between himself and Björn Borg. The only thing that interested him was being first; second didn't count. It was inevitable, then, that he would aim at the top, and Bocuse definitely was the top. But if supplanting Claude Verger in Saulieu was one thing, becoming Paul Bocuse was quite another matter.

We need a few words here to define Bocuse and his position in the French culinary establishment, because without understanding the phenomenon it is impossible to understand the scale of Bernard's ambitions. Favorite pupil and surrogate son of Fernand Point, Bocuse descends from a family of cooks in activity since the eighteenth century. Genetic modification takes longer than a couple of centuries, they say, but Bocuse's knowledge of food is so vast and his skill in manipulating it so adept that he appears to have sucked them all with his mother's milk. Born in 1926, he was making his preferred dish, *sauté de rognons*, in the kitchen of his father's restaurant at age nine, and was apprenticed at sixteen. From those earliest professional days it was apparent to everyone around him that he was headed for the top. He got there in 1965, when Michelin awarded him his third star, and his uninterrupted grasp on those stars ever since has made him the record holder for continuous years at the guide's summit.

But what is most remarkable about Paul Bocuse is not so much his longevity as his influence on the cooking trade and his fellow artisans. It is a toss-up between him and the Troisgros brothers as to whose restaurant first inspired the term *nouvelle cuisine* (there are various different accounts), but no one doubts who was the big personality of the movement, and who did the most to popularize it around the world. (When the movement spun out of control into a silly caricature, he distanced himself from it altogether. Now Bocuse cooks just Bocuse.) The man's quick intelligence, his often hilarious

wit, and immensely charismatic style led the way for a whole generation of chefs out of the servant class, where they had languished
since *ancien régime* days. Enfranchising themselves as owners of their
establishments, these artisans became model entrepreneurs at the
same time, the social equals to any of the capitalists for whom they
cooked and with whom they chatted after the *service* in their dining
rooms. So they remain today, whether they are self-financed like Bocuse, Guérard, and the Troisgros, or professionals in partnership
with outside financiers, like Alain Ducasse, Alain Senderens, or Pierre
Gagnaire.

If Claude Verger invited journalists by calculation, Bocuse did it by
the ancient instinct of the innkeeper, and all the world's press flocked
to Collonges-au-Mont-d'Or to hear his anecdotes, take in his explanations of cooking history and technique and, not incidentally, lay into
his *poulet en vessie, gratin de homard*, and *loup en croûte*. Unfailingly
he passed the good word and sent the media visitors into a circuit of
more free lunches and more explanations, history, and anecdotes in
the restaurants of his friends and colleagues, from one end of France to
the other. Bocuse was the first great educator of postwar French cuisine, doing more for its renown than all of his *confrères* put together. It
is not for nothing that Pierre Troisgros (no slouch himself) calls him
the man of the twentieth century.

When Bernard cried "I'm the greatest!" he was subconsciously
thinking: Someday I'll be Paul Bocuse. But that was a lot easier
thought than done. For the moment, he was at the point of cultivating
the great man, like a young actor hanging around an established star to
share in a bit of his glory, meet his contacts, and, accessorily, maybe
pick up a trade secret or two.

Half charmed and half amused by the overflowing vitality of his
ingenuous young *confrère* up in Saulieu, Bocuse adopted him into
the informal, protean grouping known as the Bocuse gang (*la bande à
Bocuse*), and before long the two men were telephoning back and
forth almost every day. With a few notable exceptions (Michel Bras,
for one), the great cooks of France are inveterate gossips, eager for
tidbits of news about their little brotherhood—who's in, who's out,
who's having professional or marital problems, who has come up with

something new* — and, for men who are sitting on top of the world, almost pathetically concerned about what people are saying about them. Even though shifting rivalries and jealousies are as common in this club as among starlets or fashion designers, there is a certain basic solidarity that springs to life where the food guides are concerned. The exact whereabouts of Jean Didier's red Lancia was known to every chef in every area he visited long before he drew up before any restaurant, of course, but where Michelin is concerned, this professional early warning system — *le téléphone arabe* — works double overtime. Bocuse is the world's heavyweight champion at smelling out inspectors and ringing the alarm bell.† For this, for his experience, for his enormous stature in the profession, and for all the other qualities that long ago inspired journalists to commonly (and only half jokingly) refer to him as *l'empereur*, Bocuse impressed Bernard very, very deeply.

"When Monsieur Loiseau heard that Paul Bocuse would be coming by for lunch on his way to Paris," Le Gall recalled, "it was like getting ready for a state visit by the *président de la république*. I never saw him more concerned about making everything perfect."

There's that adjective again. "Perfect" is a word that resonates incessantly around three-star restaurants, and none more so than at the Côte d'Or as Bernard charged along on his obsessive quest for recognition. That and its natural pendant, the other great house password, *"les meilleurs"* — the best. Although he had no way of realizing it, the autumn of 1980 was to be of signal importance to Bernard, because fate was preparing three momentous events for him: On avenue de Breteuil, the Michelin druids were preparing to award him a second star,

---

*They never stop. In his seventy-eighth year, Bocuse told me with real pleasure about a discovery he had made a few days earlier from an Italian cook: a new way of poaching eggs. (It involved swirling the water in a brisk counterclockwise direction.)

†Naegellen of Michelin savors the memory of a rare bit of one-upsmanship that he practiced on Bocuse. Taking advantage of a conference of the company's international staff, he played the part of an anonymous businessman in town for some anonymous meeting and sent no less than six inspectors together for dinner at Collonges. Like all his *confrères*, Bocuse is always on the lookout for *single* inspectors. This time he was flummoxed but good.

to appear in the 1981 edition; he made the acquaintance of a strikingly alluring, twenty-nine-year-old blonde divorcée named Chantal Lebras; and his *premier maître d'hôtel* hired an assistant.

As trifling as it may have appeared at the moment, it was this third event that proved to be of the greatest and most lasting importance to the future of La Côte d'Or. Hubert Couilloud, who came aboard as *second maître d'hôtel* in October of that year, was distinguished by flaming red hair, sparkly blue eyes, and a solid line of experience: hotel school, a stint at the Savoy in London, a few years aboard liners and cruise ships, and finally back to hotels in metropolitan France. At twenty-five, he was three years younger than his boss, and in character as calm and low-key as Bernard was volatile, but both men discovered that they shared the same kind of unyielding perfectionism. On a personal level, Hubert was to grow into Bernard's confidant and best friend in Saulieu. Professionally, he became by far the most important member of the noncuisine staff. What Loiseau was to the kitchen, Couilloud soon was to the *salle*.

Hubert is an interesting case, a first-rate example of the upward social mobility that the gastronomy business affords young people in France. Like most restaurant professionals—like Bernard himself, for that matter—Hubert was born into modest surroundings. Son of a farm family, he went to hotel school as a callow country boy, and depth, sophistication, and worldliness came to him in the elegant world of *grande cuisine*. As the shabby old Côte d'Or slowly mutated with the passing years into the magnificent Relais Bernard Loiseau, Couilloud's position as the boss's friend and top assistant made him, in effect, vice president of a business that totaled some sixty-five employees, with a turnover of several million dollars a year. As *premier maître d'hôtel*, he learned to move with skill and elegance in an environment peopled by clients who were usually rich, frequently famous, often high-strung, and occasionally impossible. He handled them all with ease, and the affably efficient service staff he built at Saulieu became much admired in the trade. It is very unlikely that Bernard could have built his success without Hubert.

It was a close thing, though: Bernard almost lost him right at the start. Hubert's hiring and his subsequent accession to power were both owed to his predecessor as *premier maître d'hôtel*, a man who became

briefly famous for a breach of professional etiquette so extraordinary
that it scarcely seems believable, putting Bernard and his restaurant
into deep hot water: The guy kicked a client in the ass.

It was Claude Verger who hired this choleric individual late in
1979 as the replacement for old Joseph, the last relic of Dumaine's dining room staff. A year later, he, in turn, brought Hubert in as his *second*. As much as he was a remarkable discoverer of kitchen talent,
Verger got it all wrong this time on the other side of the service door.
For reasons no one was ever able to fathom he gave his new *maître
d'hôtel* a higher salary than Bernard himself, the official *directeur* of the
establishment. Arrogant and self-assured, apparently taking his pay-
check as the token of hierarchical superiority, this former *maître* lorded
it over the rest of the staff, creating cabals and jealousies and paying little more than lip service to Bernard's orders.

Faced with a detestable and deteriorating atmosphere, Hubert was
ready to quit. Luckily for everyone, he decided instead to try to save
the situation. Taking one of his waiters with him as a corroborating
witness, he drove to Paris to warn Verger that the Côte d'Or was facing
disaster if he didn't get rid of the offending character. "I don't give a
damn about that guy," Verger barked. "Loiseau's the boss down there.
Let him work it out—but I don't want this to cost me any money."

What Verger was worried about was *les indemnités de licenciement*—
the painfully high compensation payments that France's labor laws require a boss to fork out to any employee he fires. The only way to avoid
paying the bundle of cash is to prove gross professional incompetence or
malfeasance. Which the *premier maître d'hôtel* promptly handed to
Bernard on a silver platter. God knows what got into the man's head to
perform such an egregious stunt, but Le Gall was right there when it happened, and he remembers the event vividly.

"It was in the spring of 1981. We had just won the second star, and
I was the waiter serving the gentleman in Dumaine's salon. He was
having the *aiguillettes de canard*, the duck we did in two servings, first
with peaches and then a green peppercorn sauce. The gentleman
called me over and said the duck strips were a little too firm, not
cooked enough for his taste. Naturally I told him we would change
them. I was about to take his plate back to the kitchen when the *maître
d'hôtel* came over and said: 'No—we won't change them!'

"I guess they must have had words earlier or something, but in any case he never got his duck changed. When he got up to leave after the meal he came over to thank me. 'Thanks to you, I have had a very nice evening,' he said. At that, the *maître d'hôtel* blew up. He yelled at me, said I wasn't doing my job right—and then grabbed the gentleman by the scruff of the neck, gave him a swift kick in the ass, and shoved him out the front door into the hedge. And Monsieur Loiseau was there— he saw it all, but he didn't budge. He was hiding behind the door!"

Poor Bernard. Big strapping guy, Ferdinand the Bull, afraid of girls—now this. All his life he had avoided confrontation, and this one was much too fast for him to do anything but stand there and watch, petrified with indecision. Within days Michelin was on the phone demanding an explanation. Bernard hid in the kitchen. Hubert went in to settle the matter once and for all. He found the boss calming his nerves by peeling asparagus, his favorite form of tranquilizing activity. This time the guy has to go, he told Bernard. It's either him or the rest of your dining room staff.

At last, at long last, Bernard reacted. Forcing himself into unaccustomed and unwanted aggressiveness, he charged out of the kitchen in an explosion of rage, gave the startled *maître d'hôtel* a Homeric dressing-down worthy of a marine drill sergeant, and fired him on the spot.

"Never, in my twenty-three years in the house, have I seen an outburst that could match that one," Hubert said. Without further delay Bernard appointed him *premier maître d'hôtel*. Now the way was finally cleared for the two men to team up for the attack on that third star they could already dimly perceive over the red tile roofs of Saulieu. Before the year was out, that strikingly attractive blonde joined the team. That proved to be a mixed blessing.

IX

A MARRIAGE,
AN ACQUISITION,
AND A BREAKDOWN

$\mathcal{T}$o hear Chantal tell it, that first meeting was like something from a Tex Avery cartoon: When Bernard laid eyes on her, his eyeballs popped out of his head and jets of steam shot out of his ears. Everything considered, that's probably not too far from the truth.

The time was late in the year 1980—September or October—and the place was Marc Meneau's restaurant L'Espérance (with two stars, going on three), a converted manor house in the idyllically beautiful setting of Saint-Père de Vézelay, 50 kilometers north of Saulieu. In those days Bernard and Meneau saw rather a lot of each other.* Their proximity made them almost neighbors, and they shared many similar ideas about cooking and many similar woes of clientele in the off-season. Meneau knew Bernard would be dropping by that afternoon, and he told Chantal he was going to introduce her to someone. Good, she thought. Maybe it'll be a new client. She was right, but it turned out to be rather more clientele than she had bargained for.

Chantal was quite something. Freshly divorced, she was a twenty-nine-year-old mother of two small children, and an exceedingly well-proportioned mother she was, too, with a perfectly coiffed blonde mane, flashing blue eyes, and a *soignée* manner as only French women know how to *soigner* themselves: not a hair out of place, not an accessory that

---

*As chefs, prima ballerinas, and operatic tenors often do, they had a falling out for reasons that remain obscure today, and it was never quite patched up.

didn't match, and not a square millimeter of her fetching visage that wasn't treated with exactly the right makeup, applied with a diamond-cutter's attention to detail—the sort of woman you would expect to see walking a small white poodle. And—*justement*—she did indeed have a small white poodle (its name was Sophie), but her line of business was somewhat incongruous for the rest of the image that she projected: She was selling janitorial supplies.

A native Breton, Chantal had come with her parents to the Allier region in the depths of central France when her father set up an industrial hog farm there. After ten years of marriage to a garage mechanic, she divorced and settled in the cathedral city of Auxerre, at the northern edge of Burgundy. She needed a job to support her husbandless little clan, so she took to the road, presenting a line of German detergents and industrial cleaning supplies to businesses and organizations. Which is how she came to be in Meneau's luxurious restaurant that autumn afternoon when Bernard Loiseau walked in.

"I was hardly knocked off my feet," she recalled. "But he was. He was *excité*—exhilarated—and he couldn't stop grinning—that marvelous smile of his that went all the way out to his ears. He was very, very nice and charming. He wanted to see me again."

It's not hard to imagine just how *excité* Bernard must have been. There he was, stuck in his provincial backwater for more than five years—five years of raging hormones backing up with nowhere to go—no girls, no play, no fun, nothing beyond card games and *pétanque* with the guys, and just the occasional unsatisfactory stab at the odd seduction or two that never worked out. For years everyone had been telling him that no matter how good his food was, the only way he could get three stars was to have a wife and family, because Michelin prized stability. And now, suddenly, here was this . . . this *dreamboat*, with a ready-made family! As if by magic, nearly three decades of being shy with girls disappeared in a flash. *Come to Saulieu, come to Saulieu, I'll buy every damn box of soap you've got in the car*. That was the gist of it, anyway. Yes: Steam certainly did come out of his ears.

Chantal played it cool. Rebuffing the flurry of dates that Bernard suggested over the following days, she finally accepted a meeting a week and a half later. She crossed the threshold at the appointed hour carrying her samples and wearing her business face, but it was a very carefully prepared business face. After a cursory examination of the Côte d'Or's needs in the way of sanitary equipment, the real meeting began: Lunch with the boss.

"He had everything set up in the little pink salon next to Dumaine's dining room, where we could have privacy. I got the red-carpet treatment—Hubert and Claude Le Gall to wait on us, nice wines, everything. Oh, *mon dieu, mon dieu*, I thought, I'm not going to get much business done today.

"Bernard never stopped talking. He told me his life story. He knew lots of things about me, too. Obviously he had been asking Marc Meneau questions. He wanted me to taste everything. I'm always very careful about my figure, so I don't eat much, but that day I had to have salmon and scallops and crayfish, because I told him I liked seafood. It was clear that he was interested in me—for him it was love at first sight [*le coup de foudre*]. But not for me."

For the next year and a half, Bernard courted Chantal as assiduously as he had been courting Michelin. But in the world's overcrowded and ancient history of the battle of the sexes, this little provincial chapter was strictly no-contest: Chantal was in charge all the way, as much at ease and confident in her feminine allure as Bernard was excitable, inexperienced, and groping. As if she didn't already hold all the trump cards, she noted that he had "an enormous complex" about losing his hair. (By the time he was into his thirties Bernard was almost totally bald, except for a ring around his temples.)

She made him wait—which, of course, only increased his excitability. In the great sexual equation, as any economist could have told Bernard, there's trouble ahead when the demand side outstrips supply so thoroughly as to be totally out of whack. Bernard did what he could to boost his side of the equation, in his own way. Unsurprisingly, this meant not poetry or music or long, soulful conversations, but lunch—lunch and dinner, too, when he could get away: Bocuse, Blanc, Ducloux, Lorain, Savoy. Nothing but the best. Oh, yeah, great: more foie gras, more crayfish, more champagne, more fattening desserts. Just the thing for winning a woman who watched her *ligne* like a junkyard dog watches his favorite 1983 Pontiac. Certainly there was the pleasure of sporting an emphatically decorative woman on his arm—excellent for the Loiseau image—but Bernard received precious little return for his emotional investment.

"He wanted to get married right away," she explained. "He scared me sometimes. Every single day he asked me again to marry him, but I kept putting on the brakes. He would have done anything for me, he was so much in love. But I wasn't in love with him. I had to think it over. After all, I had two children. But his melancholy touched me. He gnawed his nails until he drew blood. He was so impatient—he wanted everything, and he wanted it right away."

There's no melancholy like the melancholy of love. Poor Bernard was in deep water way over his head, a feckless amateur in *le jeu de l'amour*, chasing a woman far more experienced than he, who neither loved nor respected him. Recipe for disaster.

And yet she married him. Whether it was by his phenomenal force of persuasion, by calculation for the welfare of her two kids, or by simple fatigue from repulsing his assaults again and again, Chantal finally said yes. In June of 1982, Jean-Pierre Soisson, mayor of Auxerre and a prominent national politician, married the couple in a formal salon of his city hall. True to his word, in October, Claude Verger sold La Côte d'Or to his ex-*commis*, now a thirty-one-year-old chef with a growing national reputation, a flashy new wife, two stepchildren, and plenty of ideas. Verger's style remained typical to the end. Keeping banks out of the transaction altogether, he financed Bernard himself, gaining about 50 percent on his initial investment, plus 10 percent interest. "Pay me back whenever you can," he said, symbolically handing over the keys.

This was the situation at the end of that summer of 1982, as the Côte d'Or headed into another gloomy winter season: Bernard had two Michelin stars and was riding hell for leather toward the third, with a kitchen personnel of eight under his direction; a like number of service staff worked under Hubert as first *maître d'hôtel*, and a few local cleaning ladies and a laundress filled out the complement of employees; Chantal was in charge of the front desk, the rooms, and the decoration; and Bernard had a debt (probably at least $300,000 and perhaps as much as $500,000, but since it was a private deal, no figure has ever been given) to pay back to Verger, on his own terms and in his own time.

In that last decade of *les trente glorieuses*, France was still prospering and the restaurant trade was doing well, so there looked to be reasonable cause for optimism—all the more so in that Bernard discovered that a jewel had fallen into his hands. His name was Patrick Bertron, a calm, reserved Breton of twenty whom Verger had hired just the previous March. Starting in *pâtisserie* and then moving on to the delicate, demanding seafood post, Patrick was already displaying a prodigy's mastery of cooking technique but also, more important, an extraordinary ability to grasp Bernard's often imprecise inspirations and translate them into finished dishes. Bernard quickly named him *second*, and the dialogue between the two men—the Chef and the chef— continued uninterrupted thereafter. Bernard the idea man never failed to pay tribute to Patrick the technician. "Patrick cooks Loiseau better than Loiseau," he frequently told the press, and it was nothing but the truth. On the downside, the Côte d'Or was a wreck, but it was Bernard's wreck. From the moment of acquisition, he devoted his entire salary, and every other franc he could squeeze from the business, to paying Verger back in monthly installments over a four-year period.

Well, almost every franc. There was this thing about cars. For years he had lusted to have a Porsche like Meneau and Maximin, and while he was still courting Chantal, a secondhand beauty had come to his attention. He snapped it up. Porsches are excellent for the image. They're also ruinous for the pocketbook; completely apart from the purchase price, the little beauty cost a bundle to maintain—the insurance bill and the yearly registration fees were killers, and its mere presence on the road was an open invitation to every ticket-happy traffic cop. For once just a little bit reasonable, Bernard sold it to a client not long after his marriage.

In its stead, he bought a snappy, whippy 16-valve VW Golf GTI, and had a *garagiste* soup it up with a turbo to make it as speedy as the Porsche. That operation blew two motors. He gave up the race-driver image and settled for a black bourgeois BMW. No sooner was it delivered than Chantal ordered an identical one for herself. Hubert and the rest of the guys exchanged significant glances and shrugged their shoulders. What was going on here? They were supposed to be on an economy drive. Madame Loiseau, it appeared, was something of a spender. Bad sign.

Now that the Vergers had liberated the space, the freshly minted couple moved into their apartment above Dumaine's dining room. It wasn't much: a bedroom, a small living room, and a bathroom. Chantal requisitioned two of the hotel rooms for the kids and set to redecorating the place, drafting waiters and *maîtres d'hôtel* into hard labor as they came available. Most notable among her corps of volunteers were Hubert Couilloud and Eric Rousseau, a local boy who had come aboard as *chef de rang*—headwaiter*—the year before. Along with Claude Le Gall and Vincent Jousset, a *chef de rang* hired way back in 1979, Hubert and Eric formed the vanguard of Bernard's little army of *personnel de salle*, a tightly knit team of auxiliaries (or helpers, or associates, or assistants, or mates—finding the right word to describe their status is almost impossible, because working alongside Loiseau, they were anything but simple employees), all of whom were passionately devoted to following Bernard's quest for perfection and making those three stars happen. Stakhanovites for the cause of *luxe, calme et volupté*, they would have been the despair of any self-respecting union shop steward because, to a man, they would have walked through fire for Bernard and not charged overtime.

How could that happen? Everything about Bernard confounded the precepts of management theory, and yet he proved to be an astonishingly effective leader, motivating his people to a pitch of shared enthusiasm that was unparalleled anywhere in France. And it wasn't as if he was dealing with simpletons. Au contraire: for the most part these young men were of superior intelligence—thoughtful, perceptive, and articulate—and they all knew very well that Bernard was a human encyclopedia of weaknesses and failings. He was impossible, unstable, self-indulgent, emotional, impulsive, confabulating, confounding, often craven and childish, and a host of other unflattering adjectives, too. And yet they marched in lockstep with him all the way

---

*There is a problem of terminology here. If American usage equates headwaiter and "maîtred'" as one and the same, French *grands établissements* make a distinction between: *premier maître d'hôtel* (clearly the boss outside the kitchen); his assistant, the *second maître d'hôtel*; the senior black-jacketed waiters called *chefs de rang*; and the white-jacketed *garçons de table*, almost invariably young beginners. *Chef de rang* might also be translated as "captain," but the term "headwaiter" reflects their seniority and (relative) authority.

to the end of the road. It's difficult to explain. Nothing was ever simple with this man.

"We worked miracles for him," said Hubert. "We did ten times more for Bernard than we would have done for anyone else. He gave us ambition. He made us believe anything was possible. Every day he pumped it into our heads that we were the best and we were going to make those three stars—let's go, guys, you're the best. We finally ended up believing it. It was a permanent stimulation, an obsession."

Eric Rousseau smiled at the contradiction of it all, enjoying the memory of a thousand anecdotes that typified the Loiseau style. "He was naïve and paranoid, but at the same time he was generous and intelligent—and just so damn nice that we would forgive him for everything. Sure, he took himself for Napoleon, but he was our leader and we were with him all the way. If he yelled at us, he would come up afterward and apologize. Don't pay any attention to that, he'd say—you know, that's just the way I am. So he was the locomotive and we were the cars behind him. And you know something? We've always referred to the restaurant as *chez nous*—our place. Home. Even when we're in our own houses today we say such and such a thing happened *chez nous*. Our wives don't always appreciate that. But we were like a little family—especially when we had two stars and were angling for the third. That was a fantastic period."

While their fellow *maîtres d'hôtel* and headwaiters in Paris passed their time sliding suavely around in tuxes and shiny shoes, then, in Saulieu the guys were mostly wearing *bleus de travail*—the French version of overalls—for the first two winter seasons of Bernard's ownership. They painted Dumaine's old rooms, patched up holes, changed mattresses, fixed electricity and leaky faucets, and generally scrubbed, polished, and shined the old place up to some semblance of its past glory. Clients were rare, so they had plenty of time. When perchance some gourmet turned up unannounced, one or two of them would hurriedly dive into formal clothes and handle the *service*. Then it was back into the *bleus de travail*, with Bernard cheerleading at the sidelines.

It was heroic stuff, but everyone knew it was just make-do, what the French call *cache-misère*—covering up the poverty of it all. Dumaine's rooms were tiny, claustrophobic, and dark; the carpeting was motheaten and the toilets were those awful things called *gyrobroyeurs*—

noisy bathroom Dispose-all units designed for boats and trailers that don't have proper piping for a decent flush. (You don't want to know more than that.) And just to make things perfect, the rooms all gave out onto the road, where motorbikes sputtered and trucks shifted gears.

Never mind: Bernard had a master plan in his head. It had been there for years, in fact. If he could just get enough loans, and if he could buy some adjoining properties—notably a big old boarding house facing out on the rue Jean Bertin—he could replace Dumaine's twenty-four rooms with thirty magnificent suites, all of them turned inward toward the English garden that he would be planting in the courtyard, now just a vacant lot with some ratty old sheds. That would eliminate the noise from the street to create the *calme*. The *luxe* would come with the furniture and appointments of his future salons and dining rooms, and the *volupté* from his cuisine and his fine wines.

As Bernard dreamed of his Burgundian Abbaye Thélème, the earthly paradise of refined pleasures that Rabelais imagined in *Gargantua*, the year 1983 was preparing a series of events, omens, and portents that affected him in significant ways, throwing the dice of his destiny toward unexpected directions. The most immediately dramatic was the sudden death of Jean Troisgros, his master and inspiration but also his nemesis. Only fifty-seven years old, Jean died on a tennis court in Roanne. Examination pinpointed the cause as a coronary aneurysm, but all those uncounted hours standing in the heat of his stove and the permanent tension of making those twice-daily services perfect had to be a contributing factor. Just a cursory look around the Rhône-Alpes area shows that Jean shared his woefully short existence with some remarkable peers. Certainly Fernand Point had a weakness for champagne, but death came far too early for him all the same at only fifty-six. For Alain Chapel it was fifty-two, and Jacques Pic, fifty-nine. An even more striking example—more distant, this one—is Gilbert Le Coze, a handsome young Breton chef who took Paris by storm in the early seventies, then moved his restaurant, Le Bernardin, across the Atlantic and did even better in New York. Gilbert died in his forty-eighth year while working out in a health club not far from his West 51st Street address. Stress, overwork, and mad perfectionism can make a deadly cocktail.

In the spring of 1983, a scholarly, soft-spoken Alsatian woman named Dominique Brunet passed her CAP (Certificat d'Aptitude Professionnelle) of cuisine in Paris. It was only the most basic of diplomas of the cooking trade, but Dominique, just thirty, had no intention of becoming a chef. As a teacher (applied food sciences and hygiene) in a Parisian technical *lycée*, she already held twin masters degrees, in biochemistry and microbiology; one she had earned in Strasbourg and the other in Paris. She took the CAP in order to add a practical, hands-on knowledge of cooking technique to her long theoretical training. She was also author of three standard textbooks on hygiene in restaurants: There wasn't a food bug, a molecule, or a temperature factor on which Ms. Brunet could not learnedly discourse. People around her often said she would be the ideal wife for a cook. Fate was setting her up for a meeting with Bernard a few years later.

Also in 1983, the little food empire that Henri Gault and Christian Millau had built began to unravel. In the wake of a falling-out between the two friends, the guide and the monthly magazine were sold to the news weekly *Le Point*, and the title quickly went downhill thereafter. What had begun as a lively, original, contentious little competitor to the *Michelin*, reflecting the personality of two genuine journalists, mutated with the years into that ghastly corporate category of an "editorial product" with little but the names Gault and Millau to lend it credibility. After *Le Point* lost interest, the title was sold again and again. At last count, six or seven different owners have picked it up, the last being a French conglomerate (nickel mines, supermarkets, and vineyards) headquartered in New Caledonia, which promptly outsourced the operation to a public relations outfit. Now compressed into a single snappy brand name, *GaultMillau*, it continues an editorial existence, but there is little of the sparkle of the grand old days. With Henri Gault dead, and Christian Millau comfortably retired and writing history books, the title they founded is progressively drifting toward irrelevance.

The final significant event of 1983 was the departure of Claude Le Gall. In itself this was not a big problem—although he was very much appreciated, another competent person could be found—but it had unforeseen consequences. Claude left because his wife had found a job in Paris. Characteristically, Bernard called around and arranged a position for him as *maître d'hôtel* in one of the top restaurants in Paris.

Then he went looking for a replacement. That was where the unforeseen consequences arose.

Bernard remembered a *maître d'hôtel* with whom he and Chantal had spoken when they had dinner at a restaurant in nearby Semur-en-Auxois some months earlier. He was experienced, very capable, and spoke fluent English and Italian. He was married and had a kid, so he would surely be stable. On top of all that, he was handsome, too. That ought to please the ladies. He was, Bernard insisted, just the right one to replace Claude. Chantal shuddered inwardly, because she remembered that dinner in Semur-en-Auxois all too well; it was there that she had felt the ominous jolt of attraction, the *coup de foudre* that had been so notably absent for her in Saint-Père de Vézelay. And now he was coming to work in her place.

Today, now that so much water has passed over the dam, the "*maître d'hôtel*" is an established and yet shadowy figure of the folklore of La Côte d'Or. He is anonymous—no one even speaks his name around the premises—and referred to elliptically, as if he were not so much a person as the instrument of some preordained, dimly perceived destiny that had been awaiting them all. But the result was this: He and Chantal began a long, secret love affair. (Or one they believed to be secret.)

"We waited a whole year before our *liaison* began," Chantal told me, "and then we were able to hide it very well for two years. We had a house where we met, and several other places, too, but we never actually set up household together. We lived out our passion. But I finally broke up with him. He stayed with his wife. *C'était la vie.*"

Today, Chantal speaks of her affair with the nameless *maître d'hôtel* in terms that recall airport novels, as if it were fated and she had no choice but to yield—star-crossed lovers and all that—but her conviction that she managed to keep it secret is delusional. The close daily contact of the illicit couple with Hubert, Eric, Vincent, and the others could not help but betray a host of tiny hints, expressions, eye contacts, and subtle intonations of voice that pointed unmistakably to the intimacy she was sharing with the newcomer to the dining room crew. As usual, then, everyone knew about it except the husband. And no one dared tell him.

Considering the extraordinary symbiosis existing between Bernard and his staff, it was hardly surprising that their feelings toward Chantal should have reflected the state of her relationship with the man who was her husband and their boss. What began with warmth and good will slowly degraded into animosity.

"She didn't have much of a cultural level," Hubert said, "but that didn't matter, because she was a hard worker and very ambitious. We could appreciate that. Right from the start she pushed Bernard to buy the place from Verger and then to get the loans to fix it up. We could see that as a couple they weren't doing too well, but they shared the same ambition. Their characters were very similar, in fact. Both of them had strong outgoing personalities, but she became pretentious and started acting like a typical *nouveau riche*. She was obsessed with her appearance, so she was always dieting. When she first came here she was in jeans, but very quickly she started playing the queen and buying expensive dresses. We didn't like her. We liked her even less when she was yelling at Bernard out in front of clients, and then running off right and left to be with her lover. We were *au courant*, of course, all of us. But Bernard said nothing."

"Chantal wasn't cool with Monsieur Loiseau," said Claude Le Gall, summing up the atmosphere he left behind in Saulieu. Like Hubert, Eric Rousseau was struck by the similarity of characters of the boss and his new wife, but the allegiance of the staff was entirely to Bernard, not this woman with the white poodle who knew nothing about the restaurant business. For his part, Bernard hadn't known anything about living with a woman. With Chantal as his professor, he was fast learning that it wasn't as simple as all that. The shared ambition was fine, but where that implied the wielding of power, sparks soon flew and the disputes became more and more frequent. The staff watched and waited for it all to come to some kind of climax, as it surely would have to one day.

Headstrong, demanding, and sure of herself, Chantal never expressed regret for the thoroughgoing act of infidelity into which she threw herself so soon after marriage. As she explains it today, it is as if the simple fact of living with Bernard was enough of a trial to justify her cuckolding. (The far-reaching and long-lasting influence of Flaubert's *Madame Bovary* on French womanhood should never be underestimated.)

"Of course I was unhappy," she told me. "Living with Bernard was like living with a kid. With him I had a third child to deal with, and he did as many stupid things as my own two kids. He wasn't a woman's man. Physically it wasn't right between us, either. He wasn't a man who could make a woman happy."

"Chantal was Bernard's apprenticeship for women," Eric remarked, drawing a nice parallel between matrimony and gastronomy. "Trouble is, she got a big head—she wanted to be his equal. And in a place like this, there can only be one rooster ruling the coop. Things got worse and worse. Mind you, he wasn't easy to live with, either. But toward the end we could see it was almost hatred between them. Bernard was just too nice. She took advantage of him."

Trop gentil, trop généreux—too nice, too generous—the leitmotif returns again and again when those who knew him best speak of Bernard today. However difficult it may have been to live with his impetuous, mercurial nature, the distressing fact is that during his marriage to Chantal the only quarter from which he regularly received affection was his staff.

"Il m'a aimée," she says today—he loved me. But she never says "I loved him." The conclusion is pretty much unavoidable: During the Chantal days, at any rate, Bernard's only true marriage was to his house, his ambition, and his staff. And, ironically enough, it was a very good union, too, with an interplay of communication and cooperation that would have delighted any marriage counselor.

"Bernard had no secrets from us," said Hubert. "He involved us in everything. Whenever he had a decision to make he consulted everyone, even the dishwasher. Everything was paradoxical about him. Strength and weakness cohabited in him. He catalyzed us by his energy and enthusiasm, but at the same time he was invaded by self-doubt. If one customer out of eighty was unhappy with his meal, it could destroy the whole evening for him. He didn't need approval, he needed to be *adored*. Unanimously. And we did love him, too, in spite of his weaknesses. Or maybe we loved him because of his weaknesses. He was just so fragile and so human. A lot of people who didn't know him well enough were skeptical about his sincerity because they felt he was always play-acting, and doing a number on them. It's true. He did that. But it was only because he was trying to please them.

"More than anything else, he loved to make people happy. In all the senses of the word, he embraced everyone. Relationships with him were always strong—nobody could be indifferent to Bernard. He was a fundamentally good, warm person. He reached out to people with that native generosity of his. But he was also a great actor, so—yes—you can say he did do a number on people. He was playing a role because he wanted to make them happy. To seduce them."

He didn't seduce Chantal. With both his enthusiasm and his anxiety, he irritated her. Strangely, even his niceness irritated her. There was this quality about Bernard: he exasperated because he tried too hard. On paper, he had every quality a woman could desire: he adulated Chantal; he didn't run after other women; he took in her children as if they were his own. But he irritated her.

"He was very, very nice with my children," she admits, "and at the same time he put me on a pedestal. When I was coming down the stairs he would cry out to the staff: 'Look at my wife—isn't she beautiful?' He kept telling me I was his third star. It was hard to deal with that. He took me for his guardian angel.

"And he could be so childish. He didn't know how to shut up. When we were at dinners I always made sure to sit next to him so I could kick him under the table when he started saying stupid things. He multiplied everything by two. I used to give my kids fifty francs of pocket money a week, but then Bernard would slip them a five-hundred-franc bill. We really had a big fight about that. Then there was the thing about our diet. I was putting on weight, and I absolutely had to slim down. He was gaining weight, too, so I suggested that we both go on a diet. Well, I stuck to it and I lost those extra kilos, but not Bernard. He snuck off and ate roast chicken and French fries with my kids when I had my back turned. He was just like a kid."

Being idolized and lavishly complimented while her children were affectionately cared for might strike many women as an enviable situation—so much so, perhaps, that they might even be persuaded to forgive the occasional unauthorized fried chicken whoopee—but for Chantal it was just further evidence of the many crosses she was obliged to bear in Saulieu. And that wasn't all—Bernard wasn't a good businessman, either. Chantal couldn't stand the friends and cronies, all those journalist freeloaders and showbiz types who were eating for free. They put such a drain on the budget, she calculated, that she and Bernard could have built a beautiful duplex room in the hotel for the price of what those "guests" ate up during her time in Saulieu. Who needed these people, anyway?

Bernard did, of course. To cheer him up by their mere presence, for the notoriety that their articles gave him, for the reassurance that he really was a great chef, and for the jokes, the warmth, and the affection—much of it quite real—that flowed between him and these gastronomic courtiers who came so easily and frequently to Saulieu. Chantal was quite right: Bernard wasn't a woman's man. He was impelled, first, foremost, and entirely, by his three-star ambition and, within that, the easy camaraderie of the guys. He was never so happy as when he was off duck hunting or wine tasting or eating out with his friends in some low-life country bistro. No emotional strings attached to all that. He already had enough emotion to deal with all by himself.

There was plenty more on the way, too, but that lay several years ahead. For the moment, the overriding priority that occupied everyone was whipping their white elephant into something resembling three-star shape. In May of 1984, some nine months after his ill-judged hiring of Hubert's *second maître d'hôtel*, Bernard made another decision, a good one this time: He engaged Bernard Fabre to take over the accounts of the Côte d'Or. With that, he essentially handed the entire business side over to a man he hardly knew.

On the surface it was a foolhardy move, but as usual with Bernard, there was a certain method in the madness. He was lucid enough to know that he was no good with figures and percentages and regulations, and that even if he tried, he would be so bored and impatient that he would surely make a botch of it. Verger was clever with that side of things, but now Verger was gone. Bernard would have to get it done some other way. Meneau told him he had an independent accountant from Auxerre working for him, a man named Bernard Fabre. Bernard gave him a call, and they agreed to a meeting at Saulieu at nine the next morning.

At nine sharp, Bernard stood by the front desk as an unprepossessing, dark-haired little man wearing a purple jacket and an expression of pained anxiety pushed open the door. "*Bonjour,*" he said. "I believe we have an appointment."

"No," said Bernard. "I'm expecting an *expert comptable.*"

"But I am Bernard Fabre. I am the *expert comptable.*"

Bernard did a brief double take, laughed, and ushered the visitor into his office. "But why did you say you didn't have an appointment with me?" Fabre wondered.

"Because *experts comptables* are supposed to be old and fat and balding," said Bernard. True enough, Fabre was none of the above. Just a couple of years older than Bernard himself, Fabre had arrived in Auxerre from Montpellier, deep in the south of France, where the chewy, gargly, syllable-compounding *méridional* accents are so thick that occasionally the speech can sound almost like another language. Fabre was marked for life as a southerner by that accent, but it did nothing to diminish the acuity of his gift for juggling figures on the little calculator that he carried with him at all times, and which he whipped out of his pocket at the slightest provocation.

It is a curious, if decidedly minor, fact of history that Fabre had come north not for business but for a reason that would baffle anyone who had not spent a few months in the south of France: he was fleeing the wind. Along with golf courses, a heavy population of old age pensioners, and a few million immigrants from North Africa, the French Midi is characterized by the seasonal winds that endlessly vent their aggression on the land and the people: the *mistral* and the *tramontane* from the north, the *sirocco* and the *largade* from the south and the *levant* from the east. Some people can take it and others can't. "The wind that sweeps down from the mountains will drive me mad," sang the *méridional* poet Georges Brassens in his interpretation of Victor Hugo's poem "Gastibelza." His words weren't in jest. Fabre traded the warmth of the south for the chillier but still air of Burgundy, where he could calculate in peace.

Fabre spent the rest of that morning with Bernard and Chantal discussing how to finance the remodeling of the entry hall and building the first ten of the thirty new rooms and suites of Bernard's dream master plan. Bernard insisted that they must not be just ordinary, comfortable hotel rooms, but beautiful and beautifully appointed individual retreats, each one different from the others, small architectural works of art in themselves that would be worthy of the elite "Relais et Châteaux" category: *luxe, calme et volupté,* indeed. By the time they wrapped up the meeting, Bernard was aboil with enthusiasm.

"You look to me like a good guy," he announced. "Now you've got to have lunch with me." There spake the spiritual grandson of the man who told Robert Doisneau that no one could leave Point's place without eating lunch. At table, Bernard had a final test for his visitor. Segregating one small green element from the tiny vegetables accompanying the braised sweetbreads, he lifted it on his fork and asked: "Do you know what this is?"

"Wild asparagus," said Fabre instantly. "I've been picking them for years."

"*Toi, tu es un bon!*" Bernard exclaimed with delight. "*Je t'engage*" — you're a good one—you're hired. So there it was: done deal. Essentially, Bernard was betting his financial future on the basis of asparagus identification, but why not? Considering some of the triumphs of corporate judgment that in later years would be navigating a few enormous world-class multinational companies onto the financial rocks, a chef's gut instinct was probably as safe a bet as any high-flown boardroom strategy session. Fabre immediately opened a dossier on the first major renovations of the Côte d'Or since Dumaine's days, and stood at Bernard's side with his trusty calculator as he began negotiating his first bank loans. Nearly twenty years later, by the time they had completed the master plan to bring the Côte d'Or and its parent company, Bernard Loiseau S.A., to the final glory that he had imagined for it, Bernard would have laid his hands on just under 90 million francs (about $15 million), nearly a third of which came from the audacious unprecedented stock-market operation with which he was to cap his hustling for funds on the last day of 1998.

"In life you've got to know your limits and bring in people who know how to do what you can't do yourself," Bernard told me just as he was about to begin construction on those ten new rooms. "My wife is doing the decoration because that's something she knows about. For all the money side, I have my financial expert, Bernard Fabre. A cook can't handle everything himself."

He was getting organized. It was clear that the kid I had known in the Barrière Poquelin had matured. Once he had decided that he trusted Fabre entirely, Bernard gave him carte blanche to handle the details of the money side. He took the bit in his teeth for everything else and charged ahead full speed. Ironically, although the years 1982–86, the Chantal years, slowly deteriorated into tears, recrimination, and divorce, they proved to be richly productive for him on the professional level. It was during this period that *le style Loiseau* flowered into a fully developed philosophy with its clearly delimited goals, rules, and techniques. Blissfully ignorant for most of this period of the horns growing atop his bald pate, Bernard was bursting with a new confidence, and the three stars were no longer a chimera but a prize he could almost taste. Nothing demonstrated that confidence better than the new identity he had stamped on his place. Certainly motorists arriving from Paris would see the familiar name La Côte d'Or on the left wing of the building's face, but far more prominent, between the second and third floors, was the yard-high black cursive script: *Bernard Loiseau* and, twice as big as that, directly over the arcade of the main entrance, a huge reproduction of the curlicue *"BL"* logo that every waiter wore on his jacket lapel. The old Côte d'Or was his version of L'Hôtel Moderne, and he was effecting the same symbolic change that Jean-Baptiste Troisgros had made in Roanne when his boys took over the kitchen. But, lacking a Jean-Baptiste of his own, he acted like Napoleon at his imperial investiture and put the crown on his head himself.

"That's deliberate," he told me. "People outside of the country know La Côte d'Or much more than me. I did this on purpose for the media, so that they'll speak about Bernard Loiseau. And that's what's happening. These days you've got to personalize. You can be the best cook in the world, but no one will come if they don't know about you. I've got to fill this place up, because Saulieu's been forgotten for twenty years. When I go by the dining room and see just fifteen clients, I get the hell away from there, it depresses me so much. But I've got eighty reservations for tonight—I've already got a hard-on."

With his full-court press of personalization, Bernard was marching directly in the footsteps—once again—of his idol Paul Bocuse. The phenomenal force of Bocuse's personality had always attracted the media like bears to honey, and he had never feared to further underline his

presence by ringing declarations, huge signs or—supreme gesture of
carefree brashness—having the entire façade of his restaurant painted
in polychrome hues of scarlet, green, orange, and gold, as brilliant as a
medieval illuminated manuscript. "Everybody knows that God exists,"
Bocuse never tires of saying, "but the preacher still rings the bell."

And God knows Bernard rang his bell, too. When he made it peal,
it resounded in explosive little bursts of onomatopoeia: *Schlak! Vlan!*

"It's got to be a splendor in the mouth," he was saying. "An explosion of taste. *Paf! Toc!*"

The year was 1984, and Bernard was doing his sales talk on me. I
was buying it, of course, like anyone else who ever found himself in a
one-on-one situation six inches away from that human high-pressure
zone in the white chef's tunic, with that big, round, strong-chinned
face looming forward behind that huge smile, as arms windmilled and
fist smacked into palm to further underline what was already hyperbolic. The man was quivering with energy, so vibrantly enthusiastic, so
happy to be given the opportunity to explain himself, and so obviously
sincere that you felt a positive churl if you didn't agree with him instantly, didn't bitterly denounce Michelin for continuing to withhold
the third star, didn't marry him, didn't shake your head over the injustice of Jean Troisgros's archbishop remark, didn't do twenty push-ups,
or whatever other cause he might have been arguing for. If Bernard had
been in his father's shoes, he would have sold baby clothes to a Trappist
monastery.

He was explaining *le style Loiseau* as he marched me double-time
around his installation, showing off the improvements already completed—"pretty good, huh?"—and those that would be coming as soon
as he could persuade the banks to spring for the further millions that he
had asked for. Everything had a reason and a logic, and he wanted—he
needed—me to know that what he was applying in his kitchen was
nothing short of a revolution.

"We've got a new style of cuisine here, and it's all based on the
quality of the produce. If you're willing to pay the price, you can get
the best ingredients in the world, and with modern transportation you
can get them faster than ever. In the old days the seafood arrived three
days late, so cooks had to disguise the taste. Now we get everything
within twenty-four hours, and you can have the real taste of what they

are—*schlak!* Cooks got so accustomed to hiding the taste of the ingredients that people didn't really know what they were eating anymore.
Here I give the clients the pure tastes, the *essences* of the ingredients.
There's no sauce with my *langoustines rôties au chou*, just the prawn
and the cabbage, and they taste like what they are. It explodes in the
mouth—*clack!* When I serve salsify or celery root, you get the real taste
of salsify and celery.

"You should be able to recognize what you're eating, so I don't
deglaze with wines or alcohols, because that would change the taste.
No thickening of sauces with flour or egg yolk, either. No cream, no
fonds, no *demi-glaces*, no *fumets de poisson*, no fats at all except for a
little bit of butter when I sauté things, then I pat it off with paper
towel—there's no restaurant in France that uses as much paper towel as
we do here. When it comes to making a sauce, the other guys reach for
their pots of *crème fraîche*. Me, I reach for water. Water's the best thing
in the world. It's completely neutral, so it exactly adopts the taste of the
ingredient. You get the real taste—*paf!* Clients don't want to eat cream
anymore. Here you can eat lunch and still have an appetite for dinner.
I'm turning things upside down. In ten years everyone will be wanting
to eat this way."

It didn't quite turn out that way, but the basic idea underlying his
reasoning was perfectly sound. Big tummies were definitely *out* in the
last quarter of the twentieth century; people wanted to be slim and
were worried about cholesterol, too, so nonfattening, easily digestible
gastronomy was the way to get customers flocking to Saulieu. For this,
he would marry the best of what he had learned from his three masters,
Troisgros, Verger, and Guérard. From Troisgros, classical French
recipes with a light touch. From Verger, super-rapid, last-minute treatment of highest quality ingredients. From Guérard, his own variants on
the prestidigitation of *cuisine minceur*.

In fact, *le style Loiseau* wasn't all that revolutionary. Bernard's
menus were replete with classics of French cuisine, and more specifi-
cally the great tradition of Burgundian cooking, but it was all dramatically lightened up. Since he was excessive by nature, though, his
dedication to the lightness crusade could occasionally lead him
astray. For a few of his developmental years, Bernard became identified as the Kim Jong-Il of *la cuisine anti-sauce*, a Dear Leader manner

of absolutism that didn't always go over too well with the hungry general public. A red mullet pan fried *à l'unilateral*—on one side only—and served with a dangerously vapid deglazing with water and a thin puree of chervil might have pleased a professional restaurant critic because it was light, unusual, and absolutely free of fattening agents, but it could also shock uninitiated customers paying prices that were already hovering near the three-star range, and who had been expecting a memorable chowdown in return for their money.

A dish like this offered a pertinent illustration of an important but little understood phenomenon affecting the world of *haute gastronomie*: Professional critics are not necessarily always beneficial to the restaurant trade and the wider eating public on which the trade relies. To begin with, these worthies can be just as opinionated, capricious, and self-important as any other mortal invested with a bit of power—there are no scientific guidelines for the very personal act of judging food—and, secondly, they sit plumb in the middle of the Seraglio Metaphor: too much of a good thing. As a result, their preferences do not always necessarily jibe with the best interests of their readers. Their unavoidable, besetting problem is that they live in permanent danger of getting the blahs over wonderful food. So regularly are they fed with it that they are frequently fed up with it, too—right to the gills. After a few days of packing away, for both lunch and dinner, a succession of the most divine creations that eager chefs can thrust at them, even the hungriest *chroniqueur* can become weary and sated. A surfeit of champagne, foie gras, truffles, crème brûlée, chocolate, and all the rest of the groaning board begins to appear as an aggression to the organism. The gourmets are on overload. What should be pleasure becomes agony; they're not hungry anymore.

Certainly Henri Gault and Christian Millau were gifted, discerning analysts of French gastronomy, but their stomachs and their livers were often crying out for surcease as they plied their curious trade, and it is fair to pose a simple question: To what extent did the canons of *nouvelle cuisine*—the tiny, decorative portions, the evanescent sauces, the frequently precious and silly creations on huge plates—develop because these guys had the flagging appetites common to their profession, and were begging for mercy? For his part, Bernard was embarked on a constant crusade to please the critics who wrote the articles and awarded the stars. (Michelin stomachs, too, could tremble at the assault of two feasts a day, and the famous *crise de foie*, the most French of diseases, lurked just around the corner for all the professionals.) Consciously or not, Bernard was aiming his cuisine at the media's opinion molders, and almost without exception these were Parisian sophisticates, weary veterans of the gastronomic wars who had seen it all, whose belts were feeling tight around the tummy and who were yearning for something delicate to nibble on—something like a little red mullet on a soothing splash of chervil purée.

But was this the right kind of cooking for the Burgundian *bon vivants* living in the vicinity of Saulieu, or for passing food fans who splurged a couple of times a year for an expensive but wonderful dining experience? Clients of this sort had the right to expect a sumptuous feast, not a dietetic demonstration. For the most part they would look indulgently upon a bit of butter and cream and *demi-glace*, because they tasted great. They might not always understand or care about the philosophical underpinnings of a little red mullet.

Eric Rousseau remembered a clearly disappointed client early in the Chantal years who approached Bernard as he stood at his habitual post by the front desk, where the bills were paid and where he was accustomed to receiving compliment after compliment. This gent was a good deal more forthright than the timid soul who had dared suggest mellowing out the taste of celery root puree. "Alexandre Dumaine would turn over in his grave if he could see this cuisine," he grumbled.

His dignity affronted, Bernard mounted his high horse, made *le grand geste*, tore up the man's bill, and asked him never to set foot in La Côte d'Or again. It was surely a satisfying moment for his ego, but it was not wise. Too many customers treated too haughtily can rapidly set off a chain reaction of comment that runs like lightning though the esculent grapevine, causing damage to a reputation that's hard to undo. Even the greatest of chefs have to learn to swallow twice before barking back—and, to his credit, Bernard did. When Hubert reported more perplexed reactions to certain dishes that appeared too sparsely Calvinist and some sauces too watery, Bernard backed off and allowed the succulent richness of traditional French cuisine to flow back in.

He had only to think of Jean Ducloux, his predecessor by nearly half a century at the Côte d'Or, to be reminded of the joy that the great masses of normal customers, who do not share the spoiled-brat privileges of the full-time gastronomic professionals, experience in partaking of real classical French cuisine. When things were really bad in Saulieu, when the weather was down, the wind was whining through the cracks of his old barn, and the clients were little better than ghosts, Bernard's greatest morale booster was to grab Hubert and a couple of the guys and rush on down to Tournus, where since time immemorial Ducloux had been serving the cooking he had learned under Monsieur Racouchot in Dijon and Monsieur Dumaine in Saulieu. And there, even as they were looking forward to homicidal postprandial combats of *pétanque* and *bélote*, they would devour Ducloux's *pâté en croûte Alexandre Dumaine*, his perfect sautéed chicken, and his inimitable *quenelles de brochet*, confected of ground pike flesh, eggs, beef marrow, and suet (the thick white fat that encloses beef kidneys).

"All those pansies down in Lyon make their *quenelles* with *panade* [a mix of flour, eggs, butter, and milk], but I do it the old way, the right way, with beef fat!" Eyes blazing defiance from beneath his high *toque* and ill-fitting black wig, Ducloux would put up his dukes and proclaim the superiority of his method to anyone who wondered how he achieved the fantastic flavor and consistency of this absolutely unique dish. Pure beef fat—how perfectly shocking. Until he retired in 2004, Ducloux was probably the last cook in France to dare to cook with anything as dietetically incorrect as suet, but he knew something that the doomsayers of the flaxseed crowd will never know; its texture was perfect, and so was its taste. Call it irresponsible, call it a health hazard, but there was an honesty and nobility to Ducloux's old-style cooking that no kiwi soufflé could ever achieve.

Bernard could not have agreed more enthusiastically as he wolfed down his portion of *quenelle* and slathered his bread through the last drops of *sauce Nantua*. Alas, this kind of gastronomic daring was not an option for him in Saulieu, not when his whole sales pitch was predicated on light cooking. Still, within the bounds of *le style Loiseau*, he did himself proud with his *côte de veau fermier*. Michel Piot, at that time the restaurant critic of the daily *Le Figaro*, labeled it as simply the best veal chop in the world, ever.

To begin with, it was huge: Bernard cut the meat as far as possible to either side of the central rib, flush against the two adjoining ribs, in effect using the meat of three chops to make a single one of outsized proportions. He seared it in a hot pan, browning its surface and sealing in the juices, finished the cooking in the oven for ten to twelve minutes, set it aside to repose for ten more minutes, then returned it to the oven for a last quick moment, just long enough to glaze its surface with a strong veal "juice."

The preparation of what Bernard called his juices—whether veal, beef, lamb, or fowl—was something of a gastronomic profligacy in itself. He sacrificed prime cuts of each sort of meat by cooking them separately in a big *sauteuse* and removing the grease before deglazing them with water. He then transferred the sacrificial meats to a second receptacle and continued the cooking, with water and aromatic herbs, for several hours, until they had rendered up everything they had to give, in the form of a rich, syrupy essence, or *jus*—juice. Forty kilos of veal, for instance, yielded no more than five kilos of *jus*, but the flavor, the color, and the texture justified the sacrifice. It was with this *jus* that he deglazed the pan in which the veal chop had cooked, and with which he also brushed its surface for the final decorative glazing in the oven. This procedure—deglazing with juice from the previous "sacrificial" deglazing—he called *cuisine à deux temps* (two-stage cooking); the sauce that ennobled the chop and accompanied it to the dining room was the product of this double deglazing, bound and thickened with foie gras. The result on customers' plates may have resembled other veal chops they might have consumed, but rare, indeed, were those who could guess at even a fraction of all the fussy, painstaking steps the chops had gone through before being set down before them. It was spectacularly good, spectacularly deep in taste, and as free of nasty, indigestible fats as human culinary ingenuity could possibly devise.

"Okay, guys, let's go—we're the best. We're going to knock them on their asses tonight!"

It was with variations on this theme—exhortations as passionate as a college football coach before a big game — that Bernard began the *service* each day, lunch and dinner, during the high season of the warm months, when the roads were clogged with travelers and the Côte d'Or's dining areas filled to near overflowing. Every kitchen worker, from Patrick Bertron, his newly promoted *second*, all the way down to the lowliest *commis* and *apprenti*, had the same three-star goal etched into his brain, because Bernard never let them forget it. His disconcerting inability to hide anything was paralleled and balanced by a constant process of consultation. His practice of asking everyone's opinion on everything, right down to that of the dishwasher, would probably have resulted in a chaos of undisciplined jabbering under a different kind of boss, but with Bernard it meant a permanent dialogue. By its simple human contact, this dialogue built the ideal kind of synergy that professors with retroprojected charts try to teach in business schools; everyone around Bernard felt implicated in the life and the success of the Côte d'Or. Over the years, the staff's complicity with Bernard developed into a bond that was as much personal as it was professional.

Pierre Loiseau recalled an evening in the eighties when he dropped by Saulieu unannounced. Bernard hustled him into the kitchen like a master of ceremonies, spread his arms, and announced: "*Les gars — mon père!*" — hey, guys — meet my father. "*Bon soir, monsieur,*" they all shouted in return, as courteous as all French young men and women have always been taught to be. The father was touched by the son's gesture, but more significant for the Côte d'Or was the demonstration for the personnel that they were important enough to be introduced to the boss's close family. Gestures of this sort were never known to Bernard's guests, but they, too, formed a part of *le style Loiseau*. Where the Troisgros brothers continued the trade's ancient tradition in commanding through terror, Bernard invited his underlings into the family and even his own life. He didn't know how to do it any other way.

"I was surprised," Verger said with unfeigned admiration many years later. "He didn't do it like any of the other chefs, but he turned out to be an excellent leader of men."

During the *service*, Bernard conducted his orchestra from the traditional position of the Chef: standing at the *passe* — the stainless steel platform where he received waiters' order chits, and where the freshly prepared plates were set down beneath his eyes for a final once-over before being confided to the waiters again for delivery. It was there that he was at his most impossibly and tyrannically perfectionistic because if there is anything that sends a great chef into transports of Homeric indignation, it is the sight of an imperfection or disharmony so infinitesimally slight as to have escaped the attention of all his colleagues down the line, those who have been preparing the plate that has now reached its ultimate point of judgment before disappearing into the dining room. If Bernard Naegellen of Michelin admiringly compared Bernard Pacaud to a dog, he would have needed to consult a new bestiary to find a fitting description for Bernard in those crucial years when his second star was in hand and he was stalking the third. Something between a hawk and a tiger might do it: a griffin, perhaps.

"Mon pauvre ami, ça ne vaut pas trois étoiles." Those big brown eyes might have been moist with compassion, but he would have bounced the sweetbreads or the pigeon all the same, right back to where they came from, if his laser eye found a single atom out of place.* "My poor friend, that's not worth three stars," he would say, and he did—over and over again.

Bernard reacted that way all the time, whether he was referring to a pillowcase, a piece of furniture, or an ill-placed slice of truffle, and he said it with the implacable righteousness of a drill sergeant on inspection who can tolerate a toothbrush only when it is perfectly aligned north by northwest. The same unbending rigor was applied in the dining room, of course. If for some reason—the call of nature, the call of business, whatever—a client left the table just as a dish was set down in front of him, Hubert would order the plate returned to the kitchen, not to be kept warm but to be made all over again. You do it right. You either want three stars or you don't.

Once the *service* was well under way and Bernard was satisfied that

---

*Niggling of this sort is par for the course at this level of gastrofanaticism. Marc Meneau in Vézelay says he sends back at least a dozen plates a day. He was rewarded for his stubbornness when, in 2004, *Michelin* gave him back the third star that they had removed in 1999.

his assistants had the rest of the meal well in hand, he habitually
ducked out of the kitchen for a look into the dining room. Unlike many
of his illustrious peers (Bocuse, Georges Blanc, the Troisgros brothers),
he never entered the dining room to mingle with his guests, for fear of
interrupting their enjoyment of the meal, lest the two or three minutes
of his presence at tableside lower the perfect temperature of the pigeon
or the turbot. Standing bareheaded (he never wore a *toque*) in a corner
at the edge of the door, staying carefully out of the way of the to-and-fro
flow of waiters and *maîtres d'hôtel*, he cast an anxious eye from table to
table trying to divine, from facial expressions, from the speed of fork
and knife, from activity of the waiters, whether the clients were satisfied. When he saw a plate carried out only half consumed, he rushed
into the kitchen in its wake like a lawyer after an ambulance, and pep-
pered the waiter with questions: What did he say? Why didn't he like it?
In other words: What have I done wrong?

.That anguished query inhabited Bernard down to the marrow and,
I daresay, it lingers within some intimate recess of most his fellow
Frenchmen, garrulous and self-assured as they are on the surface, but
stricken with doubt and anxiety in the profound depths of their national soul, down there where the snakes of guilt crawl. Through all the
masses, confessions, and catechisms, the shut-ups and the hold-
yourself-straights of their childhood, French kids get the shameful, sin-
ful state of their base humanity ritually hammered into their little
heads. Bernard, with six years of living under the thumb of the priests at
Massillon, got it in double-strength doses. And just in case there was
ever an odd day when he managed to feel clean and virtuous, there was
always good old Original Sin lurking around the corner. No matter
how hard you try, you're still screwed by heredity, straight from Adam.
Guilty as charged. Saint Paul himself said so. Idealist and perfectionist,
but self-doubting behind his gasconade bluffs, Bernard was a perfect
patsy for culpability.

It worked on him twenty-four hours a day. Every afternoon and
evening, when the *service* was finished and the apprentices were beginning the twice-daily cleaning of the kitchen—scraping, rubbing, hos-
ing down, and mopping until it sparkled like a detergent ad—Bernard
ritually folded his apron into the same obsessively neat little rectangle,

wrapped the strings around it just so, and stashed it on the stainless steel shelf space that was his alone. Then he'd walk out and post himself by the front desk to socialize with the departing clients. After years of practice he learned to conceal his anger and indignation if ever some slight criticism slipped in among the flood tide of compliments, but it stuck in the back of his head, where the priests had implanted St. Paul's brilliant inspiration. Then it would come back to haunt him in the middle of the night, hand in hand with all his other demons.

"He was the most jovial person you could imagine, but then he would suddenly come crashing down from his high," Chantal remembered. "He used to wake me up in the middle of the night. 'Do you think we're going to keep the two stars?' he would ask me. He had to be permanently reassured. 'If I lose a star I'll blow my brains out,' he said. 'If you ever leave me, I'll kill myself'—he told me that, too."

So there it was. By then he must have known. The mere suggestion that Chantal might think of walking out on him indicates that he knew something was going on, even if he wasn't sure of how serious it was, and was probably afraid of finding out. The turmoil in his head would have mixed anguish with fear, but if Bernard was transfixed with jealousy, he was no Othello. He was a nice guy, not an avenging soldier. He was a cook. Fleeing confrontation as usual, he temporized and worried, bottled it all up inside him and kept up a good face. Nor was Chantal a Desdemona, for that matter. She was a girl who had been around, and she really *was* having a go with the Saulieu equivalent of Cassio. Bernard's pusillanimity in the face of her faithlessness could only increase her disdain for the man-child with whom she had imprudently agreed to share her life. The marriage was doomed.

It was a very strange period. Things were getting better and better and worse and worse at the same time. By 1985 the first nine Relais & Châteaux hotel rooms, three of them striking duplex suites, had been completed, and Bernard had bought the little *parcelles* of land lying behind the main building, torn down the old sheds there, and replaced them with the soothing greenery of a landscaped garden. Bernard was appearing more and more frequently on the radio and television shows of his freeloading media friends, racing up to Paris at the crack of dawn for a quick taping, then racing back down to preside over the lunch *service*. Highest professional recognition was arriving, too.* The *Guide Hachette* had named him "Cook of the Year," and *GaultMillau*, more enamored than ever of his light, bright concoctions, had raised his "grade" to its absolute summit: 19.5 out of 20. No one in France had gone higher.

The casual visitor to Saulieu in 1985 and 1986 would have found a vastly improved hotel, a charming, dynamic chef backed by a devoted staff, and an inventive cuisine accented with garden herbs, truffles, and light deglazings. He served his roast lobster with a shellfish *jus* "mounted," at the last minute, with butter—and even that butter would disappear in later years as he perfected his techniques. Bernard's celebrated nettles made a surprising detour to become a sauce for poached oysters, his ragout of spring vegetables and chicken livers was a piece of pure last-minute wizardry, and the baby leeks he discovered from a nearby grower, served with his fricassee of veal sweetbreads and kidneys, looked like they must have been plucked from the ground with tweezers. A generalized chorus of approval rang out from all the guides and critics. Everything seemed hotsy-totsy in Saulieu, then. Young Bernard was going places.

But the direction could be downward, too, a lot more than anyone realized. He had not completed even a third of his building program; he was still working in Dumaine's rotten old kitchen, he had maxed out on the bank loans that would permit him to carry on with the renovation, and there weren't enough new customers coming in to cover the alarming rise in expenses since his marriage. He rattled around his

---

*As articles about Bernard covered page after page of the press in those years, a younger, far less renowned *confrère* made a brief appearance in the breaking news bulletins of the national media on August 9, 1984. On that day, a twenty-seven-year-old chef named Alain Ducasse, who had two Michelin stars for his seaside restaurant at Juan-les-Pins, near Nice, survived a crash in the Alps that killed all four others aboard the light plane carrying them to the ski resort of Courchevel. After fourteen operations and nearly a year in a wheelchair, convinced that nothing worse could ever befall him, Ducasse plunged headlong into challenge after audacious challenge, building the meteoric career that saw him win three stars simultaneously in two different restaurants as he built an astonishingly successful international empire. Ducasse's brilliant career became a persistent source of worry and envy for Bernard in later years, when he fell into his deepest doldrums of self-doubt: Perhaps it was this other guy who was the best, after all.

half-empty palace talking a mile a minute, buttonholing anyone who would listen, assuring passing journalists that he was the greatest, grinning a grin that appeared ever more forced, as he posed for any silly idea any photographer threw out at him,* and the relationship with Chantal was little better than venomous coexistence. Hubert, Eric, Patrick, and the others watched and waited.

It was around this period that I experienced a little interlude with Bernard, whose distressing significance became apparent only several years afterward, when the whole tragic mess had played itself out. Following him around at a gallop from room to room, admiring what he had accomplished, hastily scribbling notes on what he had planned for the future, and simply struggling to keep track of the high-speed flow of words tumbling out in that sonorous baritone of his, I snatched a moment of respite to pose a question that struck me as obvious, but which, it seems in retrospect, had not been so obvious to many of those who were close to him. Bernard, I said, you're just so damn manic. Are you "up" like this all the time? Isn't there a pendant to this—don't you ever slow down? Don't you get depressed? The chirpy, cheerful pumpkin face suddenly went blank, and he fixed me with a long gaze. When he answered it was almost a whisper. "You've got no idea," he said, "how far down I go when I fall."

It was one of those statements that become memorable only too late, after the worst had already happened. Most others around Bernard had come across hints and premonitions of this sort, but dismissed them out of hand because only moments later he was sure to suddenly spring back to his galvanic, resolute self. Not to worry—Bernard was just being Bernard again, that was all. He was suffused with such a force of life that no one could imagine the strength of his demons, not while that explosive energy of his was charging everyone else's batteries. "I'm going to live to one hundred and twenty!" he used to boast. That was typical Bernard, and around the Côte d'Or his friends could just about believe it.

---

*His willingness to meet the press more than halfway reached something of a nadir a few years later, when he agreed to a German photographer's grotesque idea of posing with a bunch of live snails crawling on the top of his bald head. Anything—anything at all—would do if it could bring new customers to Saulieu.

To me, he had merely dropped a dark hint, a suggestion. To others he had opened up a good deal more, and a good deal more explicitly. In the stunned weeks after those doleful days of February 2003, after the worst had happened, a French journalist named Jean-Pierre Géné recalled a wild ride through the Morvan countryside a dozen years earlier, when Bernard was personally (that was typical of him, too) driving him to the town of Montbard to catch the fast train back to Paris. Bernard was holding forth, as usual, about the cooking trade in general, his experiences in it and, in particular, how he had lived the last days of the Chantal period.

"Cuisine is a business for crazies," he told Géné. "You see me at the wheel of my car here, but not so long ago I had my shotgun under my chin. I was all set to blow my top off. My *maître d'hôtel* was dipping into the till and into my wife, too. That's enough to make you blow your brains out, isn't it?"

The reference was to the trauma he had lived in the fourth year of his marriage, 1986, when the boil finally burst. Unable to hide from the obvious anymore, too deeply and thoroughly plunged into cuckoldry to try saving face any longer, worried sick about money, Bernard finally cracked on one of those cold, drizzly, hopeless winter evenings when the dining room was almost empty. Hubert, his best friend and the coolest head in the house, was the one to whom he turned for solace.

"That was his first big depression," Hubert explained. "That night, around eleven p.m., after we had wrapped up the dinner *service*, he suddenly fell into my arms, bawling like a baby. 'Hubert, I can't take it anymore,' he said. 'I'm at the end of my rope.' We went to the little salon with the fireplace to talk it out. We sat there all night, right through to six a.m., with Bernard crying and talking nonstop. I told him what counted for us was him and the Côte d'Or, because we believed in it as much as he did. We were behind him all the way, and we'd do everything to make it work.

"That reassured him. He had been afraid that maybe Chantal had taken a kind of ascendancy, and he wasn't sure where the personnel stood, for him or her. I told him we didn't give a damn about Chantal. The thing to do now was get the divorce and get out of the marriage as cheaply as possible. He was petrified about what Michelin would think and what the papers would say if he divorced, but finally he came around and agreed with me. From that moment on, he became himself again."

Within a few months, divorce proceedings had begun and both Chantal and the famous *maître d'hôtel* had left Saulieu—separately, as it turned out: he back to his wife and child and she to the Paris region, where she lives today with her third husband.

Bernard, for his part, did not remain alone for long, because something new and good was rapidly developing from a chance encounter at the tail end of 1985; he finally met Dominique Brunet, the slim, scholarly Alsatian woman whom everyone always said would make a terrific wife for some lucky cook.

X

EXIT CHANTAL, ENTER DOMINIQUE

*I*n Bernard's energetic dedication to image-building, one harmless but frequently repeated bit of exaggeration was his version of an Abe Lincolnesque rise from nothing to fame and success. The suggestion was rags to riches, but Clermont-Ferrand hardly qualified as the American frontier; the family apartment was no open face lean-to and not even the most put-upon lad could compare the hardships of apprenticeship in Roanne to the chore of clearing Indiana's virgin forest for dirt farming. In truth, Bernard was but a fairly representative son of the conservative Camembert-and-cabbage *petite bourgeoisie* that then, as today, forms the bulk of the French population and keeps alive the great old national traditions—the good ones and the questionable ones, too. Dominique Brunet's story, on the other hand, is much closer to fairy-tale material.

"Journalists liked writing that Bernard came from a poor background," she says with an indulgent little laugh, "but he never lived anything like I did."

Dominique was born in 1953 in the very chic, very exclusive Parisian suburb of Neuilly, but her family shared none of the wealth or comforts of their upper-class neighbors: her mother was a concierge and her father a laborer. After the birth of her first brother—two more would follow—they decamped to Saverne, an unlovely industrial city (foundries, machine tools, shoes) 40 kilometers from Strasbourg on the canal that links the Rhine to the Marne.

"It couldn't have been simpler," she says. "When we arrived there was no bathroom and no running water. We had to fetch it from a well in the garden. There wasn't a book in the house. Most of my uncles could hardly read or speak French—in the family they all spoke in Alsatian dialect. When I was a little girl, my dream of luxury was to go to a vacation camp someday."

Meeting with her today, it is difficult to imagine such a humble origin, but then again most of the monied swells of France's *haute bourgeoisie*—like the Neuilly apartment dwellers whom Dominique's mother served—are rather proud to trace a direct lineage to some chicken-filled farmyard just a few generations earlier. The Industrial Revolution came late to France, and much of the charm of this still profoundly rural country derives from the peasant ways and traditions that continue, just a few miles inland from the high-speed autoroutes.

Slender, elegant, and soft-spoken—you have to cock an ear, because her normal speaking volume is just a notch above a whisper—today's Dominique could have stepped straight from the modern living pages of some fashionable women's magazine. She speaks well and thoughtfully, articulating her ideas with the care and precision of the scientific method she learned in long years of studying biochemistry and microbiology for the two masters degrees that she holds from Louis Pasteur University in Strasbourg and the École Normale Supérieure Technique in the Paris suburb of Cachan. Her pensive green-eyed gaze, framed by light brown hair cut in a sensibly short pageboy, is as reserved as Chantal's flash of blue and blonde was enticing and challenging, and Dominique's delicate features recall the fine, reflective faces of a Van Eyck painting. If Chantal's allure was thoroughly twentieth-century, then Dominique's recalled the Renaissance, which was nicely appropriate for her role in Saulieu, because her arrival signaled a rebirth for Bernard from his personal doldrums and those of the Côte d'Or toward the long-awaited glory of three Michelin stars.

It was at the end of 1985 that Bernard and Dominique first laid eyes on each other, at a competition for young cooks in the central city of Vichy, famed for its mineral water of ghastly taste and its inglorious past as the seat of the collaborationist Pétain government during the German occupation. After seven years of teaching applied food sciences at a technical *lycée* in Paris, Dominique had switched to journalism and gone to work for *L'Hôtellerie*, the specialized daily paper of the French hotel and restaurant trade. She was covering the cooking competition in Vichy when she cast an eye on the jury and lingered with a more markedly appraising gaze at the big, good-looking guy with the prematurely balding head and the widest smile she had ever seen. New to the business of cook-watching, she took him for Alain Chapel, the three-star magician of Mionnay, who was also afflicted with early hair loss.

Bad start. But after a colleague wised her up, she compensated for her mistake by marching straight up to Bernard a couple of weeks later at a ceremony for the launch of a new travel guide. When she confessed her error, he was not altogether unhappy to have been confused with one of the greatest cooks France had produced since the war. There were no Tex Avery pyrotechnics this time, but she and Bernard spent most of the evening together, and when they said goodbye it was a lot more like "see you soon."

And so they did, because Dominique made sure to assign herself to cover any functions where she knew the guy with the great smile and the sad eyes would be appearing. One thing, as the expression goes, led to another, and before long she had become his friend, confidante, and lover.

"I discovered a deeply wounded person behind the jovial façade," she said. "He couldn't stand his wife anymore, the marriage was a disaster, and on top of that he was in big financial trouble."

Whenever he could get away—easiest in the long winter months when clients were rare—Bernard jumped into his car after the dinner *service* and sped up to Paris to stay for a night with Dominique in her small career-girl's apartment on the rue Claude-Terrasse. "He would cry as we talked," she remembered. "I had never seen a man cry like that, completely letting go, like a baby. It was very strange, very touching. Then he would get up at dawn so he could be back in Saulieu by nine a.m."

Those long hours of nonstop talking taught Bernard about Dominique, too, of course. Surprised and not a little intimidated by her considerable academic knowledge—while he had ingloriously quit his studies at sixteen, she had plugged away for fully a decade longer, and spoke fluent German and English as well—he was startled to learn that she, for one, really *had* come from a penurious background. What impressed him even more, though, was the strength of her ambition and the stubborn work ethic that had lifted her into the mainstream of upwardly mobile young professionals. Chantal was flashy, but Dominique was something else; she was impressive.

"When I was little, I had always wanted to get back to Paris," she told me, reflecting on her long route from her youth of straitened circumstances. "I never felt at home in Alsace, and never saw myself like the people there. At eleven I was sent to a boarding school run by nuns, the Sisters of Divine Providence. I was lucky to get there, and the whole family—aunts and uncles helped out, too—chipped in to pay my way. Some of the girls who were there came from quite wealthy families, but for us it was a big financial effort. When I was twelve—I'll remember this all my life—two sisters who were my classmates went on a cruise to Greece. Imagine—to Greece! That was like a dream for me.

"I promised myself I'd be like them someday. I already saw myself established in a big city and living in a certain manner. Not necessarily grand but . . . better. I realized I wasn't good-looking enough to succeed by my beauty, so it could only be by studying that I could get there. It's not so much that I enjoyed studies, but I knew one thing for sure, and I even wrote it in my diary: Work is the only thing that never disappoints you. Duty always comes first. Duty and work.

"So I worked. I sewed my own clothes, I fixed things around the house, and summers, I glued sneakers in the Adidas factory. Even though I've done a lot of studies, I'm still very much a manual person. Bernard and I found out that we were quite complementary. We were both ambitious, but there was a difference in our styles. When I believe in something I take great pains to achieve it, but I'm not audacious. I've always progressed carefully, step by step. I admire daring people, though, so I was captivated by Bernard. I was fascinated by the way he looked at life, by his self-confidence, and by his talent for bringing people around to what he believed in. He was like a one-man cavalry charge."

Through the remaining months of 1986 and well into 1987, as the long, dreary matter of divorce proceedings between Bernard and Chantal followed the bureaucratic route in Dijon, the semiclandestine meetings with Dominique continued in Paris. In the days and weeks between these snatches of comfort, Bernard kept in touch with

Dominique, as he always did with everyone else, by phone. Never was there a cook, or entrepreneur of any sort, for that matter, who relied on Mr. Bell's clever talking instrument more than this one.

"The phone was his office," Eric Rousseau said. "He never stopped. Often he would make calls lasting just twenty or thirty seconds, for no reason. He'd call television stars to show us that he was on intimate terms with them, but it was also to reassure himself. We would think he had something important to tell them, but then he'd just say: 'Hi! OK, love you. 'Bye.' And hang up, with that big smile still on his face, because they hadn't forgotten him. Then he would say: 'You see? I say *tu* to him.'"

Dominique remembers the many calls she received during their curious long-distance courtship of 1986 and 1987 as mostly cries of distress. "He was more and more worried about money, and if Hubert and Eric hadn't been there to support him I don't know what he would have done. By then he was afraid of his wife, too. 'I never know what she's going to say, or what she's going to come up with next,' he'd tell me. Four, five times a day he'd call so I could comfort him. It really was time for that chapter of his life to come to an end.

"Bernard told me that he learned about her affair with the *maître d'hôtel* only in that last year. People had hinted at it to him before, but he never wanted to believe them. And since he was so nice, she took advantage of him, naturally. They had a joint checking account and the credit cards that went with it, but he didn't close down the account right away. Toward the end of the marriage he got bills from the Club Med in Marbella where she had gone with her lover. I mean, it takes a certain amount of gall for a woman to do that, doesn't it? But he was afraid of her, because she could be really nasty. He could never know what she would be doing next. So he paid the bills. She even asked him for fifty thousand francs in cash to pay for a marketing course she wanted to take so she could set up a business. He paid. He gave her anything she wanted, just so she would leave him alone."

Those were edgy, nervous times for the Côte d'Or. Bernard's marriage was obviously in tatters, expenses were mounting alarmingly, and the ten beautiful new Relais & Châteaux rooms were still not bringing in enough of the expected mass of new customers. Apart from the pleasant surprise of an unexpected influx of Japanese visitors tipped off to Bernard's minimalist approach to last-minute cooking by Shizuo Tsuji, Japan's most famous gastronomic expert (apart from being an influential TV personality, he owned the world's biggest cooking school, located in Osaka), Saulieu was not yet on the map of world travelers. Where were the English, the Germans, and the Americans? Awaiting better days, Hubert led the staff in a draconian cost-cutting campaign, reducing supply orders to the minimum, delaying wine purchases, and turning off unnecessary lights in unused rooms. Between this kind of attention to detail and Bernard Fabre's rationalizing hand on the larger management picture, the gloomy situation slowly righted itself, and the Côte d'Or climbed back into the black over the following years. But it had been a close call; to keep as much money flowing in as possible, Bernard had, in essence, worked nonstop. From the time of his arrival in Saulieu in 1975 he had never allowed himself more than one day off a year—Christmas—to enjoy the luxury of closing the shop down and getting his wind back. Time and time again over those years, he speculated about taking time off and closing for some kind of vacation break, but he never dared to relax his manic grip on the tiller of his big old boat—not with all those loans outstanding. The result was pretty much inevitable; assiduity became overwork, and overwork monomania.* He had been heading toward trouble for years.

"Monsieur Trichot told me if I filled out my hotel side I'd have the place full every night," Bernard was saying, in that patented tone of absolute conviction that brooked no gainsaying. The year was 1986. As if his disastrous marital situation was not enough just then, he was in debt up to his neck (the level would soon rise to the top of his *toque*) and the clientele remained gallingly thin, but Bernard was "up" just

---

*Here, too, Bernard was following the path of his model, Bocuse, whose restaurant is open 365 days a year—but Bocuse has the entire city of Lyon as a clientele base (not to speak of the hungry and curious from every other corner of the globe, who visit his place the way they visit Madame Tussaud's waxworks or the Eiffel Tower), and he employs an oversized staff to serve them all. Bernard's comparable *confrères* all allow themselves a little reasonable breathing time. Guy Savoy takes the month of August, and the Christmas and New Year periods off, and closes two days a week. Michel Troisgros closes for four weeks of the year plus two days a week. In winterbound Laguiole, Michel Bras shuts down entirely from November through March.

then, and when he was riding the cloud of his *méthode Coué*, not even the horses of the Apocalypse could drag him down into despond. He had recently been to Paris to pay the customary call on Michelin, and André Trichot, then director of the guide, had apparently said a few nice words about his new hotel rooms. From this reticent bit of *auvergnat* encouragement Bernard had concluded that he had been right all along: salvation and the route to three stars lay in a *fuite en avant*, a headlong rush to more borrowing, more building, and more luxury.

"I don't give a goddam," he cried. "I'm just in my thirties. I'd rather be in debt now, while I'm young. The future of this business is in the hotel side. It's not enough to just to have a good restaurant anymore. People want to come to the countryside, enjoy beautiful surroundings, hear the birds chirping in the garden and relax in luxurious rooms. You've got to go up a notch. Georges Blanc is the one who really understood what marketing is all about. He pointed the way. He set the example."

Bernard was quite right. When he inherited the family *auberge* in the village of Vonnas, young Georges Blanc took advantage of the sharply reduced interest rates available through the government-sponsored *crédit hôtelier* program in the seventies to transform a little country inn into a rustic paradise of three-star food, five-star rooms, and impeccably modern appointments, including a big heated pool, a tennis court, and the restaurant trade's very first helipad—an item that drew sniggers at first but was soon copied throughout France. Behind his *poulet à la crème*, his *bar à la ligne*, and the signature potato pancakes that had been the glory of Vonnas for time beyond memory, Georges Blanc had been hiding another secret: He was a hell of a businessman.

This was what goaded Bernard, he was determined to do as well as Georges Blanc, and then he would go him one better. Blanc was not only a model, then, but already a rival as well—as were Marc Meneau in Vézelay and Michel Troisgros in Roanne and other stars of the trade, like Marc Veyrat in Annecy, who all would be making big splashes in future years. Relations within the *confrèrie* of three-star restaurants always have an edge of competitive bitchiness to them, because the tenors of French cooking are locked in a permanent contest to be the best, the most beautiful, and the most seductive before client and critic and God.

"Georges Blanc got his place from his mother," Bernard emphasized heavily, "so he didn't have that expense to worry about. Me, I've had to bust my balls to pay for this, and that's slowing me down. If I had gotten it for free, I would have knocked down the old rooms long ago. But I'll get there. The first priority is to finish all thirty of the new rooms—profitable things first. That'll bring in the money to pay for the rest."

The master plan was all worked out in his head, and he was going to get it done come hell or high water. Optimism was the call of the day, then, but Bernard couldn't resist underlining his hard luck once again, and contrasting it with the good fortune of the "golden boy" in Vonnas. "Georges Blanc has Mâcon right next door, and Lyon nearby, and he's on the route to Geneva. He's got it made. Me, I'm in this little Saulieu in the middle of nowhere, so I've got to make myself known. You can be the best cook in the world, but people won't come to you if they don't know you."

This, too, was typical of the man. That he was embarked on a permanent campaign of self-publicizing was glaringly obvious. Fair enough, an observer might say, he had an expensive house to fill up, but in spite of his excessive nature, Bernard was not entirely muddle-headed. He knew that there was a potential price to pay for all those silly TV shows he appeared on, all those pages of posed pictures in *Paris-Match*, and all those snails crawling on his bald pate: he irritated. The more he exerted himself to attract new customers to Saulieu, the more a certain segment of the gourmet public held it against him and deliberately shunned him, with a predictable kind of reaction: Who does he take himself for? Does he think he's a cook or a TV star?

More cruelly, and a good deal more erroneously, this same segment of public opinion jumped to the damning conclusion that if Bernard was in the press so frequently, it meant he was neglecting his kitchen. None of the carpers* had any idea of his near-hysterical

---

*One of the restaurant critics who spooked Bernard most thoroughly was Patricia Wells, wife of Walter Wells, executive editor of the Paris *Herald Tribune*. In his *Burgundy Stars*, author William Echikson reported Bernard's perplexity at her qualification of the food at Saulieu as "tiddlywinks cuisine," whatever that was supposed to mean. Bernard was certain that Wells bore him a personal animus for his relentlessly self-promoting style. "He was always ill at ease with her," said *chef de rang* Eric Rousseau. "She just didn't like him, and it showed up in what she wrote. She always found something to criticize."

predawn dashes to Paris or the high-speed rush to make it back to Saulieu for the lunch *service*. Few ever knew about or credited him for his valiant (and perhaps foolhardy) effort to remain open all through the week, the year 'round. Never was there a chef who worked harder than Bernard, but by trying to do too much, he was spreading himself too thin. The man was in permanent risk of nervous exhaustion.

It was on a snowy afternoon in February of 1987 that Dominique made her first visit to Saulieu, on a self-assigned mission to write an article for *L'Hôtellerie* on the cooking of Bernard Loiseau. Neither Chantal nor the *maître d'hôtel* was present at the Côte d'Or anymore, but still she and Bernard had to be careful about displaying their relationship too openly, lest this theoretically censurable intimacy lend legal ammunition to Chantal's side in the divorce proceedings. Still, hormones will be hormones, and after midnight Bernard crept into Dominique's welcoming room by passing over the railing of her terrace, leaving in the morning by the same route in reverse.

The misconceived, unhappy marriage with Chantal finally came to an end in February of 1988, when the divorce was pronounced in Dijon. As always, Bernard had Bernard Fabre at his side through the proceedings, with his quick intelligence, his knowledge of the relevant statutes, and his pocket calculating machine. He needed Fabre doubly, because he had put himself into a bind at the very start of his married life: blinded by his infatuation, he had insisted on marrying *en communauté de biens*. In other words, half of everything was Chantal's. Cleareyed and infinitely more cautious than his engaging but wildly unrealistic client, Fabre had advised him not to do it. Bernard seemingly acquiesced but he didn't give up on the idea, not with Chantal around to argue her side of the case. He set up another meeting with Fabre.

"I remember it was a Saturday afternoon," Fabre recalled, "and Auxerre was playing in the Coupe de France [the most important national soccer competition of the year]. We watched the match, and when it was over he said: '*Voilà*—I want you to give half the shares of the company to Chantal.'

"I don't agree, I said. I won't do it. And, anyway, I don't know how to do a document like that. I did know, of course, but I knew that it would be a *connerie*. I wrote him a letter the next day advising him against it again, but it never arrived. I'm sure Chantal opened it and kept it from him."

Faced with Fabre's refusal, Bernard got his local *notaire* to do the fateful paperwork instead, and within a few days Chantal was officially *présidente* of Bernard Loiseau S.A. Now, at divorce time, he was stuck with the fruit of his amorous folly. If it came down to a courtroom dirt-slinging match between divorce lawyers, Bernard probably could have carried the day, considering the relative flagrancy of Chantal's long-standing matrimonial *delicto*, but that would not remove her from 50 percent ownership of the company, and the whole messy procedure promised to be long, embarrassing, expensive, and damaging to Bernard's image—or at least his image of his image.

Fabre found a better way; he reminded Chantal that as half owner of La Côte d'Or she was also responsible for half of its liabilities. By then Bernard was more than seven million francs in debt for the first nine new Relais & Châteaux luxury rooms. He was struggling with a budget overrun of 30 percent and paying his suppliers and staff salaries on a hand-to-mouth basis with the daily receipts from his clientele. With Chantal as an expensive ornament, as long as she was still officially his wife, and a mere two Michelin stars and a frustratingly moderate flow of customers—the curse of Saulieu still held, even in the prosperous mid-eighties—he was teetering dangerously close to the knife edge of bankruptcy. There was not a banker who would spring for any more cash.

The situation was bleak, then, but its very bleakness offered Fabre the opportunity for a little southern-style persuasion to direct at Chantal. He conferred with the bankers, explained the divorce situation, and persuaded them to expedite a few judiciously unfriendly *mises en demeure*—formal demands—for payment on accounts bearing her signature as well as Bernard's. Faced with the terrifying figures, she rapidly caved in and, in exchange for the promise of an amicable divorce settlement (no blame assigned either way), left Saulieu with her black BMW, her white poodle, and two years of alimony. Bernard heaved a huge sigh of relief, and Dominique was finally able to come down to Saulieu openly for weekends in the scruffy little apartment above Dumaine's dining room.

When, on the second of December, 1988, Dominique and Bernard had a proper church wedding in Alsace, it was Fabre who was Bernard's best man. Later, at the birth of his first son, Bernard asked Fabre to be the godfather. This complicity—the dreamer and the counter—was a rare kind of hybrid symbiosis, but neither in business nor human relations did Bernard Loiseau's style follow convention.

"I considered him as my best friend," said Fabre. "Almost a brother. We felt that the two of us formed a unity. One was extroverted and gifted for publicity and the media; the other was more measured, gave advice, reined back excesses, took care of the numbers, and was careful about what he said. We felt this unity was bound to succeed."

If his devotion to Bernard and dedication to the Côte d'Or were exemplary, they were not particularly profitable for his business— "Eighty percent of my time and twenty percent of my revenues," as he put it—but there is little doubt that without Bernard Fabre advising him during the most complicated phases of the renovation program, Bernard's dream of building a Burgundian Xanadu would have been very seriously compromised.

With the departure of Chantal and the arrival of Dominique, the atmosphere in the hallways and salons of the Côte d'Or changed dramatically. What this second marriage was lacking in sexual provocation, passion, and bewitchment, it gained in reason and commitment. For their wedding night, the freshly minted couple had offered themselves nothing more exotic than to crash at Dominique's mother's little house in Saverne, and the next day they were both back at work. It hadn't been much of a honeymoon, but this was a different, far more serious, kind of union, bringing a new optimism with it. With Dominique's brains and dedication now added to his formula, Bernard was seething with energy and more determined than ever to go whole-hog and finish his dream palace. No half measures. From now on it would be nothing but the best.

Bernard was chuffed good and proper then, but, ironically enough, he didn't have Dominique literally at his side—not full-time, in any case, not at the start. For the first fifteen months of their marriage she gamely tried to carry on as before, returning to her little Paris apartment while working at *L'Hôtellerie* during the week, then hopping on the train south on Friday evenings to join Bernard for weekends in Saulieu.

There was also a new development, motherhood, accomplished by the step-by-step procedure of achieving goals that the scientific method had taught Dominique. Postulate: They both wanted kids. Given: The union with Chantal had been barren. Proposition: Seduce Bernard at the right moment. She did her calculations, chose exactly the right moment of the right phase of the moon, warned Bernard to be ready, and arrived suitably estrous in Saulieu on a Wednesday evening. Nor, for his part, had Bernard been inactive. He prepared a special *dîner intime* (what else would a chef think to do?) of a once-in-a-lifetime quality—*ortolans*. The tiny, fat, delicious melt-in-the-mouth little birdies did their duty, the plucky little things, and that very night Dominique conceived their first child, Bérangère, who was born in a Dijon clinic in July 1989.

For the following eight months Dominique maintained her back-and-forth routine between Saulieu and Paris, now with an infant in her arms. As the weeks passed, though, it became increasingly evident that this long-distance commuting wasn't right for Bernard, for their daughter, or finally, for herself. After all, there had to be another career awaiting her at the restaurant, she reasoned.

Yes and no. There was an immediate problem: Chantal's profligate ways had left their mark. The big economy drive was still on, and everyone, even Bernard, in spite of himself, kept a keen eye on the new Madame Loiseau. Would she turn out to be a spender, too? Dominique did not, of course, and she wished for nothing better than to go to work. But what work was there for her to do? Logically enough she was entirely shut out of Bernard's domain, the kitchen, but she knew nothing about the hotel side, either, and with all her years in the university, she had never done any management studies. The dining room staff under Hubert was a well-oiled machine that needed no help and was highly unlikely to tolerate any meddling from outside. Like Napoleon's *grognards*—the scarred old veterans who formed the emperor's inner circle—they had their ways and were best left alone. So what was left for Dominique?

"You're *la patronne* [the boss] now. Watch over things," Bernard said vaguely. "Mix with the clients." He meant well, but that wasn't really much help. What he really was saying, without putting it into so many words, was that consecrated old French expression: *débrouille-*

toi—work it out by yourself. He was much too busy with his grand-hotel project, his image-building and, above all, his cuisine to establish a change-of-career plan for his wife.

Dominique was no dummy, she got the message. So she watched and waited and learned. Once again, scientific as ever, she went toward her goal step by step. Her slow rise from Bernard's shadow through those early years of the marriage created a nice historical hiccup for the Côte d'Or. Whether it was deliberate emulation or pure chance, she transformed herself into Jeanne Dumaine, half a century later. The parallels between herself and Alexandre Dumaine's wife were quite extraordinary. Jeanne Dumaine, too, had been university-educated, which was very rare for French women in the thirties. She spoke German and English, and had worked as a journalist (*Harper's Bazaar*) before marrying the famous cook. Dominique soon lent the same extra touch of class to Bernard's operation that Jeanne had done for Alexandre.

Dipping her toe gingerly into the waters of the day-to-day operations of a machine of *haute gastronomie*, she began by greeting clients as they entered the dining room. With her soft voice, understated, articulate manner, and elegantly cut two-piece suits that advantageously set off her slim figure, she could not fail to impress any passing members of the Michelin crowd. Clearly, this was a three-star woman. Reorganizing the reception desk, she ruffled a few feathers with her suggestions for change, but she was *la patronne*, after all, and sooner or later she had to act the part. Bernard had never hired a secretary to watch over correspondence, had never organized a filing system or put together any properly written press material. Dominique took over all these chores. She cast around for a new team of architects to handle the big expansion plan, remembered the Paris firm of Guy Catonné from her days with *L'Hôtellerie*, and brought them down to Saulieu for a long consultation. One job led to another, and before she quite knew what had happened, she found she had more work than she could handle. That was her style—work always bred more work with Dominique. Before long she was obliged to hire her own assistant.

Then she discovered that she was pregnant again, even without the help of *ortolans* this time. Dumaine's little apartment was already crowded enough for a one-child family, but with two (or more) kids, it would clearly be impossible. She nosed around, found a big old house in town going for a bargain price (who wants to live in Saulieu?), closed the deal, and moved her little family in, extracting Bernard from the quarters above Dumaine's dining room as she would have extracted a snail from its shell. With this move, the last significant remnant of his boyish past—that sordid bachelor pad to which Verger had assigned him more than a decade earlier—was assigned to history.

Things were shaping up. In 1989 the Côte d'Or won the Relais & Châteaux prize for the best breakfast of the entire chain. A prize like that doesn't sound like much—in France the standard continental breakfast, even in quality hotels, is rarely more exalted than fruit juice, coffee, and croissants—but Bernard was out to distinguish himself any way he could. He invented a sophisticated country platter to be delivered to the rooms with pomp worthy of an *oreiller de la belle Aurore*: a pot of coffee, tea, or cocoa with freshly pressed fruit juice; a basket of warm pastries fresh from the oven (fruitcake, brioche with almonds, croissants, minibaguette with butter and homemade jams); a plate of the famous Morvan ham; a bowl of chilled ewe's-milk yogurt; another of fresh fruit salad or prunes infused in tea; and finally a third one of rice pudding, as a kind of dessert. How anyone could consume this and be able to tuck into lunch a few hours later is a mystery, but French clients, paradoxical as always, managed it with aplomb.

By the late eighties, Bernard was in full stride, confident in his architectural ideas for the hotel and vibrantly certain that he had now fine-tuned his cuisine, ridding it of its occasionally Maoist rigor and bringing it into an integrated, logical summation of his gastronomic experiences: food light and easily digestible but still gloriously rich in taste and texture and—a far more important factor than many people realize—beautiful to the eye. No great cook reaches the top without the inborn sense of esthetics that instinctively produces a pleasing, harmonious presentation on the plate. It should be pointed out, however, that certain of the culinary grandmaster crowd, some trying to outdo their competitors and some simply imitating, recently fell into weird excesses with the plates themselves. God knows who started the trend, but there was a period early in this century when otherwise sensible cooks felt constrained to serve their beautiful creations on oval plates, rectangular plates, smoked glass, and see-through plates—plates tagged with surrealistic designs and then retagged with artistically deposited streaks of sauce—not to mention a profusion of amorphous multicolor plates of the weirdest forms imaginable, resembling the prizes you win for throwing hoops over dolls in country fairs. Bernard, to his credit, never fell for this strange fad, and stuck with classical round plates discreetly decorated around the edges. His *confrères* who went for the weird stuff soon realized that they had spent ruinously for ceramic *oeuvres d'art* that no one wanted and that only distracted attention from the food.

Early in 1990, the Association of French Wine Writers voted to give the prize of the best wine list to the Côte d'Or. Something was in the air. Bernard was hot, and the wind was in his sails. Journalists and critics, ever on the lookout for the next culinary fad, began writing about him with words like "leader," "visionary," "precursor." It is an old truism that very often the most interesting cooking often occurs not in established three-star restaurants but in two-star places where the chef is on a roll and gunning for the third star. Now, in Saulieu, the smartass kid, Bernard Chirent's "worst apprentice ever," seemed to be turning into not just a trendsetter but something akin to a prophet. This was heady stuff.

"Cuisine of essences"—*la uisine des essences*—he officially called his cooking now. His use of sophisticated variants of simple deglazings with water had not slowed, but he wisely abandoned his enthusiasm for the aqueous label. For one thing, his earlier insistence on the term *cuisine à l'eau*—"water cooking"—had led to the frequent misperception that he had developed a specialty for serving boiled food, which could not be further from reality. And secondly, there was Bocuse's famous wisecrack. Although he was Bernard's mentor, model, and father figure, *le grand Paul* was and is an incorrigible joker in the iconoclastic tradition of the *lyonnais* wise guys who are always on the lookout for any bombast (preferably Parisian) to puncture. It so happened that, invited to Saulieu along with a few of his *confrères*, and taking an after-lunch stroll, Bocuse and the group crossed a little river where the trout used to swim in the days of Alexandre Dumaine.

"Now, isn't that a shame," reflected Bocuse. "We should tell Bernard about all that good sauce going to waste."

The jape instantly made the rounds of the cooking establishment, and from there it spread throughout France and even worldwide. Bernard shut up about water cooking after that. Never mind; the celebrities, the beautiful people, and the freeloaders—TV and showbiz names that made French teenagers squeal but were utterly unknown beyond the national borders—were coming to Saulieu in growing numbers eating and talking and praising. Presently François Mitterrand himself, *président de la république* and a notorious sensualist (wine, women, and politics, and plenty of great food to grease it all along) insinuated himself into a private corner of the specially secured Dumaine dining room for a dinner of crayfish fricassee, truffled celery-root "cake," and calves' liver with a fricassee of wild Morvan mushrooms.

In presentation and content, Bernard's menu by the end of the eighties had reached the mature form that thereafter would be identified with *le style Loiseau*. Graphically, the sober off-white card with the beige and brown decorative border in Burgundian tile motif recalled the façade of the building itself. La Côte d'Or *à Saulieu* held the place of honor as the first line on the cover sheet, but directly below came the personal identity: the big *BL* logo and, underneath that, his name writ large in fancy cursive script: *Bernard Loiseau*, front and center, right along the bottom of the page. Image was served.

What was being served in the dining room sprang almost entirely now from Bernard's hyperactive imagination. If the old ultraclassical entrée of smoked Morvan ham was still clinging on for a few more years, along with the beef filet with poached marrow (straight from the Troisgros experience) and the eternal hot apple tart (which traced its ancestry right back to Michel Guérard via Claude Verger), the rest was much more Loiseau and much more adventuresome. The nettle soup with snails (which could also be called snail soup with nettles) still held its starring place among the *entrées*, along with a lobster terrine served with tiny vegetables and a sauce built around its own coral juice. Little filets of red mullet now reposed on a truffle vinaigrette rather than the thin chervil purée that had raised eyebrows a few years earlier, and the sweet, tender *langoustine*—small lobster—tails were served with a fresh tomato *coulis* flavored with nut oil. One of his most curious novelties in this creative period was a caramelized cauliflower purée that he often served with his pan-fried slice of fresh foie gras. Caramelizing cauliflower was an ingenious manipulation, to be sure,

and Bernard was rather proud of, but it never quite impressed the customers as much as his own infatuation with it. Eventually he gave it up
and moved on to more rewarding culinary pursuits—*ris de veau*, for example. This unprepossessing little gland with the oddly inappropriate
English name of sweetbreads is an omnipresent classic of three-star
French cuisine, but Bernard had a problem with the soft, spongy texture of the meat, which he frankly found offensive. He solved the problem by searing it in a hot skillet until the surface was golden brown,
flipping it over to cook the raw side for a quick fifteen seconds, and finally setting it under the hot grill of the *salamandre* for a few minutes
to finish the crust to a crackly caramelized consistency.

For a modest 290 francs (about fifty dollars then), clients of the an-
timeat persuasion (but not excessively so) could by then enjoy an all-
vegetable menu of tomatoes stuffed with celery-accented basmati rice,
a ragout of mixed vegetables in a reduced beef broth (that's the "not excessively" part), zucchini flowers with creamed garlic and sweet pepper
juice, and finally, before turning to the cheese platter, a plate of
sautéed wild mushrooms. Encouraged by the success of his vegetable
experiments, Bernard would go on, a few years later, to develop an all-
potato menu—*pommes en fête*—featuring the lowly tuber in different
forms, from crisp pancakes to a smoothly seductive truffled purée, and
dancing the tango with asparagus tips sauced with his famous butter-
free *béarnaise*. Dessert was a sweet potato *croustillant* accompanied by
a green-apple sherbet. Why apple? For a wink and a play on words:
Pomme is how you say "apple" in French; *pomme de terre*—"earth apple"—is how you say potato. Bernard adjusted his potato menu with
the seasons, but his truffle-flecked purée was so sensational that he was
stuck with it from then on. In the future, Loiseau could no more give
that up than Ducloux could renounce the use of beef fat in his
quenelles de brochet, lest clients stage a dining room rebellion.*

---

*With all the technical manipulations and complexities for which they are justly
famous, it is striking to note how thoroughly some chefs are able to seduce the
most finicky *gastronomes* on earth with gestures of almost childish simplicity.
Bernard's friend (and rival, naturally) Joël Robuchon, a great master if ever there
was one, knocked Parisians for a loop with his mashed potatoes, containing
enough good Normandy butter to bend the arrow and shatter the glass of every
cardiologist's cholesterol meter.

On the seafood side, Bernard was serving his salmon filets with truffle juice and, *justement*, the fabulous truffled mashed potatoes, while his lobster medallions were delivered with caramelized carrots and a light purée of onions accented with cloves. Following the tradition-breaking modern school of gastronomic anarchists who did not hesitate to drink red wine with fish or to confound the terrestrial and the oceanic, he seized on the bland taste of *merlan*—whiting—to present their filets not in a classical seafood sauce but with a veal reduction. For poultry, he borrowed a trick from the Chinese in serving his duck breast with its skin cooked crackly and sweetly accented with honey. From two snooty Parisian palaces, the Tour d'Argent and Lucas-Carton, he adopted the old trick of preparing the sauce for his roast pigeon with the blood of the very animal he was roasting.

Like that of any great restaurant, Bernard's menu adapted to the market to offer whichever meats, seafood, and vegetables were the best available and happened to be in season. Perspicacious diners could note, around mid-April, that the color of the salty butter he served with his breads had taken on a deeper, more brilliant, hue of yellow, because the cows had gone off silage and were eating fresh grass again. If ad hoc dishes could arise from the discovery of some particularly fine mushrooms, turbot, or quail, the general rule was that the Côte d'Or presented two menus a year: spring–summer and autumn–winter. Whatever the seasonal changes, though, certain of the standards, the Loiseau classics, could never leave his card. The huge veal chop, the chicken breast with foie gras, and the pike perch with the tangy red wine sauce enjoyed permanent residence in Saulieu. But even more than these, it was another dish, an *entrée*, this one, that went on to be seen as his true banner and standard: *jambonnettes de grenouilles à la purée d'ail et au jus de persil*. If ever one dish were to be singled out as Loiseau's signature creation—like the Troisgros salmon in sorrel sauce or Bocuse's truffle soup or Michel Bras's *gargouillou* of young vegetables—it would be this one: frogs' legs with garlic purée and parsley juice. It had everything: taste, beauty, the surprise of originality, and total relevance to the region.

Ever since he arrived in Saulieu, Bernard had struggled to square the culinary circle: reconciling Burgundy's grand old traditions of lavish feasting with his own theory of a modern gastronomy that was light, easily digestible, and largely fat-free. How better to accomplish that than to take a few of the great Burgundian classics of bourgeois cuisine and set them on their tradition-bound ear with a flip of the skillet and a wink of the eye? When you think of Burgundy you think of frogs and snails and chickens in the farmyards, and trout and pike in its rivers. Well then, Bernard had already put the snails in nettles, the chickens with foie gras, and the pike with a punchy red wine reduction as intense and vigorous as his own character—but what about frogs' legs?

There had to be a new way, a better way, to attack this ancient regional specialty whose creation and enjoyment over the centuries had caused countless millions of these comically unlovely amphibians to croak, their legs ritually sautéed in hot butter and served in a super-garlicky *persillade*—parsley-green and butter-yellow, oily and delicious and slippy-sliding all over your fingers and hands, and who cares? For several months in the mid-eighties Bernard turned over in his head the idea of this dish, talking it over with Patrick and his *sous-chefs* and *commis*, but in spite of all the experiments and suggestions, the answer never came. Then, one morning in 1985, it was suddenly there.

"On est con," cried Bernard—"we've been jerks, driving ourselves crazy for nothing. I know what we'll do. We've just got to do a *persillade* without all that greasy cooked butter—that's okay for a bistro, but not for three stars."

Butter, parsley, and garlic were consecrated as absolute essentials to accompany the plump thighs of Burgundy frogs,* so Bernard could not reasonably renounce any of the three—but he could use them differently. First, the legs themselves. Keeping only the top of the thigh,

---

*The three basic elements flavoring this Burgundian classic may be immutable, but the critters they accompany and ennoble are hardly ever native anymore. Their natural habitats and preferred foods having been largely destroyed by the intensive industrial-style farming, by which France profits from the subsidies of the European Union's Common Agricultural Policy, frogs (and snails) have dramatically declined in population in the French countryside. These delicacies now have to be air-freighted in to gourmet kitchens, mostly from Turkey and Eastern Europe, where the former communist regimes had not been not rich enough or efficient enough to carry out vast programs of rural pollution with pesticides and synthesized fertilizers.

where the bulge of meat attaches to the bone like a miniature ham (the *jambonnette* of the recipe), he discarded the rest, leaving a kind of lollipop that could—should—be eaten with the hands. It's easy to spot the genealogy of this as a direct descendant of Michel Guérard's chicken wing lollipop idea in the Pot au Feu.

Now for the three great ingredients. The first part was easy. He sautéed the *jambonnettes* in butter and then, uncompromising as ever about oily excess, patted the hot, golden meat dry with paper towels. After that, the evolution of his soon-to-be signature dish became more complex. The parsley—flat parsley only, because it is thicker and has more body—he cooked like spinach in boiling water, then puréed it under the blade of a Robot-Coupe and thinned it out with water to the consistency of a *coulis*.

The hardest part to deal with was the garlic. It was unthinkable to offer frogs' legs without garlic—that's like serving cheese without wine—but how to moderate its flamethrower punch and civilize it to three-star level? Bernard's solution was to tame it by slowly leaching away its notorious bite. Following the same system that French housewives had used for centuries to remove impurities and scum from the veal of their *blanquettes de veau*, he started the garlic cloves in cold water that he brought it to a boil. After a few minutes of cooking he discarded the hot water, poured in fresh supply of cold, and renewed the process all over again. After four or five changes of water for summer garlic (seven or eight for the winter version), he was left with a pile of softened garlic cloves that still tasted like garlic but were bereft of their fiercest astringency. They had become polite. Puréed and smoothed out with a touch of milk, the garlic was ready to be assembled into its place in his little *chef d'oeuvre*.

First onto the plate was a ladle of brilliant green parsley *coulis* and then, in the middle of that, an atoll of purest white garlic purée. For the final presentation he laid the golden brown *jambonnettes* in a fetching circle around the edge of the plate. It made a gorgeous, stunningly original tableau—gold, green, and white—when set down at the table, and the *maître d'hôtel* had the pleasure of announcing to first-time clients that they should eat it with their hands, dipping the froggy lollipops first into the parsley and then the garlic. (If they felt adventuresome—go ahead, live a little—they could take it in the opposite order.)

Kids loved the dish, of course, for the opportunities for discreet play that it offered—milk-white contrails of garlic artfully traced into the sea of green—and even the most fastidious, tradition-bound French gourmets, the kind of people who eat chicken wings or bananas with a knife and fork, were persuaded to abandon themselves to the enjoyment of the world's most sophisticated (and expensive) finger food.

The *jambonnettes* was an exceptionally standout dish, remarkable in every sense of the word, but few clients in Saulieu could ever imagine the range of subterranean complexities lying behind it—or, indeed, any of the other artifacts of Bernard's new approach to cooking, neither the sacrificial cuts of expensive meats that were responsible for the depth of taste of the "juices" he cooked up every day, nor the double deglazings that reinforced the taste further, nor even the simple day-to-day gestures like the punctilious, obsessively neat dabbings with paper towel to remove cooking fats before sending a dish out. Guests who ordered the house fruit drink, a mixture of orange, grapefruit, and lemon, may have suffered an unexpected pucker at its startling astringency (uncompromisingly, Bernard suffered no sweetening beyond a small dash of grenadine syrup), but rare were those who could guess that he was also watching over their health and their waistlines with the pastries he developed over the years, containing 40 percent less sugar than the standard recipes. An even more fundamentally important aspect of the unseen manipulations underlying *le style Loiseau* was his handling of sauces.

Whatever any fashionable cooking rebels may decree in their hours of fame—and, for that matter, whatever *lèse majesté* Bernard himself had inflicted on tradition in his early days in Saulieu—sauces are and always will be the soul of French cooking. Bernard had struggled mightily to come to terms with the whole idea of sauces, so much so that at one point he veered dangerously close to dismissing them altogether. Fortunately, his native good sense stepped in and set him straight, but his essential dilemma still remained: how to reconcile the light, modern, cooking style he aspired to with all those tasty but wicked elements of stockpot reductions flavored with a multitude of extraneous ingredients, thickened with one trick or another and rendered voluptuously appealing with great infusions of cholesterol-laden butter?

The grandmother of sauces is, of course, the simple deglazing: Fry your chop in a pan and, when it is done, discard the excess grease* and pour in a liquid (plain water is the most basic) to free the concentrated cooking essences sticking to the bottom of the pan. Boil that down a bit, and the sauce is done—but it is an unappealingly runny, watery sauce. Since the days of the first baby steps of *la grande cuisine*, French cooks have sought ways to thicken their deglazings into an appealing velvety consistency. In medieval times they found they could do it with a *roux* of pig fat and flour, and occasionally even fish liver, but that was pretty gamey stuff, and not exactly *raffiné*. Ground almonds and toasted bread crumbs were better, but they gave the sauces a grainy consistency. Chopped mushrooms created a kind of thickening by adding a mass of solids, but they did not bind the sauce.

That was the big problem: the binding, the *liaison*. Flour will bind liquids beautifully, as any kindergarten kid discovers the first time he makes flour-and-water paste, but that tends to turn into a wad of chewing gum in the stomach. Arrowroot and potato flour work similarly, while cornstarch is the binding–thickening agent of choice for most Chinese cooking. Butter, egg yolks, and cream are infinitely nicer and smoother—no normally constituted human being can resist the taste of a proper *hollandaise* or *béarnaise* or a *poulet à la crème*—but none of these could exactly be called light, and their cholesterol count is redoubtable.

Bernard found the salvation for binding his sauces with vegetables—more precisely, with purées of certain vegetables cooked in water. After months of experimentation, he and Patrick Bertron settled on puréed carrots and onions for most of their sauces, and occasionally garlic, fennel, and turnip purées for others, depending on the savors they were seeking. It was an ingenious adaptation of the modern technology of the blender to solve a very ancient problem, and it was entirely successful: fat-free, velvety in texture, similar to but interestingly

---

*The English keep the fat of their famous roasts of beef, adding flour, egg, and milk to turn it into Yorkshire pudding, then deglaze the cooking pan itself with water to make the gravy they ladle generously over the meat. Roast beef and Yorkshire pudding is their traditional Sunday treat, equivalent to the French family's roast chicken and fried (or mashed) potatoes. Yorkshire pudding is homey, friendly, and tasty, but French cooks recoil at the idea of using cooked fats in their sauces. Cardiologists would probably agree with them.

different from run-of-the-mill sauces—and also delicious. (Pushing the antifat crusade to a final, logical conclusion, The Chef and the chef went on to create an ersatz but surprisingly convincing *"béarnaise"* of thickened egg yolk and mustard vinaigrette.)

Whether Bernard was fully aware of it or not, his purée-based sauces put him in the footsteps of one of his greatest masters. As early as 1972, Michel Guérard in Eugénie-les-Bains was developing the theoretical underpinnings of the dietary gastronomy that was destined to make him an international celebrity and enrich the little Landais community where he and Christine had settled. Four years later he published *La Grande Cuisine Minceur,* which included very precise directions for making sauce *liaisons* with vegetable purées. "This is one of the fundamental principles of my *cuisine minceur,*" he wrote, along with a typically didactic explanation (there will always be something of the professor in Michel Guérard) of how the bursting of cellulose cells in the vegetables avoided the deposit of acidic residues in the human organism.

Bernard, then, cannot be given the credit for inventing the system of binding sauces with vegetable purées, but he was not attempting to create a gastronomy for slimming, as Guérard had done so successfully at Eugénie. "You're not going to lose any weight here," Bernard frequently explained, "but you're not going to gain any, either—and my cuisine is so healthy and so digestible that you can enjoy your lunch and still have an appetite when dinnertime comes around."

Well, that may have been just a bit on the exaggerated side—doing justice to a couple of three-star meals a day, even of Bernard's light, minimalist style, may have been a joy, but it was not a task to be undertaken by any belly-come-lately, especially when the cheeses and desserts had been factored in.

And anyway, they weren't three-star meals yet, were they? Not officially, at any rate, because, as the eighties edged toward the nineties, Michelin had not yet bestowed its ultimate papal blessing upon the Côte d'Or. Still, with his fortieth birthday just around the corner, Bernard had come of age personally and professionally: he was well-married, father of one child, with another on the way (before long there would be a third, too), precariously solvent but solvent nonetheless, his reputation growing by the day. He had attained the stability so prized by those crusty *auvergnats* who published the only bible that really mattered for him. In short, he was an attractive candidate for the gastronomic beatification of three stars. Like his fourth decade, that was just around the corner. First, though, he had a little more building to do.

XI

THE BIG PUSH

*I*n 1987, a momentous page of French gastronomic history was turned when La Pyramide in Vienne was demoted from three to two stars. The *déclassement* did not signify a lowering of standards in food or service—neither the *sole Colbert* nor the truffle in puff pastry reposing on a winsome puddle of *sauce périgeux* nor any other of the multitude of pleasures on the day's handwritten menu had lost the edge of perfection that gourmets expected of Fernand Point's glorious caravansary by the banks of the Rhône. The reason for the demotion was simpler and sadder: the death of Madame Point, "Mado," who had maintained La Pyramide at impeccable three-star level through all the decades since her husband's "suicide by champagne" in 1955. With the last tie to *le grand Fernand* severed, Michelin applied its stern logic and clipped a star, waiting to see how the new administration would perform. As of 1987 only one of provincial gastronomy's original Holy Trinity, Pic in Valence, now in the hands of André's son Jacques, remained at the guide's top level. But year after year—hell, by then it seemed to be just about day by day—observers of the French food scene could see Bernard Loiseau in Saulieu galloping up to join the renowned pack, and getting closer with every step.

"That's what I want to buy! That's what I want to buy!"

Bernard Fabre vividly remembers the scene from that same

epochal year as a perfect symbol for the Loiseau sprint toward three stars. It was during that strange interim period when, with Chantal already out of Saulieu (but not yet formally divorced) and Dominique not yet moved in, Bernard had reverted to his bachelor ways and to the one marriage that was an unchanging constant for him: the Côte d'Or. Through Dominique's contacts at *L'Hôtellerie*, he had begun consulting with Guy Catonné's architectural firm in Paris to iron out the details of where to go next with his master building plan. Because going he was—there was no question of standing still. The nine new Relais & Châteaux rooms dating from 1985 were only the start, and he was determined to attack step two as soon as the loans he had applied for came through. This step would bring to reality every chef's most cherished dream—his new kitchen and his new dining room.

Or rather, his dining *rooms*, because by then he had learned that there was a particular logic that needed to be applied to Saulieu. There had to be a principal dining room, of course, neither too pretentiously vast nor too niggardly small. Seating space for eighty, Bernard figured, would be just about right. But on those dreaded winter days when clients were rare for even the three-star places located out in the sticks where the bankers and stockbrokers rarely roamed, he couldn't seat the day's paltry ration of a dozen or fewer diners in a room for eighty. That would make the guests feel uncomfortable while making him look bad by underlining the paucity of clientele. No: He needed two dining rooms—or even three, of diminishing size, but each one nicely located and decorated with similarly good taste, and all three of them giving out onto the garden.

And it was, precisely, in the Côte d'Or's garden that the two Bernards were tramping back and forth that afternoon in 1987, inspecting the place from behind, taking in the wretched view over Dumaine's garage and ramshackle kitchen with the goofy stovepipes sticking out of the leaky roof. This rather squalid side of the Côte d'Or was largely hidden from most clients, but Bernard saw it every instant of his life and he hated it. And that was what caused his excited exclamation.

"That's what I want to buy!" he repeated breathlessly, kicking the wall to emphasize his point. He was gesturing at Le Petit Marguéry,* one of the fifteen hotel-restaurants dating back to Saulieu's glory days, this one directly adjacent to La Côte d'Or. Like all the others, the Petit Marguéry had suffered grievously from the new north–south traffic pattern, and word was out that it was for sale. Guy Catonné and his associates had already demonstrated on paper how, by combining the space of Dumaine's garage with the Petit Marguéry, they would be able to devise a splendid U-shaped structure fronting out on the Route Nationale 6, but embracing the garden on three sides behind: hotel rooms in one wing, kitchen, salons, and dining rooms on the other, and the reception area at the bottom of the U, with more rooms above. The portion of the Petit Marguéry fronting out on the R.N. 6 could become the Côte d'Or's luxury and gourmet shop, leaving room for storage space and offices above it. The scheme was perfect.

"Buy it, buy it," cried Bernard.

"Well, that's nice to say, but let's see if we can," Fabre replied with the calm, professional deliberation of the true money counter.

They could, as it turned out. In 1988 Fabre arranged to buy the

---

*Sitting in the middle of rural Morvan as they were, the hotel's original owners had probably hoped to see a bit of gastronomic glory rub off on them from the celebrated Parisian restaurant Café Marguéry, after which they named their place. Café Marguéry became doubly famous around the turn of the nineteenth into the twentieth century for having fallen victim to one of history's most curious acts of gastronomic espionage after the American millionaire-glutton Diamond Jim Brady heard tell of the incomparable sauce—a closely guarded professional secret—that was the highlight of *filets de sole Marguéry*. Under threat of refusing his future patronage, Brady persuaded the owner of one of his preferred New York restaurants to yank his son from Cornell and send him to Paris as a spy to snitch the recipe. The boy wangled a job as a dishwasher and worked assiduously enough to be promoted up into the *brigade*, where he learned the heart of the secret: mussels. Like most seafood sauces, this one was a reduction of a white-wine-based fish stock, but heavily flavored with a reduction of the water in which mussels had been cooked. The final *liaison* was done with egg yolks and, unsurprisingly, a generous scoop of fresh, soft butter. With all of Brady's chicanery, though, it is probable that any competent cook could have doped out the broad lines of the sauce by simply going to Café Marguéry, ordering the dish, looking, and tasting. The ring of mussels ritually surrounding the poached sole would have been in itself a pretty glaring giveaway.

hotel for 1.5 million francs (about $250,000), to be paid out of Bernard's second big loan package of some fifteen million francs (a bit more than $2 million), most of which was earmarked for his dream kitchen, three dining rooms, and their attendant salons. Fabre did some fancy financial footwork to amortize and combine Bernard's outstanding earlier loans, packing them in with the new one, and setting a fifteen-year repayment schedule.

Everything seemed set. Bernard was thrilled. With the papers in apple-pie order, all that remained for him to do was meet with the seller and his *notaire*, sign the act, and take possession of the Petit Marguéry. Too easy, and too good to be true? Yes. Fabre was in his office in Auxerre that morning when his phone buzzed. Bernard was at the other end, distraught, breathless, and bearing catastrophic news: "He doesn't want to sell anymore!"

Don't move, muttered Fabre, and jumped into his car. He arrived in Saulieu forty minutes later, just in time to hit a speed trap at the entrance to town. Flagged down by the *gendarmes* and ticketed for traveling at 75 mph in a 30 mph zone, he had his car immobilized on the spot and was forced to finish the last few hundred meters on foot. He got a fine, of course, and his license was suspended for a month, but even so, the morning ended in triumph: less naïve than Bernard, he pulled off the sale with ease. Exactly as Fabre had suspected, the Petit Marguéry's owner was all too happy to sell but, like a peasant bargaining over the price of his heifer while facing another who clearly wanted it, he had just been waiting for the sweetener of a little vigorish under the table, that was all: sale concluded. Men of the world know things that cooks ignore.

Bernard was ecstatic. "What do you want to eat?" he asked Fabre. "I know you like *cèpes* [boletus mushrooms]. And you like lobster, don't you? Let's have lunch!"

By then it was past three p.m., and the last clients had finished their meals. For once officiating alone in the empty kitchen, Bernard himself grilled the lobsters and sautéed the mushrooms for an improvised *homard aux cèpes*, which he devoured with Fabre, in the company of a fine bottle of Chablis, on a corner of one of Dumaine's rotten old aluminum-topped worktables.

"Best lunch I ever had," Fabre told me, glum with the realization that there would never be another one. It was only natural, of course, for a cook to express his thanks, or simply demonstrate his friendship, with an offering of food, and Bernard did it a thousand times for different people on different occasions. Patrice Vappereau, a Saulieu native who went to work in Paris as a young man, then returned to Saulieu in 1980 and was elected mayor in 1995, recalled his first encounter with the town's star chef, an event that wowed him as keenly as the *homard aux cèpes* did for Fabre.

"My brother was president of the local tennis club, and he wanted to organize the annual dinner at Loiseau's place, but he didn't have much of a budget, so we couldn't expect anything very elegant. When my brother told me Bernard had decided to cook us carp, I was really worried. I'm a hunter and fisherman, and I know all about carp. It's a lousy fish—*de la merde*. But he boned it, cooked it in a skillet like a steak, and served it with a red wine sauce. I was astonished: It was wonderful! That carp in red wine is still one of my greatest gastronomic experiences."

That tennis club dinner of fish was, of course, an early incarnation of the Loiseau classic, the crackly skinned filet of pike perch (a more three-star style of fish) in red wine sauce that remains on the Côte d'Or's menu today, but Vappereau could not resist seizing the occasion of having a tame journalist at his side to expatiate from carp to the grander scheme of matters economic and interpersonal.

"Everyone in town loved Bernard, because he wasn't *fier*, as they say; not snooty. He was world-famous but he talked with people just like anyone else, and he laughed and joked around with passersby in the street. And he always tried to help out the town, too. For years he was our most important local employer—the Côte d'Or was the livelihood for sixty-five or more people, and he was the one who paid the biggest property and professional taxes. When I'd go abroad and tell people where I was from, they'd say 'Saulieu—ah, Bernard Loiseau!' He was our ambassador."

With the big new loan package assured, the construction crews finally got going under Guy Catonné and his team of architects in the summer of 1990. Although certain later sections of Bernard's great building plan, essentially devoted to the hotel side, were more expensive, it was this 1990 *tranche* that most swiftly and dramatically transformed Dumaine's Côte d'Or and stamped it with Bernard Loiseau's personality once and for all. The truly historical dining room where Dumaine had nourished a steady flow of movie stars, crowned heads, and political notables was not to be destroyed, to be sure, but it was relegated to the status of a museum of gastronomies past, adorned with menus, photos, and testimonials from the high, the mighty, the famous, and the stinking rich. Intelligently mixing a practical use in with the historical function, Bernard decided to use Dumaine's surprisingly small dining room (seating for no more than thirty or forty) as an intimate, conveniently placed breakfast room for those guests who foreswore the degenerate pleasure of swimming in a sea of crumbs by taking breakfast in bed.

Dumaine's kitchen, on the other hand, was obliterated—good riddance. Bernard had toiled in its creaky, insalubrious confines for sixteen years and Patrick for nine, and both of them were so heartily glad to see it go that they pitched in with the construction crews to bash down its walls with picks and sledgehammers. The entrance to the Côte d'Or's gloomy old garage became a comfortably elegant salon whose centerpiece was a fireplace of medieval proportions. Opposite that stood a vast bar and, at the far end, the entrance to the new high-ceilinged hexagonal dining room with broad windows leading to the English garden. Two smaller dining rooms, for conferences, private parties, or simply the bad days when clients were rare, continued on down at the end of the wing. Naturally enough, the entrance to the kitchen stood on the other side of the hallway, in what had been the rear storage area of the Petit Marguéry. And what a kitchen it was: spacious, glistening with stainless steel and tile, with each separate food section—fish, meats, pastry, vegetables—individually equipped with its own refrigerated space. The three cooking zones—fish, meats, and ovens—functioned now on pure, clean propane gas, and even the garbage cans enjoyed their own separate, refrigerated space out in the courtyard. Bernard had gone from a beat-up old tractor to a Ferrari.

It was an exhilarating time, and the new design spectacularly transformed and expanded the place. In all, the project required six months of work, but Catonné's planning staggered the various pieces of the architectural puzzle cleverly enough to require the closing of the Côte d'Or for no more than a single month—November 19 to December

21, 1990—at the very end of this crucial *tranche* of renovation and re-construction. It is worthy of note that apart from his reluctant one-day Christmas break, this was the only time in his entire Saulieu tenure that Bernard closed his establishment down. One month off for sixteen years of presence on the job works out to something less than two free days a year.*

When Catonné and his associates speak of those six months of working with Bernard to transform the Côte d'Or, their faces show the rueful, nostalgic smiles of those who have shared the trials of an exas-perating but still enriching common experience—army basic training springs to mind, or final-exam period in college—but the inflection of their voices bears witness to an admiration and tenderness that seem very close to something resembling love for the simple humanity of the guy who had hired them to put flesh on the bones of his dream.

He was generous and enthusiastic and appreciative and unstint-ingly energetic, of course—that was just Bernard—but at the same time, he was impossible. That, too, was Bernard. Never had these pro-fessionals worked with a client who got into their hair like this one, who niggled them so persistently or who involved himself so thor-oughly with the details, day by day and hour by hour, of what they were doing, and the how and why. In their company he haunted dealers in used construction materials throughout the Morvan and Burgundy re-gions, picking over and choosing, one by one, the elements that were to go into the building of his ideal palace. Acting with the architects, sometimes in spite of them and occasionally against them, he kept track of the pieces being put into place, the trimming and painting and polishing of them, and the final insertion of them into their positions in the remaking the face of La Côte d'Or.

"He was captivated by materials that had already had another life," said Christian Daguin, one of Catonné's associates. "He loved noble

---

*Contrary to popular (foreign) legend and the stereotypical images of three-hour lunches, endless sexual dalliance, and Latin insouciance, the French in general are an extremely hardworking people. They can be maddeningly egocentric and arrogant, but unless they happen to be engaged in one of the country's two char-acteristic national occupations—vacations and strikes—they are generally assidu-ous when they undertake a job. Bernard carried assiduity to its extended logical conclusion: nonstop work.

old wood and old tile, and he would tell us exactly how he wanted them used in the project, but it was always in conjunction with modern technology—for instance, he would demand traditional Burgundy *tommetes* [farmhouse-style hexagonal tiles], but with indirect electrical heating underneath them. 'Today's technology at the service of yesterday's materials,' he would always tell us. He used that expression all the time."

Guillaume Potel, the youngest of Catonné's team, was the one who spent the most time in Saulieu, and was doubtless the closest to Bernard. "What was remarkable," he said, "was that he always knew exactly what he wanted. He couldn't always articulate his view precisely, but he recognized best-quality stuff immediately, and he was very demanding about it. There was never any doubt about his choices. Once we were walking around a dealer's yard and he found a big old moss-covered stone lying by the side of a brook. 'I want that for my garden,' he said. None of us had even noticed it.

"After sixteen years in Saulieu he considered that he had been adopted by Burgundy, and he felt completely at home with the area's esthetic traditions. The architecture he asked us to do followed the same intellectual line as his cuisine: traditional, classical, but modern at the same time. 'I don't give a damn what people say about the culture of what we're doing here,' he told us. 'All I want to do is to give my clients the best.'"

Here, Potel was defending Bernard and his own firm from a charge sometimes leveled by fashionable chatterers of France's intellectual elite: that with the new old Côte d'Or, they had been guilty of one of the heaviest mortal sins against esthetic correctness in architecture: pastiche. Since he had borrowed such large sums of money, it was suggested, Bernard should have had the guts to make a significant statement with a kind of modern architecture that would grace Saulieu with a new, monumental identity.

Thank God he didn't. What his native good sense told him was that French modern architecture is often in glaringly stark contradiction with the unique glory of its past. It had seemed that from around the tenth century onward, just about any structures touched by French builders—cathedrals, châteaux, farm villages, market shelters, barns and work spaces—miraculously emerged from their talented hands as beautiful as they were functional. (A plausible argument could be made for the proposition that architecture is *the* great expression of French artistic talent, ranking above painting, sculpture, literature, and music.) The glass, plastic, concrete, and steel inspirations created by today's descendants of these builders, however, make a sad comparison: graceless and "cheapo," for the most part, they tend to be fragile and ill-maintained, and they age badly. Bernard wanted solid, traditional Burgundy materials and comfort for Saulieu, and he was right. The high ceilings, the handcrafted beams, the tiles, the flagstone, and the wood paneling of the new Côte d'Or offered clients the warm, peaceful sensation of leaving the noise and aggression of the twentieth century behind them and of entering a kind of rustic paradise, a soothing, perfectly preserved country manor where every pleasure of discreet refinement except one or two (there are other places in other towns for that) awaited them: *luxe, calme et volupté*.

In the end Bernard got what he wanted from Catonné and his associates, but it wasn't a picnic. "By the time we finished he had become a very good *maître d'ouvrage* [supervising client], so we could tell clearly where it was he wanted us to go next," said Potel. "But he could get carried away by his enthusiasm. He would start pipe-dreaming, and his megalomaniac side would kick in. Next thing we knew, he was talking about adding the Hôtel de la Poste across the street to his list—he wanted to buy right and left."

A bit of counting and reasonable persuasion from Fabre usually managed to cool Bernard's passion for further acquisitions, but a very definite problem emerged with the matter of authority over the work: Who was to be the final boss of the construction, the *maître d'oeuvre*. Clearly, when push came to shove, there could be only one: Guy Catonné, the founder and director of the company that had been hired to do the job, came down to Saulieu himself for the last month of work. And there he ran smack into Bernard's meddling into every detail of post, beam, tile, paneling, plug, and paint. With that, push came to shove.

"He's got to go!" Fabre remembered Guy Catonné's ultimatum all too well: If Bernard stayed around in Saulieu to *emmerder* [pester] the architects and the workers minute by minute, Catonné could not guarantee delivery for lunch on December 22, as had been planned. In fact, they might not even make it for the traditional Christmas Eve or

New Year *reveillons*—the stupefying gastronomic blowouts at which the entire French population feels obliged to eat and drink itself catatonic from 8 P.M. to past midnight, for the greater profit of the country's restaurants. And we're way over budget, too, Catonné added. You've got to find a way to cut at least a million francs.

"He came to me because he knew I was the only one who had a chance of persuading Bernard," Fabre explained. "But can you imagine telling Bernard to leave Saulieu? Leaving his baby? I began by telling him we were running over budget. I had all the figures on paper, and it came closer to a million and a half francs. He raised hell, but called me an hour later. He was very, very reluctant, but he agreed to put off the building of the monumental staircase he had set his heart on. That could come later.

"Okay, I said, but we're running over schedule, too. It looks like we're not going to finish the work on deadline.

"With that he exploded. '*Merde!*' he said. '*Pas possible!*' Now he was really panicked.

"Bernard, I said, there is a solution, but I'm embarrassed to tell you what it is: You've got to stop pestering them. You've got to leave them alone—you've got to get out of here. Go spend a few weeks with your parents.

"He blew up, flatly refused, yelled at me and called me every name he could think of. I told him to think it over. And he did, too. Called me back later. 'You're right,' he finally said. 'I'll go down to Clermont.' Two weeks later he was back, and we had lunch together on the twenty-first of December. Everything was finished and ready, but he looked around the place and decided that a lot of the floors looked too bare. That same morning he spotted the van of a door-to-door carpet seller. He flagged it down and bought fifteen or seventeen carpets. I yelled at him, of course, because the financial situation was so tight, but he saw me coming and cut me off. 'I bought them with my money,' he said, just like a contrite kid. A lot of those carpets are still there today."

As the big 1990 building program was finishing up in Saulieu, the world of French *haute cuisine* was still struggling to come to terms with two startling events that had occurred earlier in the year, both of which would have an indirect, but nonetheless real, effect on Bernard: the starburst in the gastronomic sky of Alain Ducasse's third Michelin star, and the death of Alain Chapel.

Chapel had been born to the craft. His father was a restaurateur who had already won a Michelin star in the little town of Mionnay 15 miles north of Lyon. But after Alain returned from his apprenticeships (notably at La Pyramide in Vienne), he leaped miles higher, claiming the third star in 1973 at age thirty-five. With that, the family restaurant, officially La Mère Charles but known everywhere simply as Chapel's place, became a gastronomic shrine attracting hungry pilgrims from every corner of the globe. Along with Michel Guérard in Eugénie and the Swiss Freddy Girardet in Crissier (near Lausanne), Chapel was one of those who, like Liszt, on another sort of *piano*, might have been seriously suspected of passing a Faustian pact with the devil. He was a true magician, a kitchen Houdini who dazzled, surprised, and delighted from one end of a meal to the other, from the fabulous *friture** of tiny freshwater fish (*ablettes, perches*) netted in Lake Geneva, or the innumerable ponds and clean, cold marshes of the Dombes wetlands, which he ritually sent out to accompany a glass of perfect sauvignon (a Sancerre *Monts Damnés*, perhaps) to the last sharp tang of chocolate served with the coffee.

But Chapel was also a perfectionist of the most intransigent sort, a man who worried his culinary details to death and who set his cooking times not in minutes but down to seconds, more or fewer of which would cause him to consider a dish ruined. My personal image of Chapel's perfectionism takes me back to the afternoon in the late eighties when I was briefly interviewing him over coffee, and a kaleidoscopic selection of little pastries and chocolates (these guys can never leave well enough alone), and his face froze. It froze because his laser eye had darted to a porcelain cream pitcher and spotted a blemish so tiny, so inconsiderable as to be invisible to the normally constituted

---

*Chapel enjoyed desanctifying pompous rituals of gastronomy, and instructed his *maîtres d'hôtel* to encourage guests to eat both the deep-fried fish and the delicate lacework of fried parsley that accompanied it with their hands. Just so, a few years later, did *maîtres d'hôtel* in Saulieu instruct their guests to pick up their frog leg lollipops and enjoy them that way. Bernard chose well the masters he emulated.

human gaze. Furious, he summoned the waiter who had carried the offending object to us.

"Take that back into the kitchen and smash it!" he ordered. "I'm not going to have chipped china in my house."

Chapel was only fifty-two, in the prime of his life and the summit of his glory, when he was felled by a massive heart attack. The brotherhood of *grande cuisine* was weakened and bereaved by his disappearance—as, indeed, it would be again only two years later when the great Jacques Pic keeled over in Valence—but not enough for Bernard to step back for a few moments and reflect long and hard on the nervous exhaustion that goes hand in hand with overwork. Chapel's death may have served Bernard in one unexpected and somewhat perverse manner, though. As it had done for La Pyramide when Madame Point died, Michelin demoted La Mère Charles to two stars as a sign of respect for the greatness of its defunct chef.* The guide strenuously denies that there are only so many three-star "slots" open in its pages, but even so, it was the opinion of many that this change left the region with a gaping hole to be filled, and of all of gastronomy's *dauphins* in waiting, Loiseau was the one who was exciting the most comment in those days.

As for Alain Ducasse, Bernard could not but regard with an envious and worried eye the skyrocket ascension of this extraordinary prodigy from the southwest who succeeded brilliantly, and with no apparent effort, at everything he touched. While still a boy, he had walked out of cooking school in disgust (too slow, too basic, too easy) and made his first giant steps in gastronomy by talking Michel Guérard into hiring him in his kitchen at Eugénie, an accomplishment that made him comparable to one of those juvenile geniuses who gets into Harvard at fourteen. He then went on to Roger Vergé in Mougins and—*justement*—Alain Chapel in Mionnay to polish off the training, and immediately applied it in his first restaurant, in Juan-les-Pins. In

---

*Like La Pyramide, the restaurant continues today with two stars, under the name of Alain Chapel, and is directed by his widow, Suzanne. The chef, Philippe Jousse, was Chapel's last right-hand man. His cuisine is wondrously good—certainly as good as a few other three-star restaurants one could name—but Michelin has not yet judged that the house is worth the top rating. A question of personality, perhaps.

1988 he won his first star, and the very next year he became Michelin's youngest-ever two-star chef at age twenty-seven. In spite of (or was it because of?) nearly dying in the alpine plane crash, which cost him the best part of three years to make a full recovery, he won his third star at thirty-three, fully financed in the undertaking, in the impiously luxurious Louis XV in Monaco. Moreover, Ducasse was already laying plans to conquer Paris. The rest of the planet could come after that.* (And it did, too.)

Three stars at thirty-three—and without having to lay out a *centime* of his own money! That had to be trotting in Bernard's head while he barked out orders in his gleaming new kitchen as 1990 flopped over into 1991, the milestone year that sent him into the crucial, self-questioning plateau of age forty. Just yesterday, it seemed, he had been the wunderkind everyone was talking about. Now Ducasse had gotten ahead of him, and plenty of other younger chefs were standing impatiently in line, too. Since La Côte d'Or's second star in 1981, eight others had been promoted up to the glory of three. Was the train passing him by, like the traffic on the Autoroute de Sud? Bernard chomped his nails and fretted. Why were they waiting? What more could he do to please Papa Michelin? Wasn't he good enough, after all?

Three stars *had* to come, that was all there was to it. It was one thing to have saddled himself with all those loans—by the end of 1990 he had a reimbursement schedule totaling nearly $50,000 a month (and it would go higher than that a few years later)—but more than that, he had aligned and invested his entire person and purpose and life's view to that goal. Quite literally, Bernard had mortgaged his future to Michelin. The movers and shakers of the guide heave sighs of exasperation† when they hear of chefs taking the big construction route, because it is cast-iron company policy that Michelin stars reflect

---

*"Fifteen minutes after winning my third star," Ducasse told me, "I said *voilà*, that's done. What next?" Other chefs would have considered that their life's goal had been achieved, but this one is a hybrid kind of gastronomic extraterrestrial: Speedy Gonzalez with the appetite of Gargantua. Last time I looked, he had won a total of seven stars in France, while enjoying movie-star status abroad.

†Just a bit feigned, I suspect. Secretly, they have to enjoy the power and prestige they wield.

the contents of the plate only, and that no chef can build his way up the honor roll of excellence. Even so, seized by the chimera of stardom, wealth, and prestige, chefs try it all the time, apparently undeterred by the blanched bones of preceding victims of this *folie des grandeurs gastronomiques* lying outside the bankruptcy courts.

Bernard wasn't buying any of that "company policy" business. He knew damn well that if he were to get three stars he needed more than his *cuisine des essences*, however perfectly executed. He would have to serve it on Limoges china, and in the beauty and comfort of surroundings that were apposite to and complemented the highest level of French cooking. Now, with the big 1990 building program completed, he was satisfied that he had at last arrived at that level.

Physically, the right indicators were in place, both in the Côte d'Or and up the road in his own house, where he was at last a settled family man, respectably stable. He was ready, then, but the insecurities that dogged him remained as blatant as ever. Every time I saw him in those years, he would press me with the same anguished question: "Do you think I'm going to get them, the three stars? You do, don't you? Don't you? Huh?"

His questioning had nothing to do with the many years we had known each other. That was just Bernard being Bernard. Perpetually in need of reassurance, he threw the question out indiscriminately, collaring just about anyone who crossed his path in Saulieu. I have no doubt that among those whom he grilled like that, there must have been a few bemused Michelin inspectors wrapped in their anonymous gray suits.

In his ideal palace, however, there was one aspect over which Bernard could not exercise a total and permanent surveillance: the *personnel de salle*, the hospitality and table-waiting staff. The decoration of the Côte d'Or was as he wanted it, and in his dream kitchen there was not a detail that escaped his notice, but how were his people treating the guests out there on the other side of the big swinging door? Was everything perfect? Bernard worried, and because he worried, he attempted to make himself ubiquitous. Habitués of the restaurant knew that at most meals they would stand a good chance of catching sight of the chef if they waited until the *service* was well under way and most of the guests around them had been served. At this point, a glance over at the doorway leading to the hall, and beyond that, to the entrance of the kitchen, would almost infallibly reveal the chef himself, half in the shadows, posted two or three steps back, discreetly masking his presence and taking care to stay out of the way of passing waiters: Bernard was keeping an eye on things.

He was no dope and he was no dupe. He had been around the three-star circuit long enough to know that no restaurant made it to the top unless every last detail of service and comfort matched the quality of the cuisine being served. A revealing passage in Pascal Rémy's book on his days as a Michelin inspector demonstrates that whatever company spokesmen may say, it is not the food alone that influences judgments for the guide. Even though they do it for a profession, the inspectors are just as human as anyone else, when it comes to making judgments about what they are paying for:

When we test a restaurant we take into account the environment, the quality of the welcome on arrival and departure, the surroundings, the general setup, the service and the atmosphere. For the client, a relaxed and considerate welcome is the first pleasure of a meal. The first duty of the restaurateur is to set his clients at ease. The inspector reacts to the warmth and efficiency of the first person he encounters in an establishment. The proper welcome does not improve or alter the taste of the dishes, but it puts us in a good frame of mind.

Next, if he looks around to see a well-proportioned room and a harmonious décor, he begins to feel just right in his chair. The lighting is soft, the temperature ideal, the chair comfortable. He is ready to consult the menu. The menu is clean, spotless, unmarked, easily readable, proposing dishes clearly and precisely. The tables around him, judiciously arranged, are attractive and well set. The porcelain is often good quality; the silverware is tasteful, the flowers are fresh and the glasses impeccable.

The wife of the owner or the *maître d'hôtel*, sometimes the chef in person, takes your order with a smile. The inspector asks for advice or clarifications, which are delivered with skill and interest. A pleasant and competent *sommelier* takes over. He proposes a good harmony between wines and food. A quick trip to the toilets? Obviously you can't judge a restaurant on the quality of its toilets. There is a legend that tries to make people believe that when a restaurant has clean toilets the rest of the house is properly run. But that doesn't mean you are going to eat well there.

The *amuse-bouches* arrive without delay. The water is fresh and cold. The bread crusty. The entrée arrives. Delicious. The *maître d'hôtel* inquires if you are satisfied. The main course comes at just the right moment. Some more bread? The cheeses have been carefully aged. The dessert is set out. The check arrives discreetly.

The service is rapid and efficient, finely tuned by the *maître d'hôtel* to the rhythm of each client. Conclusion: you will be more indulgent with a middle-range table amiably and attentively served than with a minuscule imperfection on an excellent plate served with arrogance or disdain.

By instinct and experience, Bernard knew all that, anyway, and he badgered his staff unremittingly to see a potential Michelin inspector behind the face of every unknown client over age fifteen. With the passing years, not only did the food on the plates and the physical appearance of La Côte d'Or come to reflect his likes and dislikes, but the staff itself became an extension of his personality. It is inevitable: Every serious restaurant is like a psychological portrait of the person who owns it and runs it. The relaxed bonhomie of the Troisgros brothers' old dining room recalled the days when local gents gathered and talked football over *pastis* in the bar, while Jean-Baptiste was serving up extra tots of cognac for the traveling salesmen at the *table d'hôte*. The always-flawless service in Vonnas today evokes Christian Millau's admiring description of the place: "Georges Blanc is the train that always arrives on time." In Laguiole, the waiters are as reserved and soft-spoken as Chef Michel Bras, and the level of their discreet professionalism is just as impressive as the boss's. Restaurant Paul Bocuse boasts so many winners of the "Meilleur Ouvrier de France"—best French worker, or artisan—diploma that the staff by itself could be taken *en bloc* as faculty for a hotel and restaurant school. If you have the occasion to visit the Tour d'Argent in Paris, you may feel constrained to kiss the ring of the

The right wing of the Côte d'Or's hotel, a bit of
the garden, and the monumental staircase with
the elevator in the middle

The main façade, looking out on rue Argentine. Note the characteristic BL logo underneath his name. All of the receptionists, waiters, and maîtres d'hotel wear this logo on their lapels.

The Côte d'Or's main dining room

Inside the Côte d'Or with the merry-go-round horse that is part of the decor. *From left to right:* Bastien, Bérangère, and Bernard

Bernard and Dominique in the garden at the back of the hotel. Roof of the dining room on the left.

Bernard and Dominique making crepes with Bérangère, *left*, and Bastien, *right*

Le Restaurant Bernard

Entrées

Jambonnettes de grenouilles à la purée d'ail et au jus de persil
Œufs en meurette au jambon du Morvan
Huîtres Belon à la compotée d'oignon et vinaigrette d'huîtres
Bisque de homard bleu, tronçons de homard au navet
Grosses asperges vertes aux vinaigrettes de pomme de terre et jaune d'oeuf
Queues de langoustines royales au jus d'ortie

Poissons et Crustacés

Sandre à la peau croustillante et fondue d'échalote, sauce au vin rouge
Tronçon de turbot rôti, sauce au jaune d'œuf parfumée à l'estragon
Bar de ligne aux huîtres Belon, pointes d'asperge verte de Pertuis
Rouget et son jus, petits farcis de légumes de saison et fleurs de courgettes frites
Queue de homard bleu poêlée à cru aux pommes de terre « grenaille »

Volailles, Viandes et Abats

Blanc de volaille fermière lardé de truffe et foie gras poêlé
   à la purée de pomme de terre truffée
Poularde de Bresse à la vapeur "Alexandre Dumaine" au riz truffé
Côte de bœuf rôtie, jus de queue de bœuf au vin rouge et à la moëlle
Cochon de lait rôti au boudin blanc truffé
Côte de veau fermier « sous la mère » de race Limousine, sauce au foie gras
Panaché d'agneau de lait des Pyrénées dans son jus au thym
Ris de veau doré à la purée de pomme de terre truffée

Desserts

Soupe de fraise et granité au muscat de Beaumes de Venise
Fine tarte chaude aux pommes
Saint-Honoré « cuit minute », crème chiboust
Tasse chocolat café et sa glace au lait
Beignets de poire pochée à la liqueur de cassis, croustillant au safran et à la vanille

Menu from 2003

Loiseau ... au fil des saisons

Les classiques de Bernard Loiseau

Jambonnettes de grenouilles à la purée d'ail et au jus de persil
***
Sandre à la peau croustillante et fondue d'échalote, sauce au vin rouge
***
Blanc de volaille fermière et foie gras poêlé à la purée de pomme de terre truffée
***
Chariot de fromages
***
Rose des sables à la glace pur chocolat et son coulis d'orange confite

Menu Gourmet

Escalope de foie gras de canard poêlée au verjus
ou
Ragoût d'huîtres et de langoustines, jus Parmentier à l'ortie
ou
Noix de Saint-Jacques poêlées aux petits légumes, vinaigrette acidulée
***
Sandre rôti au jus meunière et sa poêlée de racines
ou
Panaché de veau fermier « sous la mère », crapiau du Morvan et embeurrée de chou
ou
Filet de canette de Challans à l'aigre-doux
***
Chariot de fromages
***
Soufflé chaud au Grand Marnier
ou
Ananas Victoria poêlé au sucre muscovado, sorbet à l'ananas et croustillant de coco
ou
Millefeuille tout-vanille, sauce caramel au beurre salé

Menu Dégustation

Salade de homard bleu à la macédoine de légumes coraillée
***
Poêlée de morilles à l'œuf cassé
***
Tronçon de turbot aux asperges de Pertuis, sauce au jaune d'œuf à l'estragon
***
Pigeon fermier rôti et foie gras chaud de canard, jus parfumé aux baies de genièvre
***
Chariot de fromages
***
Sablé breton aux fraises des bois et glace au fromage blanc
***
Tarte au chocolat et sa nougatine, glace à la cazette de noisette

Bernard receiving the Légion d'Honneur
from President François Mitterrand in
1996 at the Élysée Palace

Bernard posing with a huge truffle and scallop shell over one of his signature dishes, *coquille St. Jacques au jus de persil et purée de carrotte*

The Côte d'Or's award-winning breakfast laid out in the Dumaine dining room, with the portrait of Alexandre le Grand behind. (See main text for ingredients.)

On the occasion of celebrating his third Michelin star, Bernard posing with Paul Bocuse (in apron) and Pierre Troisgros, in front of Bocuse's restaurant

Bernard triumphant, shortly after winning his third Michelin star, posing at the hotel's front door, with the new *Michelin* in his hand

Famous photo that Bocuse set up for the lunch at which Bernard invited his staff to celebrate his third star. Bocuse and Bernard atop the elephants, with the Michelin Bibendum behind, at the entry to the restaurant. *From left to right*: Roger Jaloux (Bocuse's chef in the restaurant), Pierre Troisgrois, and Jean Fleury, general manager of Bocuse's Lyon restaurants.

venerable Claude Terrail, who has frequented the rich for so long, and is so rich himself that, consciously or not, his shop generates an atmosphere of semireligious awe, making newcomers feel they should raise their hands when they want to go peepee. (The Tour d'Argent's menu has no prices marked on it. If you have to ask, you can't afford it.) For his part, Bernard had a very clear idea of how the service should be at the Côte d'Or.

"He wanted to be different from all the other places," Hubert Couilloud explained. "'We're selling happiness here,' he used to say all the time, and he insisted on a natural, convivial atmosphere. 'Just be yourselves,' he told us—there were to be no *chichis*, no putting on airs or posing as something we weren't. The greatest compliment he could get was when people told him they felt right at home. I remember once when a client lay down on one of the couches in the salon while his wife was reading a book. Bosses of other places might have been offended at behavior of that sort, but Bernard was delighted. It showed that the guy was at ease here."

Couilloud goes out of his way to credit Bernard with creating the atmosphere of unruffled competence that made the Côte d'Or's service personnel the envy of the trade, because he is too classy to shine a light on himself, but everyone in the three-star circuit recognizes this farmer's son from the very gastronomically inclined Bresse region (where the world's sexiest chickens gallop hysterically around barnyards, developing the gorgeous thighs and breasts that make them the pinups of the *Gallus gallus* crowd) as one of the best *maîtres d'hôtel** in France and the key to the excellence of the nonkitchen staff. Bernard discovered in Hubert a man who was as much a natural leader as himself, but of a diametrically opposed sort: cool and understated where Bernard was overheated and hyperbolic. (Physical stereotypes didn't fit with them at all. Big and strong and gifted with the soft brown eyes that

---

**Maître d'hôtel* was once a position of great authority and prestige in French aristocratic houses until the Revolution came along to cast down their dominant social order. Like the English head butler, the *maître d'hôtel*—master of the house—directed the owner's considerable staff and was held in such confidence that he ordered and paid for provisions, and was entrusted with keys to both the silverware cabinets and the wine cellar.

resemble those of the innumerable Charolais cattle that sun their white flanks on pastureland throughout the Morvan, Bernard might have been expected to exude easy, untroubled confidence, but he was a monument to nervous insecurity. Hubert, with his arctic blue eyes and flaming red hair, was calm and controlled as opposed to the redhead stereotype, which is supposed to be quick-tempered and choleric.) The contrasts of character made for an excellent professional marriage. One complemented the other.

The seemingly effortless efficiency of French service professionals like Couilloud often surprises foreign visitors, especially those from America, where "waiting table" is all too often ill-paid, ill-considered fill-in work for amateurs who have found nothing better to do—the summer job syndrome. Hubert represented the best qualities of this specialized category of workers, but it would have been a mistake for any guest at La Côte d'Or to assume that his skill had come easily; he had studied for it and he had worked at it. Like him, most of the men and women who hold these jobs have been trained over four-year periods of advanced studies, exactly like American college students, at one of the numerous *écoles hôtelières* around the country. Graduates of these programs are competent cooks themselves, have a CAP in cuisine to prove it, and have undergone the same long, arduous years of apprenticeship as the chefs whose food they serve. They know their business backward and forward, and at the high levels of *la grande cuisine*, they are well rewarded for it, too; in France, remember, 15 percent is automatically added to each client's bill for the service personnel. In a three-star restaurant, that can make for very nice salaries, indeed. Bernard never tired of reminding his dining room people that their work in La Côte d'Or made them *notables*, the social equals of any businessman, doctor, or lawyer in the region. They responded by taking their jobs very, very seriously.

"We're responsible for the comfort and well-being of the client," said Couilloud when I asked him to expatiate on his role. "To do that right, we have to know everything about the house, the produce used in the kitchen, and, of course, the style of cooking that we have been fighting to promote all these years. All of us are completely convinced of the concept of cuisine that Monsieur Loiseau developed, or else we wouldn't be here. You won't find anyone here who was hired just to carry plates. It's much more complex than that. We're ambassadors for a style of cuisine. We defend a certain art of living and all the culture and knowledge that lies behind it. It's our job to transmit this to the client, because we are the face of what is happening in the kitchen.

"We don't need to and we don't try to sell one dish or another—they're all equally good.* Our job is to explain Monsieur Loiseau's cooking to those clients who aren't familiar with it. We can get the message across, because we grew up with him while he was developing his style, and we know it by heart. We participated in its elaboration, too: Bernard always had the intelligence to lend an ear to the people around him. He knew that on our side of the door we were the ones who listened to the clients, and could let him know when something was going wrong. You've got to adjust. A guy who stubbornly camps on his position, even if he's a great chef, runs the risk of emptying his dining room. Bernard understood that, even if he was working to make a name for himself through a new style of cuisine, he still had to take into account what the customers wanted."†

It is an interesting exercise to follow, at some length, Couilloud's discourse on the years together with their boss, and to note how frequently the "Monsieur Loiseau" slips into the familiar "Bernard." It underlines the curious mix of intimacy and formalism that existed with this different kind of chef, one who wore his emotions on his sleeve and was unable to hide anything from anybody. Bernard's true nature was to wish to be on a first-name basis with the world's entire population, and hence to use the intimate *tu* form in speech, rather than the formal *vous*, but Couilloud's sense of professionalism led him to insist on maintaining a certain formalism in the workplace; hierarchical organizations require barriers.

---

*A veiled reference to the days of the *grandes maisons* of the traditional Escoffier style, where the likes of Bocuse, Verger, and the Troisgros brothers labored in the *brigades*, and where the *maître d'hôtel* ritually began each morning by asking the chef what the staff should push that day, in an effort to use up the expensive fish and meats that risked spoiling if kept any longer.

†Prompted by Hubert and his colleagues, Bernard rapidly backed away from his early enthusiasm for the pale, watery sauces that afforded Bocuse the occasion for his memorable wisecrack.

The result was pure dissymmetry: In day-to-day communication, Bernard addressed Hubert with *tu*, and Hubert responded with *vous*.

"That's all right," Couilloud laughed. "That never stopped me from telling him *vous me faites chier*" [roughly: You're a pain in the ass].

Exchanges of that sort happened often enough, given Bernard's unpredictably explosive personality, but both men were in agreement about the fundamentals of their work, especially the friendly, easygoing atmosphere that they wanted to establish as the mark of the house; there would be no bowing and scraping, no third-person fake *politesse* ("Is monsieur disposed to give his order now?"), none of the obsequious rigidity that obtained in so many luxury establishments, and never any kind of dress code, even implied, for clients. Gourmets made the detour to Saulieu to relax and eat, not to participate in a fashion show. In truth, though, the matter is almost always self-regulating. People who respect great food (and the considerable price they are paying for it) rarely dress like slobs. T-shirts and flip-flops have never been frequent sights in La Côte d'Or.

Thanks to Bocuse, the Troisgros brothers, Michel Guérard, and their brothers-in-arms of the *nouvelle cuisine* movement, it is the cooks who have become the undisputed stars of the restaurant trade today, each one sought after for the particular twist he or she puts on their cuisine. Everything considered, this is natural and right, but the cult of personality that has developed around the chefs tends to leave the dining room staff in the shadows, a mere half-forgotten adjunct to the kitchen gods in their high white hats. With this, the pendulum has swung too far to one side. All serious professionals know that a first-rate dining room staff is central to the success of any restaurant that aspires to excellence, because they are the ones who execute the theater that is blocked out on the other side of the swinging doors.

"Everyone's got his style," explained Couilloud. "To begin with, ours was very much against unnecessary flash. For instance, we never used silver *cloches* to serve dishes, the way Michel Guérard and Georges Blanc do. Monsieur Loiseau thought they were too showy, but in any case they would be a technical heresy for his style of cooking. When you take the trouble to get a nice, crackly crust on the pike perch, and then put a *cloche* over it, the steam will settle down on the skin and soften it up. A lot of his cuisine was based on an initial cooking, very rapid and at high heat, to get a crunchy crust on top of soft elements, like sweetbreads. If you put a *cloche* over that, it'll go soft in thirty seconds—you've defeated your own purposes.

"Bernard couldn't stand pretentious mannerisms, but he opted to have some professional display in the dining room. This is why we brought back certain old-style practices that had gone out of fashion. We decided, for instance, to do tableside carving by a *maître d'hôtel* of legs of lamb, beef ribs, and the *poularde Alexandre Dumaine.** It made an interesting little spectacle for the client to watch, and it gave the personnel a chance to show their skills. The *nouvelle cuisine* movement had pretty much devalued this kind of work, relegating dining room staff to the role of plate carriers. Bernard backed us a hundred percent in showing customers that ours was a real profession, with its own specific techniques and psychology.

"None of this happened by accident. He and I discussed these matters all the time. There would be no convoluted terms on the menu, no

---

*A very important dish at La Côte d'Or. Respectful of the national gastronomic monument that he had inherited from Alexandre Dumaine, and true to his insistence on representing an apotheosis of Burgundy home cooking, Bernard decided to offer one of Dumaine's specialties on his own menu. Spurning the *oreiller de la belle Aurore* as too ostentatious and needlessly complicated, he settled on his adaptation of the fabulous funeral pyre that *le grand Alexandre* had imagined: a fat Burgundy hen cooked in steam. But what a steam. In a big earthenware crock sealed with a cloth, the animal, stuffed with a vegetable *julienne* enriched with chicken livers, foie gras, and truffles, sits on a tripod above a rich *bouillon* composed of three "juices" of poultry, chicken wings, and veal, and a separate container filled with cognac, port, and essence of truffles. Stuffed on the inside and dressed "in mourning" on the outside—that is, blackened by truffle slices slid under its skin—the chicken is cooked in the oven by the steam rising from the *bouillon* and the truffle-accented liquors. The ceremonial delivery of the hot crock to the table is a sure attention-getter, and when the cloth is withdrawn and the lid lifted, the entire dining room is bathed in a cloud of ineffably luscious fragrances. It is so beautiful and so wrenchingly desirable that it seems almost a shame to destroy the creation by carving it up, but such is the fate of all great culinary creations. There are two services: first the breast, accompanied by truffled rice and a portion of the stuffing; and then, after a return to the kitchen for further cooking, the thighs, accompanied by either baby leeks or the famous truffled potato purée. Clients are forgiven for shedding a tear as they turn their knives and forks to the attack.

'secret' ingredients, no precious, poetical language that made clients wish they had a dictionary at the table. Each dish would be presented simply and clearly as what it was, and when we delivered it to the client we would simply announce it without going into further detail. If you spend a minute going into lyrical descriptions of the dish and its recipe, it's just getting cold while you talk, and the client has already forgotten what you've said by the time you're finished. Eating here is for pleasure, not for education. We're a restaurant, not a cultural center.

"All this was in agreement with Bernard, of course. He was enormously concerned with every last detail of what went on in the dining room, and he had a sixth sense for problems or blemishes. All of us knew that if there was anything wrong, anywhere in the house, he would find it immediately. It was as if he had a kind of heat-seeking sensor built into him. I can't tell you the number of times when he would arrive, after we had spent hours making everything absolutely perfect in the dining room, and he would suddenly pounce on one thing—a tiny detail, a speck—that we had somehow overlooked in spite of all the trouble we had gone to. So he'd yell at us and gloat over how he was the one who found the crumb, but his emotion was disproportionate in relation to the reality of the event. Other times, when some really serious problems arose, he paid hardly any attention at all and left it to us to work them out as we wanted. That was Bernard for you."

By January 13, 1991, as he quietly celebrated his fortieth birthday with Dominique, Bernard truly felt that he was ready for Michelin's empyrean. The kitchen, dining room, and salons were as perfect as he could make them. Patrick, on one side of the swinging door, and Hubert on the other, had so completely mastered their domains that Bernard couldn't imagine how they could do better, and the people under them were also beyond reproach. On the home front, Bérangère, the daughter Dominique had given him eighteen months earlier, was absolutely adorable, and now a second child, their son Bastien, was due in March.

What more could Bernard ask for? Of course the garden outside the dining room wasn't quite right yet, and he had finished only a third of the building program for the thirty or thirty-two luxurious new hotel rooms outlined in his master plan, but Michelin always said that the hotel side didn't count in the awarding of stars. Still he worried, as he mentally ran through the Côte d'Or detail by detail. How about the wines? Certainly the 25,000 or so bottles sleeping in the cellar couldn't match Georges Blanc's huge collection (Georges had inherited not only his mother's restaurant but his father's wine business, too). Even so, Bernard's own assortment was already worth more than a million dollars, and it was tended by a very dedicated *sommelier*.

Ah—the *sommelier*. Could that be a problem? He wasn't sure. Maybe. Lyonel Leconte had come to the Côte d'Or as a trainee two years earlier, a reserved, grave-eyed twenty-two-year-old fresh out of the hotel management school in Tain l'Hermitage. He was really good, too, so good that Bernard had named him *sommelier chef* only a year after that. Lyonel lived for wine, and Bernard had never known anyone with such a vast knowledge at such a young age. If anyone on his staff had clearly been born for the specialty in which he was engaged, this was the one, and furthermore, Mother Nature had proven it by providing him with the superbly efficient tool of an XXL nose: long, elegant, finely formed, and fairly twitching with sensor cells. If this nose was not quite of Cyrano dimensions, it was such a magnificent organ that if you lined up the entire Côte d'Or staff without any identifying signs, you'd pick out the *sommelier* without any problem. And Lyonel had the character to go with it, too. He was so single-minded about his work that when you asked him where he hailed from, he replied not with a place name but a wine map.

"Germolles," he would say. "Just south of the Côtes de Beaune in the Côtes Chalonnaises, about halfway between Mercurey and Givry. Pinot noir for the reds, chardonnay for the whites."

Of course no one knew it just then, but the grave-eyed lad was destined for professional glory. In 1992 Lyonel would win the Ruinart Trophy as Best Young French Sommelier, and two years after that, go on to win the Best French Sommelier competition. These honors could only enhance the prestige of the Côte d'Or—a three-star *sommelier* for a three-star restaurant—but the vague, inchoate reservations that niggled, half-repressed, in a recess of Bernard's mind were to develop into a real problem with time. As he grew to something like celebrity status, Lyonel began spending more and more time doing independent wine consulting. In the dining room, some clients occasionally perceived his mix of knowledge and youthful gravity as self-importance. Other staff members worried that his passion for enology was leading him to lose sight of what lay beyond its perimeter and to forget the most fundamental imperative in the house: to be a team player, entirely devoted to the Côte d'Or and its chef—the locomotive, the one and only star. As Eric Rousseau had said in reference to Chantal: there could be only one rooster in the Saulieu coop. In 1995 Lyonel left the Côte d'Or, not so much fired as rejected, like a foreign body. With his undeniable competence and the great prestige of his titles, he had no trouble remaking himself as a full-time wine consultant, doubtless considerably more prosperous than he ever could have been on his *sommelier*'s salary alone.

During the winter of 1991, though, Lyonel was still well integrated into Hubert's crew. As January turned to February, everyone of the Côte d'Or knew that up on avenue de Breteuil in Paris the Michelin editors were putting the final touches to the guide that would be coming out for general sale in mid-March. Through those endlessly bleak days, the staff arrived for work in the dark, heads bent against the lashing rain that the Morvan plateau inevitably threw their way, varied only now and then by a shift of miseries over to sleet or mushy snow. They would change into their tuxedolike uniforms and make their way through the burnished hallways, usually empty at those early hours— all the more so as it was winter, when no one ever came to Saulieu. Like as not they would find the boss already at his timeless post by the reception desk, telephone in hand, bantering with journalists and food critics or, more seriously, taking in the trade's gossip of the day with Paul Bocuse, Guy Savoy, or Claude Perraudin.

It was on just such a day as this—Friday, February 22, 1991, at about ten A.M.—that the morning receptionist answered a buzz and said, Monsieur Loiseau, I have a call for you from Paris: Monsieur Naegellen of the *Guide Michelin*.

Electroshock: Bernard bounded to the little bureau near the reception desk with Dominique half a step behind him and picked up the receiver, punching the loudspeaker button.

"Monsieur Loiseau," said Bernard Naegellen, "I am calling to announce to you that your establishment will have three stars in our next guide. I am telling you in advance so you will have time to prepare yourself. I know that you are very *médiatique*, but I beg you not to let the press know before our official announcement on Monday, March 4."

"*Oui, monsieur,*" said Bernard, as quietly as a chastised schoolboy.

"You will probably find that you will have more clients now," Naegellen added in the inimitably avuncular tone that thousands of restaurateurs around France cherished and feared. "They might be more difficult than before, and come looking for things to criticize, but there's no need to panic. Don't change anything in the way you work. Just keep on doing what you're doing now."

"*Oui, monsieur,*" said Bernard. "*Merci.*"

When he hung up, his eyes were brimming with tears. He took Dominique in his arms. "This is the greatest day of my life," he said.

XII

THE LOISEAU DECADE

*T*hey had to wait a while to celebrate. Superstitious as an old peasant granny, now that the prize so long awaited was at his finger-
tips but not yet palpably in his hand, and fearful of disobeying
Monsieur Naegellen's injunction about premature publicity, lest the
whole bubble burst and the Michelin fairy flutter away with its magic
three-star wand, Bernard managed to shut up for the next ten days. He
did call his parents, and of course there was no way of keeping the news
from Hubert, Patrick, and the rest of the staff, but mum was the word
around Saulieu until Monday, March 4.

When his consecration was officially announced on the radio early
that morning, though, and when archive footage of his broadly grinning face appeared on the first TV news bulletins, the dam finally
burst and Bernard was able to satisfy a twenty-three-year-old fantasy by
popping bottles of champagne for his staff in the kitchen, exactly as
Jean and Pierre Troisgros had done in 1968. By then the faxes and telegrams were already coming in by the hundreds (including one from
President François Mitterrand), and the phone lines remained satu-
rated for two days.

As it turned out, Bernard's was the only three-star promotion of a
rather severe Michelin year, and congratulatory cases of wine began arriving that very afternoon. The vinous flood continued through the
week, and by Tuesday the Côte d'Or was riddled with journalists and
TV crews, roaming the hallways with their gear, doing their reports out

by the front entrance on rue Argentine and interviewing Bernard in the little studio that had been improvised in one of the salons. To them all, he endlessly repeated the same story with more or less the same lines: I started from nothing. The only thing I had when I arrived in Saulieu was my toothbrush.* Never before had a restaurant gone from three stars to zero and back up to three again. But there's no way I'm going to get the big head now—I've suffered too much to get here.

"We entered a new world," Hubert remembered. "Business immediately went up by sixty percent." Such was the Michelin effect—and it worked, unfortunately, in both directions. In the cloistered hush of Alain Chapel's dining room in Mionnay, his widow Suzanne was already beginning to experience the bitterness of the downside: a 50 percent drop in clientele as a direct result of her demotion to two stars.

But the good times were only starting for Bernard. Just nine days after his official ascension to a stardom of three, Dominique gave birth to their son Bastien. By then magazine articles and newspaper clippings were arriving in the mail from Japan, America, and, of course, everywhere in Europe. Early in April, he was welcomed into the fraternity of big-league power hitters at the traditional new-boy dinner held in the grandiose gilt confines of the Hotel Ritz on place Vendôme in Paris. There were some two hundred guests in all, invited by the champagne house that had sponsored the event, but the most impressive place cards bore the names of the entire roster of his eighteen† three-star peers. Bernard stood to applause from the A-Team, the glitterati of gastronomy.

But the real fun came on April 24. With stars or without, Bernard's character didn't change, and his natural instinct was to spread the pleasure around. Now he wanted to give some of it back to his staff, so he decided to invite them all to lunch. What else would a chef think of doing, and where else would Bernard choose to go for it but to Paul

---

*That was how he phrased it for the TV cameras. He was being polite. According to Bernard Fabre, the standard expression he used among friends was: "I arrived with nothing but my cock and my knives."

†There were nineteen three-star places in 1991. The figure varies from year to year, according to the verdict of the inspectors at the big year-end plenary meeting in the Service du Tourisme office on avenue de Breteuil.

Bocuse's? *Le grand Paul,* twenty-five years his elder, was his godfather in the business, his friend, his mentor, and his idol, but also, in a strange, unspoken but still real way, his rival: the target he must attain if he ever was to think of himself as the greatest chef in the world—or the most famous, at any rate. Because that was in the air now, more so than ever before. It sounds silly and rather puerile—there can no more be a "greatest" chef than a greatest mother, greatest athlete, or greatest flower—but Bernard was such a child of hyperbole, and so totally immersed in the facile stereotypings of the press he had been courting for the best part of two decades, that he half believed in the pursuit of the chimera, whatever his cooler judgment might have told him. One thing is certain: He aspired to be Bocuse one day, because Bocuse was the Commander. You might as well set your sights as high as possible.

By April 24, Dominique and the newly born Bastien were in shape to make the trip to Collonges. For the first time since his arrival in Saulieu, Bernard closed the Côte d'Or on a normal working day and drove the little family down in his car, followed by the bus he had chartered for his staff: cooks, waiters, cleaning ladies, and all. "Look out," Bocuse had warned him by phone. "I've invited two heavyweight guests."

"Do you suppose one of them is Barre?" Bernard wondered aloud in the car. Dominique shrugged. Possible. Former prime minister Raymond Barre had gone on to be elected mayor of Lyon, was known for indulging generously in the city's fabled resources of fine cuisine, and his figure was not exactly that of an anorexic. If ever there was a heavyweight guest, Barre would be the one. But who could the other be?

It was neither Barre nor anyone else. Always a man who knew a thing or two about celebration, stunts, and publicity, Bocuse had shanghaied two elephants from a circus that was in town, and was riding one with a magnum of champagne in his fist when Bernard arrived. Bernard had no choice but to clamber uneasily aboard the second one with another magnum, because the photographers and cameramen were primed and waiting (Bocuse knows a thing or two about shanghaiing the press, too), and the big Michelin Man effigy had already been strategically positioned in the background, crowned with three stars. Bocuse was certain he had set up an irresistible photo op, and, as usual, he was right. The photo was published throughout the country:

more publicity for Bernard, for himself, for the circus, for the champagne, for Michelin—everyone was served.

In company with Pierre Troisgros and Claude Verger, who had made the trip to Lyon to honor the kid they had formed, the whole crew adjourned to the big panoramic salon above the main restaurant and sat down to a Brobdingnagian feast of Bocusian style and proportion. After a series of the little tidbits universally known as *amuse-gueules*—appetite ticklers—matters turned serious when the menu was presented.

Black truffle soup

Red mullet in a jacket of potato scales

Beaujolais ice

Bresse chicken in cream, cooked in a pig's bladder

Périgord foie gras

Cheeses from La Mère Richard*

President cake with strawberries and vanilla ice cream

Assorted pastries and chocolates

Champagne Moët et Chandon 1986

Château de Rully 1989

Beaune Saint-Landry 1986

Corton Pougets 1979

Nuits-Saint-Georges Clos de la Maréchale 1987

Muscat Beaumes-de-Venise Domaine des Bernardins 1990

---

*Renée Richard, the ageless, eternally blonde, perfectly coiffed, white-bloused, tart-tongued Rabelaisian mistress of the best cheese stall in the Halles de Lyon, the wholesale-retail food market in the Part Dieu section of town, became world-famous because Bocuse bought his cheeses exclusively from her. Apart from the pitiless sarcasm of her repartee (don't mess with La Mère Richard), she is revered by gastronomes for having popularized the lovely, creamy Saint-Marcellin, a cheese from the mountainous Isère region.

Author, as he was, of the most famous wisecrack about Bernard's cuisine, Bocuse did not fail to add a line at the bottom of the menu: *All these dishes have been entirely prepared WITHOUT WATER.* After the last coffees and cognacs had been sipped and it came time to pay the check, there was no check. Bocuse knows a thing or two about generosity, too.

I did not see Bernard again until eight months after his big three-star triumph. Fittingly enough, he was on the phone by the reception desk when I walked into the Côte d'Or. "Have you seen?" he was saying. "I'm everywhere!"

He gestured toward a big glossy magazine from Germany or Switzerland, the cover graced with the huge Loiseau grin. "They've discovered that I know how to cook, hee-hee-hee!"

It was a great time to be Bernard Loiseau. He was the new kid on the block who everyone was talking about, the hot story in the world of *haute cuisine*. If Joël Robuchon, the fantastic technician who took Paris by storm in his restaurant Jamin, was the cook who made the biggest splash in the eighties, the nineties might well have been called the Loiseau decade. Certainly Alain Ducasse was gathering stars aplenty, too — by 1998 he would have six, between Monte Carlo and Paris — but his was a different kind of business, more akin to an entrepreneurship in consultancy than that of an independent *aubergiste* financing, directing, and cooking in his own restaurant. There were other young luminaries in the gastronomic limelight, too, but frequently, they merely stumbled, while Bernard charged ahead. In Annecy, Marc Veyrat came to the edge of bankruptcy after overinvesting on bank loans with high interest rates. In Saint-Étienne the brilliant, poetic Pierre Gagnaire actually did go broke, and shuttered his restaurant for want of clients who would pay enough for him to recoup his investment.* The enormously deserving Michel Bras in Laguiole — doubtless *the* cook of the first decade of the twenty-first century — was not accorded his third star until 1999.

---

*Both men eventually wriggled free of their problems. Veyrat talked the bankers into renegotiating his loans, opened a second restaurant in the mountains, and went on to very successfully remake himself as the most expensive restaurateur in France. Gagnaire got a bit of financial banking, set up the Hotel Balzac in Paris (just off the Champs Elysées, in the center of Expense Account Heaven), and thrived there.

It was Bernard, then, who was to be the chef of the nineties, but unhappily for him, that entire decade was a period of slump after Europe's *trente glorieuses*, and the slowdown was especially bad in France, where *crise économique* was upon the land. Globalization had brought increased competition from abroad to inefficient French industries with bloated payrolls, and which were heavily dependent on government aid. Seesaw administration changes between socialists and conservatives had resulted in a regime of capitalism hectored by government interference in the form of high taxes and social charges and a thirty-five-hour work week. The pensionable retirement age was lowered to fifty-five and the social security system was disastrously indebted. In this edgy environment, clients who were prepared to throw several hundred dollars at a single meal became noticeably rarer. The steady forward march of bureaucracy had brought increasingly vigilant oversight by the European Commission in Brussels in matters of health and sanitary and veterinary norms, to the point of threatening unpasteurized cheeses and making it nearly impossible to make and use the classical *fonds*—stock reductions—that had been the backbone of so much French cuisine. As for the national authorities in Paris, the combination of traceable credit card payments, nonendorsable checks, computers, and a beefed-up corps of tax inspectors all but eliminated the hundreds of informal little arrangements by which entrepreneurs had circumvented bureaucratic control and kept their enterprises going.

"In the sixties and seventies, half of our profits used to be 'black'— that is, not declared to the tax authorities," a veteran restaurateur explained. "All that's finished now. You used to be able to get profit margins of seven, maybe even ten percent. Now you're lucky if you can make it to three percent. Thousands of restaurants are going broke every year. The sector's not so attractive anymore."

Jean-Michel Lorain, owner and chef of the three-star Côte Saint-Jacques in Joigny, south of Paris, on the river Yonne, told me that his profit margin was . . . zero. Like Bernard, he had invested heavily (25 million francs) to totally renovate his hotel and restaurant, with the result that he and his wife, Brigitte, were living on the salaries that their little company paid them, while ploughing everything else back into repaying their loans.

"Basically, I work for the banks and the government," he said with the ironic, disenchanted half-smile so frequently encountered among bosses of small enterprises in France. "Especially the government."

But it was André Daguin who best summed up the collective humor of the trade. "All the starred chefs are crazy," he told me. "I know all about that—I was crazy myself for thirty years."

A big, hefty, handsome rugby-playing bucko from the southwestern city of Auch, near Toulouse, Daguin had brought the kitchen of his Hôtel de France up to two stars, with a culinary *gasconnade* of dishes based on *foie gras*, and did more than any other chef to popularize *magrets de canard*, the thick, succulent cutlets of duck breast that have now become nearly as omnipresent on menus throughout France as veal cutlets in Italy. A few years ago he gave it up, sold the business, came to Paris, and took over the presidency of L'Union des Métiers et Industries de l'Hôtellerie, the national pressure group and lobby of the hotel and restaurant industry.

"As soon as I got my second star, I never made any money from the restaurant, anymore," he explained in a southwestern accent almost thick enough to require the services of a simultaneous interpreter. "After all the investment you put into the place, and the cost of the personnel, on those winter evenings when you've got two or three clients, a business like that is like a vacuum cleaner for your money. You might do OK on the weekend, but then, come Monday and Tuesday—no one, not even a rat, but you've still got the fixed charges to pay. *Ah, putaing!* So what do you do to survive? You do things on the side. You open a bistro next door. You write books. You endorse products. You do special gastronomic weeks. That's how I got by in Auch."

In Saulieu, Bernard was hustling in much the same way. His first cookbook, *L'Envolée des Saveurs—Flavors Aflight*—had just been published, and a second one was in the works. Industrialists were already hounding him about lending his name to various mass-produced foods. He would go on to accept a first contract in 1993 for a series of prepackaged soups. Soon after that he would follow the lead of older *confrères* like Bocuse, Senderens, and Guérard in signing up for a wide line of ready-made vacuum-packed dishes (beef strips with shallots and scalloped potatoes, veal with boletus mushrooms and mashed potatoes, *coq au vin*, stuffed squid, etc.) for the French company Agis. Even before his third star arrived, he had agreed to lend his name and expertise for the first Bernard Loiseau restaurant outside France, planned for the hotel Kobe Bay Sheraton on an artificial island, and scheduled to open in 1992.

Taking a break by the coffee machine in the kitchen, Hubert was telling me about another hustle that was in the works. "We're going to open a reasonably priced little restaurant next door, in the Petit Marguéry," he said. "It's going to be called Le Bistrot du Morvan, and we'll serve a much simpler regional cuisine in it, things like *céleri rémoulade, oeufs en meurette, tête de veau, blanquette*, and *boeuf bourguignon*."

The little bistro next to the expensive gastronomic restaurant was an idea that was very much in the air in those days. Both in Paris and the more prosperous provincial areas, big-name chefs were discovering that they could increase their profits by adopting an ocean-liner system of first-, second-, and perhaps even third-class dining spaces, opening unassuming annexes inevitably called bistro something-or-other, often located right next door to their main establishments, which employed fewer hands to make and serve a less sophisticated cuisine to a greater number of clients. The picky, the rich, the Paganinis of the expense account, and the unhurried would be sure to fill the expensive signature restaurants, where there was always a waiting list for tables in any case; the young and the budget-straitened hoi polloi would flock to the cheaper alternative, and probably not even steal the silverware.*

Unfortunately for Bernard, the economic pep pills that worked in Paris, Vonnas, or Lyon did not apply in Saulieu. Fishing in waters where potential customers abounded, chefs in the choicest locations could keep the two sources of income complementary and separated—*haute couture* on one side, "ready-to-wear" on the other—both of them feeding off the image of the master. In the Morvan, however,

---

*Not a joke. "*La fauche*," the theft of all sorts of objects, is a typical and recurrent problem in top restaurants. All three-star places have to accept a certain diminution of their supply of knives, forks, and spoons, the way hotels have to deal with disappearing towels. Curiously, anecdotal evidence suggests that women are more prey than men to this gastrokleptcy, and few items seem too great or negligible for their coveting. An honorable Lyonnais matron once tried to cop a candelabra from Paul Bocuse's place. Jean-Michel Lorain remembered a similar lady in Joigny who walked out with a toilet brush in her purse. An alert waiter spotted the crime, but they didn't pursue the matter, and let her have her precious souvenir.

where there were more cows than people, Bernard soon realized to his distress that the principal effect of the Bistrot du Morvan would only be to cannibalize the Côte d'Or's limited clientele. So the plan that Hubert optimistically limned for me that October morning was finally never consummated, and the idea of the bistro died a-borning.

Hubert had barely finished sketching out his illusory menu selections when Bernard rushed in with urgent concern written on his face. There were no smiles for the press this time, no jokes or anecdotes. This was an emergency. October was the season for fresh game, but he had just discovered that the hunters he had been counting on had failed him this time.

"Listen," he cried, "we've got to change the menu. The partridges aren't good enough. At least half of them aren't up to standard. We can't take chances. We'll have to substitute venison instead. Quince purée with it. Let's get going—*Il faut speeder, hein?*"

Gotta hurry up. *Speeder* was a Franco-American neologism you heard all the time around Bernard. As phlegmatic and calm as Bernard was agitated, Patrick Bertron nodded and turned to confer with his seconds about arranging the change. Hubert disappeared to handle the rewriting of the *carte du jour*—no particular problem, because menus were printed up fresh every day.

"Last minute, everything last minute," Bernard exclaimed, underlining the point with an energetic gesticulation. "This kitchen is clean as a whistle at five minutes to twelve, even when we've got a hundred seats reserved in the dining rooms—nothing prepared beforehand, nothing! There's no other restaurant anywhere in the world like this. All the other guys have their stock pots bubbling and their reductions all set to go—and, of course, their pots of *crème fraîche*. Not me. We do everything from scratch here, *à la minute*."*

In his third and smallest dining room, Bernard was going to be receiv-

---

*Not strictly true. No chef, no matter how gifted or speedy, can do *everything* at the last minute. In Saulieu as in Lyon or Laguiole or Lembach, there is always plenty of kitchen activity—cleaning, gutting, peeling, weighing, and all the other inevitable preparatory chores that come before the *coup de feu*—the moment the cooking starts. What Bernard meant to emphasize was that no dishes were cooked before they were actually ordered. Sometimes he took flight on the wings of his own rhetoric.

ing a dozen or so TV and showbiz types that afternoon, part of the shifting entourage of a record company owner who had made a lot of money with the mass distribution of pop music, and who was known to the general public mostly for his penchant for serial marriages (eight, at last count) to aspiring young singers. As we spoke, they were across the way in the public garden above the old ramparts, playing *pétanque* and building up an appetite for the special lunch that Bernard was to prepare for them.

This group was typical of the *copains*, the Paris-by-night denizens who had attached themselves to Bernard over the years since his first baby steps in press relations at the Barrières: the kissy-kissy buddies/friends/pals who were neither journalists nor food critics, and who could not necessarily help him in any direct way, but who moved in the circles of other buddies/friends/pals who could, with an invitation to a TV show here, a radio interview there, or the prospect of multiple magazine and newspaper articles. Anything that could influence more people to come down to Saulieu was grist for Bernard's mill.

"Do you think I can ask them to pay something?" Bernard asked. What in hell did I know, I who was eating for free myself that day? True, there were a lot of them and true, they weren't exactly poverty cases, but they were friends of all those other friends, after all. They had to be treated right. Bernard finally decided on a compromise to limit damages: He would make them a country-style buffet lunch featuring ingredients that were not ruinously expensive, much of which could be made in advance, in order to present them with a modest bill that would allow him to at least break even:

Fraise de veau en gelée

Salade de queue de bœuf

Terrine de volaille, jambon et saucisson

Œufs brouillés aux truffes

Irancy

But not even a picnic in Loiseau's place could ever be just a few things thrown together. *Fraise de veau*, the fatty tissue surrounding the calf's intestines, may not sound like much of a delicacy, but in the Lyon area it was commonly used as the principal ingredient in *andouillettes*, the slightly intimidating gray sausages confected of tripe elsewhere. For this country buffet, Patrick Bertron cooked it in veal stock, cut it into morsels, added tiny vegetables and hard boiled eggs, then placed everything in a mold, to set in a rich, meaty gelatin. The oxtail was also cooked in a *bouillon*, its meat stripped off and cut into small pieces, then served *en salade*, lukewarm, with hardboiled eggs, little vegetables, and sections of fried beef marrow. It was to be seasoned with a nut oil vinaigrette.

But that wasn't the end of it. Bertron had cooked an entire ham on the bone in an aromatic *bouillon*, overseen the creation of the chicken and foie gras terrine and personally tended to the excruciatingly delicate scrambling of the eggs (in a double boiler, of course, continuously turning them with a whisk as they congealed), and incorporated a fine julienne of truffles. Only the country sausage did not entirely originate in Bernard's kitchen. It could have, but since this was a one-off affair, he slightly bent his cast-iron rules and accepted an outside supplier. Irancy, the red wine he served with this little snack, was from the Yonne *département* south of Chablis. Considerably more modest (and less expensive) than its celebrated cousin wines of the Côte d'Or *département* further down to the south, it was a true Burgundy nonetheless, and an honest one, too.

I followed Bernard around for a couple of hours that morning and afternoon. His decision on the menu, and the simple fact that he finally opted to make the *copains* pay for it, gave me the chance to see how far he had come in recognizing the weight of his identity as a top chef, and assuming his responsibilities in managing what by then had become a not-inconsequential enterprise. *Largesse* there would always be, because he was wildly generous by nature and there was nothing he enjoyed more than pleasing people, but he was beginning to set some limits.

"You know," he said, "I turn down an average of seven applications a day now to work in the kitchen. Everyone wants to come here!" The tone of his exclamation was typical Bernard: half bluster (I'm the best) and half wonder (who am I?), as if pinching himself to see if it really was true. Several years later, after the whole sad drama had gone to its final dénouement, his younger brother Rémy, the calm engineer, calmly installed in a calm job in Michelin's IT department in Clermont, recalled an evening stroll with Bernard in the Côte d'Or's garden. " 'Sometimes I really have a hard time believing all this is mine,' he told me. The higher up he rose, the more worried and the more insecure he became. All that business of 'I'm the greatest' was just bluff, to reassure himself."

That morning in October 1991, as a pot of *boeuf bourguignon* (lunch for the personnel) bubbled away next to a large skillet, where shallots were slowly melting down to the *fondu* that would accompany the crackly skinned pike perch in red wine sauce, and as white-bloused *commis* and *apprentis* busied themselves with freshly delivered sticks of frogs' legs, and picked and sorted nettles from a big plastic garbage bag lying on the floor, Bernard was sipping a glass of Vichy water and holding forth on *le style Loiseau* and what went into it. To begin with, it was clear that he had learned his lesson from Bocuse's wisecrack and those clients who had wondered about the thin sauces of his famous H_2O period.

"I don't do *cuisine à l'eau*," he insisted. "Please don't call it that. It's not water cooking. What I'm doing here is traditional French cooking with a new look, updated and modernized. To be at the top level you've got to have a style, the way Michel Guérard did in the Pot au Feu. He left the scales on his sea bass and cooked it in the oven with seaweed and virgin olive oil, and served it with a watercress puree. Fantastic! He was twenty years ahead of everyone else—he created *nouvelle cuisine*.

"Now I've created my style here. Nothing is disguised with sauces the way they used to do in the old days. I do sauces, but their role is just to let the ingredients express themselves and really taste of what they are. I'll never have more than three, maybe sometimes four, flavors on the plate. I do each element separately, then put them together on the plate, and they join up—*schlak!* Explosions of taste in your mouth!

"Sixty percent of my work is finding the best providers of my ingredients. I'm perpetually at war with producers and suppliers, because I can't make my cuisine unless I have perfect materials to work with. Clients come here from all over the world, and they're expecting a miracle. A lot of them have broken their piggy banks to pay for a lunch or dinner *chez Loiseau*. They're following a dream—happiness!

"If I can't give it to them, I've failed. That's why I changed the partridges, because if I don't have fresh, absolutely irreproachable produce, I *will* fail. So I'm riding my providers' asses all the time. And they know I won't forget if they make a mistake or try to sell me second-rate stuff. I've got a memory for everything. Look at the quality of this stuff!"

He yanked open the stainless steel drawer of a refrigerated seafood compartment to present a dazzling still life of little blue Breton lobsters—*demoiselles*, they were called—and *pattes rouges* crayfish, mean little buggers waving their claws to nip at any intruder who would imprudently venture a finger. It was all so beautiful. Bernard loved it and was proud of it. His big, round, utterly persuasive moon face loomed forward, led by that strong, willful chin and a smile that brooked no arguing or gainsaying. If I had been wearing a jacket that morning, I do not doubt that he would have seized me by the lapels.

"This isn't a luxury hotel like some emirate's palace in the Persian Gulf. This is the Morvan. This is old tiles, old wood, and period furniture that smells of wax. This is the heartland, this is nature and churchyards and farms and chickens and cheeses and vegetable gardens—this is *la France!*"

The crescendo of Bernard's bucolic rhapsody was cut short when a young, white-jacketed waiter entered to announce that the *carreleur*—the tile man—had arrived. Ah, the *carreleur*, good. Bernard had a bone to pick with him. He charged out of the kitchen double time.

It was the white cloud that was bothering him.

Something of a white cloud himself in his immaculate chef's tunic and apron, he bounded out of the swinging door and fairly pounced upon the artisan who was kneeling in the hallway outside the dining room, reflectively gazing down at the red Burgundy *tommettes* that he himself had laid some months earlier.

"Look at this," Bernard cried. "White—it's gone white! It's got this"—his quick brown eyes suddenly spotted an infinitesimal speck of dust on the floor and he swooped down to remove its offensive presence from his view—"this *nuage blanc* over the red. I can't stand that! It's got to be fixed."

The mason thoughtfully ran his hands over the lovely old tiles—they looked fine to me, but Bernard, adamantly perfectionist, remained horrified—and said learned things about porosity and lime leaching out and maybe an earlier silicone treatment. Bernard contained his patience for a few moments, then abruptly brought the conversation to a close with a single lapidary command whose import everybody in France would recognize and understand.

"Well, *mon pauvre monsieur*, you've just got to make me a three-star floor."

No way to argue with an injunction like that. The matter was clear and closed. Now it was up to the mason to *speeder*.

High on Vichy, Bernard hurried me into the ladies' room to show off his latest equipment, the twin Belle Époque, *barbière*-style wash basins of glistening copper that stood under a wall-length mirror, even then reflecting a bouquet of fresh-cut flowers. He snatched up an errant petal that had drifted down to the tiled platform, profiting from a moment when the chef had his back turned, but not even this floral indiscipline could still his pleasure. He was delighted with the look of the place.

"Pretty good, huh?"

It was. It was very nice, very three-star. Bernard beamed. He led me on to the other end of the house to show me every single one of the new rooms. They were just as he had said—old stone, old tile, and old wood contrasting harmoniously with the ultramodern bathroom equipment. "Quite impressive, Bernard," I said.

"March 15, 1968," he cried, slapping his thigh for emphasis. "The Troisgros got their third star. And now, twenty-three years later, I have them, too. Hee-hee-hee!"

He loped off to badger other suppliers or sweet-talk other journalists by phone, and I returned to the kitchen for another lesson from Patrick Bertron on the realities of three-star life. Severe and unsmiling under his high white *toque*—he always wore one, and Bernard never did—he was already starting to prepare some of the lunch dishes.

"The restaurant trade in France isn't too strict about hours," he said with a shrug. "We start here at eight in the morning and there will always be someone working until at least eleven p.m. As long as there's work to be done, we stay here. That's just the way it is, if you want three stars."

He was just finishing off a filet of red mullet with olive oil (extra-virgin, of course) in a Teflon pan—one side only, two minutes exactly. He delicately patted the filet with paper towel to dry it of oil, slipped it onto a toasty-hot plate, uncooked side down—the heat of the plate would finish the cooking on that side—and passed it to his left, where a *sous-chef* added the garnish of steamed zucchini flower and laid down a few spoonfuls of sea-urchin sauce. Just as a white-jacketed waiter was bearing the offering away to the dining room, Bernard burst in, quivering with agitation. He had just tasted a sample of the country buffet for the *copains*.

"We've got a problem," he announced. "We've got to leave the walnut oil out of the oxtail salad. It's too strong—much too dominant. Kills the taste. And we've got to add carrots, and more onions—sliced, not diced, *hein?*"

Bertron nodded and Bernard dashed back out. Just before he hit the door he threw a last thought back over his shoulder. "And put in more parsley, too."

As it turned out, Bernard finally joined the *copains* at their picnic that day. It was a breach of his routine—almost unexceptionally, he took his own lunch at 11 A.M. (the universal cooks' midday eating hour), standing alone in the kitchen, with a bottle of Vichy water as his sole liquid sustenance—but, *justement*, the presence of this Paris showbiz crowd was an exceptional event, so he took himself to dining room 3 and presided at the table. Chattering, joshing, and chivvying one another, they were a joyous band who had nothing more serious on their minds that afternoon than the results of their *pétanque* tournament but, good French men and women as they were, their mood changed to earnest attention when the waiters brought the series of dishes to the table, and they listened with respect as Bernard explained their composition.

"*Les enfants,*" he intoned, as Bertron's ever so carefully scrambled and truffled eggs arrived, "these are eggs from today, laid on the farm this morning—no comparison with the *merde* that you get in Paris!"

Sausaged, truffled, egged, and oxtailed, their innards generously oiled with long swigs of Irancy, the *copains* were willing victims for Bernard's sales talk about the Côte d'Or and *le style Loiseau,* and the luncheon passed in pleasant conversation that could not have been more cheery, encouraging, or flattering to *Michelin*'s newest three-star chef. When at last he took his leave and drove up across town for his daily nap at home, it seemed to Bernard that Saulieu for once was the best of all possible worlds.

XIII

UP, DOWN, AND UP AGAIN:

Bernard's Bipolar World

"From seventy-five to eighty-two, I worked for Verger," Bernard was saying. "Starting from nothing, I got two Michelin stars and brought us up to *Relais & Châteaux* standards. That's when I told Claude the time had come to sell me the place. He did it, at ten-percent interest. After I paid him off I went to the bankers. I told them that I saw a big future here in Saulieu as a place of repose, a haven of peace and calm.

"They decided they could have confidence in me, and I started building my new hotel rooms. By the end of 1990 I had finished my program. Three months after that I won my third star. I got three Michelin stars with forty square meters of the rottenest kitchen in all of France! Now, eight months later, my turnover is up sixty percent and I've made the cover of the *New York Times*. All told, I've invested thirty million francs. I'll be paying back 250,000 francs a month through to the year 2005, but that's no problem—at age fifty-four, I'll be home free."

Looked at that way, it all seemed so natural, sequential, and almost automatic—bing, bing, bing, the logical steps of his recipe to happiness, wealth, and renown. The traveling salesman's son was selling me, as he had long ago sold himself and everyone around him, on the quasi-inexorable process that had brought him safely to destination. No one ever subscribed more enthusiastically than Bernard Loiseau to the credo and mythology of traditional capitalism: Everything is possible for those who strive; success is a flower just waiting to be plucked; a hard beginning maketh a happy end. All that.

It was a euphoric moment, but Bernard could not suspect, as he happily laid out his past, present, and future for me in that autumn of 1991, that he was only at the start of something very much like an infernal spiral, that within ten years the 30 million francs of borrowed money would balloon to nearly three times that amount, as one project and one acquisition led to others, that he would find himself owner of not one but four restaurants, or that, in a scramble for more cash, he would be taking the unprecedented step of floating his own company—that is, himself—on the stock market. Within that period he grew more and more *speedé* with each new responsibility, running himself to the edge of nervous exhaustion as he struggled to keep pace with his burgeoning ambitions. Certainly he progressed toward his goals, but as their proportions grew increasingly grander (or megalomaniacal, as some commentators suggested), each step forward brought him only the view of his personal chimera—the easy resolution of his problems by age fifty-four—disappearing over the horizon.

There was money out there in the banks, and Bernard put his finger into the gears of the machine. His original ambition had been only to become a successful *aubergiste* crowned with three Michelin stars, but somehow it always turned out that there was more to be done—nothing was ever quite good enough, not yet perfect. To create a physical setting and an ambience worthy of *Michelin*, it was clear that he had to renovate some and build a lot, but the standards of Alexandre Dumaine's days were no longer acceptable at the end of the twentieth century. He had seen the Troisgros brothers, Georges Blanc, and Michel Guérard putting together caravansaries of world-class luxury, and he could do no less. Hell, he could do more, and better!

So he borrowed. He saw Bocuse expanding from Collonges-au-Mont-d'Or to Epcot to Tokyo, and into downtown Lyon, where one after the other, he opened a series of gloriously successful *brasseries*. In Vonnas, Mâcon, Bourg-en-Bresse, and Lyon, Georges Blanc did the same. Jean-Paul Lacombe, owner and chef of the marvelous two-star Léon de Lyon (his cooking deserves three stars, by the way), metastasized in and around Lyon with a gaggle of money-spinning cafés and restaurants, and in Paris, Guy Savoy was building a mini-empire of satellite restaurants even before he had won his third star. And of course, above all there was Alain Ducasse, the gastrocomet, the man who was causing culinary thunder and lightning around the whole damn planet.

Cuisine's First Division was a rich, racy, glamorous place. None of these adjectives could conceivably apply to an isolated Morvan cow town like Saulieu, but Bernard worked and invented and wheedled and borrowed until he had brought the Côte d'Or's level of esthetics, comfort, and service up to, or even better than, those of his most distinguished colleagues. Once he had launched his program, its progression barely left him time to draw breath between the succeeding steps. In 1994 came five big, handsome, balconied rooms giving directly out onto the central garden, a new garage, and a "technical center" for a central air-conditioning unit. A year later, abandoning the idea of a bistro, he opened the Bernard Loiseau boutique on the ground floor of the ex-Petit Marguéry. In 1998 he completely renovated the main building's façade, raised the top floor 1.5 meters, and built nine new rooms.

With that same *tranche* of construction, Bernard at last got the beautiful, handcrafted circular staircase after which he had lusted for so many years, and which quickly became the Côte d'Or's *marque* and identifying symbol. A spidery latticework of noble woods pegged and tenoned together, it was an artisanal *chef d'oeuvre* designed and erected by the Compagnons du Devoir, the present-day descendants of the medieval artisans who had built France's great cathedrals. Locked in the staircase's embrace was a spacious modern elevator, all glass and shimmering stainless steel. Bernard was thrilled with the contrast— today's technology and yesterday's materials, indeed, in one gorgeous ensemble.

In 1999 he knocked down Dumaine's old hotel with its cramped quarters, and added nine new rooms and suites, a billiards room, a library, and a salon for conferences and seminars. In 2001 came the Côte d'Or's grand finale: a spa and fitness center, and a completely redesigned garden with a heated swimming pool, tucked away in a discreet glade down at the bottom. By that year he had also considerably spread his wings beyond Saulieu, having expanded into Paris with the successive purchase of three restaurants in 1998, 1999, and 2000, which he redecorated, manned with personnel he had formed, and re-named as the first exemplars of his "aunts" concept of high-level bistros, suggesting the homey food of family visits to an aunt who was a serious Cordon Bleu cook: Tante Louise, Tante Jeanne, and Tante Marguerite.

And so it came to pass that by the first year of the new millenium, Bernard the penurious apprentice had spent 88 million francs (more than $10 million) of other people's money to bring his dream to reality. But a cruel irony was lying in ambush for him in an alleyway of his route to success; however impressive his debts appeared to be, it was not the money that in the end would hound him to the most desperate of measures. Obsessed as he was with building his ideal palace and at-tracting enough clients to pay for it, he could not imagine that after the "Loiseau decade" had come to a close, it would be his creativity and his cooking—that is to say, his very identity—that would be called into question by lesser men than himself. And the worst aspect of the irony was that the attacks would come not from bankers and creditors, but from the coterie that he had assiduously courted through his entire ca-reer: the gastronomic press.

When I met with him in that autumn of 1991, though, Bernard was riding the cloud of his personal *méthode Coué*, and everything was falling into place as it should. The Côte d'Or was beautifully remod-eled, and before long it would be even more beautiful and a good deal bigger, too. Everyone was talking about his cuisine, and he had be-come a true media star. Classy, devoted, and as hard-working as him-self, Dominique was seconding him in every way possible, removing the burden of paperwork and picky details that he, the Big Picture man *par excellence*, had always hated. The technical money matters that were beyond Dominique's purview were being handled by Bernard Fabre. Bernard now had two adorable kids (a third would be born in 1996), a big, comfortable old house on the hill, a first-rate staff, and the respect of his peers in the business. In short, he had made it.

In a few pithy phrases, he summed up his path to success and the rationale that had guided him. "I was in an impossible situation," he explained. "I was in Saulieu, and I had a gas station opposite my front door,* not the Mont Saint-Michel or some majestic view of the Alps. To bring people down here I had to do something new and different, so that's what I did—*le style Loiseau*. It took me eight years of trial and error to develop it, but I did it. Today, people recognize my snails in nettle soup and my frogs' legs the way they recognize Robuchon's mashed potatoes, Troisgros's salmon, and Bocuse's black-truffle soup. Now that I'm at the top, I'm going to cash in by selling my name the way the other guys have done."

Which is exactly what happened. In addition to his deals for soups and ready-made vacuum-packed dishes, featuring his face with that Loiseau grin on the outside of the package, Bernard would go on in years to come to collaborate with Nestlé for a new mayonnaise recipe, consult on wines for Savour Club, sign up for a speaking job for a weekly chronicle on a popular Paris radio station, write a column[†] for a Sunday paper, and lend (or rather, sell) his expertise as a consultant to a Swiss hotel group. But perhaps more interesting and prestigious than any of these was the deal he struck through JTB, the Japan Travel Bureau, that country's top "destination management" company: the Côte d'Or–Bernard Loiseau Restaurant on the top floor of the hotel Kobe Bay Sheraton that was being built. Against a remuneration (undisclosed but clearly handsome), he would provide the recipes, train Japanese cooks in Saulieu, send one of his own French *sous-chefs* to live and work in Kobe, and make a personal appearance of two weeks each year.

Passionate, infinitely curious, and superbly organized travelers, the Japanese have long been fascinated with French cuisine. In addition to the Hermès scarf, the Vuitton bag, and obligatory visits to certain must-see highlights (the Eiffel Tower, the Louvre, Notre Dame, the Opéra, and a few select Loire Valley châteaux), no self-respecting Japanese tourists felt their visits complete without at least one high-

---

*Since then, the funky little gas pumps have disappeared, but the garage and car dealership are still there.

†Bernard signed the column, but it was Dominique who wrote it. Ghosting articles and books is as common a practice among top chefs as it is with athletes, politicians, and movie stars. Bernard was always a delegator, and who better to delegate this chore to than a wife who was a journalist and food expert?

end gastronomic experience. For the wealthier among them, this meant a *Michelin* three-star restaurant. Naturally, Paris was the prime destination, and the Vrinats, Terrails, Senderenses, and Passards could count on their share of clientele from the land of the rising sun as a matter of course.

In the provinces, though, there were two restaurants that the Japanese gourmets particularly favored: Paul Bocuse's in Lyon and Bernard Loiseau's in Saulieu. This was largely the doing of the late Shizuo Tsuji, the extraordinary Mister Food from Osaka. The École Technique Hotelière Tsuji had begun as a small training center for Japanese cooking alone, but Tsuji built it into a behemoth—the world's largest cooking school—teaching Japanese, Chinese, French, and Italian cuisine to often as many as five thousand students a year. An indefatigably productive writer and promoter of fine cuisine (twenty-nine books, a national TV show, and a flood of articles), Tsuji had been taken in hand in the early sixties by Paul Bocuse, who introduced him to the aristocracy of the French gastronomic establishment. Over the years their friendship developed into a professional symbiosis that saw Bocuse flying regularly to Japan to open restaurants, consult, and sell a personalized Paul Bocuse product line, while Tsuji bought two châteaux in Beaujolais country, to which he shuttled hundreds of his students for on-site training in *haute cuisine française*. Long before globalization had become a catchword of management gurus, Tsuji and Bocuse were practicing it to their mutual profit.

The Franco-Japanese trail blazed by this unlikely pair of friends— Tsuji was as restrained and demure as Bocuse was playful, adventuresome, and extroverted—was soon trod by most of the great names of French gastronomy, and it was hardly surprising that the Japanese Travel Bureau would come knocking on Bernard's door as he rose toward three-star prominence. Both Tsuji and Bocuse had recommended him highly, his media stardom had long since spilled over into Japanese press and TV and—the final convincing stroke—his minimalist style of fast-cooking high-quality ingredients at the last minute bore certain resemblances to Japanese culinary techniques.

So the contract was signed, Bernard made a preliminary scouting trip and, late in January of 1992, flew back to Japan for his first full tour of duty in the Kobe Bay Sheraton. On the flight over and throughout the ensuing two-week obligation, Hubert Couilloud was at his side. But if Bernard's pertinacious questing after glory and success made him appear like some gastronomic Don Quixote, Hubert was no Sancho Panza. If anything, the aptest analogy would be that of Virgil guiding an overwhelmed and terrorized Dante as he lived the dreadful experience of his visit to the Inferno. Because a dreadful experience it was, that first Kobe trip, and a very significant one, too: Bernard fell to pieces.

Six years earlier, Hubert had seen his friend and boss break down when he finally faced Chantal's infidelity and admitted it to himself and the world, but that had been readily understandable; Bernard was exhausted from overwork, the restaurant was on the knife-edge of insolvency, and he was the humiliated husband who could no longer hide his horns. Who wouldn't be tempted to break down under those circumstances?

But this collapse in Japan came like a bolt out of the blue. Bernard was remarried, he had his third star, the Côte d'Or had done sensationally well all spring and summer after going to the top of the Michelin class, and now in Kobe, cohorts of bowing Japanese admirers were blanketing him with honors. Everything seemed perfect, but there, on that artificial island at the other end of the world, Hubert abruptly saw the dark side of the entrepreneurial dream that was supposed to bring Bernard home free and living happily ever after at age fifty-four.

On their second night in the hotel, Hubert was awakened from a deep jet-lagged slumber when his phone began ringing insistently sometime after midnight. *"Je ne suis pas bien,"* cried Bernard, his voiced trembling with panic — "something's wrong. I don't know what's happening to me. I'm depressed. You've got to come down and sleep here."

Still in his pajamas, Hubert pulled on his Sheraton dressing gown and shuffled down to Bernard's room. Once again, as he had done in 1986, he sat for the rest of the night as Bernard poured out an anguished litany of doubts and fears. Everything was wrong, everything was hopeless — his cooking, his business, his marriage, his health — and wherever he turned, there was nothing but black, irredeemable failure. He had seen the third Michelin star as the magic bullet that would resolve all his problems, but Saulieu had turned out to be Saulieu, after all; the euphoric spring and summer seasons had given way to the same cold, wet gloom of clientless winter days. Had he made the wrong choice right from the start in 1975? Had he committed his life to an error?

"It was like a decompression," Couilloud remembered. "He was away from everything he was familiar with, out of his cocoon of the Côte d'Or, and the recognition and adulation that surrounded him there. Suddenly Bernard found that he was alone with himself in a strange new environment. People were honoring him, but that honor wasn't love, you see. Admiration wasn't enough—he had to be *loved*. That was what always supported him. Now he was like a puppet whose strings had been cut, and he collapsed."

It didn't get better. Through the next two weeks, Bernard plodded mechanically through his contractual obligations in the kitchen and with the press like a human soufflé that had fallen. The electric personality, the very one that could thrill blasé Parisian intellectuals with an impassioned description of a snail or a sweetbread, now mumbled lifeless platitudes and returned to his room. The exotic vibrancy and color of Japan that had fascinated his heroes Paul Bocuse and Pierre Troisgros left him cold and inert.

Bernard was in a pit. Fearful and suspicious of Japanese food— even under normal conditions at home, a slightly undercooked shrimp could be enough to trigger a suffocating allergy attack, and the mere idea of raw fish rolled with cold rice made him shudder—he spurned every refined little delicacy that some of the world's finest sushi and sashimi cooks were hoping to introduce to the great French master. Worse yet, his appetite for any kind of nourishment at all disappeared. Bernard—the big mouth, the big eater, the big personality—Bernard wasn't hungry, and he didn't care. It was as troubling as it was astonishing. For two weeks Hubert ordered him room-service pasta, the only thing he would consent to put in his mouth. Sometimes with tomato sauce, sometimes with cheese, but mostly just plain, the twice-daily ration of noodles went into the gullet of the great chef as he sat, head down, torpid, and silent, virtually spoon-fed by his *maître d'hôtel*.

At the end of the contractual ordeal, Hubert nursemaided his boss back to Saulieu and told Dominique what she already knew: Her husband needed some kind of treatment, and fast. A specialist in Paris prescribed Prozac. Bernard obediently took the pills.

"Bipolar disorder" is the currently accepted term for what medical people used to call the manic-depressive syndrome. There is great variation in the onset and force of its symptoms, but it occurs equally in men and women, and various experts estimate that it affects about one percent of any given population. An illness marked by periods of sustained disruption of mood, distorted perceptions, and impaired social functioning is about as broad (and vague) a definition as any med school primer might give, but it is in the enumeration of its well-documented symptoms that a picture of Bernard emerges. He could have stood as the archetype.

The "up" symptoms are inflated self-esteem or grandiosity; racing ideas; extreme talkativeness; excited, elated behavior; increased goal-directed activity; excessive pursuit of activities that carry the risk of painful consequences—spending lots of money is frequently cited; distractibility; decreased need for sleep; and general extravagance. For Hubert, Eric, Patrick, and the others, this could not be the description of a sick person. It was simply the Bernard they had known from the moment of their hiring. If it was illness that had engendered his zealously uncompromising perfectionism, then they could only applaud the illness, because that was what had made the Côte d'Or what it was.

Like a machine without an over-rev governor, Bernard was "running hot" all the time—it was simply what everyone identified as his normal behavior. When he plunged into the abyss, then, it was doubly disturbing, because it happened so rarely. What no one could suspect was that the abyss might be as deep and black as the elation was exalted.

Medical science has a laundry list of the bipolar personality's "down" symptoms. Among them are a generally depressed mood; sluggish manner; diminished pleasure in activities; fatigue, energy, and weight loss; indecisiveness; and feelings of worthlessness or guilt. Hubert saw the whole panoply of symptoms in Tokyo, just as he had in Saulieu in 1986. What he could not believe, what he could not even conceive of—not with this force of nature, this human monument to positive energy and optimism—was the last symptom invariably described in all literature on the bipolar syndrome: recurring thoughts of death or suicide. "The life expectancy of individuals with bipolar disorder is significantly reduced," one expert succinctly put it. "Between 25 and 50 percent of people with this diagnosis attempt suicide, and 15 percent die by suicide."*

It never crossed anyone's mind. Not Bernard. He loved life too much.

For three or four months in that winter and spring of 1992, the staff of the Côte d'Or anxiously watched as the boss struggled with himself and with Eli Lilly's mind-bending molecule. Of course they all knew everything about his treatment because, even in a diminished state, Bernard told everything to everyone. And he was diminished, too; the pill had calmed him down, certainly, but the electric personality was replaced by an amorphous Loiseau caricature who needed a lot of sleep but still complained about feeling constantly tired. For the first time in seventeen years of activity, the Côte d'Or's staff saw what it was like to work with a "normal" boss, one who wasn't endlessly yelling at them and cheerleading for them and finding fault with them—in short, one who rode their asses, to use Bernard's consecrated expression— from eight in the morning to midnight. But they didn't like it a bit.

Neither did Bernard. The spark may have gone from his character, but it was still there somewhere within the chemical cloud, and he hated his situation. He took his treatment back into his own hands with a razor blade; day by day, he carefully sliced away incremental parts of his Prozac pill.

"We all encouraged him, of course," said Eric Rousseau, using the nice French expression *pour lui remonter les bretelles*—to raise his suspenders—"because he saw his illness as shameful, as if he had the clap or something. Appearances were everything for Monsieur Loiseau. The idea that he, this big, strong, famous chef should be on Prozac was intolerable for him. We told him that there were plenty of business leaders and big-name politicians who were doing the same thing, but that didn't make any difference. He was Bernard Loiseau, after all. What if it got into the press?"

The press—*quelle horreur!* The mere idea of an article suggesting any kind of psychiatric treatment drove him to an obsession with liberating himself from the pill. And he succeeded, too. By May, he had

---

*Jeffrey Stovall, MD, in *Uptodate*, clinical information service on the Web: *utdol.com*.

razorbladed the dose down to a sliver, and little by little, the real Bernard Loiseau reappeared. "The machine started up again," said Hubert. "He recovered his taste for life."

With all due respect to Eli Lilly, to the Paris specialist who prescribed Prozac, and to Bernard's methodical razorblade, it was in all likelihood mostly thanks to the tilt of the earth's axis that Bernard recovered: winter turned to spring, and with the dry, balmy days, the clients began returning to Saulieu like migrating birds. There is nothing to warm the cockles of a chef's heart like a full dining room. To generalized grins around the Côte d'Or, Bernard became impossible again.

Re-energized and apparently secure in his three-star prestige, his lucrative contracts, his fecund marriage, and his enviably skilled, supportive staff, Bernard coasted—no, that's not right, he couldn't coast, he galloped, Loiseau-style—through the nineties, king of his ideal castle, national TV and radio personality, international ambassador of French cuisine, buddy-buddy with President François Mitterrand, who frequently came by for dinner and to spend the night (he slept in the duplex room 31, and he was partial to crayfish with tarragon, the huge veal chop, and the *poularde Alexandre Dumaine*), and leading light of the French culinary establishment. How thoroughly and indubitably Bernard had become a leading light was underscored in pop culture when, in 1996, fresh after Mitterrand had awarded him the *legion d'honneur* in a formal salon of the Élysée Palace, his effigy joined Bocuse's—*le grand Paul* himself—in the Musée Grevin's waxworks in Paris. Quite a time. Top of the world.

Even an apparent disappointment proved to have a silver lining. In 1995 the Kobe earthquake had so shaken the Sheraton and its owners that a rethinking of their long-term plans made them decide to end the Loiseau restaurant experiment, but that was fine with Bernard, because it gave him a face-saving excuse to free himself of that dreaded two-week Japanese exile.

Probably the most extraordinary year of all was 1996. In March, the mighty, haughty, hoity-toity Tour d'Argent—Claude Terrail's unassailable temple on the Quai de la Tournelle opposite Notre Dame de Paris, where gastrotourists from everywhere in the universe mentally genuflected before the *maître d'hôtel* who carved their portions of *canard au sang* with solemn priestly gestures—was demoted to two stars. Bernard's place was above the Tour d'Argent! A dream. Unbelievable.

Baby Blanche was born in that same signal year—Bérangère, Bastien, and now Blanche, three little BLs to add their juvenile presence to the little gold $\mathcal{BL}$ logo in cursive script that the *maîtres d'hôtel* and *chefs de rang* wore on their lapels, and with malice toward none and any latent schadenfreude well contained, Bernard could not help but notice the setbacks of two of his young three-star *confrères* whose energy and media prominence inevitably made them rivals in the glory game. First Pierre Gagnaire, the poet-cook in Saint-Etienne, was forced to scuttle his restaurant for want of clientele. It was the first time ever that a three-star establishment had gone broke, but Gagnaire's problems were soon shared by Marc Veyrat in Annecy, who was very publicly teetering on the precipice of bankruptcy and crying for help.

For many in the trade, it was a time of introspection. Beyond the fierce competition reigning within the brotherhood of top restaurateurs—a real beauty contest, and frequently a bitchy one at that—increasingly rigid government regulations and supervision were making it harder and harder to turn a profit without raising already high prices up to absurd levels. The restaurant trade is hard, unrelenting sleep-deprived work to begin with; at its highest level, fatigue is compounded by the same kind of nervous tension that drives operatic divas to seek relief in the extravagant behavior that frequently characterizes their ilk. After Alain Chapel's and Jacques Pic's premature exits, the brilliant Joël Robuchon in Paris concluded that the strain of three-star perfectionism twice a day was too much to expect of mere mortals. He quit his great restaurant on avenue Raymond Poincaré* and retired from competitive cooking to write books and lend his name and considerable talents to television cooking shows. Far too many great cooks were dying young, he said. I don't want to join them. You've only got one life.

---

*And who should take it over but Alain Ducasse? By installing his hand-picked crew and drawing even more enthusiastic media attention than Robuchon had enjoyed, he initiated one of the capital's most celebrated antagonisms. Robuchon versus Ducasse is gastronomy's Guelfs versus the Ghibellines.

If Bernard was introspective around this time, it certainly didn't show, not to the world at large, at any rate. *Monsieur Speed*, he was up and down simultaneously, all day every day, in a permanent saw-tooth pattern: everything was either *fantastique* or *nul*. Hyperbolic, Manichean, and absolutist, Bernard was Bernard, and that was that. But what the clients saw was only the "up" Bernard, standing in his immaculate white garb by the reception desk as they came and went, boyishly attentive and helpful, shaking hands, opening the door for them, explaining his cooking and his career with all the easy skill of a seasoned vaudeville trooper, repeating the same stories with the same lines that his staff already knew by heart, all the while grinning that irresistible Loiseau grin—looming chin-thrustingly forward to make his points,—then crying *Voilà! Voilà! Voiiii-là!* as his interlocutors agreed with him, as agree they must, under the irrefutable, surging plenitude of his affirmations.

It was in this auspicious period of the mid-nineties that a few questions I wanted to ask him about culinary matters brought me to Saulieu again. I had thought we could handle my queries by phone, but after some minutes Bernard said, look, this is getting too complicated, why don't you just come on down to Saulieu and we'll talk it over at lunch, OK? I suppose I was secretly hoping he'd say that, but when he added that we'd be sharing the table that day with his accountant and his lawyer, I thought, ah, hell, there goes the fun.

The main action in the dining room that afternoon was being provided by a woman from the medieval fortress town of Semur-en-Auxois who was marking her ninetieth birthday by inviting fourteen of her family members to ingest enough food to stupefy a wild boar. French grannies know how to celebrate. Skirting this gaggle of senior sybarites, Bernard ushered me into the smallest of his dining rooms, where a round table was set for four. The lawyer and the accountant—none other than Bernard Fabre himself—were already in place.

By all rights, it should have been a pretty doleful affair. Between taxes, mortgages, interest rates, and ironing out some final details of his divorce settlement with Chantal, the afternoon hardly augured to be bathed in jollity. I took my seat, inwardly fearing a tiresome hour or two.

I should have known better. The French are the French, after all, and if that nonagenarian granny had the good taste to celebrate her long life in style, lawyers could be like Hubert de Montille. On the downside, the charges against him were heavy: He was the former president of the Dijon bar association, had pleaded innumerable cases, and had been guilty of an incalculable flow of whereases and *res ipse loquiturs*, in his long and distinguished career, but that was all right, because there was a major extenuating circumstance—he was also a wine maker. Scion of a line of *vignerons* who had been making a superb Volnay as long as anyone can remember, Hubert had subpoenaed two pieces of evidence to place before our jurisdiction at the start of proceedings. To wit: Exhibit A, a Puligny-Montrachet 1993 and Exhibit B, a Bâtard-Montrachet 1988. In choosing these two bottles he was making something of a professional pirouette, in that he hadn't brought along any of his own Volnays. Everyone with any enological culture already knew the de Montille's Volnays, *n'est-ce pas*, but how about these babies? Hubert had just acquired some strips of vineyard in Puligny, and he was excessively proud of his new production, even if the 1993 was admittedly a little thin compared with, say, '88, '89, or '90.

Bernard was trying hard to be a good boy. Blindingly white in his chef's blouse and the dazzling smile that not even a tax declaration could erase from his visage when he was face to face with his own culinary creations, he listened obediently to de Montille's figures, as Bernard Fabre sighed and clucked, but it was obvious that it was all going in one ear and out the other, because Bernard's attention was riveted on the plate of hors d'oeuvres that a waiter deposited before us: tiny *tartelettes* of rabbit liver on a *brunoise* of young vegetables, and breaded snails deep-fried with parsley and star anise.

"Taste that!" he ordered, passing the plate my way and making sure it continued through the circuit until there was nothing left. *"C'est bon, hein?"* he said, dropping an anvil-sized hint to which the only truly acceptable answer would have been a standing ovation, but which we watered down to mere unconditional approbation. I have often wondered at the pressing urge for seduction that inhabits all great chefs, as characteristic of the species as a dog's bark. With Bernard, it was very much like lifeblood.

"C'est bon, hein?" he repeated, and it was. It was wonderful. Bernard beamed.

With the arrival of the first course, it became apparent that Bernard had honored us as ad hoc (but still more or less official) tasters, willing guinea pigs on whom he could try out some new ideas that he and Patrick had been tossing around in the kitchen. Serious matters began with a lentil soup thick with duck giblets, served in wide flat bowls, each of which had a poached egg reposing like a sunset in the middle of the deep amber liquid. Bernard fixed his bright brown eyes on my dish, growing visibly impatient as the seconds passed and I still had not taken the essential step for bringing out the cascade of flavors he had so carefully planned.

"*Casse-moi ça dedans!*" he ordered, reaching over with his fork to mimic the gesture I was to accomplish. I had to act fast, or else he would have done it for me. It was only after I had mashed the sunset down into the leguminous dusk—orange-yellow fingers of yolk flowing like solar eruptions into the pottage's celestial night—that he was satisfied and I was permitted to proceed with the savoring of the contrasts and mellow interminglings of taste and texture. I had hardly mingled my own self with it all by the time Bernard was already wiping his plate squeaky clean with a piece of bread, unwilling to lose the least atom of goodness before the waiter spirited his bowl away.

When the second dish arrived, creeping *déjà vu* arrived with it, the old, familiar apprehension of an exam that turns out to be harder than one had bargained for. This one was pure Loiseau, a construction as hard-edged, linear, and complex as a Schoenberg string quartet: a ragout of baby green asparagus with scallops caramelized in olive oil and a sauce of blended sea-urchin tongues bonded by a celeriac purée. Chewing under Bernard's imperious gaze, I mentally weighed my responses to the exam. Was this dish: ❑ good ❑ excellent ❑ extraordinary ❑ none of the above?

"The asparagus are from Blanc," he felt constrained to point out.

"Georges Blanc?" I wondered in dull-minded incomprehension. The ageing wunderkind of Vonnas had so many irons in the fire that I couldn't help wondering if he had gone into the grocery business, too.

"No, no, Blanc the farmer. Best vegetables anywhere. Just *taste* them—nothing's disguised there. The taste springs out at you—*schlak!* That's what it should be like each time you take a mouthful. It's the taste—the real taste. Each time, it should be like an explosion in your mouth. *Paf! Clack!*"

I mentally marked the third box.

Under de Montille's disapproving eye, Bernard briefly upstaged the lawyer's wines by thrusting a bottle of mineral water my way. He wanted to be sure I knew this one—Châteldon, it was called—because it deserved attention, swimming as it was against a flood tide of the more widely known Perriers, Evians, Volvics, and Vittels.

"*Goûte!*" he ordered. "Taste. It's the best mineral water in the world."

Of course. What else could it be at his table?

Now, in spite of himself, in spite of the facts and figures tumbling from de Montille's agile memory, in spite of Fabre's sighs and frowns, Bernard had slipped totally into his Joyous Provider mode, the only one he was really comfortable with. He gave dutifully unstinting praise to the 1979 Corton that de Montille had also brought along to accompany the main dish—it's always a pleasure to see old folks standing tall—but it was the appearance of the roast chicken that captured his sincerest attention.

"Look at that!" he cried. "Isn't that beautiful? That's the real barnyard fowl, the kind you'll never find in a store." He bent as reverently as a supplicant over the steaming platter. "It even smells a little bit of *merde*, just the way a real chicken should. Wing or thigh?"

Serving us, he explained that immediately after graduating from the oven, the bird had been injected with truffle juice, a neat application of the hypodermic syringe that might usefully be added to medschool curricula for the benefit of future gourmets among the corps of French doctors. With each portion of chicken he scooped us a generous ladle of stuffing (boned pigs' feet, truffles, and foie gras), decorated with little golden chips of thrice-blanched, and then deep-fried, garlic. Alongside lay individual *galettes* fashioned of potato and the bird's chopped giblets.

By the time the great wicker-basket loads of cheeses, nuts, and figs arrived for our perusal and choice, the divorce settlement got only the shortest of shrifts and taxes were as well as forgotten. De Montille made a stab at returning to business by checking something or other on Bernard's cell phone, but his heart wasn't really in it. When dessert followed—the house's own silky off-white version of real bean-rich vanilla ice cream (beans from Madagascar and Tahiti) Bernard's Joyous Provider mode was beginning to veer dangerously toward feeding frenzy.

"Take a *tuile*, take a *tuile*," he insisted, passing around the table a gleaming plate of pastries, chocolates, and *petits fours* and watching every single one of them disappear into our maws. *Tuiles*, named after their resemblance to meridional roof tiles, have always been something of a mystery and bafflement at La Côte d'Or, marrying metaphysical lightness (look out—they rise to the ceiling if you let them go) with a depth of taste that—every rule's got an exception—bespeaks not only almonds and sugar, but, yes, butter as well, and plenty of it.

Around and around the pastry platter went, the most dissolute of gormandizing excess for a lunch crew already deeply plunged into satiety. On came the coffee and the cigars and the delicious *mirabelle*, the world's most sophisticated white lightning.

The afternoon was drawing to a close, but Bernard didn't want it to end. His cooking, his pursuit of food's purest essences, had made him famous around the world, but now his role as host—the ultimate expression of that cooking—was on the line, and there was nothing more that he could offer us.

He couldn't accept it. There had to be *something*.

"Have another *tuile*," he said.

I couldn't. Not even that.

"How about another glass of wine?" Already, a young *sommelier* was hovering with a bottle of beet-red Maranges Clos des Loyères.

No, better not. I had to drive, after all.

"Some more *mirabelle*? Another cigar?"

No thanks. I felt positively guilty in refusing.

"You sure you don't want to rest before you go? I can have one of the maids turn down a bed for you."

Not a bad idea, but I really had to be getting back.

Bernard was close to desperation. What else could he try? There had to be something else to offer, but what? He darted his eye around the room, then back to the table. Aha! He spotted the cell phone.

"Here," he said, thrusting it across the table to me. "Don't you want to make a phone call? Long distance?"

So there it was, Bernard being Bernard more emphatically than ever. Several years afterward, the scene of this cascade of offerings jumped back into my head when Eric Rousseau, reminiscing about his years at the Côte d'Or with this singular boss, summed him up with a single lapidary phrase. "Monsieur Loiseau was so generous himself that he just couldn't understand it when people weren't generous with him in return."

That little lunch with Fabre and de Montille could not have offered a better view of Bernard at his best, in every direction: his cuisine, his enthusiasm, his total dedication to quality, his charismatic character, and his amiability—the simple, downright *niceness* of the guy. Never was there a chef who genuinely liked to make people happy more than this one. "If I could afford it, I'd like to give away the meals here," he frequently said, and he really wasn't lying.

Bernard was flying high in those days, no doubt about it. His depression of 1992 was a thing of the past, and he was once again tall in the saddle, looking forward to the next challenge. In 1998 he came to the foot of a big mountain to climb, and he scaled it, too, but, Bernard being Bernard, he did it *direttissimo* style, taking a route that no one in the restaurant business had ever thought of before—the stock market.

This was how things stood as the year began: Bernard had his new kitchen and dining rooms, his beautiful, monumental staircase, twenty-three *Relais & Châteaux* rooms of the highest standards of luxury, but the Dumaine wing of the hotel—the very one whose rotten old rooms Hubert and Chantal and anyone else they could shanghai into hard labor had painted in the eighties—was still in place, prettied up as well as he could make it but still cramped, dark, and unprotected from street noise. His development plan absolutely called for an additional nine spacious first-class rooms, the library, the billiards and conference rooms, the pool, sauna, fitness center, and a relandscaping of the garden—not to mention a couple of other restaurants in Paris that he had his eye on, the future Tante Marguerite and Tante Jeanne.

Trouble was, he had maxed out on traditional bank loans and had an outstanding debt of nearly five million euros. At this point, a client suggested (in the euphoria, we may suppose, that invades one after a great meal accompanied by great wines) the intriguing idea of raising a war chest for finishing off his building program by going public. Conservative as ever, Fabre was against it—too many imponderables, too complicated—but Bernard was predictably seized with enthusiasm. He took the plunge.

So it happened that in the very last days of business in December 1998, the 129th and final initial public offering on the Second Market of the Paris Bourse was something called *le Groupe Bernard Loiseau*, which was able to boast a turnover of less than 5 million euros a year. Counseled by BDO Gendrot and underwritten by the Caisse Centrale des Banques Populaires, Bernard offered himself, his restaurants, his contacts, his industrial gigs, and his prospects for the future for sale— 600,000 shares at 7.42 euros apiece.

Damned if it didn't work. There were plenty of drawbacks—changing from a private to a public company entails a vastly increased amount of paperwork and bureaucratic detail, but Bernard was careful to keep 53 percent of the stock in his own pocket, thereby protecting himself from possible future takeover bids and meddling from stockholders. He had to go through the rigamarole of electing officers to the new company, opening up his books, presenting annual reports, and holding stockholder meetings, but at least no one could oblige him to put *crème fraîche* in his sauces. All the hassles were offset, though, by the wonders of the stock market that a few entrepreneurs had discovered before him: the IPO gave him enough cash—4.5 million euros— to finish off his building program and buy his last two Tantes.

Unsurprisingly, many of the new stockholders were affluent sorts— bankers, brokers, doctors, and business and professional people who had been frequenting the restaurant for years, who had succumbed to Bernard's overwhelming charm, and who felt something like a national duty to support the man who had brought the grand old Côte d'Or back to glory.

"A lot of it was emotional—*affectif*," said Bernard. "They knew me and they knew my cooking. Many of them bought shares to give away as Christmas presents."

Within a few years the revenue of the group had more than doubled (up to 11.6 million euros by 2001, for instance), and the overall business was turning a respectable profit just shy of 1 million euros a year. In later years the stock generally followed the downward trend of the Paris Bourse, but Bernard was quick to point out that his shares fell less than most, and that on average he proved to be a better performer than any number of mighty industrial giants and golden-boy dot-com flashes in the pan.

"Those jerks with their *start-ups de merde* are gone now, and I'm still here!" he crowed with a defiant Mussolinian chin thrust. A few seconds later, though, he plummeted right down into the other pole of the bipolar personality.

"I pass my time trembling," he admitted, *sotto voce*.

In mid-December of 2002, I came to Saulieu again to do a little article for the *Wall Street Journal* on the whys and wherefores of his stock-market adventure. Most of the details of that reporting job—the facts, figures, and dates—have by now slipped into the approximations of vague memory, but I recall with perfect clarity the scene of my lunch that day.

As luck had it, I enjoyed the signal honor of sharing lunch with Dominique in the best seat of the house—the chef's table in the kitchen with its red leather bench and stainless steel top, set on a raised dais just a couple of meters from the *passe* where the chef makes his last examination of plates before passing them on to the waiters. As a gastronomic teaser before the rest of the lunch, Bernard had decided on an off-menu treat for me that afternoon: *huîtres chaudes*, six huge (triple-zero) Belon oysters quickly grilled under the *salamandre*, and sauced with a reduced *coulis* made of the oysters' own juices, to which a little touch of balsamic vinegar had lent a slightly acidic bite.

On my side, the conversation with Dominique was lively and rich with factual information; while taking notes, I earnestly endeavored to limit my sips of the chilled, lemony, deliciously alluring Chablis in my glass, lest I bungle on some date or figure.

On his side, behind the stainless steel counter separating us, Bernard officiated, inspecting and barking orders as he supervised the succession of plates going out to the dining room. He was a very busy guy, as chefs invariably are twice a day, but at the same time he was preparing my oysters himself. He was in profile as he stood holding his hand under the orange glow of the *salamandre* to test the heat, when suddenly, out of nowhere and for no apparent reason, he whirled around, looked me somberly in the eye, and made an announcement.

"*C'est jamais gagné*," he said—the battle's never won.

At the moment I took it for a total nonsequitur, and a rather puzzling one at that, because there wasn't a trace of a smile on his face. Two months later, I learned that it wasn't a nonsequitur after all.

XIV

THINGS FALL APART

*I*n October of 1995 François Mitterrand made his last trip to the Côte d'Or. Out of office since May, the ex-president knew he was dying of cancer but intended to enjoy the good things in life to the end, so he came for dinner* and to spend the night. Taking his leave the next morning, this frequently enigmatic little man reached up and, for the first time ever, embraced Bernard with the traditional kisses on either cheek that have been the French presidential accolade ever since the country went from monarchy to republicanism. At that moment, Bernard understood he would never be seeing him again in Saulieu. Less than three months later, Mitterrand was dead.

Without erecting too-obvious signposts of omen and portent here, Mitterrand's last visit may be viewed as a foreshadowing for Bernard, something like the beginning of the end of the palmy days when he enjoyed a special relationship with the critical establishment while also being lionized by the general public that saw him on TV, heard him on the radio, and could barely escape his smiling face in newspapers and

---

*What does a moribund ex-president of France order for one of his last serious gourmet meals? It was calf's liver in Mitterrand's case, seared in a hot skillet until lightly crusted on the outside, then slow-cooked so the inside remained pink. Sauced with a reduction of successive deglazings of "sacrificial" veal, it was accompanied by a purée of Bintje potatoes shot through with chips of black Tricastin truffles. He washed it down with a glass of Blagny from the vines of Thierry Matrot, an excellent *vigneron* from Meursault.

magazines. He was still riding high on a wave of popularity and critical acclaim, but times were changing in gastronomy as much as they were in politics, and habits, tastes, and fashions were shifting along with them. *Un clou chasse l'autre*, they say—a new nail drives out the old. Until then, Bernard had known only the experience of being one of the new nails.

French gourmets can be as fickle as adolescents adoring, then casting aside, pop idols, and the foodie journalists and guide critics who influence these gourmets were the same in the nineties as they are today: undeniably knowledgeable, competent, and refined of palate, but suffering from repetition of too much of a good thing—in a word, cloyed. Sated with great fare and egregiously flattered by chefs and *maîtres d'hôtel* wherever they turned their august attentions, and redoubtably powerful by the force of their published words, they were at permanent risk of self-importance and the haughty indifference engendered by a nearly permanent professional exposure to the sorts of delicacies, oh dear, how tiresome, that ordinary mortals might encounter a few times a year at best. Like the movers and shakers of the "rag" trade, members of this caste were constantly on the lookout for new trends, new faces, and new ideas—anything to whip up jaded appetites and provide an unexpected new spark or angle to write about. (It is maddeningly difficult to write a sexy story about Taillevent in Paris, for instance, because everything there is professional, traditional, and flawless. An adventuresome chef who is constantly coming up with new culinary fireworks—even if some of them misfire—is infinitely preferable as a source of interesting copy.) Unimpressed by the same direly expensive serving of turbot or *foie gras* that they had on their plates a couple of nights earlier, these critical ladies and gents could sigh impatiently at lobster, pout at truffles, and roll their eyes with sovereign contempt at classics like a *steak au poivre*,*

---

*In August, 2003, a long, devotional cover article in *New York Times Magazine* by Arthur Lubow hailed the very inventive Catalan cook Ferran Adria and his acolytes as saviors of the great tradition of Western gastronomy, grown old and stagnant in France, in Lubow's opinion. "One look at the conventional *steak au poivre* sizzling grimly in a skillet," he wrote, "and you feel in your gut [the] panicky *sauve qui peut* impulse to escape Paris at all costs." Clearly, the author—a shining example of this breed of professional anorexics—had never enjoyed a *steak au poivre* prepared by the likes of Pierre Troisgros.

however perfectly executed. Professional eaters can be a blasé crew, indeed, inevitably recalling Cocteau's famous command to his friend Diaghilev: *Étonne-moi*—Astonish me.*

In Clichy, Paris, and during his struggling early years in Saulieu, Bernard had astonished the critics, especially the influential Henri Gault, who was charmed by his youthfully ingenuous enthusiasm, his capacity for nonstop work, his hypertrophied will to please, and the overpowering force of the sales rhetoric that he could never resist laying on. It took grumpy old Michelin a while longer to be similarly impressed, but eventually they came around, too, and *le style Loiseau*, this evolution from Troisgros via Verger and Guérard, became generally accepted as a discrete and coherent entity. With that, Bernard might well have persuaded himself that he was king of the mountain.

But even as he sat on his summit in Saulieu, slow tectonic shifts were rumbling beneath him. Elsewhere in Europe and then, unexpectedly, in America, the U.K., Asia, and Australia as well, brash young cooks—some expatriated from France but most of them native-born—were taking the techniques that the French had pioneered, adding their personal touches and their national ingredients, and coming up with an excellence in gastronomy that was unquestionably equal to the best that the French were doing themselves. France was no longer alone at the top of the fine food chain.

"We're not the best, we're just more numerous," Ducasse told me with a shrug, not displaying the least hint of alarm. "The competition is global now. There's talent everywhere, and the most widely shared thing in the world is *savoir-faire*. In almost any major capital now you can eat as well as you do in France. Great restaurants are no longer a French monopoly. The only difference is in numbers—there are just more of them here than anywhere else."

---

*When Alain Ducasse took over Joël Robuchon's former place on avenue Raymond Poincaré in Paris, he proved that he had a sense of humor—or provocation—by including on his card that antediluvian chestnut, a *tournedos Rossini*, an act approximately equivalent to Limp Bizkit adding a Boccherini minuet to their repertoire, or perhaps a driver entering a 1947 Ford in the Le Mans race—and winning. (It was terrific.)

Bernard didn't care about the world at large; he wasn't a voyager like Ducasse. As far as he was concerned, New York, London, and San Francisco could take care of themselves. His place was France and his ambition was to shine in France—but the tectonic shifts were at work there, too. France was not immune to the globalization in which Ducasse was so merrily and successfully swimming. And that was worrisome.

"Fusion," a strange and rather ominous word signifying a breach of the comforting national boundaries within which *la cuisine française* had been sequestered for so many centuries, was entering the national culinary vocabulary, and the *Guide Michelin*'s new director, Derek Brown, was said to be favorable to it. In Roanne, young Michel Troisgros, Pierre's son and Bernard's great rival, was offering a menu heavy with Japanese influences, while speaking unashamedly of his admiration for that country and its culture of gastronomy. In Cancale on Brittany's Bay of Mont Saint-Michel, Olivier Roellinger (still only two stars but a sure bet for three) was wowing gourmets young and old by thumbing his nose at endogenous tradition with his profligate use of spices and exotic flavors and textures from everywhere in the world. The admirable Pierre Gagnaire, master of a wildly imaginative, futuristic culinary sleight of hand, had bounced back from his failed Saint-Etienne venture to win three stars in a new Parisian location, and the succession of little ramekins that became the trademark of his artistic expression—a main theme in the central dish, echoed by supporting variations in a semicircle around it—was pure sensation, unlike anything going on anywhere else. In Laguiole, the equally admirable Michel Bras, marathon runner, ecologist, and natural philosopher, tramped austerely through the austere hills and meadows of his native Aubrac Plateau to pick wild plants and herbs unknown to Escoffier traditionalists, sniffed them, tasted them, and then incorporated them into his dazzling cuisine. In his twinned restaurants in Annecy and Megève, Marc Veyrat took notice of Bras's favorable publicity, concluded that his *confrère auvergnat* was on to a good thing, glommed onto it himself, and elevated his version of "natural cuisine" into an entire system backed by a relentless PR campaign, while comparing himself to Mozart and denouncing the rest of French cooking as "has-been." A mountain mountebank of the purest sort (Veyrat was born and raised in the Alps), he postured outrageously in the signature black peasant hat that never quit his head, indoors or out, while charging stratospheric prices (a couple could expect to be separated from $1,000 for their supper). But his act was new, different, and exciting. It worked. Clients flocked to him, mouths and wallets agape.

Less outrageous but perhaps even more significant was what was happening just over the border in Spain on the other side of the Pyrenées, where a brotherhood of Catalan cooks led by Ferran Adria was fast becoming the cynosure of the eyes and palates of the wealthy international gourmet set. Adria's surrealistic space-age cuisine—codfish foams, ginger sprays, truffle lollipops, foie gras sherbet, and hundreds of other equally strange inspirations—inevitably invited comparison to two of Catalonia's earlier artistic wild men, Salvador Dali and Antonio Gaudi, and was marked by extraordinary manipulations that were more reminiscent of a high-tech industrial research lab than a classical kitchen. Adria's restaurant, El Bulli, had a waiting list that stretched not over months, but years, and his dishes frequently required not only explanations of content but instructions on how to go about eating them. The world-weary been-there-done-that crowd of gastronomic sophisticates from every corner of the planet scrambled for tables the way their kids had done for Cabbage Patch dolls and fairly swooned with gratitude at being allowed in. They obediently did as they were told and concluded that they had at long last discovered gastronomic Nirvana.

But what about plain old eating of plain old ingredients that you could actually recognize? Was that even what restaurants were for anymore? Doubt could be permitted in certain chic quarters of Paris— always the most capricious and fashion-obsessed of gastronomic venues—where something with the moronic name of *le fooding* was catching on fast with the hip young professional crowd. This vaguely defined lifestyle movement was to classical restaurants approximately what video games were to old hi-fi sets: an overarching fashion statement heavily influenced by earlier trends in America. Built around décor, music, lighting, and style, restaurants devoted to *le fooding* specialized in bizarre and surprising dishes* light-years removed from French cuisine's classical vocabulary—just right for the beautiful and almost beautiful people who flocked to the latest hot addresses to see and be seen. *Étonne-moi*, indeed, but preferably in surroundings where TV personalities, models, and movie stars show up.

The old road was rapidly aging. Just a few years earlier Bernard had been the one doing the astonishing, but now a new generation was coming to the fore, and he wasn't about to impress this notoriously capricious, short-memoried bunch with a bourgeois dream house of Burgundy tile, waiters in tuxedos, and *choufleur caramelisé*.

This one deserves some further explanation, because it says something about Bernard in relation to the protean world of gastronomic fashion. Caramelized cauliflower was a late creation, one in which Bernard took great pride but that ultimately failed to deliver on the promise he saw in it. True to his mantra of reinforcing his ingredients' taste—the *real* taste, the one that ends with a *schlak!*—he evolved a three-step process for souping up the bland taste of this supremely modest vegetable. The process began where ordinary home cooking usually ended: with the cooking in boiling water. After draining the cooked *choufleur*, he forced it through a fine sieve, hung the resulting purée in a cheesecloth, collected the liquid that seeped out, and reduced it to a concentrated essence. Step two was to remove the purée from the cheesecloth and cook it down on the stove nearly to caramel texture, helped along by a generous lump of fresh butter. Into the blender it went for step three, now admixed with the reduced *bouillon* that had been collected from the cheesecloth. The end result was a rich, buttery *velouté* that he could serve as an accompaniment to several different dishes, but most frequently appeared on the Côte d'Or's menu in partnership with lobster medallions in a lobster coral sauce.

In spite of all the thought and effort that went into it, though, his

---

*The excesses of culinary invention by would-be *artistes*—in France and anywhere else in the world, for that matter—inevitably invite comparison with degenerate Rome. Monty Python got it just right with the scene in *The Life of Brian* where Brian, hapless stadium vendor, goes through the crowd shouting his wares: "larks' tongues, wrens' livers, jaguars' earlobes, Tuscany fried bats, otters' noses, ocelots' spleens."

labor-intensive inspiration proved to be of doubtful value; after all that work, all he had was a dish that tasted like cauliflower, only a bit more so, and happened to be in a smoother form. Basically, Bernard had put in a heroic effort to lend interest to a vegetable that was—face it— intrinsically boring. *Choufleur caramelisé* could be no match for all the excitement going on elsewhere. Had he gone off on the wrong track? Was he losing the touch that had so impressed critics in the seventies and eighties?

Knowing the man, it is easy to imagine panicky thoughts like this jabbing into the blanket of optimism with which this most insecure of all of France's gastronomic tenors draped his person. Let us now con- tinue a little farther down that road of speculation. *Nouvelle cuisine* had been something of an ersatz revolution to begin with—essentially the smart ideas of a few young chefs, pumped full of air into a commercial soufflé promoted by Henri Gault and Christian Millau, and whose ex- cesses went right through the top of the silliness meter. Well, what was *le style Loiseau* but a personalized offshoot of *nouvelle cuisine*? Did that mean he was just pumping more air into the air at La Côte d'Or?

Not really—he was a serious cook absolutely dedicated to his craft, and anything but a phony. But there was a more fundamental truth lurk- ing behind that moniker of *le style Loiseau*: For all his (very persuasive) talk of being different from other chefs, *basically, Bernard was just cook- ing classical French cuisine.* His veal chop, *foie gras*, sweetbreads, chicken breasts, pigeon, pike perch, his celebrated frogs' legs, and his snails in nettle soup—even the more rarified, pricey items like turbot, scallops, and lobster—his entire menu, in fact, was rooted in the great wellspring of provincial recipes, ingredients, and techniques descended straight from their origins in a thousand farmhouses and villages, elabo- rated and refined over a couple of centuries by professional cooks. He took infinite pains to make his menu light, healthy, and honest—deglaz- ing with water to ensure that true tastes would be preserved, eschewing *crème fraîche*, fastidiously patting off cooking fats with paper towel, and all the other purist/Maoist/perfectionist habits and tricks that he devel- oped over the years—but when the rhetoric was stripped away, what clients at La Côte d'Or were getting on their plates was *cuisine de terroir allegée*—traditional French country cuisine dressed up *à la Loiseau*.

Meanwhile, away from the *luxe, calme et volupté* of tradition that

Bernard had so lovingly installed in the Côte d'Or, the earth was turning faster and faster. Pierre Gagnaire's marvelously good but often baffling procession of little ramekins was echoed and amplified by Ferran Adria's thirty-two-dish meals lasting five or six hours, while a thousand other smart guys were fusing Japanese, Thai, Chinese, and you-name-it with the venerable seven-thousand-odd recipes of *Gringoire et Saulnier*, the standard reference book of French chefdom. Alain Ducasse, top gun of the smart guys, was referring to himself as a *zappeur*, and in the herky-jerky TV-dominated www-world of the short attention span, instant gratification, MP3, and video games, the Sony generation was gobbling up novelty and begging for more. Where the Beatles created masterpieces on two-track recorders, now pop music weaved its path through a labyrinth of sixty-four tracks, and the arrangers somehow managed to fill every single one of them, tweaking dials and sliding slides to make silicon sing out in a whole new vocabulary of freaky sounds and special effects, synchronized with the computerized graphics of the clips that went with them. It was all part of a whole, and there was a perfect logic to it, globalization was at work, ideas and trends shot around the planet with lightning speed, and there was no stopping progress. The world had become a kaleidoscope.

"People used to come here to eat," said a gloomy Marc Meneau in Saint-Père de Vézelay. "Now what they want is *la fête*."

Unspoken: Clients used to be connoisseurs who would recognize and appreciate the craftsmanship of a cook who could turn out a perfect *homard à l'américaine, chartreuse de perdreaux*, or *sauce grand veneur*. Now they want to be amused, surprised, and delighted by novelties. They want a show. *Étonne-moi*.

So: The chicken or the egg? Was it the chefs who were imposing the giddy new trends of *cuisine tendance*, or were they only responding to the demands of a new generation? Who knows, but in any case, Meneau was right. *La fête* (aka in neo-French: *le fun*) was fast becoming the order of the day, and it was happening wherever you looked. Christo was wrapping, Damien Hirst was formaldehyding, Nigel Kennedy was playing Bach with his hair punk-spiked in superglue, Marc Veyrat was getting raves for lichen mousse (*mousse de mousse* — would it surprise you to hear it tastes just like moss?), and in conservative, bourgeois Joigny, Jean-Michel Lorain, freshly recrowned with the three stars he had lost in 2001, was serving oysters in porridge and getting rewarded for it by *GaultMillau* with a grade of 19 out of 20.

Any chef who stuck by tradition and classicism risked the most terrifying adjective of all: *ringard*—corny, rinky-dink, passé. The smart guys were rockin' and rollin', but on his *piano* down in Saulieu, Bernard was still playing Debussy, Ravel, and Satie. The old certainties were slipping away fast. *Les trente glorieuses* had brought modernization and a new kind of prosperity to France, but with that prosperity had come Britney Spears, a thousand and one *MacDos*, and the dream-joys of the PR industry, while a stunningly rapid proliferation of meretricious, cheapo commercial architecture every day further blighted the serene beauty of the countryside that Bernard loved and where he had netted the crayfish and harvested the snails that were no longer there. In the few short years since his adolescence, he had seen France swing from a land of *matières nobles*—stone, wood, slate, and tile—into one of steel, concrete, plastic, and plasterboard. Times were a-changing.

Consumerist *gigantisme* was upon the land, and now it was the M.B.As who ruled. The French one-upped the Americans by leapfrogging the supermarket phase right into the immensely bigger hypermarkets, which in turn provided the cue for the birth of the behemoth Wal-Marts and Kmarts over on the other side of the Atlantic. Women abandoned their kitchens to labor, nine to five, in the factories and hypermarkets in order to buy the very goods they produced in their factories and sold in their hypermarkets: a perfect symmetry; the loop was looped. As the stoves at home grew cold, the famous back burners transmuted into black ceramic induction plaques expressly designed for heating up prepared industrial foods, while the adjacent microwaves thawed and cooked the now-ubiquitous frozen stuff. The national identity that was once built around the family, the hearth, the table, the village, the church, and *le petit commerce* had disappeared in a wink—*poof!*—and with it went the cheery feeling of belonging to a community of like-minded citizens.

The center wasn't holding anymore. French cuisine had always been both regional and seasonal, and there was a comforting regularity in the eternal rhythms. When the season for oysters ended, you could count on the fat white asparagus arriving to take their place, and then the strawberries, the melons, and the cherries. Then autumn would come, with its venison and wild boar and the return of the oysters. The celestial wheels turned, as Newton said they should; spring would follow winter, and summer spring; things were in their place and God was in his heaven. Now all that was falling apart. With globalization and the efficiency of modern transportation, everything was available all year 'round, flown in by air cargo. It was progress, no doubt, but all that "out-of-season" stuff, now so available, was expensive and didn't taste as good as the real thing—and for all anyone knew, it was genetically modified, too. Whatever happened to the taste of naturally grown tomatoes? Why were French kids beginning to suffer from obesity? Somehow it didn't seem right. Down in the southern city of Millau, a peasant leader named José Bové skillfully exploited the nation's vague, inchoate longing for the authenticity of the old days by leading a raid that demolished a new McDonald's outlet. Bové's raid made him something of a Robin Hood hero in France and a media star around the world, but the true significance of the event was that Bové himself, surrounded by his very telegenic PR image props—a Lech Wałesa mustache and a Joe Stalin pipe—was not a peasant at all, but rather a left-wing intellectual whose conscience had been raised as a child in California; he was an imposter.

In Annecy and Megève, Marc Veyrat's folksy restaurants were mere decorator recreations of down-home rusticity, and his *cuisine naturelle* was made famous via the state-of-the-art communication techniques of his wife's PR agency. In sum, it was a perfect example of a Disney experience.

Down in Saulieu, a fitting irony had come down upon Bernard's head. The dynamics of the consumer society brought him, the purest purist of a Maoist *cuisine des essences*, into the service of the beast with the ready-made industrial dishes to which he lent his name and which were sold in hypermarkets throughout the country. In fact, it was largely the remuneration he got for his industrial flings that allowed him to keep his head above water financially. He was compromised, in contradiction with himself. A philosopher might have used the word alienation.

Everything put together, there were plenty of reasons for him to feel an inner turmoil, and they reached all the way down to his cooking, the very heart of his professional identity. The truth was that he wasn't particularly good at it, not from a technical point of view, at any rate. Jacques Maximin had been affectionately chaffing him when he launched his challenge in the kitchen, but he was right: Bernard was not one of those cooks who could whip you up a *béarnaise* or a *hollandaise* with his eyes closed, the way any master chef could. He had gone straight from apprenticeship to the position of chef at La Barrière Clichy without putting in the intervening years of on-the-job training—*commis, sous-chef, chef de partie, second*, the normal stepping stones of professional competence—that marked the careers of most of his colleagues. As a result, he had large holes in his technical know-how. He was a good inventor because he was an idea man, but for sheer creativity he was not in the league of Chapel or the three magic Gs: Guérard, Girardet, and Gagnaire. To develop his style he had relied on an extraordinarily sure and sensitive palate—he was an exceptional taster of both food and wines—but his innovations were mostly refinements of what was already there, taking what others did and going a step or two further: perfecting.

There it is, the central point: Above all, Bernard was a perfectionist. Do or die, he was determined to build not just a wonderful hotel, but the best damn country palace in all of France, the best maintained and the best staffed; to have in his kitchen only the finest ingredients, regardless of price; to cook them and present them so impeccably, so limpidly, that nothing of their essential qualities of taste and texture was hidden or disguised; and to persuade his clients that they could never, anywhere else, enjoy an experience to match a meal and a night at the Côte d'Or.

Through all the borrowing, building, decorating, cooking, and persuading, it was perfectionism that drove him. And being a perfectionist, he naturally doubted himself. Beneath the bluster, he was the guy wandering through his garden with his brother, wondering whether all this really belonged to him. He pranced and posed for the press, but, because he was intelligent, he knew in his heart of hearts that he would never truly be *le top*—neither an Alain Chapel in the kitchen nor a Paul Bocuse on the world's stage as the leader and figurehead of the trade.

So of course, the more self-doubt assailed him, the more he blustered and the more he caricatured himself. By the time he passed his fiftieth birthday, the Bernard who greeted guests by the reception desk, like the Bernard who appeared on radio and TV, emitted a nonstop sales pitch for La Côte d'Or, for himself, and for *le style Loiseau* that had become so passionate and perfervid that his body could scarcely keep up with the machine-gun flow of words. He audibly gasped as the excited flow of phrase and exclamation tumbled from his mouth, gulping air in a vain attempt to keep going without a pause.

"He scared me," admitted Bernard Naegellen, the Michelin honcho who had awarded him his third star. "Everything was too fast, too much. I couldn't help wondering if he ever got any sleep."

Dr. Ladislas Kiss, a Lyon-based psychiatrist, first became aware of Bernard by chance, when he caught one of his television appearances, and was struck by the surging, twitching energy of the man. He was fascinated. Like a baseball fan keeping track of a favorite player, he informally followed Bernard's career for more than a decade after that, gazing at him from a distance with a mix of admiration and apprehension. His professional diagnosis was the same as Naegellen's human one, but he knew a good deal about the clinical symptoms as well, notably the bipolar personality's alarming tendencies toward self-destruction.

"The way he was going," he told me, "I would have had him forcibly interned for his own good if I had been treating him."

Well, in light of those apprehensions, I asked him, didn't you ever consider approaching Dominique, or even Bernard himself, to warn of the dangers that lay there in the offing? Dr. Kiss gave the fatalistic shrug of a man who has been around. "I know just how he would have reacted if I ever wrote him. He would have immediately thrown my letter in the garbage. You know—just another shrink trying to make money off me."

As he wound himself up tighter and tighter, Bernard made work the remedy for all things—nonstop work for improving the Côte d'Or, for persuading customers to come to Saulieu, for overcoming self-doubt, for forcing back the bipolar's angst at the simple fact of existence. Phobias developed. His cleanliness became excessive and his rituals compulsive. He changed his chef's blouse several times a day, and the tiniest spot or speck on his apron consigned it instantly to the laundry. His shirts were never white enough, the creases of the iron never sharp enough. A hair out of place or a crumb stuck on the side of someone's mouth—even a client's—unnerved him to the point of his desperately wanting to brush it away himself, and Dominique, Hubert, or Eric could sense that he was restraining his nit-picking instinct. He always parked his car in exactly the same place when he came to work in the morning, then passed directly into the pantry of the breakfast room, where he took his espresso standing in order to remain fully operational. After gulping it down, he poured his orange juice directly into the same cup. That avoided sullying a clean glass—*il n'y a pas de petites économies*, runs a favorite saying of the French—no savings is too small; every little bit helps. When a trip to Paris, Dijon, or some other destination outside of Saulieu called for a change into civvies, he consulted everyone who crossed his path about his choice of necktie. The least expression of doubt from the lowliest waiter or kitchen worker was enough to send him into a paroxysm of indecision and had him sprinting back to his closet for the selection of another. When the shoe was on the other foot, predictably he would become a punctilious master sergeant. Any *maître d'hôtel* assigned to accompany him—even Hubert, the most senior and privileged of the entire staff—had to stand inspection before the chef's stern, inquisitorial eye. No one could appear in public at Bernard Loiseau's side with scruffy shoes or a badly ironed shirt. Twice a day, before quitting the kitchen after each *service*, he played out an unvarying mania to the staff: folding his apron just so, always precisely the same three-step demonstration of military precision, ending with a white rectangle resembling a flat loaf of bread, around which he carefully wrapped the strings before stashing it in the same spot in the same stainless-steel drawer.*

He was big and strong, but he was chicken. When Dominique was away with the kids, he left the big old house in town and came down to sleep in the hotel, his $10-million security blanket. In fact, he could hardly bear to be away from Saulieu at all, because it was the only place where he felt entirely safe and sure of himself. His famous mad dashes to Paris in his black BMW—a zoom up the R.N. 6, arrow-straight to the hamlet of Etrée, a swift right over to the autoroute, then a 220-kilometer pedal to the metal to the TV studio or radio station five

---

*A bronze reproduction of his folded apron adorns Bernard's gravestone in the Saulieu cemetery today.

minutes before time—were almost never one-way trips. Whatever time it was when he finished, Bernard rushed frantically back to home base, usually with time enough to supervise the next *service*. These dashes allowed him to multiply his image throughout France, but it was this very image-multiplying that misled a steadily growing corps of critics into believing that Loiseau spent his time basking in the Parisian limelight when he should have been back in Saulieu tending to his cuisine. Far from being the glory-hunting dilettante that his censors saw in him, he was so fanatically devoted to his establishment that he literally felt sick when he was away from it. The Côte d'Or was his cocoon and his life.

Slowly, almost imperceptibly, all the little things were adding up; uncertainties edged toward doubts, doubts toward worries, and worries toward anguish, all of it compounded by a level of physical and spiritual fatigue that veered dangerously into the red zone. In spite of—or because of—his three stars, Bernard was never sure whether he was doing enough to please his clients.

"Tell me what's wrong, tell me what's wrong," he begged every time I stopped by Saulieu, and he was absolutely sincere. It was almost as if he was seeking a cause for self-flagellation—the good old original-sin instinct of the born perfectionist who can't make anything too good or too right. On one of those occasions he even managed to turn a comment that I had meant as a compliment into a source of worry. I like the way you use salt, I said. Your flavors really have zing. "Yeah," he said, "I salt right to the maximum, don't I?" Ostensibly he was agreeing with me, but the tone of his voice, his body language, and his facial expression said: *maybe too much.*

Unwittingly, I had touched on a subject that some years later was to prove heavy with consequence. In 2000 or 2001, Hubert, Eric, and the others began reporting back to Bernard and Patrick a rise in critical comment from the dining room about the seasoning of dishes, notably the sauces. A certain number of clients had found them too strong for their palates, too salty. Bernard perked up, because sauces had been a hot topic since the nineties. Certain prophets of *cuisine tendance* demeaned them across the board as a hangover from the traditional school, out of place in modern cooking. Since the Middle Ages—long before the concept of restaurants even existed—sauces had been of capital importance to French cuisine, and they had constantly evolved in reflection of the broader society. In the days of Escoffier, sauces were generously poured over the meat or fish they were designed to enhance, but with *nouvelle cuisine* they had migrated to a less important position, while at the same time becoming lighter and less copious. In the nineties, Bernard saw many of his modern colleagues imitating Pierre Gagnaire, who spooned them out only in deft, delicate lines or little dots around the principal ingredient, more as an element of decoration than the central message of taste.

As a young heller in Saulieu, Bernard himself had toyed with something like a sauceless cuisine, but rapidly abandoned that inspiration as he matured into a serious professional. Even the most fervent or obtuse revolutionary could see that French cuisine virtually defined itself by its tremendous vocabulary of sauces, and that getting rid of them would be not just sacrilegious but probably commercial suicide, too. (Not everyone can be Pierre Gagnaire—and even Gagnaire himself went broke before he came to Paris.) The hyperminimalist approach of the antisauce movement didn't affect Bernard, then, but the rise in negative comment from the dining room did; it was worrisome. No more than five or six clients had complained about saltiness, but that was enough to open up a whole new source of anxiety. He had evolved *le style Loiseau* in response to people's concerns about gaining weight and building up cholesterol. With this salt business, it looked like there was something new: Now people were worried about their blood pressure, too.

Bernard then told Patrick to cut back on the seasoning, especially the salt. It was a decision that would come back to haunt him. Very soon, he received a great big heavyweight haunting of the most distressing sort.

"I was rather disappointed by a meal at Loiseau's place. I can't remember exactly when, but it was a few years ago. There was nothing *dramatique* about the experience, but I just wasn't moved by what I ate. It was no problem, really—certainly not a threat to a star—just a little disappointing. Every restaurant has days when things don't seem as sumptuous as before. Maybe the atmosphere wasn't good because there were hardly any clients, maybe the weather was bad, I don't really know what it was. Anyway, he took it quite well when I spoke to him about it. I always got on well with him."

Bernard Naegellen was recounting, with the typically relaxed bonhomie of the seasoned warhorse of gastronomy, what for him had been merely one meal of thousands that he had taken over the years, first as an inspector and later as boss of the *Guide Michelin*. An astute gourmet, if ever there was one, Naegellen is also a pleasant and remarkably easygoing man for one who wielded the Jovian thunderbolt power of decisions over stardom in the guide he directed for so many years. For him, one slightly disappointing, now anonymous, lunch (he couldn't remember what he ate) at the Côte d'Or was hardly worth more than a shrug, a mere blip in a long career.

For Bernard, though, that friendly little chat after lunch could only have been a calamity, a nightmare through which he called on all his outstanding talents as an actor to maintain a façade of equanimity. Was it the sauces that Naegellen found disappointing? Who knows—he couldn't even remember himself—but it is more than likely, because the sauce is the heart of a dish. In any case, Naegellen's ho-hum reaction could only have been like a punch in the stomach for Bernard, one of a critical series of big-league reproaches that would come to erode his self-confidence. A few years later, in recounting the career that had brought Bernard to such great renown in Saulieu, a Parisian journalist found a nice historical parallel for his hypersensitivity. When some now-forgotten notable asked young Mozart to play a piece, the child apparently replied: "First tell me you love me."

That was Bernard, dead on. When love wasn't there, the big guy was lost.

The first, early creations of *cuisine tendance* hadn't bothered him in the least. He laughed at them, in fact, Patrick Bertron remembered. That fusion, all those silly foreign ingredients, those tricks and those chemical manipulations, struck him as pure idiocy—*des conneries*— that was going nowhere. For his part, Bernard was engaged on the true, the noble, and the shining path, the timeless verity of *la cuisine française*.

"He was sure that *cuisine tendance* was just a passing fad," Bertron said. "Let the others do it, he said, but if I want to eat wasabi and seaweed, I'll go to a Japanese restaurant. French cuisine was deeply rooted in our culture, and Monsieur Loiseau was certain that it was the best in the world. Why try to imitate Japanese or Chinese or Spanish cooking? Why do globalized cooking? That was OK for Paris, maybe—and he had a lot of respect for Pierre Gagnaire—but not here in Saulieu, not in the French heartland. It would be completely out of place."

The trouble was, *cuisine tendance* was in the air, and it was making the professional anorexics giddy with excitement. And Bernard was an ageing wunderkind, now past fifty, still cooking classical French stuff—perhaps nothing as culpable as a *steak au poivre*, but still all-French and very classical. From there it was but a short jump to other adjectives, murderously cruel ones, this time: stodgy; has-been; *ringard*. Suddenly Bernard wasn't laughing at the smart guys anymore. A note of desperation crept into his psyche.

"I can't do that," he told Bertron bleakly. "I don't know how."

Hubert Couilloud, Bernard's companion in the gastronomic wars for more than twenty years, was also his best friend, the advisor whom he respected the most, and the de facto second in command of the Côte d'Or. He knew Bernard as no other man did—and no other women, for that matter, until Dominique came along with her quiet, unassuming perspicacity. He saw Bernard's dilemma developing with a logic of its own as he progressively locked himself into the certainties that had created *le style Loiseau*.

"First of all," he said, "Bernard cooked for himself—the things he liked and the way he liked them prepared. Crayfish, for example. He had found that the best way to do them was to fricassee them, and do a simple deglazing with the little *jus* he had made from their carcasses, along with shallots and tarragon. He couldn't eat them any other way, and he felt as if it would be taking his pants down to even try. With this approach, he ended up repeating himself. His menu was rather limited, but he stuck with it, so the critics thought he wasn't evolving. Toward the end he finally did make an attempt to join the movement for novelties, but he absolutely refused to do 'world food.' He was very much aware of the perception that he wasn't moving along, and he began to fear that the spring of inspiration* was drying up. He talked about it all the time.

"Things go faster today, don't they? You can't keep serving the same dishes for years and years, because people are hungry for new things. Bernard was heading in the direction of a renewal, but depression got to him and he lost sight of where he was going. He lost his lucidity. We should have tried to force him to go away for a month of vacation, but it would have been no good. He wouldn't have done it. He had never taken a real vacation. All he ever thought about was the Côte d'Or. His place."

That held true for his marriage, too, and his family. For Dominique, it was a marriage grounded above all on work, the true center of their partnership. It never was easy. When she decided to leave her Paris journalism behind and come down to Saulieu full-time, she found it excruciatingly difficult to break into the routine of Bernard and his brothers in gastronomic arms and make a meaningful role for herself in the Côte d'Or. The guys were set in their ways, and they didn't make way easily for this interloping Wife Number Two. They treated her like a new passenger trying to squeeze into a jammed subway car. For all they knew, she might be out of there after a few years, too.

That was underestimating the strength of character and the determination lying behind that impassive green Alsatian gaze of hers. She approached this challenge with the same methodical application that she gave to her role as wife and mother of Bernard's children, his hostess in the restaurant, his press and publicity agent, and director of planning for the Côte d'Or. Dominique plugged along, never whining, never crying, never losing control—the exact contrary of her husband—until she had become quite simply indispensable. Indispensability did not mean, though, that the union of these opposites was a primrose path.

---

*The last recipe he created was *pigeon fermier, sauce au sang:* a boned pigeon stuffed with a mixture of pigeon meat and liver, roasted and served, *à la Tour d'Argent,* with a sauce thickened with its own blood. He presented the bird lying on a light, velvety purée of peas, a variation on the whole peas that French tradition had served with roast pigeon since time immemorial. This dish nicely symbolizes Bernard's professional dilemma. He was doing something different, but at the same time it was eminently classical.

"He found me cold," she said candidly. "Sometimes he would kiss me in front of the personnel. I didn't like that—in front of the employees, can you imagine? I'm a girl from the east. My character and my upbringing have given me this obligation of reserve. It's not my nature to be explosive, like Bernard. I'm an Alsatian. Ever since I was a little girl people always taught me that I shouldn't make too much noise, or even laugh too loudly. So I learned to live my strongest emotions within myself.

"We both knew what we were getting ourselves into, right from the start. Bernard took a risk, too—he didn't know whether I would adapt to life in Saulieu. When I came down here, all the others had been in place for years. I was aware of how hard it might be for me, and after all I didn't have to marry him. I could have left. And I had no illusions about Bernard being an ideal Prince Charming, either. I was a grown-up. But I knew that he worked on a long-term basis. Me, too. I've always been a long-term person. I knew what he was trying to accomplish here, and I wasn't about to hold him back by complaining that he didn't spend enough time with me, or pay enough attention to me. No, what do you take me for?"

When Dominique describes the couple's hectic everyday life at the Côte d'Or, a strikingly significant phrase pops up from time to time: "*On se croisait*," she says—our paths crossed. These are exactly the words that Pierre Troisgros used to describe his parents in the early days of L'Hôtel Moderne in Roanne, when Pierre Loiseau was sharing the memorable *table d'hôte* with his fellow traveling salesmen. No stars or three, the job of maintaining top quality in a hotel-restaurant is an endlessly repeated slog of long, exhausting, sleep-deprived work. Clients check in and check out, deliveries arrive, hunger comes as it always does, and meals won't wait. There's no surcease to the routine. Feeling sorry for yourself won't help, so you get on with it.

Dominique got on with it, but occasionally she couldn't help wondering whether Bernard's devotion to his work and his ideal palace wasn't a bit much. She had no illusions about her place in his affections—the Côte d'Or would always win, hands down—but he was a faithful husband, not a womanizer, he didn't drink, he had sired her three beautiful children, and he provided well for the family. What more ought a woman to expect? She could build a good life around that. Even so, his habit of appropriating objects she had bought for the house and putting them in the hotel was a little hard to take. And then there was the matter of the kids. Bernard's workplace was only a few hundred yards from the house, but he could hardly ever spend any time with them, because when he wasn't working, he was sleeping, and he had no days off; the Côte d'Or was open seven days a week. It was a numbing regimen, but Bernard was obsessed with paying off his mountain of debt, and every extra client he could hustle into his dining room contributed a little bit more. In this, too, as with the basic thrust of his cooking, he was only following the lessons learned from his redoubtable mentors, the brothers Troisgros. Even the most put-upon apprentices in Roanne had been obliged to admit that of the entire kitchen crew, it was Jean and Pierre who worked the hardest and put in the longest hours. But there were two of them. When Jean absolutely needed time off there was Pierre, and when Pierre was weary there was Jean. In Saulieu, Bernard had only himself. Certainly Patrick Bertron could cook Loiseau better than Loiseau, and certainly Hubert Couilloud had the dining room staff under firm control, but who could watch over them? Who else would see the crumbs on the side of mouths? Obviously, no one but poor, manic, stressed-out Bernard.

"He was adamant—completely impossible—about the slightest imperfection in the Côte d'Or, but he wouldn't notice a broken door up in the house even if it was staring him in the face," Dominique recalled with a rueful little laugh. "Everything was for the hotel. If I asked him to watch the children for just an hour, he couldn't do it—he had to stay permanently available in case there was a problem in the restaurant, or a phone call from a journalist. The only thing I absolutely insisted on, the only change I was able to force into his routine, was to have an early dinner at the house with me and children one day a week—every Sunday at six thirty. He accepted that, but it was a trial for him. As soon as we had finished he rushed back down to the hotel to supervise the dinner *service*."

A chef so singlemindedly attached to his job inevitably recalls Vatel. Everyone in France knows the story, even if it harks all the way back to 1671, because it is a rare and dramatic symbol of devotion to duty carried to the ultimate extreme. Like Hubert Couilloud, François Vatel was a *maître d'hôtel*, but his boss was rather grander: Louis II de

Bourbon, prince de Condé, cousin of King Louis XIV. Among other properties, the prince owned the breathtaking island château of Chantilly, 30 miles north of Paris, and it was in this stunning setting that he received the king and his retinue of two thousand or so courtiers. Exhausted and sleepless from days of making ready for the royal visit—he was responsible for the whole show, including a dinner with perhaps three hundred different dishes spread out on twenty-five tables—Vatel was crushed when he learned that two tables at dinner Thursday evening had lacked roasts. It wasn't even his fault. Several unannounced nobles had crashed the party, but he was the one who took the blame. That night, he lost face when the fireworks display he had organized fizzled on account of cloudy weather. Up before dawn Friday morning, he was determined to redeem himself with a lunch that would delight not only the notoriously gluttonous* monarch but his thousands of underlings as well. Disaster: He was appalled to discover that only two carts of fish had arrived from the Atlantic seaport towns where he had sent orders several days earlier. Madame de Sévigné told the rest of the story in one of her famous letters.

> The great Vatel, this man distinguished with abilities above all others, whose well-made head could contain all the needs of a state; this man, then, whom I knew quite well, seeing that at eight o'clock this morning the seafood had not arrived, was unable to bear the reproach that he was sure would be visited upon him; in a word, he stabbed himself to death.

In Saulieu, few could suspect that there was a Vatel lurking within Bernard. By an ironic historical parallel, it was Hubert, the fellow *maître d'hôtel*, who saw farther than others did, and worried about how far things might go.

"Bernard used to ask me what I thought about life after death," he

---

*Louis XIV's sister-in-law, the Duchess of Orleans, one of the regulars at court in Versailles, has left us a gripping description of the royal appetite: "I have seen the king eat, and this on many occasions, four plates of different soups, an entire pheasant, a partridge, a large plateful of salad, a helping of mutton with garlic, two healthy slices of ham and a plateful of pastries, followed by fruits and jellies."

said, "but he never said the word 'suicide' to me, and he never spoke about Vatel. Over the final year, year and a half, though, there had been presages. He became obsessive about nailing everything down here, making everything so perfect, once and for all, that he would be immune to attack. He had never been so present in Saulieu as during this last period—no vacations, no more leaves, no more hunting trips, no more nights playing cards, no more visits with his friends. Finally, toward the end, he even stopped making his phone calls. He convinced himself that by sweating more than ever before he could make himself untouchable. But in fact he was at the end of his rope. I started warning the other guys to look out for him. I told Dominique I was worried. Look out, I said. He's not right."

Dominique knew Bernard wasn't right, but she didn't know what to do about it. He refused to go on Prozac again, and there was no question of seeing a psychiatrist—no shrink for Bernard Loiseau. And anyway, she noted that he was sleeping quite well. That looked like a good sign. She had been accustomed to seeing him falling into insomnia when things were going badly; now his long hours dead asleep reassured her. What Dr. Kiss could have told her was that one of the well-documented symptoms of the bipolar personality in crisis is paradoxical; someone teetering on the edge often sleeps unusually long hours.

It was in September of 2002 that another doctor, Doron Zeeli, an Israeli specialist in geriatrics and internal medicine, came on a gastronomic tour to Saulieu with his wife and stayed for forty-eight hours in the Côte d'Or. He loved the food—"it was music in the mouth"—but his professional reflexes led him to some disturbing conclusions about the man responsible for making it.

"In my specialty I very often have to assess patients' behavior by their body language," he explained, "because they are not always able to speak. During dinner on our first night, I made a diagnosis of Bernard Loiseau on the spot. I told my wife he was on the verge of a collapse.

"I caught sight of him at the other end of this magnificent dining room, standing at the exit to the kitchen. He was absolutely still, immobile, but I could see the tension in him, and his eyes were darting from right to left. I had a good look at him for maybe half an hour. The man was like a spring that was wound up as tight as it could get, just before it exploded.

"The *maître d'hôtel* recognized us as Israelis—I don't know how, but I was very impressed by that—and he told me there was another Israeli in the room. This was Avital Inbar, a famous writer of travel and food books. I went over, introduced myself, and invited him to join us, since he was eating alone, so we readjourned to our table. Maybe ten minutes later his plate was ready, and when the waiter delivered it, Mr. Loiseau cried out an order: 'Avital,' he shouted. 'Eat. You'll talk later.' I could see that they were old friends, but this was like a military order. The picture was quite clear to me, and quite distressing. I felt sorry for the man. It was obvious he needed a couple of months in a desert oasis somewhere to regain his forces and recharge his batteries. He was like a car that was running on the last fumes of gas from an empty tank.

"The next morning, when we went for breakfast, he was there at the reception desk, looking at the reservation book. You should have seen it—he wasn't turning the pages, but frantically slashing through them, checking the names to see if there was any VIP he should give special care to. He was like a tiger crouching before his prey. I'm usually very outspoken and direct, and I'm not afraid to approach people and give my views, but I couldn't bring myself to start talking with him, because I was pretty sure he would brush me off. But I told Avital that this was the shadow of a healthy person."

The closest Bernard got to an oasis was a four-day break in Cannes. He and Dominique checked into a good hotel and just slept. They had meant to take time off for a real vacation, but in 2002, as in all the previous years, one thing or another got in the way, and it never happened. In Cannes as in Saulieu, the ease with which Bernard dropped off into sleep reassured Dominique. In the big 1992 depression, he had been constantly assailed with insomnia. Now, she thought, with four days of good sleep under his belt, he ought to be able to bounce back in good shape—manic, hyperactive, and impossible, but great at the same time: the old Bernard. Something else was encouraging, too. For the first time ever, he was beginning to talk about being more reasonable about work. Maybe they could close down for a day or two, like Michel Troisgros in Roanne. First, though, one last push. Just to get things perfect. Absolutely perfect.

XV

DÉNOUEMENT

*L*ate in the autumn of 2002, a town councilor mentioned to Dominique that a few grave sites would be coming up for sale in the Saulieu cemetery. Being a woman who had always conducted her life rationally, she decided it would be a good idea to get it over with and buy one. Sooner or later someone had to think of things like that, so why leave it as a chore for some other undetermined person at some indeterminate later time? As a devout Catholic who was raising her kids strictly within the faith, regularly attending Sunday mass with them and sending them away weekdays to church-sponsored boarding schools, she saw a family tomb as a place where they could come and pray for her and Bernard's souls in future years.

She went to have a look. Walking past the pretty little fifteenth-century church of Saint Saturnin just inside the wall at the bottom of the hillside cemetery, she climbed the steep grade up toward the newer section and found an available site high up on the right-hand side. Turning her gaze downward, she was pleased to see that it commanded a direct view out over the rooftops of Saulieu. This would do nicely. She snapped it up.

There were no premonitions or anything of the sort behind the purchase. Dominique was simply being Dominique: sensible, foresightful, efficient. At the same time, however, down in the Côte d'Or, Bernard was being Bernard, and that was altogether a different story.

He wasn't doing well. The cold weather, the rain, and the end of the tourist season had brought the dreaded empty days back to Saulieu, the days when only three or four of the sumptuous new rooms would be occupied, when clients had to be shifted over to the small dining rooms lest they feel uncomfortable alone in the big main room, when Hubert and the rest of his staff rattled around the luxurious palace, with the sound of their own footfalls on the waxed Burgundy tiles echoing in their ears. It was a time for the hibernal blues, and the introspection that comes with it. Now the boss wasn't pumping them all up and telling them they were the greatest anymore. Whatever had happened to that last big push that he had promised Dominique? It never happened.

"He shut himself off," said Stéphanie Gaitey, Dominique's administrative assistant. "He became unattainable. We couldn't reach him anymore."

Everyone in the house was struck by Bernard's slow withdrawal from the world, especially as time accelerated toward the end of that 2002 season. According to Hubert, "a huge lassitude" had come over him. Eric Rousseau saw it more as a deep paranoia. "It was infernal," he said. "He went deeper and deeper into his own space, down into himself. From time to time he would emerge from the pit and listen to us. We told him over and over that he ought to take a good, long break, and he'd say I know, I know, you're right—but then he would see an article in the press about some other chef who was doing well, and he would fall right back down into the hole."

Bit by bit, the solace of the *méthode Coué* abandoned him like a protective skin flaking off. Albert Nahmias, a well-known Parisian restaurant consultant, recalled the moment when he realized that Bernard had given up the illusion of ever being the top dog of the trade. "It was one of those Bernard calls," he said. "Very short, less than a minute. 'Ducasse is the best in Paris,' he said, 'but I'm still the best in the provinces, right? Right?'"

So he was already compromising with reality. This version of Bernard, bereft now of the motivation of his driving illusions, was the shadow of his former self. No longer buoyed by the certainty of his own great destiny, he began taking comfort in the dubious negative pleasures of schadenfreude: so and so is divorcing, another has big money problems and—have you heard?—yet another is in line to lose his third star. It wasn't very elegant, but he was grasping at straws.

As those short, chilly days of late autumn edged into winter on the Morvan plateau, the black spiders set earnestly to work in Bernard's head, nibbling away at whatever confidence, balance, and judgment remained there. The least problem became a disaster, and molehills turned into mountain ranges. For a whole mix of reasons, 2002 had been a lousy year. In the wake of the 9/11 calamity in New York, the idea of travel was suddenly fraught with new perils, especially travel by plane, and reservations by foreign visitors—particularly Americans—had dropped precipitously. To make matters many times worse, a strange, totally unexpected vendetta had erupted between France and the U.S., seemingly out of nowhere. A host of policy disagreements—Iraq, environment, international trade, farm subsidies, industry tax breaks—had degenerated into a barely concealed slinging match between Presidents Bush and Chirac. On the surface, the french fries–freedom fries punchup looked like nothing more than a silly bit of puerile posturing, but it was soon aggravated by heavy jingoistic huffing and puffing on both sides of the Atlantic. Now Americans were hardly coming to France anymore, and even less to Saulieu. For the Côte d'Or, that was nothing short of disastrous. Foreigners represented nearly half of the hotel's clientele, and Americans were the most cherished of the lot. European hoteliers love Americans—they have plenty of money, they aren't complainers, and they tip well. Where Bernard was concerned, the love story was reciprocal: as much as his ebullient, outgoing personality, his boasts, and his self-publicizing often grated on French sensibilities, Americans recognized it and felt a kind of kinship with it. They accepted him as one of their own, and they adored his cooking, too.

But where were they? All through the spring and summer of 2002, Bernard awaited them, his grin and his sales talk primed. It was mostly in vain—the Yanks appeared only in disappointing dribs and drabs. Nor were there enough German, Swiss, Belgian, or British visitors to fill the empty space they had left, because economies were stumbling throughout Europe, and spending for necessities asserted its inevitable precedence over luxury hotels and gourmet meals. Certainly the Côte d'Or wasn't alone in its misery—hotels and restaurants were suffering everywhere in the provinces—but somehow Saulieu seemed even more provincial, more out of the way and less visited than the other places. By the end of that blasted 2002 summer season, Bernard wasn't bothering to post himself at the window anymore to watch for cars.

As if matters weren't depressing enough just then, an awful piece of news arrived. The lugubrious icing on the cake for 2002 came at the end of October: Lionel Poilâne and his wife were killed in the helicopter he was piloting off the coast of Brittany. This quick, elfin, intelligent Parisian baker, producer of the sourdough bread that had made him rich and famous, was a friend to the whole French gastronomic establishment, living proof that an artisan who dedicated himself entirely to quality could succeed, make lots of money, and gain international fame without compromising his principles.

"Bernard seemed emptier every day," said Dominique. "Empty and defeatist. Sometimes his behavior became downright extravagant. He enjoyed scaring me, because my calm irritated him. A couple of times, when I came by the house in the afternoon, I found him lying on the bed looking exactly like a dead man. When I started to panic he got up with a laugh—ha, ha, I got you!—pleased with himself that I had fallen for the joke. But then he would disappear into his world again, and leave us behind. Other times, out of the blue, he would suddenly make completely outrageous statements: It's finished, forget it, we're never going to make it. That kind of thing."

One afternoon at home, as Dominique was reading the papers, Bernard sat absently gazing at television. À propos of nothing, he suddenly spoke. "I think I'll commit suicide," he said, as casually as if he were talking about a little errand to run. Dominique scolded him for his playacting. Bernard was being Bernard again.

The last time I saw him was in mid-December of that year. I'd like to say I found his smile forced or his manner strange, but there was none of that. If anything, he was more *speedé* and defiantly proclamatory than usual. He had been born with tremendous gifts for acting, and it was always hard to judge whether he had switched them on or whether he was being his real self. For me this time, he found the resources to heave himself up out of his slough of depression to put on a fireworks display of volubility, seemingly as sure of himself as a man of destiny could be. It was quite a number he did for me, leaping from subject to subject with an alacrity that was hard for me to keep up with, in spite of my scribbling notes as fast as I could. His whistling in the dark was of Beethovenian proportions.

"I'm the star!" he cried. "I've passed Bocuse. He's number two now. What got me to the top was my determination. I decided at age seventeen to be the best, and no one's going to stop me now—*je les em-merde* [screw them]. My life is giving happiness to others. Nothing's permanent, we're all just renters down here. They don't make coffins for two or three people—we all die alone.

"I'm chauvinistic—sure, I'm chauvinistic. I'll never do world food here, because my clients come to Saulieu to eat *French* cuisine. I'm defending my country and my culture with my cooking. Globalization just leads to uniformity—in cuisine, in wines, in decoration, everything. I won't do that. I'll never lose my soul!"

Wow. Bernard was really switched on, and when he seated me in the place of honor at the chef's table in the kitchen, he was every inch the master of his domain, as he directed the *brigade* in the preparation of that day's lunch. But with all the vainglory of his pronouncements and his dominating presence in the kitchen, the essential fact of the day was this: His dining room was almost empty. It was at this lunch that he suddenly whirled around and blurted out that jarring nonsequitur: *"C'est jamais gagné"* —"the battle's never won."

I now realize, of course, that it wasn't a nonsequitur at all; I had just been too thick to pick up on its significance. "The battle's never won," indeed. In sum, what it signified was that he had made up his mind about something dramatically important, his quest had been illusory. He could never make himself strong enough to be immune to attack. He could never attain perfection.

Things were telescoping fast. A month or so before my visit to Saulieu, Bernard and Dominique had made a pilgrimage to Paris to bend a knee before Michelin. It is a common practice in the trade— even Paul Bocuse, the Emperor, does it on a yearly basis—but for Bernard, this time there was rather more urgency than a mere courtesy visit would indicate: Rumors had been spreading through the gastronomic grapevine that he was somehow, in some vague, undefined manner, in trouble with Big Red.

Not at all, not at all, Derek Brown assured them with exquisite politesse in the gray, faceless inquisition room where he received them. Rather gray and faceless himself, after so many years of deliberately blending into the woodwork as an inspector, Brown addressed them in a suavely vernacular French that bore only the slightest hint of an English accent. Vividly in memory of Monsieur Naegellen's expression of disappointment at lunch some time before that, Bernard soaked up every one of his words like a petitioner before the Pythian oracle at Delphi.

After the predictable generalities and social graces, Brown got closer to the point in response to Bernard's prodding. There is one thing I might call to your attention, he said with courteous English restraint, consulting the Côte d'Or's dossier. We have received a certain number of letters suggesting that perhaps the sauces weren't as tasty as before, that somehow they had less, how shall I say, less *niac*. Constitutionally unable to hide anything from anybody, Bernard reacted with such evident consternation that Brown felt obliged to calm him. But don't worry, he said, *il n'y a pas le feu au lac*—the lake's not on fire. This sibylline expression was the closest he would allow himself to come to letting Bernard know that his third star was safe for the 2003 guide. But was it? Upon returning to Saulieu, he rushed into the kitchen and told Patrick to immediately go back to their old level of salting.

"Ever since he won the third star, he had been haunted by the idea of losing it," Hubert said. "The idea of being demoted, of becoming just a two-star chef, was intolerable. His whole *raison d'être* had been the glory of the top position—I'm the best, everyone loves me. But after the interview with Brown he came back thinking it was all over. It was pathetic to see. He dragged himself around the kitchen saying, I'm finished, I'm no damn good, I'm *nul*. It was the infernal spiral. He was like a zombie."

"He was a victim of his own idealism," Dr. Kiss posited. "He had this vision of an ideal world that had not come to pass. Of course he never reached his goals—almost by definition, he never could. This was an exalted personality whose megalomania was in the pursuit of an unattainable ideal. He couldn't understand that you can also have a life of just plain excellence. He was caught in the trap of his own perfectionism."

For an accountant whose life was built on numbers and percentages and the clackety little pocket calculator that he would whip out of his pocket on the least occasion, Bernard Fabre delivered a remarkably perceptive analysis of the culinary side of the impasse into which his friend's idealism had driven him.

"His cooking was purity—always just three ingredients and three savors on the plate, complementing one another, tied together by a sauce that hid nothing, because it was the concentrated essence of the main ingredient. For him, a chef who wasn't sure of himself added extraneous elements that masked or altered the taste of that principal ingredient. But his cuisine was what it was, and he couldn't make it into anything else. He couldn't change, he couldn't add foreign flavorings, and he couldn't invent gimmicks to persuade critics that he was renewing himself. He was, therefore, in a state of paradox. He was up against a wall, and didn't know how to get past it.

"Naturally, this dilemma spilled over from the cooking side into the financial side. He started building a scenario of catastrophe. I'm going to lose my third star because I can't renew myself. That's going to make me lose money and drive me into bankruptcy, and they'll take my hotel away from me. He was looking at everything negatively, seeing one step leading to another, right up to the fatal conclusion of losing it all. I told him we had already weathered the hardest times and were in better financial shape than ever, but he couldn't see it that way. You're sick, I told him. Go take a long vacation, see a psychiatrist—do something. He said, OK, OK, but of course he never did anything about it."

What he did do was the worst tactic imaginable, but it was pure Bernard. In the melancholy, unpeopled days at the tail end of 2002 and the beginning of 2003, he had plenty of time on his hands to telephone around and tell his friends (and supposed friends) about his meeting with Brown, repeating his conviction that he was about to lose his third star. In few fields of human endeavor (fashion springs to mind) is professional gossip so rich and so avidly propagated as in the tight little world of *haute cuisine*, so of course Bernard's anguished speculation fed into the circuit and rapidly made the rounds, north, south, east, and west. It inevitably came to the attention of the specialized journalists who ride that circuit. They threw in whatever information they had from other sources, drew their conclusions, and then put pen to paper.

Quickest off the mark was François Simon, the quinquagenerian *enfant terrible* of gastronomy, restaurant critic for the Paris daily *Le Figaro*. On January 18, he signed an article giving a short rundown of what was new in 2003 for a selection of well-known names in the trade. After gently chaffing Marc Veyrat for the pompously named "Global Laboratory of Aromas and Spices" that he was proposing to open in the new year, giving a mention to Joël Robuchon's new "atelier" restaurant in the seventh *arrondissment*, and repeating the old news that the hotel and restaurant industry in general was going through a very rough patch, he came to the speculation that always seizes France around this time of year: the promotions and demotions that Michelin might be deciding for the 2003 guide.

> Bernard Loiseau (La Côte d'Or, in Saulieu), had a big scare in this respect, since the word was going around that he was losing his third star, like the Pourcel brothers of Le Jardin des Sens in Montpellier; which, everything considered, would not have caused any sincere surprise, since the Pourcel brothers are definitely worthy of two stars. It appears that both these restaurants will keep their stars. They can heave a huge sigh of relief . . . until next year.

Simon ended his column with the remark that Bernard Loiseau, decidedly the man under fire these days, would also be docked two points, from 19/20 to 17/20, in the 2003 *GaultMillau* guide.

By early February, when both guides laid down their cards for 2003, it appeared that Simon had been right on both counts: both the Côte d'Or and the Jardin des Sens in Montpellier maintained three stars in the *Michelin*, and *GaultMillau* did, indeed, knock Bernard back down to 17/20. But where had that item of Bernard's "big scare" come from? Not from *Michelin*, if Derek Brown is to be believed.

"We had no problem at all with Bernard Loiseau and three stars," he insisted to me. "If the restaurant had three stars this year, we wouldn't have given it if we didn't think it was deserved. The man had three stars since 1991, and we don't do that lightly."

And Simon's insistence that Bernard had been in danger of losing a star? Brown's urbanity briefly shifted to vexation. "Where do these things come from? If I knew, I could stop them, couldn't I? People make these things up. I really have no idea. We obviously ask ourselves the question: Where could such a thing start? And we don't know."

Unless Brown was lying through his gleaming teeth, then, while it was François Simon who was telling the true scoop via a highly placed mole inside the Michelin fortress on avenue de Breteuil, the conclusion that must be drawn is the saddest one of all: by his panicked phone calls, an exhausted, despondent, and totally negative Bernard had started the ball rolling and created something of a self-fulfilling prophecy. Like protagonists in Greek tragedy, he did it to himself; picking up a vague rumor, he vastly amplified it and shifted it over to the specificity of losing the third star. And what went around came around.

If he could have taken heart from seeing the three lovely stars still attached to the Côte d'Or's listing in the 2003 edition of *Michelin*, a second article by François Simon on February 7 was enough to plunge him back down into the pit. "Michelin follows a policy impregnated with marketing," Simon wrote in an apparent attempt to justify his January predictions. "Like many of its *confrères*, it singles out a chef more for the image he will bring to the guide's notoriety than for his intrinsic value. Similarly, the stars aren't lifted until the public is prepared. This could explain why the guide left three stars this year with two addresses that were legitimately under threat. Bernard Loiseau in Saulieu [La Côte d'Or] and the Pourcel brothers in Montpellier [Le Jardin des Sens]. They know that they are living on borrowed time."

This was something of a journalistic tour de force, typical of Simon and his own *confrères* of the French intelligentsia—the most deconstructionist, conspiracy-obsessed crowd this side of a Kremlinful of Marxist-Leninists. Contemplating the seemingly placid, truffles-and-tummies world of restaurants and restaurant guides, he had managed to discover a cabal: Chefs were being used and the public manipulated for nefarious purposes (probably related to capitalistic profiteering). With all of Simon's tortured ratiocination, though, what really hurt Bernard was that brutally cruel little phrase "legitimately under threat." This was not only a public humiliation but proof of his worst fears; he was doomed. The execution had only been stayed. Until then he would be left to twist in the wind.

Worse was to come. Although *GaultMillau* was far less important than *Michelin*, this quirky, personalized, and hyperopinionated guide held a special place in Bernard's heart for the amazingly enthusiastic support it had given him throughout his early career, right from the days of the old Barrières, when Michelin had scarcely even heard of him. Bernard had put Henri Gault up for long, chummy weekends in Saulieu, feeding him (and his dog) his finest, lightest take on new *nouvelle cuisine*, and Gault had responded with dithyrambic paragraphs in the guide, elevating the young and inexperienced chef to the firmament of cooking's aristocracy.

From the start, the guide's great specialty had been to use the shock value of surprise—make headlines, get people talking—to boost its circulation, and the best way to create surprise was to smash traditional icons while plucking relative unknowns from their anonymity and parading them as *GaultMillau*'s "discoveries." Of all the unknowns and little-knowns, it was Bernard who had been promoted the fastest and had risen from nowhere to the highest. He had been their golden boy.

But times, people, tastes, and companies change. Since 1983 and the departure of its two founding fathers, the guide had bounced around the corporate circuit, changing owners more frequently than Elizabeth Taylor changed husbands, bought and then sold by one company or another, mostly losing money, readership, and credibility along the way. The new millennium found *GaultMillau* in the hands of yet another international conglomerate, one that this time had farmed out the creation of the guide to seven or eight service providers, with a public relations company based in Rouen handling the restaurant critiques. All the while, Michelin had sailed along at its same dignified, stately pace, occupying the high ground as a virtual monopoly, imperturbably low-key in the face of *GaultMillau*'s shock tactics.

Two big headline grabs marked the release of the 2003 *GaultMillau*: the demotion of Bernard by two full points, down to 17/20; and the beatification of Mark Veyrat with the grade of 20/20.

Veyrat's 20/20 was unheard of. Never before had *GaultMillau* dared to so honor any chef, not even all-time greats like Alain Chapel, Michel Guérard, or Freddy Girardet, because 20/20 signified historic perfection; no one could ever do better. (Previous editions of the guide had always limited its top laureates—Bernard among them—to 19.5, on the sensible reasoning that absolute perfection was unattainable in mortal matters.)*

More than any other chef, more even than Pierre Gagnaire, Veyrat represented the postmodern school of *cuisine tendance*. Heavily influenced by Michel Bras and the astounding manipulations of Ferran Adria's Catalan school of laboratory cooking, he served many of his dishes in liquid rather than solid form; injected ingredients by hypodermic syringe at tableside into other ingredients; occasionally presented sauces in the form of ice cubes; used strangely shaped plates; had clients drink through organic straws or out of test tubes; put dry ice chips in the bottom of a glass to create smoky-hokey billows of clouds; made deliberately provocative mixes of taste (*mousse au chocolat* with wild thyme); and in general carried on like a carnival Houdini. It must be said that for the most part his food was extremely good, and worthy of the three stars that Michelin awarded him, but it was also marred by all the hocus-pocus. *Étonne-moi*.

Veyrat's 20/20 crown of ultimate glory, announced simultaneously with his own degradation, was a crushing blow for Bernard's ego. His world had been turned topsy-turvy. In 1985, when *GaultMillau* had first awarded him 19.5, and a year later, when they had named him "Cook of the Year," Veyrat had been little more than an interesting, self-taught regional chef with a loud voice and a penchant for experimentation. Now both the man and the style of cuisine he represented had zoomed far past Bernard. Veyrat restaurants were the most expensive in France, but they were full every night, and the waiting list to get in was two to four months. In those rain-lashed February days, the Côte d'Or was as good as empty, and the chic crowd was dismissing its cuisine with an awful, murderous word: classical.

And it was true. With all his sales talk about being different, Bernard's cuisine was as straightforward and as limpidly classical as the culinary grammar that he had learned under the Troisgros brothers, and never abandoned. Just as Fabre had said, it was a cuisine of purity.

---

*Most observers of the French restaurant scene agreed that the 20/20 mark was a silly stunt, because it left Veyrat stranded and the guide hoisted by its own petard. From that point on, the Savoyard cook could only be marked down—either that or *GaultMillau* would be obliged to keep him at 20/20 forever.

But by the year 2003 that kind of purity wasn't amusing the professional anorexics any longer. Worse, the PR outfit charged with making *GaultMillau*'s restaurant critiques had decided to get at Bernard personally, and the paragraph devoted to the Côte d'Or was an undisguised *ad hominem* attack on him. All his years of hustling and gesticulating to persuade people to leave the autoroute and make the detour to Saulieu came back to roost in sixteen lines of oblique and occasionally baffling prose that fairly dripped with contempt.

> When Bernard Loiseau forces his smile to the cameras, hammering every syllable as if he were driving a post into the ground, the will to charm seems to be accompanied by the subliminal angst of not carrying it off, for the stakes are of industrial dimensions. To make a go of it in Saulieu without help, without multinational backing, the world created around his name has to function at full speed, neither omitting to cite the names of his Paris bistros (Tante Marguerite, Louise, etc.) on his switchboard's recorded message, nor forgetting that the environment built around the meal must be so reassuring that the visitor is practically condemned to satisfaction. Nothing will remain for him [the visitor], then, but to swoon before the pike perch in red wine sauce, the lobster with boletus mushrooms and the farm chicken with foie gras and truffled purée, uncomplainingly swallowing a check that is certainly astronomic but one which, we may be sure, is indispensable for balancing the books. And if we may be so bold today as to write what more or less everybody knows, that this cuisine constructed on a patiently consolidated base is hardly dazzling but simply very well made and agreeable, it is also to point out that if you have the money to invite your family or some friends who are not accustomed to great tables, La Côte d'Or still constitutes one of the best initiations to very high level restaurant eating.

What praise there was lying within these lines was about as faint as what could still be considered the stuff of responsible restaurant criticism. But like Veyrat's beatification, Bernard's demotion did make headlines, and it did, indeed, make people talk about *GaultMillau*.

"Taking away a single point was one thing," reflected André

Daguin, president of the hotel trades lobby group, "but two was an aggression, that can be explained only by two hypotheses: either it's an error of judgment or it's a marketing stunt aimed at reinvigorating their weak sales. When a guy as emotional and depressive as Bernard sees that, it does things to his head."

The rating of 17 points repositioned Bernard from the exclusive circle of a handful of great chefs to a vague grouping among the one hundred or so who were simply well considered. "I'm not the best any longer," he said. "I'm not even second best."

Never two without three. The new *GaultMillau* reserved one final fillip for Bernard: Michel Troisgros was named "Chef of the Year." For a number of reasons—his proximity in age and geography, the fact that he was Pierre's son, his sober, withdrawn personality, the polar opposite of Bernard's—Michel was the one that Bernard instinctively viewed as his great rival, and with whom there was an intense although undeclared professional competition. But what separated them most thoroughly was their cuisine. Having traveled widely and worked in the *brigades* of the numerous great restaurants where his father had successively sent him, Michel had soaked up years of learning under different masters with different cooking styles. These were precisely the formative years that Bernard had missed because of Chef Jean's antipathy. Certainly Claude Verger's miraculous intervention had saved him from professional oblivion—and, indeed, had rocketed him up to quasi-instant fame—but he had missed an essential part of his artisan's training all the same.

When Michel returned to home base in Roanne, he was a well-rounded, fully formed professional. His professional baggage allowed him to turn his back on his father's French classicism to opt instead for an inventive, hypermodern cuisine with a frankly international accent. Where Pierre's signature dish was salmon in sorrel sauce and Bernard's was updated frogs' legs, Michel's was a poached sea bass with Koshi-hikari rice. Where Bernard built his country palace in traditional Burgundy comfort and style, Michel decorated his in Japanese lacquers and modern art. Where Bernard was cooking according the Troisgros bible, Michel went all-out for fusion. In Saulieu, Bernard had neither the culinary culture nor the desire to switch over to foreign cooking styles. He didn't want it, didn't know how to do it, and for years had laughed at it with easy scorn. But now, faced with what he perceived as

a growing disaffection for purely French cuisine, an awful thought res-
onated persistently in his head: Had he missed the boat?

It was a listless, distraught chef the staff watched that February,
stumbling around his kitchen. Bernard barely spoke, and when he did
he was usually mumbling self-reproach. He stopped his marathon
phone calls, letting others pick up the wall phone in the kitchen when
it rang. Bernard the talker was shutting down.

"Ever since 1973, we had exchanged phone calls every two weeks,"
Claude Verger said. "But from the summer of 2002—July, exactly—I
called him nine times without getting through to him. Every time it
was someone else who answered, and there was always some excuse—
he was in a meeting, or with a client, or any other invention like that.
In December I called four times on the same morning. The first time,
they told me to call back in ten minutes, and when I did they said call
back again. Finally after two more calls, I yelled at them and gave up.
He had gone to ground in his kitchen and wasn't taking calls anymore.
Why? Because he had *emmerdements*—big troubles—and didn't want
to talk about them with me. As long as things were going all right he
was fine, but as soon as he got some bad news, it was *floof!* He was like
a soufflé that had fallen."

Big, important indication here. Closing himself to Verger, his spiritual father in the trade, indicates just how deeply Bernard had
plunged. And since his phone shyness harked all the way back to July,
at the same time as Bush and Chirac were shouting insults at each
other across the Atlantic and the Americans were staying away from
France in droves, it meant that the plunge had begun well before Simon's Michelin insinuations and the *GaultMillau* sledgehammer had
come down on his head. But all through those months neither Bernard
himself nor those who were close to him could perceive the throb of a
deadly warning: He was becoming dangerous to himself.

"The dream of Icarus," is how Dr. Kiss characterized Bernard's
pursuit of his ambition. "He was in a state of neurobiological exhaustion, only he didn't realize it. People of this sort very often cannot recognize their psychological fatigue—they believe they're thinking
straight, but the more exhausted they become, the more their thinking
goes off track. They don't recognize the pathological state they're in, so
they don't stop. Sometimes they become even more active when

they're exhausted. It's a vicious circle. Bernard Loiseau was one of the innumerable victims of the depression of exhaustion. He had used up his physical and psychological reserves. It's what Dr. Freudenberger* called 'burnout.'"

His circle of refuge grew progressively more constricted. Early in the new year he limited himself to Saulieu and the hotel. Presently even that was too vast. By February he took to his last redoubt, the kitchen, avoiding people, entering and leaving by the back door. There were no more of those theatrical appearances of the great chef by the reception desk, no more of the ritual visits to the doorway of the dining room to watch over his guests. There were hardly any guests there, anyway.

Hubert was deeply troubled. Having lived through the 1986 breakdown over Chantal and the 1992 collapse in Kobe, he had experienced Bernard's depressions more closely than anyone else, but this one was worse than ever. Look out, he told Dominique. I've never seen him as bad as this. I know, I know, she said. I'm doing what I can.

On Saturday, February 22, Hubert called a special meeting of the dining room staff. "I'm asking all of you to redouble your efforts," he told them. "Monsieur Loiseau is not doing well at all. I don't know if you realize how bad it is. All of us have to do everything we can to help him. We've got to keep an eye on him at all times."

That same night, Bernard finished the *service* and got home around eleven p.m. Upstairs in their quarters, Dominique was reading in bed. As Bernard was unsnapping the pressure buttons of his chef's blouse, he blurted out a new idea, a conviction that had been trotting in his head through the day. "Now I'm sure of it," he said. "The media want my scalp."

"Oh, come on," she said testily, putting down her book. "Cut it out. You've kept your third star. Who cares about what a few journalists say?"

Bernard shut up and went back inside himself. What was going on inside his head was the same litany that he had been repeating aloud

---

*The American psychiatrist Herbert J. Freudenberger, who died in 1999 at the age of seventy-three, coined the term "burnout" to describe a state of fatigue due to excessive devotion to a cause or ambition that failed to produce the expected reward. Perfectionism, he wrote, can be a malediction.

over the past few days: I'm no damn good. I shouldn't have tried to be a cook. I can't even make up a new menu.

On Sunday, freshly returned from a business trip to Japan, Paul Bocuse called from Collonges. Bernard took the call. Therein lies a sorrowful little premonitory story.

"I even remember the time," Bocuse told me, "because I looked at my watch and saw it was ten past twelve and thought it's probably too late because he'll be at his lunch *service*. But I got him and I said what's new? Paul, I'm desperate, he said. With all this business of losing two points in *GaultMillau* and the Simon articles about *Michelin*, I just don't know what I'm going to do. And then last night I had just nine clients. Half of that was a family with kids. They wanted to eat in their room, and they just ordered cold slices of ham and bread and mineral water.

"He was really down in the dumps. Terrible. I said, Bernard, I've got a picture to cheer you up—you can put it in your office. He and Dominique had been down to Collonges a little while before, and I had this nice blowup of a photo of them with me and Raymonde at the table together. I signed it and wrote on the back: '*Bernard, la vie est belle*' [life is beautiful]. I had it mailed the next day. He never got it."

In February, the Côte d'Or's clientele inevitably thinned to a trickle—the curse of Saulieu seemed to be immutable. On Mondays, guests were even rarer. And Monday lunch was always the scantest of the week. On that Monday, February 24, there were only ten or twelve clients for lunch. Most noticeable among them was a couple of young American cooks en route to Chagny, where they were slated to spend a few weeks observing the kitchen of Bernard's three-star Burgundian colleague Jacques Lameloise. The Americans ordered the *poularde Alexandre Dumaine*, the steamed and truffled chicken made famous by his illustrious predecessor. Bernard oversaw the intricate preparation of the fat Bressane hen and sent the big ceremonial crock out to the smallest of the dining rooms. Patrick and the rest of the crew finished up and scrubbed the working surfaces before leaving for their afternoon rest. Shortly after two o'clock, Stéphanie Gaitey passed through the kitchen on her way up to work.

"*Vous avez une sale tronche*," he told her—you're looking tired.

"And you're not any better," she said. It was true. He seemed bizarre.

"Yeah," he said with a self-deprecating little laugh. "When we see each other tomorrow, we'll talk it all out."

By three o'clock Bernard was all alone. On her way to join Stéphanie in the office one floor up, Dominique cut through the kitchen to the spiral staircase at the rear wall. Bernard was standing in silent thought in his commander's position, hands planted on the stainless-steel *passe*, staring into space. After a few long moments he took off his apron, meticulously folded it—one, two, three—wrapped the strings around it just so, laid it in its place in the cupboard, ducked out the back door, and drove home for his nap.

A perfectionist, especially a bipolar perfectionist, does not forget details. Bernard had promised Bérangère, a budding photographer at twelve, to pose for a picture intended for a local museum's brochure. He sought her out at home and reminded her of the photo call. That was a nice surprise—Bernard was usually reluctant to let anything interfere with his nap time. The girl posed him with some of the household's menagerie of animals, took the snap, and walked happily back to the hotel's boutique, where she was helping out. Bernard mounted to the master bedroom, where eleven-year-old Bastien was comfortably installed on the bed watching a soccer match on TV. Bernard joined him for a few minutes, then brusquely sent him out. Go play in the garden, he said. I want to sleep.

At about quarter past five, Dominique drove home to pick up a document she had left in the master bedroom. She found the bedroom door locked. Never mind—there was another door that connected it to the girls' room, and that one was so old that the lock didn't even work. Curiously, though, when she pushed the door it didn't give. Something seemed to be blocking it. This time, she gave it a good shove, and it budged enough to open up a crack. She saw something white: Bernard's chef's blouse. Still not understanding, she shoved harder and saw the barrel of the shotgun she had given him as a birthday present two years earlier. Blood was everywhere.

XVI

THE THIRD LIFE OF
LA CÔTE D'OR

*W*edged against the door where he had collapsed, Bernard was already long gone. When a local doctor arrived a quarter of an hour later, he could do no more than certify death by gunshot to the head.

There was no note. This might suggest a *coup de tête*, an impulsive spur-of-the-moment act that might just as well not have happened at all, but Dominique remembered that a week earlier almost exactly the same scenario had taken place: Bernard had sent Bastien out of the room with oddly uncustomary gruffness. Had that been a near thing? Had he taken up his weapon then, but backed out at the last minute? Who knows. But today, reflecting back on her husband's behavior during those final months, she is convinced that for some time he had been inwardly caressing the idea of a grand departure *en pleine gloire* while he was still crowned with the glory of three stars, like a great athlete hanging up his spikes after an Olympic gold medal.

"A question of honor," she mused. Because, fundamentally, it was honor that he had been chasing throughout his entire insecure life, at least since that ignominious *feuille blanche* he delivered at his BEPC exam in Massillon. For his part, Hubert shrugged fatalistically. He had seen the fatal issue brewing for weeks, without ever really knowing enough, being quite sure enough, or having enough authority to do anything about it. But of one thing he is certain: When Bernard went through that one last ritualistic folding of his apron that Monday, the story was already played out. It was a dead man who walked out of the kitchen's back door.

The news was out that very evening, and the country reacted with stupor. Bernard's suicide was the top item on every TV news program and in every newspaper. The illustrated weekly *Paris-Match* ran two cover stories on *le drame Loiseau*. Inevitably, all the stories recalled Vatel, but somehow this event was even more stunning. Vatel was merely an employee of the king's cousin. Bernard had been of the reigning family, one of the royals of *la haute gastronomie française*, and probably the most widely known one of the lot. For all the general public knew, this was cuisine's Sun King himself, the man with the ideal life, the ideal wife, the ideal kids, and the ideal country palace, which was so beautiful that it knocked all his provincial competitors back into second place. But what that same general public could not suspect was that their Sun King was in fact a big, scared kid with an incomplete professional formation, a terrifying load of debt, a mostly empty dining room, and a psyche that he had run to exhaustion by trying to keep pace with the personal mythology he had created. *Luxe, calme et volupté* was for the clients, not the provider.

The trade reacted with considerable emotion, of a sort and degree that came as a surprise to many. Like a cathartic, Bernard's desperate act released a torrent of feelings—anger, resentment, injured pride, a sense of injustice—that had been bottled up within the profession for decades. "We can say, we can even affirm, that they killed Bernard Loiseau," impetuously wrote Jacques Pourcel, president of the Union of Haute Cuisine Française and co-owner, with his brother Laurent, of the Jardin des Sens in Montpellier. Like Bernard, the Pourcel brothers had suffered from Simon's criticisms and from a strangely equivocal, lukewarm text in the *GaultMillau*, which had awarded them only 17 points. Paul Bocuse*

---

*Bocuse was also noted at 17 in the *GaultMillau*, but he was accustomed to their disfavor, and he didn't give a damn. After having inspired Henri Gault and Christian Millau to coin the term *nouvelle cuisine*, he continued serenely on his professional route while they and their successors plunged into the risk-charged practice of seeking out novelty above all things. The Fauves of the kitchen are the pinups in *GaultMillau*, but Bocuse, who has been everywhere, seen everything, and done everything, has forgotten more about cuisine than the novelty makers and the culinary poetasters ever learned. The same cuisine that was *nouvelle* thirty years ago is now considered classical. That's all right with him, because it is also perfect.

publicly agreed, singling out *GaultMillau*'s commentary on Bernard as excessive and needlessly cruel. In short, murderous. "They play with us," charged the usually placid Jacques Lameloise in Chagny, "raising us up then knocking us down. I think that's what made him crack."

There was plenty more comment of the same tone, but rarely as poignant as the words of Jacques Guillo, a modest sixty-year-old chef in the village of Mûr-de-Bretagne. Guillo's turnover had leaped up 35 percent when his restaurant, Auberge Grand' Maison, won a Michelin star in 1984, and he had cherished it ever since, offering an impeccably executed classical menu heavily angled toward seafood and local Breton products. But, like Bernard, it was apparently this classicism that did him in with *GaultMillau*, for in 2000 he was blindsided by an astonishingly malicious critique: "La cuisine of Grand' Maison is a total failure."

"I cried for forty-five days," Guillo said. "I know why Bernard killed himself: It was for his honor. The day of his burial, I took fifteen minutes out of my day to go to the church here in Mûr. I lit three candles and prayed for him, all alone."

More celebrated names than Guillo came forward to testify to the man-killing pressures of the trade. In Saint-Père de Vézelay, Marc Meneau, looking worn-out and old before his time, admitted to insomnia so severe that he was obliged to regularly knock himself out with sleeping pills, and having entertained thoughts of suicide. André Daguin told me about a less-known cook, a journeyman in the Paris region who blew his brains out a few months after Bernard. And, he added, there was the case of Jean Bardet, a wonderful chef who holds two Michelin stars in the cathedral city of Tours-sur-Loire. He was saved at the last minute only because his wife caught him in the staircase, gun in hand. Bruno Olivier, chef and grandson of the great Raymond Olivier, who had brought the Grand Véfour in Paris from zero to three stars, declared that the loss of a Michelin star did more than any health problem to kill his grandfather.

"It's difficult to live with [the critics]" said Guy Martin, the present chef of the Grand Véfour, once again holder of three stars. "You're there, carrying on normally, working your heart out, and they tell you that you're one of the best. Then suddenly the next year, you're not. You can't take those people seriously. They are the ones who should be asking themselves questions, and who should do their mea culpa."

There weren't many mea culpas. The critical establishment cir-
cled the wagons and defended itself with fervor, inevitably invoking
freedom of the press. *GaultMillau* hemmed and hawed and said it
wasn't our fault, and mighty Michelin took a chastising hit when Pascal Rémy, the rogue inspector who wrote a book about his life in the
citadel, revealed that there had been eleven inspectors when he was
hired, but only five when he was fired sixteen years later.* François Simon had the elegance to admit to me that he was touched to the quick
by Bernard's suicide, adding that he had suffered a *crise de conscience*
as a result. Curious guy: In the very same article where he had spoken
of Bernard's third star "legitimately under threat," he added a couple of
lines demonstrating something very much like compassion. "Someone
who has not seen a chef on the day of the loss of a star," he wrote, "cannot imagine the dread that has entered his life."

Fundamentally, Simon's fault, if fault there was, lay more in the direction of deontology than any legal malfeasance: He had written rumor rather than fact. Having been limited to restaurant criticism
throughout his career (*GaultMillau* before *Le Figaro*), he didn't have a
feel for the ethical restraints of journalism. Like so many in his curious
craft, he had acted more like a gossip columnist than a journalist. And
in truth, it wasn't Simon who killed Bernard, any more than it was
GaultMillau. There was more to it than that. But the concomitance of
their negative comments that February, coming after eight or ten

---

*Doubtless influenced by the reigning business wisdom of the M.B.A. culture,
Michelin unwisely went for the short-term gain of cutting costs by paring back the
payroll of the Service du Tourisme and sharply reducing the number of inspectors.
While this may have been a plausible strategy for optimizing certain office operations, it was disastrous for the guide, in consideration of the unique image of un-
failing rectitude that it had projected ever since its founding by grandpappy André
at the start of the twentieth century. For the sake of a few paltry schoolteachers'
salaries, Michelin took the risk of squandering its most precious jewel, the
hundred-plus years of the unquestioning trust that it had enjoyed in the bosoms of
gourmets (and, by extension, tire buyers) everywhere, and dashing the last hope of
Homo gallicus, that most disenchanted and mistrusting of individuals, that there
still remained at least one institution in the country that was not altogether rotten.
Michelin went on a hiring campaign to rectify its grievous mistake, and perhaps
an M.B.A. or two was fired to make room on the payroll spreadsheet.

months of hard times and bad news for Bernard and the Côte d'Or, was doubtless the proverbial final straw on the camel's back.

Finally, when all the coals have been raked over and all the jealousies, rancors, and self-serving ambitions have been appeased and the pettiness swept away, there are only two real culprits to be blamed for Bernard's death: the twentieth century and his own tortured psyche. The laws of the market, the endless competition of the star system, the myth of material success, the easy accessibility but terrifying transience of fame—he joyously swam in it all, but it proved to be much deeper and the currents much stronger than he had ever imagined. He lost his way and drowned from sheer exhaustion after keeping afloat all the way into the early days of the twenty-first century.

Whatever the tragedy and whatever the chagrin, the show has to go on in the restaurant trade as much as it does in show business, so they served dinner that Monday evening in the Côte d'Or to the few guests who had already reserved. Patrick cooked while Hubert and the rest of the staff plugged along on automatic pilot, doing their best to act normally. Dominique slept with the kids in the hotel that night, all four of them piled into the huge master bed of room 35, the biggest in the hotel. Before and after sleeping, they prayed together for Bernard's soul. At first she didn't have the courage to unveil the whole truth; she told them their father had died of a heart attack. A few days later, as gently as she could, she told them the full story, which in any case they would not be able to escape in the media or simply in talk around town.

They closed everything down for the next four days while the staff arranged the funeral. Whatever Bernard's failings and weaknesses had been on the intimate human level at which they knew him, they were determined to give him a send-off as grandiose as the wildest flights of fancy on which he had built his personal legend.

On Friday, Bernard was the uncontested star of the cooking world one last time, accompanied by an honor guard composed of all twenty-four of the country's three-star chefs, who had responded magnificently to Hubert's and Eric's calls. Michel Bras flew in from vacation in Peru, and Joël Robuchon, a "virtual" three-star since handing his place over to Alain Ducasse, came from Japan. Ducasse was there, too, and some celebrated names of cinema, radio, and TV, plus an official representa-

tive of the government (secretary of state for commerce and light industry), but they were swallowed up by the swarm of three thousand–plus mourners who flowed into Saulieu that afternoon, most of
them spontaneous arrivals who had not been formally invited. The
twelfth-century basilica of Saint-Andoche, with a theoretical capacity
of six hundred, had probably never been as full as on that Friday, going
a hundred or more over capacity with the mass of humanity that occupied every inch of standing room on all sides of the central seated area.
When no more could possibly be crammed in, the crowd spilled out
onto the square in front of the basilica's monumental entry, or took
themselves to the adjacent park, where a giant television screen showed
a rebroadcast of the ceremony.*

The government rep spoke, and the mayor, and Paul Bocuse, but it
was the great, hulking André Daguin, the voluble rugby-playing Gas-
con with the impossible accent, who got it just right. Hunched over the
lectern—it looked like he could splinter it into pieces if he just
squeezed his fists a little harder—he gazed down toward Dominique,
self-controlled and erect, sitting with the children in the front row next
to the coffin with Bernard's white apron folded on top. Daguin spoke as
a fellow restaurateur who had intimately known the pressures and
pains of the race after stars, but also as a friend who, like so many others in the audience, had enjoyed the warmth and generosity that
Bernard loved to shower on anyone who took the trouble to come see
him in Saulieu.

"For the first time we're with Bernard and he's not making us
smile," Daguin said. "For the first time we're with him and we feel terrible. There's always a final rendezvous, and now it has happened, but
it's really too soon. The artist has left the stage in full glory. We feel as
much like applauding as crying."

The funeral cortege halted for a few moments before the front entrance of the Côte d'Or on the way to the cemetery, as the staff stood
bareheaded in homage. Then the family and a few close friends buried

---

*Chantal was there in the crowd, as was Claude Perraudin. Even though he had
been Bernard's friend since apprenticeship, Perraudin did not attempt to elbow his
way into the basilica to join his more renowned fellow chefs. Modest and unassuming, he opted to remain one of the anonymous watching from without.

Bernard in a hastily arranged tomb on the site that Dominique had purchased only a few months earlier. Following immutable French custom, the bereft were expected to offer a *collation*, or light snack, to the mourners. A couple of thousand persons walked down to Saulieu's cavernous exhibition hall where, on an endlessly long line of linen-covered tables, Gaston Lenôtre, France's most famous caterer, had laid out a Pantagruelesque selection of cold meats, cheeses, pastries, sandwiches, mixed *hors d'oeuvres*, and a selection of wines and fruit juices. It wasn't exactly a party, but Bernard's staff had made sure that no one would face the drive back home on an empty stomach. They had no doubt that this was exactly the way Bernard would have wanted it.

The media people threw themselves at Dominique, of course, and she received them with the same graciousness that she had always proffered when it was Bernard they had come to see. She gave interviews to reporters and sat for the TV cameras in a hot, brightly lit studio that the technicians had improvised in the little library next to the billiards room, speaking with calm, thoughtful reserve, reflecting on each question, and trying to answer it as forthrightly and intelligently as possible. There were no histrionics; she sought to create no effects or pull any emotional heartstrings. Dominique remained Dominique. She did not weep for the camera. She refused to. She was too proud and too honest to hoke it up.

She paid for her pride and honesty. In the days after the funeral, a kind of national consensus developed. Wherever you went those days and spoke with anyone who had watched her on TV—and who hadn't?—the comment was almost automatic. She was so calm. She didn't cry. She's cold. She's heartless. Men were generally willing to at least give her the benefit of the doubt, but women, like the *tricoteuses* clicking their knitting needles at the foot of the guillotine, were implacable. They had been prepared to lend tearful sympathy, but they had been cheated of the wailing they wanted. Dominique hadn't fulfilled her side of the bargain.

Guy Savoy, Bernard's closest friend and longest professional companion since the days of apprenticeship in Roanne, had a better, much closer view. "During the whole awful thing, Dominique was much stronger than any of us. A few days after the *drame*, one of the waiters came to get me in the kitchen—Madame Loiseau is there, he said. Oh,

God, I thought, I don't know if I can handle that. We're all such wimps. I was sick, sick. I couldn't keep from crying. When we sat down together, I couldn't help her at all. Finally it was Dominique who comforted me!"

Savoy's handsome bearded face twisted into a grimace as he recounted the experience, and before I quite knew what was happening, he burst into tears in front of me. "Excuse me. We're in the business of happiness. We're no damn good at handling grief."

On Saturday, the Côte d'Or opened its doors again, and the kitchen and dining-room staff plunged back into their well-oiled routine. That weekend and all the rest of weeks and months of 2003 fulfilled the distressing augury presented by Bernard's death: clientele was down 20 to 25 percent over 2002. Even with this, though, they could count themselves lucky. In 2003 the entire hotel-restaurant sector in France was devastated by one of the worst years in memory, and many of their colleagues suffered 30 and 40 percent losses of clientele.

Withal, 2004 opened with great news, the best that they could possibly hope for: as it had done when Fernand Point died and Mado took over the reins of La Pyramide, Michelin maintained the Côte d'Or's third star.

"We looked at Saulieu very carefully in 2003," Derek Brown assured me. "In all, the inspectors had ten or twelve meals there during the year. Obviously it was a very emotional time, but we had to try to be completely clear and objective about what was happening—you can't make judgments on sentiment. We saw no reason to change our rating. They were really motivated, and everything was at a very high level. If that continues through 2004, I see no reason why they shouldn't maintain their three stars in the 2005 guide."*

Since that awful February, a lot has changed but at the same time very little has changed. The biggest difference is a new name. To honor her late husband, Dominique has officially renamed her establishment Relais Bernard Loiseau. The final touches of decoration that Bernard had been overseeing with the architects that winter have been carried

---

*And so it happened: When Dominique opened the 2005 *Guide Michelin*, the Côte d'Or's three stars were still shining as brightly as ever.

out, and now the hotel is pristinely finished to the last detail, exactly as he wanted. Naturally enough, Dominique has become the new president of the publicly quoted Bernard Loiseau Group. The group is debt-free, because the 20-odd million francs that Bernard owed to the banks at his death were covered by the insurance policies that Bernard Fabre had been prudent enough to take out several years earlier on Bernard's head. Bernard was aware of this, of course, when he committed suicide, and it is anyone's guess how much, if at all, this influenced his terrible decision.

Ironically enough, Fabre is no longer associated with the operation. In the months after that February it became increasingly apparent that without Bernard, he had become something of a dinosaur, a holdover from the free-swinging old days when the chef as the jovial commander-in-chief delegated entire sections of his domain to those whom he instinctively trusted. Working out of his accountancy office in Auxerre, Fabre had handled all the money matters that bored and baffled Bernard and, as the sole signatory for most important documents, had virtual carte blanche over the enterprise's finances. His manner was Dickensian, his tools were pen, pencil, and pocket calculator, and he hated computers. This approach would not do with diligent, attentive, up-to-date Dominique. As president, she was responsible not only for the livelihood of the Côte d'Or's sixty-five employees, but to the shareholders of Groupe Loiseau S.A. as well. She asked Fabre to come and set up his office in Saulieu and demanded her own overview of the books — naturally with a joint signature for all major documents. In short, she decided to demonstrate that she was the boss. At that, Fabre quit.

Reorganizing the company's administration, Dominique replaced him with Isabelle Proust, a dynamic young graduate of the prestigious École des Hautes Études Commerciales, in the new position of *directeur general*. What the group has lost in the sympathetic folklore of Bernard's easygoing personalized business style, it has gained in Proust's computer-wise efficiency. Dominique also took stock of the times when clients had always been rarest in Saulieu and made a decision that was long overdue but impossible while Bernard was charging around, working himself to death: to close shop for two mornings a week (Tuesday and Wednesday); and to shut the place down entirely for a month between January and February. It is entirely conceivable that Bernard would be alive today if he had dared to take this step and allow himself the time to relax and decompress.

"The old team had their way of working, but I had trouble imposing my ideas," Dominique said. "It wasn't easy. They were accustomed to a little enterprise that was essentially the restaurant in Saulieu. Now we're more than that. We're a group that's quoted on the stock market, with an image to manage and everything that goes along with that. Now I have very qualified people, each one working in a particular domain."

Madame la présidente Dominique surely is, then, but as far as visitors to the hotel are concerned, the role in which they knew her is unchanged. Twice a day at mealtimes she descends from her office above the kitchen and, dressed in the conservative monochrome *tailleurs* that she prefers, circulates in the dining room to greet guests, answer questions, and exchange comments about the menu. Her temperate, composed manner is about as different from Bernard's as could be imagined, but the explosive days ended with her husband's death. Today's style of *luxe, calme et volupté* is more low-key, more feminine, and more refined.

The menu, too, has undergone a sea change. Now entirely in the hands of Patrick Bertron, it is evolving in reflection of his own tastes and inclinations. At forty-three, after more than twenty years of working under Bernard, he is as zealous as ever about the quality of the ingredients that suppliers bring into his kitchen. *Le beau produit* was the basis of Bernard's culinary philosophy, and the network of suppliers he built up in Saulieu was unsurpassed anywhere in France. Although sticking generally to Bernard's low-fat, cream-free approach, Patrick is taking liberties with his Maoist purism for the unembroidered, hard-edged essence of each ingredient. Patrick does not fear to deglaze with wine or stronger alcohols, employs many more riffs and minor chords than did Bernard with his C-major cuisine, and is far more open to the spices and herbal accents that his former boss rejected *en bloc*. He has already been known to include *péquillos*—lively little peppers—in certain of his creations.

"I don't rule out any ingredients at all," he says. That's hot news for the Côte d'Or. The menu is now about two-thirds Bertron and one-third Loiseau. A special separate section is devoted to Bernard's great classics, starring the obligatory *jambonnettes* of frogs' legs, the crackly-skinned pike perch in red wine sauce, the crayfish with tarragon, and the golden sweetbreads with truffled purée. While allowing that he is open—in principle, at least—to any ingredient he deems useful, Patrick remains devoted to *cuisine à la française*, and studiously avoids the fusioning world-food craze that has enthralled so many of his *confrères*. On the other hand, he is a far more technical and sophisticated cook than Bernard, and he is leaving behind the quasi-puritanical absolutism of his former boss's old culinary style and striking out on his own into new territory.

"In the old days," he explained, "when we were showing new ideas to Monsieur Loiseau, he always went straight to the heart of the dishes and refused all the touches we had put with them and around them. 'Take this out, take this out, take this out,' he would say: 'I don't want it, that serves no purpose, *c'est nul à chier*' [no damn good], and one after another, they would all disappear from the plate. But the client today wants to see *du travail*, some inventiveness and fantasy on his plate."

After more than two years as sole master of the kitchen, Patrick has incontestably imposed *le style Bertron*, and by all indications it is going down very nicely with the clients. Those who stay for a day or two often opt for a two-meal solution: lunch on the Loiseau menu, dinner on the Bertron, or vice-versa. On Patrick's menu they might start with crayfish tails and a jellied infusion of their reduced essences with fresh pea shoots and a winey *savagnin* mousse, or a slice of *foie gras* quickly seared in the skillet, served with a rhubarb *charlotte* and tiny candied onions with a gingerbread vinaigrette. Popular seafood courses include a filet of *féra* from Lake Geneva cooked *à l'unilatérale*, with a "melt" of young onions and *fromage blanc*. His duck filet with caramelized skin is already on the way to becoming a Bertron classic, and his stuffed pigeon breast is a professional tour de force whose complexity of preparation would doubtless have sent Bernard into scandalized tirades, but Patrick's eyes light up and something very much like a lilt comes to his voice when he describes the steps that go into its making.

"First we remove the two breasts. With the meat from the thighs we make a stuffing, compounded with foie gras and a bit of lard. We place this stuffing between the two breasts, which we roll together, cover with a little sheet of *crêpine*, and tie up. Then we roast it, very gently so it remains nice and pink inside. While this is going on, we make a little *jus* from the carcass, lightly accented with vinegar—just enough to excite the taste buds. We make a side dish of tiny *girolle* mushrooms with snow peas, and another of a potato 'marrow bone.' This is a potato that we have cut and hollowed out to resemble a marrow bone; in the cavity we put the pigeon's heart and liver, which we have sautéed, and we close the cavity with a little potato 'biscuit' that we have cooked separately. This goes on the *jus*, which we have further flavored with a bit of sage, and next to it is a candied shallot which has been slowly cooked in the oven on a bed of rock salt, until it is soft and creamy on the inside. We half open it up, like the petals of a flower, and lay inside it the pigeon's wing tips, which we have previously glazed in the *jus*. I like to send out a somewhat more complex finished product like this. It shows the client that we have been working for him, that we've really put some thought into his plate."

Were it not for his native Breton reserve, Patrick would be veering close to the rhapsodic here, and it is abundantly clear that he feels and is cooking like a man whose handcuffs have been removed and knows exactly where he is going. He has the kitchen well under control with a new staff that he has handpicked, and his head is full of ideas. With that, with Hubert's practiced management of the dining room staff, with Dominique presiding over the business side, and with the memory of Alexandre Dumaine and Bernard Loiseau imprinted on every square inch of the place, the rebaptized Côte d'Or is well launched into its third life. How it fares now is entirely up to the new crew.

In the dining room, the crew is still composed mostly of Bernard's old soldiers, but with new impetus and the new style of management, the manner and course of the big old boat are gradually changing direction. The last time I was in Saulieu, Hubert set up a menu for me that was half Loiseau and half Bertron. Between the *jambonnettes* of frogs' legs and the golden brown filet of John Dory accompanied by an artfully stuffed little tomato and a brochette of glazed young fennel, I could scarcely have imagined a better or more refined lunch, but the memory I retain most strongly of that afternoon concerns not so much the food on my plate as the ghost of the man who had created the ineffably pleasant atmosphere that pervaded the place.

I was not, of course, the only one to feel the presence of that ghost. It was all around me, in the traditional architecture that Bernard had loved, in the refinement of detail in the food being served, in both the dignity and natural friendliness of the staff, and the fluent professionalism with which they were busying themselves everywhere in the dining room: no rigid mannerisms, no forced gestures, no obsequiousness, nary a pat, predigested phrase. They were as their old boss had formed them, each one acting out his or her part in the theater of gastronomy as an intelligent human being, independently shouldering responsibilities, and damned if it didn't seem like they were actually enjoying their work.

About halfway through the meal, Manu, the *sommelier chef*, dropped by the table to check my glass, but after refilling it, he did something that I think could only have occurred in the Côte d'Or that Loiseau had built. Very quietly and discreetly, he broke a cardinal rule of the trade: He had a drink with me.

Or rather, a toast. It was very quick, so quick that no one else even noticed his gesture. He took another glass, filled it halfway, lifted it and gently clinked it against mine. "To Bernard," he said, and drained the glass.

He turned and went back to his business with the other guests, cool and faultlessly professional. But the unrehearsed and unfeigned sincerity of Manu's breach of normal rules only underlined how amazingly successful Bernard had been—big scared kid that he was—in motivating his people to excellence. With all his childishness and glaring faults, they really had loved him, admired him, and been inspired by him. More than his Maoist recipes, his media stardom, or his fervent sales talks, this was the most important, and certainly the most moving, legacy he had bequeathed to the historical old Burgundy palace that he had taken over and transformed by sheer force of will. He had breathed life into it, renewed it, and given it a genuine personality.

"Restaurants are the last refuge of civilization on the planet," Guy Savoy likes to say. There's a good dose of exaggeration in an affirmation as broad as that, but Guy can be forgiven for it, because it's not so far from the truth, either. Certainly, restaurants are businesses engaged in seeking profit, but it is remarkable how often they can be something very much like a calling, how often the artisans engaged in that calling are stricken by the artist's imperative to transcend the dreadful, passionless bottom-line mentality that more generally rules the modern world.

It's an odd kind of business, taking money to give pleasure, but no one who has spent some time observing these artisans—people like Jean Ducloux, Michel Bras, Pierre Gagnaire, or Jacques Lameloise—can doubt for an instant the utter sincerity with which the best of them approach their craft. In the big cities, given the nature of big cities, the pleasure is frequently centered on the dazzle and flash of novelty, but in a great provincial inn, the restaurant is only the centerpiece of a larger whole: an escape for a few hours or a few days into an enveloping haven of peace and repose: *luxe, calme et volupté*.

By the centuries of tradition lying behind them, by their matchless treasury of culinary expertise, and by the sheer weight of their numbers, the inns of the French countryside are an unequalled example of that civilization of which Savoy speaks. It's a moot question, I suppose, whether in the greater scheme of things, a provincial chef's life may be placed in the same balance alongside the grand, the rich, and the lofty of the world, but Bernard Loiseau made a passionately sincere and very respectable contribution to that civilization. He is to be honored for it. Indeed, as Guy Savoy cried that afternoon in his restaurant on rue Troyon, he gave his life for it.

He's not too far from the truth there, either.

INDEX